Pascal

PASCAL

The Man and His Two Loves

John R. Cole

NEW YORK UNIVERSITY PRESS
New York and London

NEW YORK UNIVERSITY PRESS
New York and London

Library of Congress Cataloging-in-Publication Data
Cole, John R. (John Richard), 1941–
Pascal: the man and his two loves / John R. Cole.
p. cm.
Includes biographical references and index.
ISBN 0-8147-1510-9
1. Pascal, Blaise, 1623–1662. 2. Philosophers—France—Biography.
3. Scientists—France—Biography. I. Title.
B1903.C64 1995
230'.2'092—dc20 95-4381
[B] CIP

New York University Press books are printed on acid-free paper,
and their binding materials are chosen for strength and durability.

Manufactured in the United States of America

10 9 8 7 6 5 4 3 2 1

Love makes itself felt better by deprivation than in enjoyment, and there is no better way of understanding the disorder of our affections than by our separation from the object. We quit without pain what we possess without pleasure—but we judge the excess of our love by that of our suffering, and we never feel our attachment to perishable things more acutely than by our regret at their loss.

Man is so unhappy since the Fall that to accomplish something significant, he must lose his reason. Madness is so natural to him that the greatest minds are the most disordered. There isn't one of them who is unaffected by some admixture of disorder. The same temperament that makes sages also makes madmen, and the melancholy that makes the finest works also makes the highest extravagances.

—Jean-François Senault, *L'homme criminel*

Contents

Acknowledgments

Jean Mesnard has informed and guided all lesser students of Blaise Pascal, and my greatest scholarly indebtedness is to him. Lane Heller offered encouragement at a crucial juncture. Erna Furman and Robert Furman read a preliminary version of my first chapter, and Donald Goodwin and Samuel Guze offered counsel on questions of diagnosis. Drake Bradley helped me with statistical analyses. Anonymous readers of earlier drafts offered many helpful criticisms. I learned what I could from these persons, and the book would have been the better if I were capable of learning more from them.

Librarians, including Thomas Hayward, Laura Juraska, and LaVerne Winn, have been patient with me and generous with their time and knowledge. At Harvard and Yale, especially, others have helped me to use more specialized collections. In France, the Bibliothèque Nationale and the Bibliothèque Municipale et Universitaire de Clermont-Ferrand have shared their treasures.

The Penrose Fund of the American Philosophical Society, the Roger C. Schmutz Fund for Faculty Research at Bates College, and the endowment of the Thomas Hedley Reynolds Chair in History provided financial support.

The bottom line in a book like this is not financial but familial. I offer it in loving memory of my mother, Margaret Hall Cole, a historian who set aside her own career for her family, and my father, William Henry Cole, a priest who preached and practiced the Two Loves.

Introduction: Two Conceptions of One Life

"The last thing one discovers in writing a book is what to put first." Blaise Pascal put it best, but, come to think of it, just where did *he* put it? First? Last? Somewhere aside?

Pascal's fragment seems to be less a "thought" than an afterthought. What to put first in his Apology for the Faith? Of course, the great man himself never completed his great book, nor even so much as a first draft of a first part or a first chapter or a preface. Indeed, he left his manuscripts in such apparent disorder that his heirs had to make their own book, selected and arranged in their own way: *Pensées de M. Pascal sur la religion et sur quelques autres sujets, qui ont été trouvées après sa mort parmi ses papiers* (1670). For this first edition, they set aside the fragment on first things and last things. Eight years later, they did include it in their chapter 31 of "Various Thoughts," placed arbitrarily but suggestively between their chapter 30 of apparently impersonal "Thoughts on Death" extracted from Blaise's letter to his elder sister Gilberte after the death of their father, Étienne, and their chapter 32, which was his intensely personal "Prayer to Ask God for the Good Use of Illnesses," written in his own last years of illness.

At the turn of the century (1897 and 1904), Léon Brunschvicg made Pascal's afterthought, which he numbered Pensée 19, part of an editorially conceived first chapter of "Thoughts on the Mind and on Style." At midcentury (1951 and 1963), Louis Lafuma renumbered it Pensée 976 and included it among last things, toward the end of a section of "Fragments not Registered" that he appended to an edition otherwise based on the order of fragments in the manuscript First Copy. Toward the close of the century, Philippe Sellier (1976 and 1991) has re-renumbered it Pensée 740 and replaced it toward the beginning of a similar appendix in an edition based on the alternative order of the Second Copy. I make Pascal's afterthought my first word because its afterlife symbolizes the extent to which we make and remake the great book of the Pascal whom we all admire and love.

The image of the man Pascal (1623–62) has been far more stable. It goes all the way back to 1662, the year of his death and Gilberte Périer's memorial *Vie de Monsieur Pascal*.[1] This seventeenth-century "Pascal" was the product of his sister's two loves, for her brother and for the God of their shared faith. Late in the twentieth century, her image of the great man is still authoritative. Brunschvicg, Lafuma, and Sellier have agreed, for all their editorial differences, that "the first thing" for readers of the works of Pascal ought to be this life of Pascal.[2] Gilberte Périer's conception was simple, and subsequent scholarship has proven it to be supple. Looking backward in the months after his death, she reconstructed his life in this way: Youthful Genius, Midlife Conversion, Mature Saintliness.[3] I shall call this the canonical conception.

Understandably, the grieving sister was tempted to put last things first. She emphasized her brother's mature devotion, saintly suffering, and holy death, and she slighted his childhood and denied his attachments to family members, including herself. Her little memoir was set down for her family and closest friends alone at their particular request, but it was also her offering to God and to her brother's memory. It still edifies even as it informs. Thanks in large part to the conception of Pascal's life that it did most to form, the *Pensées* are almost unimaginable as anything other than a work of the most powerful intelligence in the service of the Christian Faith.

I, too, have long hesitated. How best to begin? Perhaps it would be best for me to begin with a profession and a confession. In the beginning was the Word, and the Word was Love. But historians, who have long lavished such attention on wars, crimes, follies, and misfortunes, still find it difficult to give human love its due, in part because its aspirations have been so high and in part because its roots are so deep and so tangled. Psychologists and psychiatrists, to whom we turn for counsel, often seem anxious to reduce love to an infantile dependency or a pansexuality and to do so on no firmer basis than patients' evanescent words interpreted in terms of the doctors' elaborate theories.

I want to understand the great Pascal, his life and work, and I believe that the keys are his loves of the other Pascals and of the Christian God. I believe that the former love not only preceded but also supported the latter, and I will try to show why I believe that this was so. Finally, I believe that the disciplined historian can methodically regain access to "his heart and his mind and his soul" toward the beginning of his life, at its crucial turning point, and toward its holy end. Yet, however perversely, I find that I must oppose Pascal and the Pascals on these most fundamental matters. The "Two Loves" of my title are those of the Two Great Commandments, the Love of God and the Love of Neighbor (Matt. 32:36–40). For good Augustinians, these objects are opposed; sinful man is self-centered even in his love "of others," and God is jealous.

More perversely, I find that the Pascalian text of texts, the *Mémorial* of his ecstatic encounter with the God of Abraham at the time of his decisive conversion, calls me to "take and read" not only the Scriptures that filled the convert's heart, mind, and soul but also *The Interpretation of Dreams* by that most notorious atheist Sigmund Freud. This is not the profession of a psychoanalytical counterfaith. Method, not theory, may be Freud's more enduring legacy. Extending the reach and documenting the effectiveness of his associative methods of interpretation, I believe that I make a contribution to the analytical study of human affects even in a book that makes no further reference to such shibboleths of psychoanalytical theory as the Oedipus complex.

Freud regarded the interpretation of dreams by means of the dreamer's associations as "the royal road" to a knowledge of the unconscious. As a clinician, he could not imagine how to extend this road to the knowledge of dead dreamers who rest in the silence of the tomb, unable to contribute associations.[4] A historian, I believe I have discovered how to recover associations methodically in the case of Pascal's visionary experience on 23 November 1654. "Take and read." We can still retrace Pascal's powerful memory into the Bible that he knew virtually by heart and therein find not only his god but also empirical evidence of his associations and of the regular workings of his unconscious mind. This may be the greatest perversity: it is in Pascal's Bible that we can *see* evidence of the unconscious processes that Freud had to infer, namely, condensation, displacement, and visual representation.[5] And it is in the historical study of the great modern Thinker-and-Believer that we can *test* statistically the validity of Freud's greatest discovery, the method of interpretation by associations.

The sin of sins is pride, and every author, perhaps especially the student of the great Pascal, must somehow come to terms with his own vanity. I confess that I have strong opinions about this fascinating man and his written work. The strongest is that the precondition for an understanding of the work is a historical understanding of the life. Remarkably, no English-language historian has ever pursued serious and sustained inquiry into the surviving evidence on this man's life. "Pascal" has remained in the hands of students of literature, philosophy, and theology, strong hands that shape what they hold. He who never finished his great book and who wanted to appeal as a man, not an author (Pensées 675, 745), still less a reasoner, has been bound up with the *Pensées* as the archetypal Thinker-and-Believer.

In Pascal's life, the child came before the man and lived on within the man. His mind included the "psyche" as well as the "intelligence" and the "spirit." Within this psyche, his mother, father, and sisters met fundamental needs and aroused the most powerful emotions, but his parents died and his sisters left him. The author's enduring works, his polemical *Provinciales* (1656–57) and fragmentary *Pensées* (primarily 1656–58), come between his father's death (1651) and his own eventual incapacitation in the last years of illness (1658– or 1659–62). I present a new and rather darker conception of this life: Youthful Attachments, Separations and Losses, Mature Depression.

In this revisionist conception, specialists may recognize some traces of the Pascal envisioned by Voltaire as his great antagonist and "eulogized" by Condorcet in Voltairean terms, a figure whose mature devotion and written work alike were shadowed by pathological melancholy.[6] However, neither Voltaire nor Condorcet attempted anything like a history in modern senses. They did not make good use even of the limited documentation that was available to them, and both were such doctrinaire opponents of the faith that inspired Pascal that profound misunderstandings were inevitable. Furthermore, their attempts to dismiss his last years and late writings as those of a "madman" reflect the biases of their own rationalist philosophy, not the findings of an empirical psychology or a modern psychiatry.

I want to reintegrate Pascal's life, before and after conversion, and his life and work, youthful mathematics and science as well as mature written work. I also want to reconcile, insofar as that is possible, opposed conceptions of Pascal's life, those of the Jansenists and of the Voltaireans. The canonical version and the philosophical alternative both tend to reduce the younger man's life to his sovereign intelligence and to make a radical scission at midlife. I focus on familial relations and affections or, in a word, love. In my history, the great facts of this man's life are his familial attachments, separations, and losses. His early experience left its mark on his later life and work. I argue that he was a great genius and a melancholy sufferer who made good use of his illness.

The Canonical Conception and the Orthodox Tradition

Jean Mesnard has been the preeminent specialist since the publication of his *Pascal: l'homme et l'oeuvre* (1951). This wonderful little book begins with a vigorous reaffirmation of Gilberte's reliability on points of fact and ends with his own tribute to Pascal's "heroism and saintliness."[7] In his magisterial edition of the *Oeuvres complètes* (1964–), Mesnard comes very close to endorsing her conception as his own:

> [She] alone presents an account of the whole life in which the various parts are balanced. . . . [F]ew persons could have known Pascal so intimately. . . . [Her work] is a biographical masterpiece, as estimable for its charming style as for its penetration and profundity. . . . Understandably, it has become inseparable from Pascal's [own] works and . . . has shaped the historical image of the author of the *Pensées*.[8]

In this retelling, Pascal's life falls into two parts of unequal length and interest. For longer years of lesser import, he was a mathematical and scientific prodigy. At twelve, without instruction or reading, he amused himself on the playroom floor by retracing the steps of

Euclid. At sixteen, he published work on conic sections that was said to surpass anything done "since Archimedes." By the age of twenty-four, he had invented the Arithmetic Machine and conducted the Vacuum Experiments. Gilberte calls the Machine "a new thing in nature"; with it, anyone could use the rotations of wheels to perform operations of thought. She passes rather quickly over the Experiments, remarking only that they established "the weight of the air" as the cause of effects hitherto attributed to "the horror of the vacuum." This is an understatement; they provided the first experimental disproof of Aristotelian—and Cartesian—physics. Pascal was well on his way to becoming the most eminent savant in France, if not Europe. Instead, after a spiritual conversion in two stages, he abandoned the Machine and the Experiments, too.[9]

In the eight short years before his early death, the mature Pascal became a devout author and saintly exemplar. He wrote the *Provinciales* and began an Apology for the Faith. In the former, he defended Augustinian conceptions of grace and attacked the Jesuits' supposed moral laxism. In the latter, he would have devoted his remarkable talents to the task of "refuting the strongest arguments of the atheists." Incapacitating illness interrupted this writing before an early death terminated it, but this same illness was the condition for his further spiritual development. The greater part of Gilberte's narrative is devoted to her evocation of his exemplary faith, hope, and charity.[10]

The crux of this life is conversion, but the very faith that inspired Gilberte also limited her history. She had been taught by the abbé de Saint-Cyran and others that God—only God—can make a heart "new" (Ezek. 36:26), and it would not have occurred to her to seek human explanations.[11] She emphasizes "an occasion" in his twenty-fourth year when Providence "obliged him to read pious literature." That occasion was a serious injury suffered by his father, but neither she nor later scholars have well considered the domestic context for spiritual change. In any case, having read, she says that Blaise renounced "all other studies so that he might devote himself to the one thing that Jesus Christ calls necessary."[12] This is to hear the Word and prepare for eternal life (Luke 10:42; John 6:27). However, Pascal's experimental science followed the providential occasion and devotional readings, not vice versa.

Gilberte's complementary account of the Second Conversion represents the great man as having been called by God "to quit the world absolutely."[13] This, too, is problematical. Looking forward, her language suggests a more decisive withdrawal than is consistent with the factual evidence. Looking backward, there are other problems. In Paris in 1662, Gilberte probably worked from her memory of letters that she had received in Clermont in 1654 and 1655; in them, her sister, then a nun at Port-Royal, had reported her brother's change of heart. Jacqueline de Sainte-Euphémie believed in the sinfulness of man and the grace of God, and she reported the conversion without much of a role for herself or any for other family members. For her, the past was something to be overcome.[14] Gilberte, too, divides Blaise's life at the conversion rather than uniting it.

More remarkably, even in a narrative centered on spiritual conversion, she keeps perfect silence on the spectacular evidence discovered on his person after his death. From within his doublet, where he had secured and secreted it under the lining, the Périers recovered the *Mémorial,* a scrawled Paper folded into an elegant Parchment copy. After a meticulous heading with a precise notation of the date and time comes the record of an ecstatic experience, beginning with a single, centered word, "fire." We confront the "God of Abraham, God of Isaac, God of Jacob."[15] Pascal's heirs appreciated the significance of the *Mémorial,* which they placed first in the album into which they mounted his manuscripts. Mesnard has now edited "the most extraordinary writing that Pascal ever penned." He believes that it documents "the immediate presence of God . . . , a personal revelation . . . , the beginning of a new life."[16]

The *Vie de Monsieur Pascal* prepares readers to revere its subject. Its conception of the life was true to Pascal's own faith, and it has been very fruitful for later interpreters. But it is also limiting insofar as it has etched too deep a line between the man before and the man after conversion. It is limiting insofar as it has encouraged readers to find only intellectual and spiritual content in the "Thoughts" of this "King of Minds."[17] And it is limiting insofar as it directs attention only to the powerful faith of the Apologist and pure spirit of "our saint,"[18] while regarding his illness as something physical, apart from his mind and spirit, an obstacle to thought if a condition for further spiritual development.

A Revisionist Conception

I have found empirical evidence, open to others' critical review, that the Pascal of the Night of Fire was *unconsciously* preoccupied by continued attachment to his deceased parents, even as he was *consciously* committing himself to his God alone. It would not be necessary to make such a point of this were it not for the denial of such attachments in the orthodox tradition.[19] In the *Vie de Monsieur Pascal,* there is no hint of a mother-son relationship before the early death of Antoinette Begon (1596–1626), leaving three young children. However, in an oral anecdote, Gilberte provides additional testimony that can be analyzed methodically to show Blaise's infantile attachment to his living mother. Modern studies suggest that early loss can have long-deferred psychiatric consequences.[20]

Étienne Pascal (1588–1651) has always been allowed a more prominent place in the story of his son's life. It ought to be dominant. In historical memory, he has become "Pascal's father," but in historical fact it was Blaise who was "Pascal's son." Étienne was sole parent after his wife's death in 1626, head of the household until his own death in 1651, and Blaise's sole source of financial support ever, sole teacher ever, mentor in mathematics and the sciences, and so on. Paternal love and pride were the essential conditions for Blaise's rapid intellectual development and great early accomplishment. Then Étienne died.

Blaise wrote a long letter of consolation to Gilberte, which she treasured. However, in her memoir of his life, she considers this most painful loss only in a displaced reference in the Second Version, where she quickly makes the spiritually correct but historically erroneous point that "he loved without attachment."[21] Critically reread, the letter in which Blaise instructs Gilberte in the Two Loves also documents his own continued attachments to his father, explicitly, and both sisters, implicitly.

Jacqueline, the youngest of the Pascals (1625–61), was the favored sister. Traditionally, Blaise led her to God at the time of his First Conversion in 1646, and, after his relapse into relative worldliness, she led him back at the Second in 1654. Yet it was she who had shown the earliest signs of devotion. His attachment helped to inspire his First Conversion, probably, and Second, certainly. He followed her, figuratively, even after she put on the veil (a decisive rupture) and took her vows (a civil death). Gilberte reports that when she died in 1661, Blaise displayed no grief himself and tolerated none in others.[22] The question is how to interpret such behavior.[23]

Gilberte, the eldest child (1620–87), married away in 1641. This was just when, as Blaise was repeatedly to remind her in later years, his chronic pain had begun.[24] Whatever he meant, she felt unloved. He failed to show affection or to acknowledge her tenderness. This troubled her greatly until the day of his death, when she was disillusioned by "a very worthy person" who "told me that it was his fundamental pious maxim *never to allow anyone to love him with attachment.*"

After his death, we discovered still another proof of how much he had taken this principle to heart. So that he could have it ever-present, he had written this out in his own hand on a separate little paper. We found it on him [N.B.] and recognized it as something that he had often consulted [N.B.]. Here's what it said:

> It's wrong for them to become attached to me, even if they do it freely and with pleasure. I would deceive anyone in whom I were to arouse such a desire, for I'm no one's end, and I can't offer anyone satisfaction. Aren't I ready to die? And so the object of their attachment will die. I would be guilty of passing off a falsehood as if it were the truth, even if I were to persuade them most gently, and they were to accept it with pleasure, and in this they were to give me pleasure. I ought to warn those who would be ready to consent to the lie that they should not believe it, however much I might benefit. In much the same way, then, I would be guilty if I were to make them love me or to attract people to attach themselves to me. They should not attach themselves to me; they must devote their whole lives and every effort to pleasing God or searching for Him.[25]

So, Gilberte concluded, Blaise's apparent indifference had actually been a sign of his perfect charity.

The fate of this Separate Little Paper well illustrates the strengths and weaknesses of the traditional understanding of a man remembered for his sovereign intellect and Christian spirit. Gilberte wrote that it represented "divine illumination given him for the perfection of his Christian life."[26] The first editors of the *Pensées* more systematically rationalized and depersonalized this intimate text. As principled Pascalians, they removed *all sixteen* of Blaise's first-person pronouns from the brief paragraph, then bound their corrected version along with other "Christian Thoughts" into an editorially conceived chapter 28.[27] This was to strike the person from the Paper, having already stripped the Paper from the person.

Of course, scholarship has progressed. Modern editors have restored Pascal's pronouns, and everyone would probably accept that there is more to Pensée 396 than numbered thought. However, rationalistic biases remain remarkably strong. In his *Pascal et Saint Augustin* (1970), the most learned theological study, Sellier discusses the Separate Little Paper as one abstraction among others, Pascal's reflection on the Augustinian distinction between use and enjoyment, *uti/frui*. In his respected edition of the *Pensées* (1976 and 1991), Sellier presents it as part of a planning dossier for the Apology.[28] In his *Pascal* (1951), the best life and works, Mesnard compares its ideas to those of Descartes and other great thinkers. In his *Pensées de Pascal* (1976), the best commentary, he suggests that its intimacy is only apparent, "masking" general principles.[29] I suggest contrarily that the general principles mask a deeply personal response to his history of unacceptable losses.

Strictly historical scholarship on Pascal has moved away from such considerations. Mesnard has produced by far the most original and most learned work on the great man's life: *Pascal et les Roannez* (1965). His premise is that Gilberte and her daughter Marguerite guarded Blaise's memory somewhat jealously and so misrepresented historical reality, posthumously clasping him to the bosom of the family and so holding him back from friends. His declared purpose is "to *detach* Pascal as much as possible from this family and to reconsider him, so to speak, through the eyes of his two great friends," Artus and Charlotte de Roannez.[30] Thus, Mesnard redirects scholarly attention away from the Pascal and Périer households and toward the duc de Roannez and his entourage. Focus on this friendship, which did not become close before 1653,[31] inevitably diverts attention from the first thirty formative years of Blaise's life. Furthermore, the research in the notarial archives that has been so instructive on so many points of fact contributes little to our understanding of the heart.[32]

A large body of psychiatric literature investigates the hypothetical relationship between early parental loss and later depressive disorders.[33] No one imagines a one-to-one correspondence of sufficient cause and necessary effect, and, in Pascal's case, the long years between his mother's death and his own incapacitating illness surely mattered. However, clinical, epidemiological, and theoretical studies combine to encourage the closest possible scrutiny of the great project left on his writing table when work was suspended by illness.[34]

Seeking significant affective content in Pascal's work, I do find evidence strongly suggestive of a depressive disorder. This is not to dismiss his writings; it is to contribute to their interpretation. *Pascal's* last, most original, and most brilliant scheme for the projected Apology is the two-part plan sketched in Pensée 6, outlined in the table of contents, and partially realized in the "classified" fragments, Pensées 1–382. Part 1 was to have been a naturalistic argument for "the misery of man without God," an appeal to self-knowledge that would lead the worldly reader toward religion. Part 2 was to have been a scriptural argument for the Christian Redemption, which promises eternal "felicity with God." Pascal still moves readers with his expressive fragments on human misery; the *Pensées* include no comparable evocation of happiness.

Pascal's paradox of the useful illness, reported in the *Vie de Monsieur Pascal* and developed in the *Prière sur le bon usage des maladies,* is celebrated.[35] A valetudinarian believer, he supposed that physical illness could serve spiritual well-being. A respectful student of his life and work, I suppose that subclinical hypomanic traits served him as a polemicist and as a lay thinker who dared to project a grand Apology. Apparently, a more severe depressive disorder then helped him to experience and to express much that is deepest and darkest in the *Pensées*.[36]

John Bowlby's attachment theory has suggested general lines of inquiry and interpretation. Although few working historians or other students of Pascal can be familiar with it, its concern with elemental affects and observable patterns of behavior makes it at least potentially very useful. Dr. Bowlby's magisterial trilogy is entitled *Attachment and Loss* (1969–80) (see appendix 1).

I suggest that the mature Pascal suffered from an affective disorder, the course and causes of which cannot be fully known. Yet episodes in 1647, 1651, 1654, and 1658–59 are probable and probably related to his experience of separation and loss. Admittedly, I am separated from my subject by a wide ocean and three and a half centuries. There can be no true diagnosis from such a distance. Any historical assessment must be tentative. Having said that, I add that the *Diagnostic and Statistical Manual,* Fourth Edition (DSM-IV, 1994), of the American Psychiatric Association does provide an atheoretical and operational tool that is potentially very useful (see appendix 2).

I would also recommend the psychological and psychiatric literature on what seems to be the disproportionate amount of affective illness observed in writers, including the most gifted, and, inversely, the exceptional creativity displayed by many writers who are also sufferers from manic-depressive illness, especially in milder cyclothemic forms. Kay Redfield Jamison, author of *Touched with Fire: Manic-Depressive Illness and the Artistic Temperament* (1993) and coauthor of the monumental *Manic-Depressive Illness* (1990), is among those who have called attention to this "silver lining" of otherwise dark clouds (see appendix 3).

PART ONE

ATTACHMENTS

The two great events in the young Blaise Pascal's emotional life were the loss of his mother, who died when he was only three years old, and the subsequent transformation of his relationship with his father, who became all-important and remained so until his death twenty-five years later. Unfortunately, Pascal's heirs, our informants, focus so sharply on Blaise's intelligence and spirituality that they virtually isolate him even within the household. Even his father remains an indistinct figure in this representation, and his mother is lost in the shadows.

Gilberte Périer mentions Antoinette Begon's name in the second sentence of her *Vie de Monsieur Pascal*. That is all, absolutely all, that she has to say about the living woman. Mother enters to give birth to Genius, then quickly exits to make way for Father's education of Genius:

> My mother having died in the year 1626, when my brother was only three years old, my father found himself alone. He devoted himself more fully to his family, and, as he had no other son, his great affection for him was a matter not only of the child's evidently great intelligence but also of the boy's status as only son. [My father] could not bring himself to entrust his education to anyone else, and so he then resolved that he himself would instruct him, as he did.[1]

Readers seem to be left with only rhetorical questions concerning the mother's place in this little family. What difference could her short life and early death have made to her one son, who suffered the loss when he was so young? And, given such a father, what child could ever have needed a mother?

Chapter 1 serves to make a historical case for the anxious attachment of the young boy to his living mother. It returns readers to the alien world of the seventeenth century, when the most sophisticated savants lapsed into the grossest superstitions about the facts of life and powerful heads of genteel households lorded it over women and children. Yet this world, like our own, was another in which mother-child bonding was elemental, another in which separations and losses could be catastrophic.

Chapter 2 reconsiders Étienne Pascal's situation as a bereaved widower. It was Étienne, not Blaise, who headed the family, and this father made at least three significant decisions after his wife's death that radically altered his relationship with his one son. He would not remarry, would not remain in his native city, and would not send his son to a *collège*. The bare facts have long been well known, but their consequences for Blaise's emotional life have not been well understood.

Chapter 3 reconsiders Blaise Pascal's genius as a precocious savant in light of his relationship with his father. It begins the argument that his particular history of familial attachments preconditioned his most impressive intellectual achievements.

CHAPTER I

The Ghostly Mother

Blaise Pascal was anxiously attached to his mother before her early death. This conclusion rests on the analysis of testimony concerning his first years that has always perplexed everyone familiar with it. It tells an "utterly strange story" about "the strangest illness in the world," which was apparently the effect of an old witch's mortal spell. The Strange Story survives in two versions, here designated the Ménil Version and Marguerite's Version.[1] The former is regulative. It was recorded by an anonymous hand "at Ménil on 14 August 1661."

The historical filiation of this oral tradition can be reconstructed, and it is very reassuring. The initial testimony can only have been that of Étienne himself, a uniquely well-qualified participant-observer. His elder daughter, Gilberte, must have heard the story from her father directly, and she was the sole intermediary between this participant-observer and the eventual recorders. The recorder of the first written version is identifiable only by the time and place, but these, too, are reassuring. Ménil or Mesnil is a common place name, but the search can be restricted to the Paris region by Gilberte's presence in August 1661.[2] Ménil-Saint-Denis makes sense geographically, socially, and culturally.

Geographically, Ménil-Saint-Denis was just a league to the west of Port-Royal des Champs, where Jacqueline Pascal was a nun.

Socially, this was Ménil-Habert, and the Haberts were among the oldest and closest Parisian friends of the Pascals. Culturally, the most important fact is that Henri-Louis Habert de Montmort had succeeded Marin Mersenne and Jacques Le Pailleur as the central figure of the most important scientific society in France, with which Blaise Pascal was still identified even after his conversions.[3] The particular identity of the anonymous recorder at Ménil does not matter nearly as much as the general sophistication of the whole milieu of curious savants.

The Strange Story of Baby Blaise and the Old Witch

This oral narrative apparently aroused the recorder's interest because the scientific credentials of the Pascals and the Périers compelled others to take seriously Gilberte's tale of a witch and her spells:

Mme. [Gilberte] Périer told us an utterly strange story about her brother. He was still only two years old when he fell to the strangest illness in the world. He couldn't stand the sight of water or other liquids, and he couldn't endure his father and his mother together, although he could perfectly well accept either one separately. He was as emaciated as a child *en chartre,* so much that death seemed the only outcome.

So extraordinary an illness made many say that he had been the victim of a spell, and suspicion fell on an old woman who had received the charity of the household and to whom the nurse had sometimes brought him. Rumor became so general that M. Pascal the father decided to find out about it. He drew this woman aside, threatened to take her to court if she did not cure his son, and ordered her to do it with no new spell.

After apologizing, the old woman promised it. But she said that some other creature must die in the place of the child, for the spell was mortal. He wanted to give her a horse, but she was content to take a cat, and, as she was carrying one off, she met persons on the stairs who opposed her. Taking fright, she then threw the cat out the window. Although it was rather low, the cat fell stone-dead.

Then she went to the garden to choose a few common herbs, which she mixed with flour, making a sort of cake that was placed on the child's navel. As soon as it was put upon him [by her?], he fell into a lethargy in which he seemed to be dead. Having been called, the doctors pronounced him dead. His father alone maintained that the child was *not* dead, and he prevented them from shrouding him.

Shortly afterward, the old woman knocked at the door. When he saw her, the father was unable to control himself. He rushed over and struck her. Without showing any surprise, she said that he was right to have hit her, because she had forgotten to tell him what to expect. She assured him that his son wasn't dead and that he would remain in this condition [only] until midnight, when he would be found cured.

They waited until then, reassuring themselves all along that the child was *not* dead. Finally, at two o'clock he began to revive. He saw his father and his mother together without alarm, which showed that he was better. Nevertheless, he was still a little afraid of water. But soon he was playing with it, and in four or five days he had so recovered that he seemed never to have been ill.

The old woman confessed that she had been driven to cast the spell on him, because M. Pascal the father had refused her, when she begged him to solicit unjustly for her in a legal matter.[4]

The witch and her spells, actual or alleged, need not continue to mystify a medical case history, observed, remembered, and recorded by credible persons: "He was emaciated like children who are *en chartre,* so much that death seemed the only outcome."[5] Seventeenth-century lexicographers offered a babel of labels for the medical problem(s), but their definitions suggest at least an imperfect understanding of the etiology and proper treatment of the deficiency disease(s) popularly termed *chartre:*

Debilitating disease that consists in such an emaciation of the entire body that there seems to be nothing left on the bones but skin. "To be *en chartre* . . ." "We appeal to St. Mandé for those who have fallen *en chartre.*"[6]

"A wet nurse had to be given to the sick [child], because he was falling *en chartre.*" . . . This term apparently derives from the preceding word [*la chartre,* prison], because incarceration causes dejection and emaciation.[7]

The provision of wet nurses would certainly have helped those children who suffered from *chartre* or, in a modern term, marasmus. The basic problem was the inability of adult caregivers to supply adequate protein, calories, vitamins, and minerals. The breast milk even of a woman who is herself malnourished supplies these essential nutrients, but weaning can leave a child without an adequate dietary replacement. No premodern economy could supply cheap, plentiful, widely distributed, and safely pasteurized cows' milk.[8] Although the Pascals' native Clermont was located near to the highlands of Auvergne with their herds, what came down to market was cheese and not milk, and the plainland of the Limagne was devoted to the cultivation of cereals.[9] Gruels filled weanlings with carbohydrates while failing to meet basic nutritional needs for proteins and calories, not to mention vitamins and minerals.

Furthermore, unsanitary feeding practices led to gastrointestinal infections and "weanling's diarrhea."[10] Malnutrition and infection combine in a synergistic relationship. Malnutrition lowers bodily defenses against infections, and infectious diarrhea, in turn, inhibits providers from offering the necessary food and drink and then, before nutrients can be absorbed, evacuates too rapidly whatever is ingested. The child loses subcutaneous fat, then muscle tissue, as the body consumes its own reserves. Progressive losses in weight are accompanied by a retardation of further growth, a fractiousness that complicates feeding, and a perverse loss of appetite itself.[11]

Much of the advice offered by the doctors of the Old Regime was very good, however imperfect their understanding. They advised that weaning be postponed until the age of eighteen or even twenty-four months, which is very late by modern Western standards but very sensible if the weanling cannot be assured of adequate nutrition without breast milk.[12] Furthermore, they counseled against the *bouillie* or gruel that was the principal supplement and dietary alternative. This counsel, too, was sensible because only in the ideal world was *bouillie* always a mixture of white flour or bread crumbs and fresh cows' or goats' milk, first baked and then served on a clean finger. In the real world, the flour or bread was nutritionally inadequate, the animal milk was often insufficient or unsanitary, the baking might be omitted by a dry nurse who found it easier to warm and moisten the mixture in her own mouth, and the finger. . . .[13]

In the Strange Story, Baby Blaise displays the symptoms of what we would call marasmus. He is emaciated at the age of two years (Ménil Version) after a progressive wasting in his second year (Marguerite's Version), and he rages at parents (both), while rejecting "water" (both) and "other liquids" (Ménil).[14] These reports support the inference that he suffered from malnutrition. Although the remote and proper narrators have nothing to say about diarrhea, gastrointestinal infection, too, is probable.

The malnutrition itself is absolutely certain. The knowing eye could have seen conclusive evidence of this in the autopsy performed after Pascal's death. The distraught Gilberte may not have witnessed this somewhat grisly effort to comprehend the incomprehensible, but she did record "the opening of the body."[15] Some things she understood; others, she did not:

The skull lacked any other suture than the [the blank left here by the copyist suggests a corresponding gap in Gilberte's anatomical knowledge],[16] which was probably the cause of the headaches from which he suffered his whole life long.

At this point, if not in the previous clause, Gilberte digressed to reminisce about her brother's development:

To be sure, the suture called the *fontale* [anterior fontanel] had once closed [in early childhood]. But, having [reopened and] remained open for a very long time in his childhood, as often happens at that age [sic] it had not been able to close again. A substantial callus [cartilage] had covered it completely, as you could easily feel with your finger [presumably during his later childhood].

Then she returned to the doctors' discovery of the skeletal abnormalities that she seems already to have known before the postmortem examination, without having given them much thought:

As for the coronal suture, there wasn't a trace of it. The doctors observed that there was a prodigiously massive brain, the substance of which was so solid and so condensed that, in their judgment, this was the reason why, since the *fontale* hadn't been able to reclose [over so massive a brain], nature had provided this callus.[17]

The seventeenth-century doctors thought that Pascal's "prodigiously massive brain" had been too big and too solid for his skull to enclose. Hence the open fontanel, hence the chronic headaches, and hence the triumphant intellect. In short, they observed genius. But a modern pathologist would see the consequences of childhood dietary deficiencies, particularly vitamin D and calcium. The diagnosis would be rickets:[18]

Pathologic changes in children [with rickets] consist essentially of defective calcification of growing bone and hypertrophy of the epiphysial cartilages. . . . In chronic deficiency the cancellous bone of the diaphysis and of cortical bone may be resorbed.[19]

More general deficiencies of proteins and calories may also have been involved in this case. Marasmus is "a bone disease as well as an 'everything disease.' " The malnourished body consumes itself, and the skeletal child who is "nothing but skin and bone" actually loses even that:

Protein-calorie malnutrition can result in a thin shell of bone or reduced mineral mass, and even a loss of bone. In the extreme situation, actual bone "dumping" may appear as the hard tissues as well as the soft are lost in the course of nutritional disease.[20]

Today, when weaning is usually earlier than it was in the seventeenth century, dietary deficiencies often simply delay the closing of the fontanels, which is normally completed by the ossification of the anterior fontanel sometime between ten and sixteen months.[21] In Gilberte's time, when weaning was later and weanlings' diets were routinely deficient, it was apparently very common at least in Lower Auvergne—"as is often the case at this age"—for the fontanels to close in the second year, while children were still on the breast, and then to reopen after the nutritional catastrophe of weaning.

The Terrible Two-Year-Old and His Terrifying World

The physiological crisis of malnutrition was compounded by a social and psychological crisis after weaning. The two behavioral symptoms of this one "strangest illness" admit no other single explanation. First, the Ménil Version says that the child "could not stand the sight of water or other liquids." Marguerite's Version gives a livelier description of exaggerated protests, "very great fits of passionate rage."[22] Second, the Ménil Version says that he "couldn't endure his father and mother together, although he could perfectly well accept either one separately." Again, Marguerite adds detail: "He responded with pleasure to the caresses of either one alone, but when they approached one another, he cried and struggled with an excessive violence."[23] Weaning relates these two behavioral patterns to one another and to the physiological evidence of malnutrition.

Much of the strangeness of the Strange Story is a consequence of the fact that the child's behavior was observed by adults. Blaise must have seen the cup and reacted vigorously against this symbol of deprivation, but Étienne saw "water or other liquids." Adults then defined "weaning" as a "prevention" and derived *sevrer* from *seperare*.[24] Weaning was an active prevention by means of separation. The father knew very good reasons for preventing the boy from continuing to nurse, but the son could only have known that the breast and all that it had represented had been taken from him. In favorable circumstances, the routines of nursing would have included all sorts of interaction (looking, touching, vocalizing), not just a passive receptivity. Any sudden disruption by means of social separation would have been a disaster for the child.[25]

Blaise's second "strange" behavior, his loud protests at his father and mother together but not at either separately, also makes perfect sense, but only from the weanling's perspective. Étienne surely saw himself and his wife as a perfectly proper couple to whom no one, young or old, could possibly take exception. Blaise presumably saw either that his mother, who was somehow lost to him after weaning, now approached with his father (Ménil Version) or that his mother, holding but not nursing him, welcomed the approach of his father (Marguerite).[26] In either case, *that* was the insult following the injury of weaning itself.

Other factors aggravated insult and injury. Blaise's experience in the year 1624, which began when he was six months old, helped to prepare the crisis that came to a near-fatal climax sometime in the next calendar year. In 1624, Étienne was the *premier échevin* of Clermont, but he spent most of this year in Paris, far from home. There was a first trip in the winter, then a second that lasted the seven and a half months from 6 May to 26 December.[27] For his son, this would have been a period of rapid social development characterized by great dependence on his mother (or possibly a primary surrogate) and anxiety at the approach of strangers. When Étienne finally returned to Clermont, he would have felt fully entitled to reclaim *his* wife and *his* son, but, to Blaise, he would have been an intrusive stranger.

Étienne's very long absences in 1624 may have owed something to a veritable taboo that precluded sexual relations for nursing mothers or nursing for the sexually active.[28] An eldest son was often favored with his mother's breast, which was recognized as the safest means of feeding even for those families who could afford to hire wet nurses.[29] Although it is a secret of the nursery, not the boudoir, that I am trying to discover, the two were related. When Étienne finally returned, he promptly took his place in his wife's bed, as we know from the fact of Jacqueline's birth just over nine months later.[30] This means that Antoinette could not have continued to nurse her son, had she done so for his first eighteen months.

I have supposed that Blaise was nursed by his own mother. This inference may be erroneous, although the combination of strange behaviors strongly suggests it. The Ménil Version of the story includes a nurse who had "sometimes" brought Blaise to the old woman. Marguerite's Version also includes a nurse who gave him the breast intermittently after he had finally passed the crisis of his illness.[31] But the nurse was never the focus of Baby Blaise's attachment, as the second behavioral symptom makes very clear. Mother was Mother, whoever had nursed the child before his father's return.

The weanling would have had to endure further stresses in the second half of his second year in addition to the return of his father and the withdrawal of the breast, his mother's or a nurse's. Although serene developmentalists can write of this as "the stage of autonomy," harried parents use different words, "the terrible twos."[32] Infantile terrorism actually peaks before rather than after the second birthday. Experts agree: "Negativism" is "far and away the most significant new behavior" in the second half of the second year. "The emergence of negativism is inevitable."

> All parents should be prepared for a fair amount of friction. . . . Why a child has to become ornery and stay that way for a minimum of six or seven months is one of the mysteries that make the study of early human development so rich and fascinating.[33]

In the best of circumstances, this stage of development demands a new sort of parental discipline, precisely because the child has begun willfully to test the limits of his social being.

Blaise Pascal was full of the devil. After Étienne had returned to Clermont in December 1624, he, the intrusive and powerful "stranger" who had retaken Blaise's mother as his own wife, was clearly responsible for disciplining his son and defining the limits. How did he perform his paternal duty? We do not know. It means very little that, in the desperate circumstances of his son's strange illness, he was willing to strike down an old woman in his own home.[34]

It does mean something that this was a society in which parental violence was sanctioned for every child, even ordered for the young prince who matured to become Louis XIII. In the words of King Henri IV to the governor of the Dauphin:

> I have a complaint to make: you do not send word that you have whipped my son. I want you and command you to whip him every time that he misbehaves or is stubborn, knowing full well that there is nothing in the world better for him than that.[35]

The good King knew this because he knew so well that he had benefited so much from the whippings of his own childhood.

The best evidence on disciplining in the Pascal family comes from Jacqueline, who addressed Gilberte on the subject in a letter dated 25 April 1655. Gilberte's inquiry has not survived, but the known composition of her household permits informed inferences on the nature of her problem. The mother's question must have been this: In keeping with the love of God and the love of man, how can I discipline my troublesome young sons? Firmly, even severely, her cloistered sister advocated a counterterror:

> Try to make yourself loved, reproving them [children and servants] without bitterness. Nevertheless, you must always do it with severity and firmness. . . . Whenever they offend against God, against their master [the head of the household], or against the charity and union that ought to prevail among them, then you must show yourself to be severe to the point of inspiring terror. You must know that the [common] people and [all] children are like the Jews, who are moved only by threats and by promises. . . . You cannot tolerate any offenses in these respects; rather, inform their master and exhort him to punish them severely. . . . It is very good that your greatest threat be to have them cast out.[36]

Jacqueline's counsel presumably reflects her own upbringing in Étienne's household.

In any case, Baby Blaise could not have raged with impunity; the good father would have responded to his son's "stubborness" with his own vigorous "wisdom." The recommended alternative to physical punishment could have been even worse. Some thirty years before Jacqueline's letter, he had indeed been "cast out."

The Young Mother and Her Early Death

This brings us back to the Old Witch. Her age means that she cannot have been another wet nurse; the Pascals' charity means that she must have been considered poor; her request for Étienne's support in a legal matter implies that she thought that she had some claim on his protection. All this is important, but not nearly so important from Baby Blaise's perspective as the fact that his nurse had left him with the old woman "sometimes." How many times, how long at a time? Hours? Days? Weeks? Months? It hardly matters. Even brief separations can be traumatic for young children, even in the best of circumstances.[37]

These were not the best of circumstances. The poor old woman was probably a *sevreuse:* "There are women in whose houses one places children as boarders in order to wean them."[38] That is, the old woman's social function was to separate the child from his mother and any other wet nurses. It was a desperate business. An older widow, especially, who could not even pretend to offer her own milk for sale and who might not have any other way to earn a living, could take in a younger and wealthier woman's child, with his tantrums and his diarrhea, hoping to receive as payment at least the small donations of the great household. In this case, how much worked against the success of this surrogate caretaking, the old woman and the little boy! Consider his angry temper, his strange surroundings, his wasting illness, her confessed hostility, her acknowledged poverty, her limited understanding . . .[39]

Keith Thomas has written persuasively about the social context of early modern witchcraft. Regularly, victims and their families suspected a particular person, and, regularly, this person was an inferior with a plausible grievance. Real women did cast spells in the effort to enlist the aid of higher powers. Their witchcraft was a pathetic form of vengeance in which they as otherwise impotent sufferers of "injustices" rose up against the stronger.[40] The reported facts of the Strange Story fit this theoretical model perfectly.

The Pascals and their neighbors blamed the old woman for the child's decline, presumably in her none-too-tender-loving care. But this was only their side of the story. From the old woman's perspective, the powerful Pascal had refused to help her in court, despite her past services. So she may actually have done her nefarious worst, actually casting the spell, as she confessed. It is also possible that she was a witch only by reputation and that her nominal confession actually represented only a frightened compliance after the suspicious magistrate had accused her. In any case, in the story as told by the Pascals, when Baby Blaise saw her coming, he swooned away.

He did survive. Marguerite's Version is more satisfactory than the Ménil Version in its account of the recovery, allowing weeks and not just days. Additional details make perfect sense historically and psychologically. Desperate attempts were made to nourish the baby by placing an herbal cake over his navel (the Old Witch before the crisis) and to replenish lost fluids by offering him sugared wine to drink (Mother or nurse after the crisis).[41] Then came the wet nurse's breast. And then came Mother's arms:

> At about six o'clock in the morning, he began to open his eyes and to recognize the people around him. Seeing his father and mother together, he began his usual crying. This showed that he wasn't yet cured, but it was at least some consolation that he wasn't dead, and six or seven days later he began to tolerate the sight of water. Returning home, my grandfather saw him pouring water from one glass to another in the arms of his mother. [Hoping that this was a sign of a complete cure,] he tried to approach them [mother and child together], but the child wouldn't allow it. A few days later, he [Blaise, again apparently in his mother's arms] did. In three weeks, the child was fully recovered and fleshed out once again.[42]

The Strange Story is not so very strange, after all. It makes very good sense, even if it is a sense that eluded its tellers. Their world seems alien and dangerous, too, especially for the very young. Nevertheless, at the heart of the story there are these two most familiar and most comforting facts: the great power of a mother's love for her young child and the stubborn force of the young child's love for his mother. For the historian, Antoinette Begon may still be much more a ghost than not, but, for Baby Blaise, she was life itself.

Then she died, leaving her husband and their three children, Gilberte (six years old), Blaise (three), and Jacqueline (one). Analysis of the Strange Story now shows that Blaise had been anxiously attached to his mother, but no informant tells how the little boy reacted to her death, either at the time or later. Pascal's historians must choose or, if you will, wager.

The choice that seems more cautious is actually quite risky. We can proceed directly to later and happier parts of this life story that are better known or apparently known, especially Étienne's attentive parenting after his wife's death. Following Gilberte, every scholarly historian of Blaise's life has made this choice.[43] However, this is to wager that what family members did not observe, remember, and record about the little boy and the impact of his loss cannot have been very significant. The wager is doubled by the additional bet that no understanding derived from the psychology of our time can pertain to this past. This risks Panglossian optimism and psychological obscurantism.

There is an alternative. We can proceed indirectly, considering psychological generalizations before returning to the historical case. There are three sorts of studies on the general problem of early maternal loss in the contemporary world: first, clinical studies of parentally bereaved young children; second, an important body of theory on the human experience of attachments, separations, and losses; and third, epidemiological studies of the incidence of early parental loss among populations of adult psychiatric patients.[44] For a brief review of the clinical studies and of attachment theory, see appendix 1.

CHAPTER 2

The Widowed Father

Étienne Pascal made three particularly consequential decisions in the decade or so that followed his wife's death. They are best introduced as negatives: first, he decided that he would *not* remarry; second, he decided that he would *not* remain in Clermont, the home city of the extended family; third, he decided that he would *neither* send his son to any school *nor* bring any other tutor into the household. These three negative decisions had one very important positive consequence: they powerfully reinforced the bonds of attachments within the reduced household.

Even Étienne himself may not have fully understood his own motivation, and no historian could presume to divine all of the many factors that must have contributed to each decision. It seems quite likely that much of this decision making, especially the decision not to remarry, must have been made more by default over a period of time than by conscious resolution at any one time. No one knows. But ignorance of "causes" cannot trouble knowledge of "effects," and those effects seem so predictable that at some level he must have wanted to do just what he did do. He attached his children, especially his son, ever more closely to himself.

By 1635, the year in which Blaise turned twelve, Étienne had cut himself free from most nonparental responsibilities. He had taken no second wife and so, not incidentally, fathered no further children after Gilberte, Blaise, and Jacqueline. For most of every year, he had no regular relations with his extended family in his native city. For the foreseeable future, he would have neither office himself nor corporate affiliations with other officers. Indeed, he appears to have had neither prospects for employment nor the sort of investments that would have required his attentive supervision. I am tempted to rewrite the long sentence from Gilberte's *Vie de Monsieur Pascal* in which she made the long jump from her mother's death to her brother's education: "Having lost his wife, my father resolved to hold his children, especially his only son, especially closely."[1]

Étienne's Decision Not to Remarry

The elder Pascal chose not to remarry after the death of his wife in 1626. He was then thirty-eight years old.[2] Under the demographic conditions of the Old Regime, it was not at all unusual for a husband to lose a wife in her childbearing years. A quarter or more of all married men were widowers by the age of thirty-five years, and another quarter or more of the total were widowed by forty-five: "We should note the frequency of widowerhood suffered between 30 and 40 years, especially between 35 and 40 years."[3]

What was unusual in this case was that Étienne did not remarry promptly. For widowers in their thirties, the registers of parish after parish document remarriage rates of about 70 percent within the parish, without counting additional remarriages outside the parish. The median intervals between spousal losses and subsequent remarriages are consistently less than one year.[4] Remarriage rates were higher for urban widowers and for fathers of young children. All this explains the mild surprise registered by Pierre Durand, a seventeenth-century compatriot, when he noted that the young widower, father of three small children, had not remarried.[5]

No informant specifies how Étienne cared for the children in the five-year interval between his loss and his move to Paris (1626–31), but recourse to other members of the family or to servants could not possibly have nullified the significance of the great fact that he did not remarry. If Étienne were to have remarried, there would have been not only a new wife-and-stepmother but also, probably, new sons and daughters, brothers and sisters. In fact, there was to be nothing of the sort. For Étienne, that meant that there were no close rivals in his affections for the privileged place occupied by his three children, especially his one son. For these children, that meant that there was one parent and one only, with no mother-surrogate of anything like the father's importance.

In these circumstances, the bonds between the single parent and his children certainly became the tighter, and there was probably a similar effect on the relationships of the older sister with her younger siblings. Gilberte was three and a half years older than Blaise, almost six years older than Jacqueline. In the motherless household, her relationships with the younger children probably took on some aspects of a mother's role even at a relatively young age. The capacity of orphaned children to provide support for one another has been closely observed in our own century of death and dislocation—but the same capacity also makes these children more indispensable to one another than would otherwise be the case.[6]

The presence of female servants in seventeenth-century households meant the availability of other persons who might be supposed to have served as surrogates for the lost mother. But any such comforting suppositions, if taken to mean the formation of lasting attachments between Blaise and a servant or servants, cannot be supported from the evidence at hand. In the *Vie de Monsieur Pascal,* Gilberte manages to tell the story of Blaise's youth without so much as alluding to a single domestic, named or not.[7] In the *Vie de Jacqueline Pascal,* she does credit an unnamed female retainer with having "raised" both younger children, but even this passing remark, rightly understood, probably tells more against than for the sort of specific, enduring, and emotionally compelling relationships that alone qualify as attachments.[8]

Louise Delfault was the woman in question, and the documentary record verifies that she served the Pascals in Paris for the last twenty years of Étienne's life (1631–51). But this means that she did not serve the family in Clermont during Blaise's first eight and a half years (1623–31).[9] Of course, anyone is perfectly free to suppose that the younger boy had already formed an attachment, properly speaking, with a motherly domestic before 1631. So much the better for him—until 1631. Then, to allow for the retention of the known Delfault in this role in the remote city, the supposing historian would have to suppose a further separation from the supposed mother-surrogate. So much the worse for him.

After 1631, the proprieties of gender relations would have militated against too close an association between Blaise and Delfault or any other young woman. It would have been one thing for a careful father to entrust his six-year-old daughter to the care of a young *Parisienne,* quite another to treat his eight-year-old son in the same way, ignoring the gender and maturation of the boy. A boy of this age was already a bit old to have been left in a woman's hands, and, with each passing year in the 1630s, moralistic arguments against a promiscuous association of the son and the servant would have become the stronger.[10]

Étienne's Decision Not to Remain in Clermont-Ferrand

The elder Pascal's second consequential decision was not to remain in Clermont but to move to Paris at the end of 1631. Gilberte explains that this relocation greatly favored Blaise's education by freeing his father from the distractions of provincial society and work in the tax court.[11] Consider the former. During the period when he remained in Clermont with his children as an unremarried widower (1626–31) Étienne's extended family would have been a significant resource for his children. His own perspective seems to have been that he suffered from an embarrassment of such riches.[12]

The great size of the family was legendary. Étienne's Aunt Jeanne Enjobert lived on until 1641, when one of her sons, Étienne's Cousin Blaise, counted out *469* of her "nephews and nieces" who were then still living. This amazing number can be verified,[13] but a genealogical recitation of the relatives who could have helped Étienne with the children in Clermont is not necessary and would distract us from the main point: the move from Auvergne was a move away from the other Pascals, notably Étienne's five brothers and sisters and their families.[14] Among them, the closest was the elder Blaise, chosen as the great Pascal's godfather and, as tellingly, Étienne's successor both in his house on the rue des Gras and in his office in the Cour des Aides.[15] It was also a move away from his in-laws, the Begons, particularly Antoinette's brother Jean and his wife Jacquette Durant, each of whom was godparent of a Pascal daughter.[16] After 1631, Blaise could not have had easy, regular access to uncles, aunts, or other surrogate-parents from the extended family. Students of history, literature, religion, and other disciplines now focus on the figure remembered rightly as the great Pascal; however, the boy himself must then have focused on the dominant figure in the family, his father.

Étienne's adult social world at Clermont inevitably involved him in much wider engagements, and some knowledge of these engagements can help explain his decision to leave his native city. He had long held office in a lower tax court, the Election of Clermont (1610–25); he had been the *échevin premier* of the city (1624); and he was at the time of his removal to Paris a *second président* in the Cour des Aides, the sovereign tax court for this part of the Kingdom (1626–34). All this made him one of the town's most powerful persons, but his prominence had various costs in years of crisis for the financial officers, the city government, the local school, and public health itself.

The varied troubles of Étienne's public life would have favored his evident reorientation toward private concerns in the late 1620s and early 1630s. In April 1626, he had purchased the charge in the Cour des Aides, which brought personal nobility to him as the officeholder and promised transmissible nobility to descendants, should a son and a grandson follow him in the heritable office. His future and that of his family seemed assured. But then disaster followed disaster, starting but not ending with his wife's death later in the same year.

In 1627, the Crown created seven new offices in the Cour des Aides, which had been a ten-man court. Sales of these positions lessened the social exclusiveness of the old court by introducing new persons, reduced the appreciation of old offices by glutting the market with new, and lowered the income of old officers by distributing shares of court fees to the new men as well as the old. At the same time, the Crown imposed forced loans that it euphemistically billed as "augmentations of wages." The net effect was that Étienne had to pay more for an office that seemed to be worth less.[17] In 1630, another "augmentation" forced him to loan the King an additional quarter of the capital value of his office.[18]

The year 1630 did bring the welcome news that the Cour des Aides would be moved from Montferrand to Clermont, a royal compensation to the larger city for losses suffered by its Election.[19] However, the royal Edict of Union, by which a distant King arbitrarily ordered the two old communities, each proudly independent, to join as one new municipality, Clermont-Ferrand, must have brought more aggravation than satisfaction.[20] First, to remove the Cour des Aides from Montferrand was to offend or even to injure those officers who had resided in that previously separate city. To compensate them, the evenhanded King again reached deeper into the pockets of his subjects, including Étienne Pascal and the officers from Clermont.[21]

Second, to introduce the sovereign financial court into Clermont was to exacerbate tensions between its members and those of the civil court, the Sénéchaussée-and-Présidial, which had previously enjoyed an undisputed preeminence. Both power and precedence were now contested, and one local historian from the seventeenth century makes Étienne the unsuccessful nominee of his colleagues in an electoral contest for the *échevinage* and explains his relocation to Paris as an effect of bitterness at this political failure.[22]

Third, more importantly for the parent of a son fast approaching the age for formal schooling, the Edict of Union further *divided* the two cities by granting a new Jesuit *collège* to Montferrand, which was otherwise very much the loser in this "bizarre" exercise of royal authority.[23] It would have made no sense to authorize opening a new school for Montferrand, if the King had not also ordered closing the old school in Clermont. Any good Clermontois with a son of school age would have been outraged, whatever he thought of the Jesuits. Blaise passed his seventh birthday in mid-1630; his closest uncle, Étienne's brother Blaise, was a leader in the unsuccessful defense of the old municipal school.[24]

I have used the term disaster, but, from this distance, the vicissitudes of venal officeholding, local politics, and Latin schooling may seem little more than aggravations. A disaster fully worthy of the name did strike the entire city in 1631. This was a plague year. The Cour des Aides retreated to Thiers, and Étienne as *second président* must have gone with his fellow officers, taking his children.[25] What happened in the Clermont that they left behind is so far removed from our experience as to be beyond modern comprehension.

Consider the record of births in the one parish from which registers survive for the period of the crisis. There were ninety-six baptisms in the calendar year 1630, but only fifteen in the twelve months from 30 June 1631 to 30 June 1632.[26] There is no complementary

TABLE 1
Population Loss at Clermont in the Plague of 1631
Property Tax Assessed (in *livres*)

	<4 l.	*4-10 l.*	*>10 l.*	*Totals*
Names struck	130	41	28	199
Retained	95	41	73	209

Pierre Charbonnier, "La peste de 1631," *Revue d'Auvergne* 79 (1965): 124.

record of deaths, but we can count the names struck from the tax rolls of 1630 in the course of preparing those for 1632. In the Pascals' parish, Saint-Pierre, 199 of 408 taxpayers were removed, suggesting a loss of almost half the population. Taxpayers assessed at higher levels did have a marked advantage, but even they died in great numbers (see table 1).

The names struck may include some heads of households who fled and survived, but most refugees would have returned, and no tax assessor abandons hope without cause. Contemporaries did understand some things about the terrible epidemic and their inability to control it. Confronted by the plague, they knew no remedy so effective as the three adverbs from the old maxim:

> Haec tria tabisicam tollunt adverbia pestum;
> *Mox, longe, tarde,* cede, recede, redi.[27]

Leave *quickly;* go *far away;* return *slowly.* The epidemic at Clermont must have contributed to Étienne's decision to relocate to Paris for however long a time. The month of the Pascals' departure, November, was the end of the plague season.[28] This would have been the first occasion when Clermontois who had retreated to some nearer refuge could have returned home to prepare for the longer journey to Paris—or when they would have been welcomed elsewhere on the road northward.

Whatever caused Étienne Pascal to move to Paris, these effects are certain. This single parent took himself as well as his children away from the extended family and from any other significant relationships in Clermont. He left behind the corporate world of the Cour des Aides, the disputes and complications of the Edict of Union, and all the problems for the city and its leaders that arose from the plague. He was freed to begin an active sort of parenting in Paris that would have been virtually impossible in his native city, where his relationships and responsibilities were so much more extensive.

Although Étienne himself returned home each fall for several years (1632–36), his move was both permanent and consequential. The 400-kilometer distance between Clermont and Paris was much greater in the seventeenth century than it is now, when transportation is so much safer, quicker, cheaper, and more comfortable. There was no regularly scheduled or minimally dependable conveyance of any sort between the two cities.[29] The trip was always long, costly, and difficult, and it could be dangerous, too.[30] These would have been good reasons for Étienne not to have taken his young children along with him on annual trips back to Clermont. Even if they, too, revisited their homeland and its people, which is far from certain, they had lost easy access to the extended family, the principal effect of which must have been to intensify attachments within the already reduced household.

Étienne's Decision Not to Send Blaise to a School

The elder Pascal's third significant decision was neither to send his son to any school nor to bring another tutor into the household.[31] He himself would teach the boy at home. In the familial tradition, the father's decision followed the mother's death; it was accepted as a matter of course and explained by his recognition of his son's genius. However, so extraordinary a decision could not have been a matter of course, and no simple explanation can suffice.

The question of Blaise's schooling must have been raised at least as early April 1630, when the royal Edict gave to Clermont the Cour des Aides but took away its Latin school.[32] Despite royal and judicial prohibitions, townsmen fought long and hard to maintain their own municipal *collège*. They succeeded only in part, and the Latin schooling at Clermont that had been made insecure in 1630 was not to be secured again until 1662, the year of the great Pascal's death.

Montferrand was united with Clermont after 1630 in form only, and this smaller and less favored community—part of the "unified city"—fought for the few compensations that had been given by an ungenerous King. This meant opening up its own new *collège* and, just as importantly, closing down that of Clermont. The Jesuits would have preferred to teach in the larger city, but, unwelcomed there, they finally agreed to organize the new *collège* in Montferrand, where classes did open in the fall of 1634.[33] Among the members of the Society who helped to establish the new school was the young François Annat, later the Confessor of Louis XIV and the named antagonist in Pascal's last two *Provinciales*.[34]

Quite apart from more narrowly personal motivations and corporate frustrations, the utter devastation of the plague and the extreme uncertainty of educational opportunity in Clermont must have helped to drive the Étienne Pascals from their native city. The municipal *collège* at Clermont had become a local battleground, and partisans from Montferrand had been supported by the Crown and the *Parlement*. In Paris, Étienne could have placed his son in a more secure and prestigious institution. Had he done so, Blaise would have been educated *by* other masters and *with* other students in a social environment that was deliberately all-embracing. Classes were very large, but close supervision was the rule, and hierarchical structures organized the leading students under the masters.[35] In the course of years spent in any such school, the boy would have formed significant relationships with masters and students. Inevitably, these engagements would have withdrawn him from his father's household.

However, Étienne chose not to send his son to any school even in Paris, where he would have had every opportunity to do so. This was truly extraordinary. Philippe Ariès has written that only the King's own sons were educated at home after the age of about ten.[36] Of course, even these exceptional boys were not directly governed or tutored by their own father, as was the case for Blaise Pascal.[37]

Even Adrien Baillet, a seventeenth-century librarian who seems to have read almost everything and an author whose own work suffers from the fact that he forgot almost nothing, could suggest only one other instance of paternal home schooling. Blaise Pascal's education remained, in his word, a "singularity." Only Jérome Bignon's (1589–1656) was at all comparable, and the circumstances of the Bignons and Pascals differed instructively.[38] Paternal and domestic education in the Bignon household had begun only in chaotic years of the 1590s when the normal functioning of both the courts of law for Roland, the father, and the schools for Jérome, the son, had been interrupted. Furthermore, when the boy was ten years old, the elder

Bignon agreed that Nicolas le Fevre, tutor of Henri II, prince de Condé, might take in Jérome as an inspirational light for his high-born but dim-witted pupil.

Jérome Bignon then spent two years with le Fevre in the Condé household away from his father's daily supervision.[39] The younger Bignon became well known both at Court and among the savants of Paris, and, although he returned to his father for further studies, including some jurisprudence, he was never again limited to the society—or the instruction—of his father and his father's close friends. Indeed, he studied law at the University of Orléans, where his close contemporary, Étienne Pascal, also studied.[40] From there, he returned for a brilliant career marked by the highest offices and by sympathy with Port-Royal.

In contrast, there was nothing in the Paris of the 1630s that would have prevented Étienne Pascal from sending his son to functioning schools. He chose not to do so. Therefore, Blaise never escaped parental tutelage and never experienced another teacher in another household or institutional setting. His sole parent in a city remote from his extended family was also his sole teacher. It goes almost without saying that no more traditional seventeenth-century education succeeded better, if the measure is to be the pupil's original, varied, profound, and enduring intellectual accomplishments in later life. But Pascal's unique upbringing also risked social and psychological constriction for its beneficiary. These risks were the greater because under his father's governance Blaise never had an independent residence, never an independent income, never training for an independent professional life, and never, apparently, parental encouragement for a marital alliance.[41]

What was going on in the years when most boys of his class stepped decisively beyond close relationships limited to members of the family and toward the broader society encountered in the *collèges* and universities? Modern scholarship on the phenomenon popularly known as "school refusal" suggests explanations. The deeper problems are often those of the *parent,* not the child. A mother or father may cling to a beloved child out of an intense need for companionship or a vague anxiety that something dreadful might happen. Even when the child's fears cannot be explained by parental anxieties, the real problems tend to concern leaving home, not going to school. In short, school refusal has more to do with the family than with the school and as much to do with the parents as with the child. It is a sort of attachment behavior best understood as a manifestation of separation anxiety.[42]

What was going on in the Étienne Pascal household? The rapid paragraph in which Gilberte proudly introduces her father's domestic instruction of her brother mentions these good reasons in this order: the loss of his wife, which left Étienne "alone"; the lack of another son, leaving only Blaise; and the precociousness of the little boy, which promised such great things. But good reasons may not be explanation enough for this father's "so great affection" or, in another language, his parental attachment. Étienne "could not bring himself to entrust his [son's] education to anyone else."[43]

Why did Étienne Pascal *not* remarry, *not* remain in Clermont, and *not* entrust Blaise's schooling to others? It would be too simple an answer to say, "because he loved his son." But it would not be wrong. Étienne's extraordinary paternal devotion extended beyond Blaise's childhood. Father and son together returned to their native city in 1649, where they spent Étienne's sixty-second and Blaise's twenty-seventh year together. The father had been badly injured in a fall on ice a few years earlier, and he was already old. The son, too, was infirm, even if no longer quite young. The already-old Étienne seems to have cared for the no-longer-quite-young Blaise as if he were still a child. Gilbert Domat, son of the latter's closest Clermontois friend, much later recorded this bit of local lore: "The father of M. Pascal the Genius . . . took extraordinary care of him."[44]

CHAPTER 3

The Precocious Son

The *Manuscrit Durand* associates the now forgotten father with his still illustrious son in a reference worth recalling: "Messieurs Pascal, illustrious mathematicians."[1] It is one of the peculiarities of this subject that Gilberte, the primary architect of the familial tradition, actually obscured Blaise's intellectual identification with and filial attachment to his father. Her narrative portrays the greater genius as a solitary discoverer and inventor, with Étienne's role virtually reduced to that of a properly appreciative witness.[2] She knew that Blaise had loved his father, but he had taught her that this had been a love "without attachment."[3] I argue contrarily that even in his most-celebrated feats as a mathematical and scientific prodigy, this son followed and honored his father, owing most and repaying most to this one most-beloved man. Paradoxically, it is in the works of genius, especially the Arithmetic Machine and the Vacuum Experiments, that the heart first discloses itself.

Blaise's "Invention of Mathematics"

As his sister tells the story of the great Pascal's education, the important fact was neither his ready comprehension of others' subject matter nor even the precociousness of his own maturation. It was rather the startling revelation of his genius. Nature, not nurture. Her one extended anecdote quickly became celebrated.[4] Her point in this story of the Twelve-Year-Old Euclid was that the boy-genius had "invented mathematics" without anyone else's help, but this same story provides the most dramatic evidence of the place of *Étienne* Pascal and *his* intellectual enthusiasms in his son's development. Nurture as well as nature:

VMP 8 His genius for geometry first manifested itself when he was only twelve years old in an episode so extraordinary that it deserves a detailed retelling.

9 My father was learned in mathematics, and he used to discuss this science with all qualified persons, who often came to his house. However, because he planned to instruct my brother in the languages, and because he knew that mathematics fills and greatly satisfies the mind, he didn't want my brother to have any knowledge of it. He feared that it would make the boy neglect his Latin and his other languages. . . . For this reason, my father shut away all of his books on the subject and refrained [even] from talking about it with his friends in his presence. The child's curiosity was aroused despite these precautions, and he often begged my father to teach him mathematics. My father refused. Instead, he promised that he would teach it to him as a reward, just as soon as he had learned his Latin and his Greek.

10 In the face of this opposition, one day my brother asked my father what was mathemetics. . . . He told him that, generally speaking, it was the way of making precise figures and finding the proportions among them. At the same time he forbade him from asking any more about it or from ever thinking about it. But, given even so slight an opening, this mind could not remain confined within the prescribed limits. By himself, he began to ponder the mathematical science of making perfectly precise figures.

During his playtime, while alone in the room where he usually amused himself, he took a piece of charcoal and drew figures on the tiles of the floor. For instance, he tried to find the way to draw a perfectly round circle, an equilateral triangle, and other things of the sort. He accomplished all of this. Then he tried to find the proportions. But, because my father had taken such pains to hide everything, he didn't even know the names. He had to invent his own vocabulary, and he called the circle "a round," the line, "a bar," and so on. After these definitions, he made himself axioms, and finally he made perfect demonstrations. As one progresses from one thing to the next in such matters, he pursued his research so far that he reached the thirty-second proposition of Euclid's Book One.[5]

11 While his son was absorbed in this task, my father entered the room. My brother didn't hear him enter or notice his presence for some time. You couldn't say who was the more surprised [when at last he did]. Was it the son, who was caught doing just what his father had ordered him *not* to do?

Or was it not the father, who happened upon his son in the midst of all of *this?* My father's surprise was all the greater when, in response to his question about what he was doing, the boy answered that he was seeking such and such a thing that was the thirty-second proposition of Euclid's Book One. My father asked him what had made him think of such a thing. He answered that it was because he had found something else, and, in response to the same question about that something else, he went though some other demonstration that he had conceived. Finally, retracing his steps and always using the names of "rounds" and "bars," he got back to his definitions and his axioms.

12 My father was so astounded by the greatness and the force of this genius that, without another word, he left the boy and went to the house of M. [Jacques] Le Pailleur, who was his intimate friend and who was also very learned. When he got there, he stood motionless, like a man transported. Seeing his transport and his tears, M. Le Pailleur became quite upset and begged him tell the cause of his sorrow. My father told him: "I'm not crying from grief, but from joy! You know the trouble that I've taken with my son to conceal from him geometrical thinking, for fear that it would distract him from his other studies. But look what he has done!" Then he explained what he had found, which was that his son had, so to speak, invented mathematics.

Blaise need not have worried. Instead of being punished for having disobeyed his father, a serious offense whatever the temptation, he was rewarded with a copy of Euclid's *Elements* for his further amusement in leisure hours. Lest her readers miss the point, Gilberte concludes with a reiterated claim that even this book learning was Blaise's own, mastered without help and without any of the disciplined effort usually associated with schoolwork: "He read it and he understood it all by himself [during his free time], without ever needing any instruction." Soon, she says, all the mathematicians of Paris could witness the precocious intellect of the boy who attended and participated fully in their learned gatherings.[6]

For Gilberte and other admirers of the Genius, the crux of this story comes in paragraphs 10–11, recalling the revelation of his incomparably powerful intellect. While at play, this child had recreated the thought of the ancient father of geometrical thinking. She stops short of claiming that he had independently reinvented Propositions 1–32 from book 1 of the *Elements* or that he had recited it all to his father, but it seems clear enough that she understood there to be only one such geometry and that she thought that Blaise had made an epochal leap from drawing perfectly regular circles and triangles to rethinking the perfectly regular processes of Euclid's thought.[7]

Whatever the boy told his father when surprised in the enjoyment of forbidden games, he may already have gotten his hands on a French translation before his father presented him with the *Elements* as a prize for his mathematical genius, perhaps in Latin as an inspiration for further language study.[8] Alternatively, he may have adopted only the figures from a Greek or Latin version in which he could not easily read the text.

There is better evidence of Pascal's genius from later years; the fascination of this story as Gilberte tells it lies in the relationship of the narrative frame (par. 8–9 and 12–16) to the central scenes (par. 10–11) and in the assumptions made by Étienne Pascal about Blaise's achievement, which help to support Gilberte's affirmations concerning his own intellectual passion for mathematics and his emotional attachment to his son. Mathematics was *Étienne's* preferred occupation in his Parisian retirement, so much so that he feared that an intelligent boy, once exposed to its full and perfect satisfactions, would forget every other interest and lose all other discipline. Blaise, for his part, played the game of games when he drew his circles and triangles on the floor and conceived related demonstrations. He played grown-up. In his own mature words: "[F]ollowing the example of the *sieur* Pascal, his father, . . . he showed from his youngest years a particular inclination for the mathematical sciences."[9]

By the date of this episode, mathematics linked his father to the royal government itself. On 6 February 1634, Cardinal Richelieu had appointed him to a seven-member group commissioned to discuss and evaluate Jean-Baptiste Morin's technique of determining longitude at sea. Richelieu—like Morin—seems to have hoped that the affair could be quickly and happily concluded "in my presence." Not so. But by 1635 Étienne Pascal had played a principal role, mathematical, scientific, and quasijudicial, in the determination that Morin's ideas were neither new nor practical.[10] All of this must have impressed Blaise, not just with his father's prominence in others' eyes, especially the Cardinal's, but also with his father's subject, mathematics, which sustained that prominence.

Blaise Pascal's later accomplishments as a geometer, inventor, and physicist reflected work with his father, work that developed his father's intellectual interests, that served his father's political interests, and that honored his father as much as himself. His two most spectacular achievements as a new scientist, the Arithmetic Machine and the Vacuum Experiments, provide the most telling illustrations of the much more general point: the intellect of the prodigious genius was inseparable from the heart of the loving son.

Blaise's Arithmetic Machine

The great Pascal's invention was occasioned by his father's service as a tax commissioner, which required the most onerous and tedious fiscal calculations. This has always been recognized, but there is much more to the father's role in the story of his son's first mechanical calculator, which has not been recognized. From first to last, Blaise's machine was the work of Étienne's son. This point is not made in Blaise's own *Lettre dédicatoire* and *Avis nécessaire,* in the royal *Privilège,* or in Gilberte's *Vie de Monsieur Pascal.*[11] What follows briefly explains the occasion for the invention and then resolves what was really a process, not a single flash of inspired genius, into four steps.

The occasion was this. In 1639, Étienne Pascal had been named a tax commissioner for the *généralité* of Rouen. This appointment sent him into a province that had dared to rise in rebellion against the Crown. From a Norman perspective then or a detached perspective now, he was an alien agent of royal repression.[12] In 1639, he had advanced along with the haughty Chancellor, Philippe de Séguier, on the heels of troops who called *themselves* "the scourges of God." In 1648, he was to retreat only in the face of the more serious rebellion that threatened the government of Queen Anne and Cardinal Mazarin.[13]

During his years in Normandy, Étienne's most important and most delicate task was the *departement* or "division" of direct taxes. Total amounts to be collected from the Kingdom as a whole and from each of the *généralités,* the largest parts of that whole for these purposes, were determined in Paris. Then the partial burden to be borne by each *généralité* had to be divided into the shares of regional *élections* and further subdivided into the shares of local parishes. At the end of the process of assessment, the parish itself had to decide how much each of its households would have to pay. The determination for the kingdom as a whole naturally considered first the wartime needs of the Crown. This was clearly the responsibility of the King and his ministers. The relative economic capacities of the taxpaying subjects could be determined, if at all, only by members of the local communities themselves. That left crucial decisions at the level of the *généralité* and the *élection* that could neither be made in Paris nor be entrusted to subjects, especially Normans tainted by rebellion. Given the total assessment for the *généralite,* how should it be divided by *élections* and subdivided by parishes?

No fixed set of proportions could determine these divisions and subdivisions for all time, however important was past precedent in making these decisions. "Bad years," as various as they were unpredictable in the agrarian economy, required various accommodations in particular cases, and, once a concession was made favoring any given region or locality, subtracting from subtotals due, corresponding additions had to be made to others' assessments because the grand totals had been *imposed* from above.[14] Supervision of the *département,* the processes of division and subdivision, followed by subtractions, additions, and new divisions and subdivisions, required from the commissioner the highest political skills, moral integrity, and personal stamina. It also required elementary monetary calculations and recalculations and re-recalculations of a sort that routinely confounded even the best seventeenth-century administrators.[15]

These servants of the Crown needed some sort of adding machine. The traditional alternatives, paper calculations with pen and ink or freehand manipulations of *jetons* or "tokens," could not add or subtract as quickly and accurately. The younger Pascal's pride in meeting this need is evident in his *Lettre dédicatoire à Monseigneur le chancelier* (1645):

> If the public interest is served by my invention [of a machine with which] to perform all of the operations of arithmetic in a way that is as new as it is convenient, more credit is due to *Votre Grandeur* than to my little labors. I can boast only of its conception, and it is the honor of your commands that is wholly responsible for its birth. The tediousness and difficulty of the traditional methods of calculation that I experienced during the past several years [1640–45] in the many matters connected with the commission with which you have honored my father . . . made me think of finding a quicker and easier way.[16]

There can be no question about the occasion for the invention or the intentions of the inventor. Blaise Pascal did not first serve the interests of science, commerce, or banking; he served *his father* and his father's superior in public finance.[17]

The first step toward the invention of an "arithmetic machine" was conceptually the most difficult. The inventor had to believe that, in principle, thought could be mechanized, that is, that the mental operations of arithmetic could be performed by the physical rotations of wheels. In the years immediately after Descartes's *Discours de la méthode* (1637) and *Méditations* (1641), such a belief ran counter to the best new mathematical philosophy. This conceptual leap would seem to require Genius, and Blaise Pascal would seem to be just the right thinker.

However, it is certain that Wilhelm Schickard, professor at the University of Tübingen, had conceived and designed a workable machine by 1623–24. Schickard later corresponded with Mersenne on other matters, if not, insofar as we know, on his machine or its conception.[18] Furthermore, Mersenne most admired *Étienne* Pascal not for his strictly mathematical competence, but for a "very excellent marriage . . . of the practical with the theoretical."[19] Finally, we know that the practical-and-theoretical father dispatched his mathematical son to Paris in the early winter of 1642–43, when he was busiest with the *département* of the taxes for that year.[20] His son was then nineteen years old, just the age when he invented the Arithmetic Machine, according to Gilberte. So much for certainties. Without some evidence that Blaise got the idea for a machine from his father or his father's friend, they do not quite add up.

Credible testimony does exist. It comes from a well-informed and sympathetic fellow-townsman of Florin Périer, who had assisted Étienne in Rouen from 1640 to 1642, married his elder daughter in 1641, and returned to assist him from 1644 to 1645:

> [When Blaise Pascal was] nineteen years old, Father Marin Mersenne told him that for the past two years, he had had in mind a sort of arithmetic machine by which one could perform all of the operations of arithmetic [i.e., adding and subtracting] without using pen and ink or tokens. He [Mersenne] was confident that such a machine was possible, but he hadn't yet succeeded in actually finding [designing? producing?] one.
>
> M. [Blaise] Pascal remembered Mersenne's idea. He reflected on it, and within a few days, he was done [first working design?]. This was the wheel that he [Blaise] first called the Séguier Wheel in honor of the Chancellor. . . . Contrary to his intention, it has since been renamed the Pascal Wheel.[21]

Mersenne seems to have had the idea for some sort of arithmetic machine as early as 1640–41, whether or not he was indebted to Schickard, and he seems to have shared his thinking with the Pascals by 1642–43. He may have broached the idea for a machine in earlier conversation or correspondence with Étienne, who knowingly sent his son to discuss it further when the occasion of his work demanded it. Alternatively, without having any prior hint, Blaise may have visited Mersenne in Paris, described his father's administrative labors, and then been given the idea to bring back to Étienne at Rouen. In the first scenario, his father would have been his immediate source for at least the initial conception; in either scenario, his father's friend would have been the deeper source. As Blaise was later to write about Mersenne, after again following and again surpassing him: "He had a most remarkable talent for raising interesting questions—but he wasn't so successful in answering them."[22]

The inventor's second step was to produce a design from which artisans could construct a prototype of the actual machine. The third step was for inventor and artisans together to modify the designs, experiment with various materials, and develop improved machines. Speed, accuracy, and convenience of operation were all essential, of course, and any truly useful machine had also to be both durable and portable.[23] It took about two years for Blaise to satisfy himself in these respects, but by 1645 he was ready to dedicate a perfected machine to the Chancellor.[24]

We can only speculate about Étienne's role, if any, in this long process, which Blaise directed from within his household. It must have been of the greatest interest to him as a person notable for his "happy marriage" of mathematical theory with mechanical practice. His employment as a tax commissioner overburdened with calculations could only have increased this interest, and his paternal pride in the mathematical gifts of his only son would virtually have guaranteed his expression of that interest. Even if Étienne did not collaborate actively, his wealth, status, and power were essential to these stages of his son's invention. The importance of the funding is obvious: because he could draw without apparent limit on Étienne's resources, Blaise could command *over fifty* successive, handcrafted prototypes from the artisans who worked with and for him. Étienne's status and power aided him incalculably.[25]

There was a fourth step, the promotion of the machine. This has been badly misunderstood by latter-day admirers who have generously ranked the Étienne Pascals as lesser noblemen, without critically reevaluating the basis for the supposed nobility and without sufficiently realizing the limitations imposed on nobles by the principle of derogation.[26] In fact, Étienne was not legally a nobleman before 1645, and anything like modern marketing of the Pascaline would have been absolutely incompatible with his own and his son's noble status after 1645.

Much was obscure in a society in which the fiction was that nobility was a matter of descent and the fact was that it could be acquired by individuals and families, too, in a regular process that usually took three generations. But this much would have been particularly clear to Étienne after his years in the tax courts at Clermont and Montferrand. His patrilineal grandfather, Jean Pascal, *marchand-bourgeois,* had surely been a commoner.[27] His father, Martin Pascal, a *trésorier général,* had held an office that ennobled him *personally* but could ennoble descendants *transmissibly* only if they had held it for two generations more.[28] They did not. It was a social distinction for Étienne that his mother, Marguerite Pascal de Mons, had been born a noblewoman, but this was not a legal basis for his pretensions to nobility.[29] Her children were born commoners.

Étienne's first office, *conseiller* in the Élection (1610–24), was not ennobling. His second office, *second président* in the Cour des Aides (1625–34), was ennobling personally but not transmissibly, according to the once familiar provisions of *patre et avo consilibus* (ennoblement for the officeholder's descendants only if both the father for twenty years previously and the grandfather for another twenty years before that had also held the office).[30] Étienne's father and grandfather had never owned the ennobling office, and he himself had sold it. The former *second président* went to Normandy as a man of great personal distinction and political importance, but he was not a nobleman. He was a commoner. His commission itself changed nothing in this respect.

What mattered were Étienne's letters as a member of the conseil d'État, which conferred fully transmissible nobility upon him and his family by the stroke of a pen on 27 December 1645. However absurd the notion of a world upside down in which *a son's genius* could earn for *his father's blood* a nobility that this father immediately transmitted to his grown son, that seems to have been the real world for the Pascals. Of course, nothing is simple. Étienne's own services to the crown may have merited further reward. And Louis XIV's minority was a time of political weakness when the Queen Mother and her Minister did try to strengthen themselves by distributing honors more freely than had been customary.[31] Having said so much, I add that Blaise's *Lettre dédicatoire* to the Chancellor ended with a rhetorical effusion about Séguier's willingness to accept a presentation-model of the machine and to say nice things about it. Blaise could hardly find words enough to express his gratitude, but he was able to remind the great man of the faithful services (and just deserts) of the Étienne Pascals:

> In the impotence to which the excess of your goodness has reduced me [my inability adequately to express my gratitude and joy . . .], I am content to revere it by my silence[!]. The entire family whose name I bear is as interested as I am in this benefaction and in many others. Every day, we renew our prayers for your prosperity, doing so from the heart, so ardently and so continuously that no one could boast of being more attached than we are to your service.[32]

It was only after (but very soon after) Blaise Pascal had so effusively dedicated his extraordinary Arithmetic Machine to Chancellor Séguier and so formally presented him with a handsome model for his cabinet that Étienne Pascal was given an honorary seat on the conseil d'État and the transmissible nobility that went with it.[33] Thereafter, he was a *chevalier,* his son, an *écuyer,* both of them, noblemen. It would be naive to suppose that the presentation to the Chancellor had no motive of social promotion.[34] The machine was a triumph for the Pascals as a family, and it is difficult to imagine that, without his father, this twenty-two-year-old son would have been so forward or could have been so successful in exploiting his wonderful invention. We can still see the noble arms of the Pascals de Mons, now more or less legitimately adopted by the Étienne Pascals and proudly affixed to Blaise's machines.[35]

Blaise's Vacuum Experiments

The better evidence on the Vacuum Experiments allows a better appreciation of roles played by Étienne and his friends than is possible for the history of the Arithmetic Machine. Blaise suggested to his readers that he confronted "the agreement of all laymen and the crowd of the philosophers" that nature abhors the vacuum and that he was the lonely partisan of a new truth, namely, that "nature has no repugnance against the vacuum."[36] However, it is absolutely certain that his father had preceded the young man who represented himself as a lonely partisan and that this father provided essential support for his son's work. Pierre Petit's letter to Hector-Pierre Chanut on 26 November 1646 shows that *Étienne* Pascal was already a theoretical partisan of the vacuum long before he or his son had seen any experimental evidence:

Passing through Rouen [in September 1646], I [Petit] told your good friend and mine, Monsieur [Étienne] Pascal, [about his own previously unsuccessful attempt to replicate the Torricelli vacuum experiment]. He was delighted to hear about it, both because of its novelty and because, as you know, he has admitted [the possibility of] the vacuum for a long time.[37]

According to Petit, it was *Étienne,* not Blaise, who was most eager to witness his second attempt to replicate the experiment, with better glassware and more mercury, and who assisted him as the principal experimenter. It was *Étienne* who took the liveliest satisfaction when the second attempt succeeded:

Monsieur [Étienne] Pascal [had been] convinced for a long time that the opinion shared by Hieron [of Alexandria] and many other philosophers was true, and he was delighted to see what he considered to be its confirmation in this experiment. I told him that I did not think that everyone would be so satisfied, because, influenced by the received opinion that doesn't admit the possibility of a vacuum, they will still say that what remains above the mercury in the tube is very rarified air.[38]

As Petit reported it, Blaise's role on the occasion of the first French replication of the Italian experiment was to voice the objections of "the Simpletons," that is, the Aristotelians.[39]

Of course, Blaise Pascal soon proved himself to be the most brilliant defender of the experimental methods of the new science—and of the theoretical opinion maintained by his father. In 1644, Mersenne and Chanut had talked of wanting to perform the Torricelli experiment. In 1646, Petit and Étienne had actually done it with a four-foot tube made to their specifications by the glassmakers of Rouen. But in 1647, the younger Pascal was imaginative and audacious beyond comparison in a series of New Experiments. Less than a year after the letter reporting this modest success, Blaise was ready to boast in print of spectacular successes with mercury-filled tubes twelve and even fifteen feet long and of water- and wine-filled tubes forty-six feet long that had been attached to masts and displayed to the curious.[40]

More importantly, Blaise conducted a coherent program of more sophisticated if less spectacular experiments, publicized his work promptly, and discussed its significance clearly and cautiously. No French contemporary approached his talents as a brilliant theorist, tenacious experimenter, or persuasive expositor. There is ample evidence here of what Blaise himself called "my own genius," and there is also more.[41] This son's science defended his father's opinion; his costly experiments were fully funded by his father's purse; and his published *Expériences nouvelles touchant le vide* were "dedicated to Monsieur Pascal, *conseiller du roi en ses conseils d'État et privé,* by *le sieur* B. P. his son."[42] Appropriately, our one extended composition from Étienne Pascal is his letter to Père Noël on his son's behalf. In it, Étienne refers to the unemancipated Blaise, then almost twenty-five years old, as if his son's "obedience" and his own "condescendence" still defined the relationship.[43]

Blaise's early intellectual accomplishment pleased Étienne above all others. Gilberte reports: "My father took a sort of satisfaction that you can easily imagine in my brother's great progress. . . ."[44] I go further. I suggest that Blaise's Arithmetic Machine and his Vacuum Experiments were offerings to his father, first of all, and to the rest of the learned world, only secondarily. They are all the outward manifestations of an inward love. My evidence is not just Étienne's known response to the first signs of Blaise's genius but also the son's pursuit of his father's prior interests and his effective abandonment of these pursuits after his father's death.[45]

PART TWO

SEPARATIONS AND LOSSES

The exceptional youthful attachment of Blaise Pascal to his father left him exceptionally vulnerable to the pains of separation and loss. Indeed, it is the analysis of the evidence on his behavior when Étienne's death was a perceived threat (1646) and then an awful actuality (1651) that provides the best argument for the strength of the prior attachment.

By definition, attachments are particular, enduring, and highly emotional.[1] This means that the loss of one particularly beloved person cannot simply be made good by relationships with others. Nevertheless, especially when the bond with his father was stretched and broken, Blaise's sisters were also dear to him. When Gilberte as the last of the Pascals looked backward, she saw in her mind's eye a union of Blaise's and Jacqueline's hearts:

> He couldn't have loved anyone more than he loved my sister—and he was right. He saw her often and told her absolutely everything. She satisfied him every time, without exception, for there was such a perfect correspondence in their feelings that they agreed on everything. Surely, their hearts were one, and they found in one another consolations of a sort comprehensible only to someone who has experienced the same happiness and who knows what it is to love and to be loved with such trust, fearing no division and experiencing every satisfaction.[2]

Gilberte's paragraph tells us a lot about Blaise and Jacqueline, but it is perhaps even more interesting for what it suggests about her own sense of apartness from their intimacy.

This part 2 concerns three periods of crisis for the Pascals: 1638–39, 1646–48, and 1651–53. At the beginning of 1638, Étienne was in his fiftieth year, an official who had retired early so as to allow time for intellectual pursuits and a very active parenthood; insofar as we know, he was healthy, and, insofar as he knew, he was financially secure. Blaise was only fourteen, but his promise as a mathematician was already evident and his health, too, seems to have been good enough. Gilberte at eighteen and Jacqueline at twelve were still living more or less contentedly at home. Then the crises began. Each threatened Blaise's attachments both to his father and to his favored sister. By mid-1653, Étienne had died (1651) and Jacqueline had entered the convent (1652) where she took her vows (1653). That left Gilberte in remote Clermont. Or did it leave even her?

Gilberte was so modest and so humble that she hardly enters the memoirs by which she honored her more celebrated siblings. Nevertheless, she had been a very significant figure in the paternal household before leaving it for marriage to Florin Périer on 13 June 1641.[3] Blaise was later to tell her repeatedly that he had never passed a day without pain after reaching the age of eighteen; whether or not she made the connection, the fact is that he had turned eighteen on 19 June 1641, within a week of her wedding.[4]

Chapters 4, 5, and 6 concern the three periods of crisis. Knowledge of each is essential to an understanding of the great turning point of 1654 and the heart of the matter with respect to Blaise Pascal's life and work.

CHAPTER 4

The Crisis of 1638–39

The Pascals looked inward upon themselves more than most other families. This was especially true in the mid- and late-1630s, after Étienne had removed them from their native Clermont and when Blaise was being educated at home in Paris. Étienne had not yet accepted new administrative responsibilities; Gilberte had not yet married away; and Jacqueline had not yet left the world for a new life in religion. But even in the 1630s, there were reminders that the family was not alone and that its members were not secure in their mutual attachments. In the crisis of 1638–39, Étienne had to flee from his own home and children, having suddenly become a fugitive from what passed for royal justice. In his absence, Jacqueline suffered a near-fatal case of smallpox. This double crisis led to a double resolution: Jacqueline recovered her health if not unspoiled beauty, and Étienne was pardoned for having defended his rights.

It is a measure of Gilberte's selectivity in the *Vie de Monsieur Pascal* that she does not mention these events. It is also a measure of the limits of other historical sources that their immediate impact on the young genius cannot be documented. But there is good evidence that Jacqueline's perceptions of the world and her place in it changed significantly in the course of the crisis, becoming much more religious. This seems to have had a very powerful deferred impact on her brother at the time of his First Conversion (1646), when, apparently, he took the lead, initiating the conversions of his sister and father. Actually, his later initiative followed her earlier lead. Knowledge of the First Crisis (1638–39) and its compounded threats helps to explain Blaise's behavior at the time of the Second Crisis (1646–48), the Third Crisis (1651–53), and, still later, the Second Conversion (1654).

Étienne's Outlawry and Jacqueline's Precious Poetry

The First Crisis began with a capital misfortune. In the years 1633 and 1634, Étienne had sold his two principal assets from Clermont, his house on the rue des Gras and his office in the Cour des Aides, and then in 1635 he had placed available capital in government securities.[1] However, 1635 also just happened to be the beginning of French military intervention in the Thirty Years' War with its catastrophic implications for public finance. Payments of quarterly interest soon became irregular, and the market value of the *rentes,* particularly those like Étienne's that were nominally secured by the *tailles,* simply collapsed.[2] These incomes represented a capital calculated at the *denier* 18; that is, the government had pledged to return an income of 1 *livre* per year for each 18 *livres* invested. However, in the circumstances, since the government was not honoring this commitment, the market value plummeted to the *denier* 3 or 2. The investor who tried to sell depreciated *rentes* could have expected to realize at most three and possibly only two times the nominal income from a more optimistic speculator, not eighteen times.

Étienne had legal title to an annual income from the *rentes* of 3,648 *livres, 2 sous;* at the *denier* 18, this would have made them worth some 65,665 *livres.*[3] It is quite unlikely that he had actually paid so much for them, because the Crown wholesaled them at discounted rates, and his relationships in the financial world would have ensured him the most advantageous terms. This makes the royal arbitrariness of a partial suspension of payments more comprehensible if not more justifiable. However, whatever Étienne's rightful expectations, his income had been slashed, and, worse, the market for his insecure securities had crashed. His *rentes* could not have been sold for more than 10,944 (at the *denier* 3) or even 7,296 *livres* (at the *denier* 2), so that he had suffered a paper loss of 5/6 or even 8/9.[4] It is no wonder that, having put so much of his fortune into the *rentes* at so unfortunate a time, he got a little excited.

The outraged Pascal participated in an angry demonstration in March 1638 at which, in his faithful daughter's delicate words, "some actions took place that were a bit violent and seditious."[5] Other protesters were thrown into the Bastille, and Étienne evaded arrest only by flight. This left his children to fend for themselves with the assistance of domestics and friends. The challenge for the latter was to return him to the good graces of the Court and the Cardinal.

Shrewdly, they attempted to exploit the personal appeal and poetic talent of his littlest and sweetest and prettiest child, Jacqueline. Verses dated from the first months of Étienne's disgrace suggest both a youthful courtier's mere flattery of the greats and a heroic daughter's fierce devotion to her father. Here, from April 1638, is an impromptu quatrain on the subject of a great lady closing the shutters of her chamber; the poet's conceit is that the beautiful but modest woman must know that, unshuttered, her eye would dazzle the sun:

Voyez la bonté de Madonte:
Son oeil, qui n'a point de pareil,
Ne veut pas souffrir le soleil
De crainte de lui faire honte.

In the next month, she addressed an epigram to her father, expressing her confidence that no enemy could dim his glory:

Cher père, ne crains point l'effort
Du temps, ni même de la mort;
C'est en vain qu'ils te font la guerre.
Ils peuvent bien ravir ta présence à nos yeux;
Mais ton âme à jamais vivra dedans les cieux,
Et ton renom dessus la terre.[6]

Jacqueline had shown a fondness for the artifices of the salon and the passions of the theater, and there was reason to hope that her poetry might be turned to her father's political advantage.

In May 1638, Étienne's supporters introduced Jacqueline to the Court of the Queen at Saint-Germain, where the twelve-year-old poetess composed impromptus for an eleven-year-old princess, the Mademoiselle de Montpensier. Here, the conceit is that her subject is too beautiful for words:

Muse, notre grande princesse
Te commande aujourd'hui d'exercer ton adresse
A louer sa beauté; mais il faut avouer

Qu'on ne saurait la satisfaire,
Et que le seul moyen qu'on a de la louer
C'est de dire en un mot qu'on ne le saurait faire.[7]

This preoccupation with prettiness is banal but also poignant, given the facial scarring that Jacqueline was soon to suffer. She returns to the theme again and again, here in an impromptu for Madame d'Hautefort:

Beau chef-d'oeuvre de l'univers,
Adorable objet de mes vers,
N'admirez pas mon prompte poésie.
Votre oeil, que l'univers reconnaît pour vainqueur,
Ayant bien pu toucher soudainement mon coeur,
A pu d'un même coup toucher ma fantaisie.[8]

Jacqueline had also prepared more studied pieces for the Queen herself, Anne of Austria, who was then pregnant. We now know that the unborn child was in fact a male, the future Louis XIV. The Dauphin was not to be born until 5 September, but his first movements had been felt on 22 April.[9] This Great Event was a very good sign in a pregnancy that had seemed miraculous in its origins and was to be Providential in its effects both for the foreign Queen who had not borne a child in twenty-three years of marriage and for the troubled Kingdom that had so recently suffered a generation of civil wars.[10] Therefore, it was a heaven-sent opportunity for the Pascal child to make an appeal on her father's behalf. She did her best:

Cet invincible enfant d'un invincible père
Déjà nous fait tout espérer;
Et quoiqu'il soit encore au ventre de sa mère,
Il se fait craindre et désirer.
Il sera plus vaillant que le dieu de la guerre,
Puisqu'avant que son oeil ait vu le firmament,
S'il remue un peu seulement,
C'est à nos ennemis un tremblement de terre.[11]

Even this was not enough. The fetus who was to be the Great King exercised his little muscles and the little girl sang his praises in her little verses, but her father remained in hiding. The judge was an outlaw.

Jacqueline's Smallpox and Earliest Devotional Poetry

Later in the same most stressful year, Jacqueline suffered a grave illness:

> In September 1638, she came down with smallpox. Her condition was perilous. In these circumstances, my father put aside all thought for his own safety, saying that, whatever were the dangers to himself, he wanted to be in his own house to oversee her care with his own eyes. And, indeed, he never left her side for a moment, even sleeping in the same chamber. She recovered, but she was completely spoiled.[12]

Blaise is our proper subject, not Jacqueline or Étienne. What did he make of this episode, then or later? Gilberte does not say. In any case, the fifteen-year-old boy could not have felt the same love for his little sister that the mature man was to feel for the grown woman ten or twenty years later. Gilberte did notice and remember two great facts, namely, Jacqueline's survival only after having reached "the extremity," and Étienne's dramatic display of parental attachment to his afflicted child. Blaise must have noticed and remembered, too.

Gilberte also recalled Jacqueline's overt reactions to the facial scarring by which "she was completely spoiled":

> She was thirteen years old and quite sophisticated enough to be able to appreciate her former beauty and to bewail its loss. Nevertheless, she was utterly unaffected by this accident. Quite the contrary: she regarded it as a favor. She composed verses to thank God for her scars, the [holy] guardians of her innocence and the certain marks that He wanted to preserve it for her. This was all her own idea.[13]

Jacqueline's verses survive. Another reader would make a better judge of the literary merit of her poetry itself or of the historical interest of her puritanical preciosity. But the student of the Pascals' familial attachments and Blaise's later development can make the following points.

First, *Jacqueline* is the family member who provides the earliest evidence of anything like spiritual fervor within the Pascal household. This fact would not mean so much if it were not also true that she had not been presented to a bishop for confirmation before her conversion at the age of twenty.[14] In his *Petit catéchisme,* Saint-Cyran had specified "the age of discretion" as that at which communion is a Christian duty. The catechist acknowledges that this age may come earlier or later in individual cases, "at seven, eight, or ten years, and sometimes even later, sometimes earlier."[15] The case of Jacqueline Périer, Jacqueline Pascal's niece and godchild, provides a well-documented example of a "late" confirmation and first communion in a scrupulous community where the sacrament was approached with proper reverence; this niece was presented to the bishop at Port-Royal at the age of eleven years.[16] Yet the aunt had been unconfirmed at twenty. The inference that her father had been inattentive to such matters seems inescapable, despite Gilberte's much later assertion in a pious memoir that he had always shown "very great respect for religion."[17] In fact, Étienne's teaching, example, and governance of the family in earlier years cannot have been very devout.

Second, Jacqueline's *separation* from her father, even before the illness, was the condition for her first known offerings to the Christian God rather than to lesser idols, the "beautiful" Montpensier, the "adorable" Hautefort, or the "virtuous and sacred" Queen.[18] I do not infer that Étienne would have disapproved; I do infer that her increased sense of social vulnerability favored her spiritual development.

Third, her *vocation* for a religious life was already implicit in the poem of thanksgiving composed after her recovery, however juvenile the sentiments of a wounded thirteen-year-old who was still nine years away from a mature and "perfect resolution to renounce the world."[19] In the verses quoted below, she already regards her facial scarring as the guarantee of her virginal innocence.

Jacqueline's first devout verses were two poems of thanksgiving for "the gift of poetry," both dated just before the medical crisis. They compound a great deal of obvious vanity with at least a little apparent humility, a sense of unworthiness and even guilt that may owe something to her human feelings of abandonment after her father's flight. The poem of thanksgiving after her recovery, dated November 1638, is far more significant:

Moteur de ce grand univers,
Inspirez-moi de puissants vers,
Envoyez-moi la voix des anges,
Non pas pour louer les mortels,

Mais pour entonner vos louanges
Et vous remercier au pied de vos autels.

Votre souveraine bonté
Du haut du ciel a visité
Le plus chétif ver de la terre,
Et garanti du coup fatal
Un corps plus fragile que verre,
Parmi tous les excès d'un incroyable mal.

Ainsi l'on voit qu'en vérité,
Grand Dieu! votre bénignité
S'est montée en moi bien extrême,
Me garantissant d'un péril
Où sans votre bonté suprême
Mes ans allaient finir dans leur plus bel avril.

Oh! que mon coeur se sent heureux,
Quand au miroir je vois les creux
Et les marques de ma vérole!
Je les prends pour sacrés témoins,
Suivant votre sainte parole,
Que je ne suis de ceux que vous aimez le moins.

Je les prends, dis-je, o souverain!
Pour un cachet dont votre main
Voulut marquer mon innocence;
Et cette consolation
Me fait avoir la connaissance
Qu'il ne faut s'affliger de cette affliction.

Mais, grand Dieu! Mon travail est en vain;
Il faut un esprit plus qu'humain
Pour bien raconter vos merveilles,
Et ce grand excès de bonté,
Charmant les yeux et les oreilles,
Excède mon pouvoir et non ma volonté.[20]

Gilberte much later recalled Jacqueline's verses as evidence of her acceptance of her disfigurement, but this cannot have been simple for the admired adolescent who had so praised others' beauty. In the fourth stanza quoted above, before Jacqueline's conversion, vocation, profession, and edifying life and death as a nun, she had held a mirror before her own once pretty face. Gilberte's narrative reports behavior that strongly suggests social withdrawal and psychological regression:

She spent the whole winter without ever leaving home, being in no condition to mix in society. But she wasn't in the least troubled, busying herself with her dolls and her trinkets.[21]

As for Blaise, there is no more reason to suppose that he then shared Jacqueline's newly matured taste for religious poetry than that he then shared her childish play with dolls and trinkets. But he must have been aware of her greater devotion, which persisted and which led to more celebrated compositions. From 1640 alone, we still have the "Sonnet de dévotion" (February), the epigram "A Sainte Cécile" (November), and the stanzas with which she won the competition of the Palinodes at Rouen, "Sur la Conception de la Vierge" (December).[22] This last led to drums, trumpets, and congratulatory verses in her honor from the great Corneille himself.[23] There were also to be precious verses "Contre amour" (1642 and 1646), which give a worldly statement to the theme of blessed virginity also known from the explicitly religious poems.[24] Nothing about this First Crisis was more important for Blaise in the long term than Jacqueline's increased devotion, known from her poetry, and Blaise's awareness of it, inferred from the closeness of the family and the public acclaim given her poem for the Conception of the Virgin.

L'amour tyrannique *and the Cardinal ex Machina*

Different sorts of love impelled the little girl and the Cardinal Minister, but they combined happily, and the crisis was resolved in the spring of 1639. Jacqueline emerged from the household to accept a bit part in a command performance of Georges de Scudéry's *Amour tyrannique* at the Palais Cardinal.[25] She was Cassandre, a Queen's confidante and messenger, and she seems to have performed well enough on stage, although it is hard to imagine how anyone, however young and petite, could have stolen the show with lines like hers.[26] In the crucial fourth act, for instance, she would have spoken exactly one unheroic line:

> Cassandre: Que votre Majesté se dérobe un moment.[27]

When the playacting was done, the real-life drama began, all stage-managed for Jacqueline by Étienne's friends. But the child-actress herself did have to approach the all-powerful Cardinal Minister on her father's behalf. Jacqueline played to perfection her own historical part, that of a courageous and passionate young girl whose appeal could move even the redoubtable Richelieu. There was pathos aplenty: the little Pascal had lost her mother in infancy, only to be separated from her father while still a child. Then had come her disfiguring illness and her father's flight to the relative safety of his native city, a full week's travel from his children in Paris. Now, through her tears, the petite girl, who looked even younger than her years, dared to ask for the return of her surviving parent. Of course, she had prepared a poem for Richelieu, in which her nervousness became his tribute:

> Ne vous étonnez pas, incomparable Armand,
> Si j'aï mal contenté vos yeux et vos oreilles;
> Mon esprit, agité de frayeurs sans pareilles,
> Interdit à mon corps et voix et mouvement.
> Mais pour me rendre ici capable de vous plaire.
> Rappelez de l'exil mon misérable père.
> C'est le bien que j'attends d'une insigne bonté;
> Sauvez cet innocent d'un péril manifeste.
> Et lors vous me rendez l'entière liberté
> De l'esprit et du corps, de la voix et du geste.[28]

Richelieu may already have decided to pardon Étienne. In any case, after Jacqueline's appeal he took the adolescent girl on his eminent lap and gave her hugs and kisses, "unimaginable and extraordinary caresses," then turned to her older sister for "many [more] caresses," and, finally, returned to the charming petitioner for yet more "unbelievable caresses." The daughters had triumphed. Their father could return, if only he brought back these adorable girls.[29] The chastened protester did return, accompanied by his children, and he was duly pardoned. Within the calendar year he was to be sent to rebellious Normandy as a royal commissioner. As such, his principal responsibility was to supervise the assessment of the direct taxes that funded not only the King's wars but also his own *rentes*.

What did an observant Blaise learn from all of this? Easy truisms about the instability of human fortune or the corruption of worldly power? Probably not. The First Crisis as a whole should have taught much harder lessons about the insecurity of human attachments and the possibility, perhaps even inevitability, of separations and losses.

CHAPTER 5

The Crisis of 1646–48

The crisis of 1646–48 began with Étienne, Blaise, and Jacqueline together in the Pascal household. In January 1646, Étienne was fifty-seven years old, a powerful *commissaire départi* who had just received letters as a *conseiller d'État,* which meant more money and higher honors. Blaise was twenty-two; he had no immediate prospects for anything like independence, but, as the inventor of the spectacular Arithmetic Machine, he was already well on his way to surpassing his father's reputation for learning. Finally, Jacqueline was twenty; she was the apparently unconcerned object of others' marriage projects.

Marriage Projects for Jacqueline

Gilberte had already married away, far enough away that the rest of the Pascals did not see her again after her departure for Clermont in late summer 1642 until her return to her father's household in Rouen at the end of 1646. When she did return, it was to stay for almost two years. Thus, she was well informed about the events of these years, allowances being made for Blaise and Jacqueline's return to Paris in the summer of 1647. But information is not everything. Gilberte's understanding mattered more, and she understood what I call a familial crisis solely in terms of spiritual conversions.

In the *Vie de Jacqueline Pascal,* Gilberte prefaces a brief account of her sister's conversion with a vague but authoritative report concerning "many" abortive marriage projects:

> During this period [prior to January 1646], there were many occasions when she might have married. But God so ordained that there was always something that prevented it. She herself remained completely submissive to my father's will, showing neither affection nor aversion.[1]

Whose were the projects? Within the family, they can only have been Étienne's. In 1641, he gave his elder daughter to another Auvergnat, a blood relative who assisted him in the service of the King, Florin Périer. In later years, the Pascals would have made a more attractive alliance, although Normans would have known Étienne as an alien agent of the royal fisc. In any case, something always went wrong with marriage projects for Jacqueline. She remained marriageable but unmarried.

Marguerite Périer's much later *Mémoire* is more specific but less reliable. Nevertheless, she must have been able to draw on memories of her mother's stories, and her assertion of a particular marriage project for Jacqueline at the beginning of 1646 is perfectly consistent with Gilberte's generalizations and quite plausible in its own right: "Mademoiselle Pascal the daughter was then sought in marriage by a *conseiller* in the Parlement of Rouen."[2]

This would have been an appropriate alliance for the daughter of a former *second président* (a higher-ranking office) in the Cour des Aides of Clermont (a less prestigious court). Étienne was at the time a *commissaire départi,* and he might have profited enough from his commission that he could endow his second daughter somewhat more richly than his first. In June 1641, he had given Gilberte only an income of 750 *livres* in depreciated *rentes,* unrealistically evaluated as a capital of 13,500 *livres.*[3] After December 1645, whatever were his fortunes or their limits counted in hard money or measured in real property, the new *conseiller d'État* himself was a *chevalier* and his unmarried daughter a noblewoman.

No one knows how Étienne balanced issues of wealth and status when considering this possible marriage alliance. And no one knows what Jacqueline may have felt in her heart of hearts, she who showed neither affection nor aversion. But we probably do know enough to appreciate Blaise's position: he would have had everything to lose and nothing to gain in any imaginable marriage of Jacqueline into the Norman Robe. Even a modest dowry or a paper dowry would have had to come from the family strongbox, and any corresponding gains in real wealth or local status would have been hers, not his. Above all else, Jacqueline herself would have left the Pascal household for a separate Norman residence in order to form the new marital union.

Étienne's Accident and the Pascals' Conversions

A threat of significant loss was added to this threat of significant separation when Étienne suffered a serious injury in a wintertime fall. Gilberte is our informant, although she was still in Clermont when her father fell in Rouen. Furthermore, her narrative purposes and historical presuppositions limited the account in the *Vie de Jacqueline Pascal*. She was telling the dramatic story of her sister's conversion from worldly preciosity to religious sanctity, and she apparently supposed that God must have had that end in view when her father fell on the icy streets of Rouen. She rationalized as much as she spiritualized when she made the physical injury suffered in this fall the providential occasion for reading good books and this reading, in turn, the occasion for spiritual conversions:

> In January 1646, my father fell on the ice and dislocated his hip. He would not entrust his care to anyone other than MM. de La Bouteillerie and des Landes. They had the goodness to remain with him for three months. . . . The whole household profited from the presence of these gentlemen. Their edifying discourse and good example made my father, my brother, and my sister curious to read the books that had guided them. Thus, they all became acquainted with the works of M. Jansen, M. de Saint-Cyran, M. Arnauld, and other writings with which they were . . . [This ellipsis represents "a seven- or eight-line" gap in the manuscript copy of Gilberte's lost original.][4]

Gilberte further rationalized the conversions in her *Vie de Monsieur Pascal*. Étienne Pascal, his injured body, and his gentleman-doctors drop from sight. Jacqueline goes, too. Blaise alone remains with the good books:

> Immediately after these experiments and before he was yet twenty-four years old, divine Providence brought to birth an occasion that obliged him to read pious works. God so enlightened him by these readings that he came to a perfect understanding that the Christian religion requires us to live only

for God and to have no other object but Him. This truth seemed to him so evident, so necessary, and so useful that he terminated all his [mathematical and scientific] research.

My goal is not to scold Gilberte yet again for having so badly mistaken the chronology of Blaise's experimental science (which he began seriously to pursue only late in 1646 *after* the First Conversion earlier in 1646) and religious devotion (to which he had converted *before* the Vacuum Experiments of 1647). It is to use information that goes back to her in order to go beyond her own retrospective preoccupation with her celebrated brother's intellect and spirit. Gilberte must have been Marguerite's informant for two much later versions of the same crucial event. Neither is neatly integrated into a clear vision of Blaise's life, but the two together provide materials for a more critical analysis. This is the more concise version:

Having gone out for a charitable act, he [Étienne] fell and dislocated his hip. He wanted to entrust his care to two gentlemen, M. Deslandes and M. de La Bouteillerie, who were very good at that sort of thing and who were also remarkably pious. They used this occasion to convert first M. Pascal the son and then Mlle. Pascal the daughter, who was then pursued in marriage by a *conseiller* from the Parlement. . . . When my grandfather's injury had healed, the two of them persuaded him, too, to give himself wholly to God. He did so with as much joy as they had felt.[5]

Marguerite tells more than she may have known. The chronology is the key: first, the marriage project for Jacqueline; second, the accidental injury of Étienne; third, the series of conversions: Blaise, then Jacqueline, and finally Étienne.[6]

Marguerite's other version of the conversion story had much more to say about the lay doctors:

They each had a natural gift for the resetting of broken bones and dislocated joints. . . . [In addition,] they had both made a perfect study of medicine, surgery, and anatomy. After they had resolved to give themselves wholly to God, they had both built little hospitals on their estates. . . . M. Deslandes, who had ten children, had placed ten beds in his hospital, and M. de La Bouteillerie, who had none, had set up twenty. In these thirty beds, they received all the poor who came to them and, as good doctors, treated them without charge for all sorts of illnesses. They also instructed others in their science of resetting limbs.[7]

This helps to explain why Étienne should have refused care from anyone else. These laymen were not doctors, but they had great experience in treating orthopedic problems, and their nobility and their charity, too, helped to recommend their science. Étienne awaited their coming, although this was to leave his injury untreated for an unspecified time.[8] There may well have been complications, then or later. In any case, whatever the wisdom of the patient's decision and the skill of the laymen's care, Blaise feared the worst. His father might die, and then *he* would be lost, literally lost.[9]

It is worth trying to explain why the gentleman orthopedists should have been willing to leave their estates and hospitals for the Pascal household, the suffering poor for the injured Étienne. The Périers may later have forgotten these nameless others, but charitable concern for them could have justified exceptional attentiveness to the privileged patient. Étienne Pascal was not just any old man or any old rich man; he was the tax commissioner of Louis XIV, newly appointed to the conseil d'État, and he and his son were also notable savants. For the Norman gentlemen to have healed the former in body and spirit could have done more good for many more of the Norman poor, whose lives were pulverized under the grindstones of the royal fisc, than they could have done beside their thirty charity beds. And for them to have converted such eminent men could also have been expected to have—as it did have—further consequences for still others inspired by the devotion of such notables.

Their Jansenist spirituality had much to offer to the Pascals. Gilberte says that Deslandes and de La Bouteillerie brought unspecified works by Jansenius, Saint-Cyran, and Arnauld. Antoine Arnauld's *De la fréquente communion* (1643), which now seems so ponderous, was once very popular, and it may have appealed to the Pascals particularly as the work of another Auvergnat whose family had also resettled in Paris in the parish of Saint-Merri. Cornelius Jansenius's *Discours de la réformation de l'homme intérieur* (1644) and the abbé de Saint-Cyran's *Coeur nouveau* (1643) were tracts much better suited to beginners.[10]

Jansenius's *Discours* begins with a rather heavy emphasis on human mortality and sinfulness after the Fall, developing this image of the natural gravity of corrupt man in ways that might have seemed figuratively appropriate to the Pascals in the winter of 1646. Then comes a preliminary discourse on the Two Loves, the Augustinian opposition of the creature's rightful love of the Creator and wrongful love of the dear self in its many guises. The discourse proper concerns the three sorts of concupiscent self-love from I John 2:16.[11] This text is powerful in itself and more powerful in context:

I John 2:15 Love not the world, neither the things that are in the world. If any man love the world, the love of the Father is not in him.
16 *For all that is in the world, the lust of the flesh, and the lust of the eyes, and the pride of life,* is not of the Father, but is of the world.
17 And the world passeth away, and the love thereof; but he that doeth the will of God abideth forever.

As Jansenius explains the three impermissible loves, they are sensual pleasures, intellectual curiosity, and, worst of all, the pride that makes fallen creatures seek independence for themselves and dominance over others. In his conclusion, he returns to the theme of the Two Loves, stressing the impermanence of worldly loves, defined in the broadest way to include all voluptuousness, all science, and all vainglory: "Give God all the love that you have withdrawn from the world, . . . and make him the unique object and the one center of your affections."[12]

Saint-Cyran's *Coeur nouveau* is a little tract for new converts who are engaged "in the world and in marriage." It takes its title from the verse that also serves as its epigraph:

Ezekiel 36:26 A new heart also will I give you, and a new spirit will I put within you; and I will take away the stony heart out of your flesh, and I will give you a heart of flesh.

Again, here are the Two Loves in passages teaching that the new convert must detach himself from earthly objects of affection:

This [new] heart is nothing other than His Spirit and His Grace, by which our soul is detached from the objects of the senses and raised to God by all sorts of good thoughts and holy affections. This Spirit and this Grace, which establish this new heart, are called "charity" and "love" in Scripture. . . . The entire new life consists in loving God and in relating all our works to Him. . . .

All devotion consists in serving and adoring God spiritually and truthfully, by a love that is interior, sincere, and true. This love detaches us from the love of creatures and unites us to God alone in ways that are wholly spiritual and divine. This heart and this love can be compared with the tenderness of a tiny infant still in his mother's womb or newly-born. . . .

The first exercise and the first occupation of this [newly converted] soul is to strive to retrench all that it considers contrary and harmful to the new love of God, whether what must be cut away is within or without. If there is any earthly object that it loves by obligation, it must take care to purify its former intention. It must begin to love [this object] for God alone, with a firm resolve to refer all affections to Him as their source and their end.[13]

What was here for Blaise Pascal? For Jacqueline? For Étienne? Let us start with Jansenius's emphases on fallen man's mortality and sinful man's concupiscence. As 1645 ended, the great facts of family life were, in roughly chronological order, the marriage project(s) for Jacqueline, the recent triumph of Blaise's Arithmetic Machine, and the letters naming Étienne to the conseil d'État. Then, in January, had come the shock of Étienne's serious injury after his wintertime fall. This was an occasion for anxiety as well as reflection.

A neglected detail of family history is surely pertinent. On 24 December 1639, after a wintertime fall, Étienne's brother Blaise had died.[14] Étienne himself was the eldest of three brothers, Blaise, the second, and Bremond, the third. Étienne had honored this Blaise as his son's godfather in 1623.[15] He had then sold him both his house on the rue des Gras in 1633 and his office in the Cour des Aides in 1634. The terms had been favorable enough that the cloistered Jacqueline was later to recall them as a "miracle" of charity among the worldly.[16] This adds up circumstantially to a very strong case for the closeness of this elder Blaise Pascal to the Étienne Pascals. News of Uncle Blaise's death after his Christmastime accident in 1639 must have had stunning impact on his nephews and nieces at this time. The long and traumatic separation entailed by their father's life as a fugitive had finally ended that spring, but a new separation had begun in the fall when he had left Paris for rebellious Rouen. The children could have rejoined him there only after the province had been pacified.

In January 1646, it had been Étienne Pascal himself who had fallen on the ice, injured his hip, lain untreated while awaiting the lay doctors, and suffered unknown further complications during and after the three months of intensive care. He may well have broken bones, not merely dislocated the joint. He was not necessarily bedridden for the entire three months, but he must have been severely incapacitated for some time, perhaps much longer. This, in turn, must have meant care not only by his doctors and domestics, but also by his cherished daughter(s).

Sometime in 1646, Étienne's one remaining brother and Jacqueline's godfather, Bremond, also died back in Clermont.[17] It is quite possible that this had not yet occurred and was not yet foreseen in the wintertime of conversions at Rouen. But there is reason to suppose that Étienne's own condition was alarming, and it was in this context that his devout doctors found receptive readers for their spiritual literature.

There was something for everyone in Jansenius's text, I John 2:16. First comes the concupiscence of the flesh. Jacqueline had *already* turned away from her own adolescent sexuality after her case of smallpox, when she had responded with thanksgiving *both* for her recovery *and* for her scars, which would protect her innocence. In the intervening years, she had celebrated the perfect purity of the Virgin Mary and written verses "Contre amour." And she had shown what her sister later considered a remarkable indifference when the occasion(s) for marriage had arisen. Given this past, it would not have been surprising if *she* had been the first of the Pascals to have embraced Jansenist spirituality. But she was not the first; Blaise was.

Jansenius's exposition of the text from John also addressed a second form of concupiscence, the "lust of the eyes." Blaise would have been most directly affected after his maturation had allowed him a more ambitious intellectual life and Étienne's public responsibilities had absorbed most of his energies. But both Pascals were great sinners, insofar as their "forever restless curiosity" reflected a "vain desire of knowledge" that was inexcusable, whatever the fair name of "science." For fallen man, there could be no such thing as a pure science, certainly not mathematics. Although Jansenius did not recognize the New Science as a rival to his traditional faith, he did condemn experimental methods and expose the pridefulness of any pursuit of "novelties" or "inventions." So much for both the *Traité des coniques* and the Arithmetic Machine?[18]

Finally, there was the "pride of life." Jacqueline and Blaise, too, were very proud persons, but Étienne may have been prouder still, proud of his remarkable children, prouder of his own dignity as a *commissaire,* and perhaps proudest of his recent qualification as a *conseiller du Roi.* From the perspective of a rigorist spirituality, he had been culpably disobedient in the affair of the *rentes,* then as culpably dominant in any pleasure that he had taken in governing others as the royal Commissioner. There was also the very awkward fact that Étienne's household had been so little devout that Jacqueline, who was now past twenty, had yet to be presented for confirmation.

Quite apart from its appeal on other, higher grounds, the Augustinian spirituality of the Two Loves offered these three good persons these two additional good things. First, the rigorist demand that God be the unique focus of all love gave the Pascals religious sanction for rejecting a marriage that would have meant Jacqueline's withdrawal from the paternal household. A son, even this son, would have had no voice in the premarital negotiations, and this daughter had been perfectly submissive to her father's will. But Blaise must have known that Jacqueline had already shown her inclination to reject the false love of the salons and to embrace the true love taught by the Church. When he had appealed to her after his conversion, she had been receptive, and this, in turn, had cast a new light on the proposed marriage. Brother and sister together could then approach their father at a time when his physical condition had made him especially receptive to their persuasion. The first good thing in our retrospective assessment of the conversions is that they led to the abandonment of marriage projects for Jacqueline. What was left of the family was kept together.

The second good thing is that the Christian promise of the heavenly Father's eternal love offered a basis for hope even when Étienne's life was threatened. The Pascal children had already experienced the loss of their mother and separation from their father. These experiences and the death(s) of their uncle(s) would have heightened their insecurity in 1646, after Étienne's accident. No one knows what wonders the pious laypersons and the good God may have done to strengthen the frail man's bones. But Gilberte and Marguerite do say that they did do wonders for his maturing children's souls. Their message, universal as it was, met the particular needs of these persons at this time. They could repeat the promise of promises, the undying love of an eternal object, God.

That familial attachments were fundamental to Blaise's First Conversion—and to its limitations—is suggested by the fact that he was so quick later in 1646 and 1647 to pursue the Vacuum Experiments with and for his father. He had just been converted by a Jansenist literature that was rigorous in its spiritual denunciation of scientific "curiosity." Nevertheless, his father and his father's friend initiated experiments with mercury filled tubes at Rouen, and his father's theoretical convictions were at stake. Blaise followed him and soon far surpassed him. Apparently, this later made so little sense to Gilberte as the author of edifying memoirs, that she "corrected" her memory of the events that she had witnessed in order to fit the demands of the spirituality that she, too, had come to share. But it makes perfect sense in terms of Blaise's enduring attachment.

Blaise's Illness of 1647 and Jacqueline's Vocation

This illness is not well documented, and its symptoms are neither described with anything approaching clinical accuracy nor dated with historical exactness. Marguerite Périer much later left the following account of "a very extraordinary state" that her narrative places after the First Conversion (winter 1646) and the Vacuum Experiments (winter 1647):

> It was caused by his overwork as a scientist. The spirits having risen [from his legs] to his brain, he was left paralyzed from the waist down. The result was that he couldn't walk without crutches, and his legs and feet became as cold as marble. Every day, they had to dress him in brandy-soaked stockings, so as to return some warmth to his feet. In the circumstances, the doctors ordered the family to forbid him any sort of [intellectual] work.[19]

Thus, the fact of his Genius explained the sufferings of the Genius; the doctors and the family tradition after them supposed that the afflicted legs had been emptied of vital spirits rising to the great head.

Marguerite's chronology means that this "very extraordinary state" must also have come after the abortive marriage projects for Jacqueline, after the accidental injury suffered by Étienne, and after the return to Rouen of Gilberte. We are dependent on the hearsay testimony of a lay observer (Gilberte), repeated long after the fact by a garrulous anecdotalist (Marguerite). Nevertheless, this "strange story," too, makes a historical sense unappreciated by its tellers. It suggests the threatened son's desperate identification with his injured father. How like Étienne, who had dislocated or broken *his hip* after a fall *on ice,* for Blaise, too, to suffer in the following year *a sort of paralysis from the waist down,* with "*legs and feet as cold as marble*"!

Characteristically, Marguerite was so preoccupied with the strange phenomenon that she did not bother to record less extraordinary symptoms. As Gilberte tells it, Blaise suffered from vague "incommodities" after turning eighteen in June 1641, the month of her marriage: "He sometimes told us that he hadn't passed a single day without pain since reaching the age of eighteen." She suggests that the "illnesses" were both chronic and degenerative, although she also describes prolonged periods of intensive work on the Arithmetic Machine (1643–45) and the Vacuum Experiments (1646–47), and for most of this time she was not present to observe her brother's condition.[20] She does give us one paragraph specifically concerned with the beginning of his great "indispositions" in 1647, when, during her prolonged visit, she was in a position to observe him very closely:

> Among other incommodities, there was his inability to swallow liquids unless they were heated; even then, he could take them only drop by drop. In addition to that, he also had insupportable headaches, overheated entrails, and many other ills. The doctors prescribed purgation every other day for three months. For this he had to take lots of medicine, all of it heated and administered drop by drop. This was a veritable torture, which touched the hearts of everyone near him, although he himself never complained.[21]

The "uncomplaining" victim of so many ills rejoiced that his sufferings enabled him to understand Christ crucified.[22]

Gilberte must also have observed and remembered much more, but her written record in the *Vie de Monsieur Pascal* was limited by her propriety, her medical incomprehension, and especially her memorial purpose to tell the edifying story. She refrained from describing in any detail "*other* incommodities" and "*other* ills." From September 1647, when Jacqueline was nursing her brother in Paris, there are reliable reports that Blaise had difficulties speaking and experienced headaches, night-sweats, and insomnia.[23] The several reports on the illness are intriguing, but they are also so vague as to prevent anything like a retrospective diagnosis.[24]

One thing is sure. Pascal *gained* in various ways from his loss of health. He himself emphasized that his illness prevented him from continuing his work in the physical sciences and so served him as a saintly sufferer and student of Christian perfection.[25] Negatively, it made it impossible for him to continue the scientific experimentation that had exhibited and further excited his prideful curiosity. Positively, it inclined his heart toward penitence, focused his spirit on God alone, and allowed a truer imitation of Christ's sacrifice.[26]

There was more to be *gained*. The invalid who suffered so in the presence of his sisters received loving care from these sisters. I have emphasized Blaise's first great loss, that of his mother. Twenty years later, it would have been a predictable gain that his illness required Gilberte, who had already married away, and Jacqueline, for whom there had been marriage projects, to care for him as his mother had done so long beforehand. His most striking symptoms suggest a gross regression and submission to a nursing that was at least quasi-maternal. This could explain *both* his inability to walk *and* his intolerance of any food other than liquids that were heated and served drop by drop.

Étienne had become Blaise's sole parent, sole teacher, and sole support. The boy had grown into manhood without leaving his father's household, but Étienne's accident in 1646 then suggested the awful possibility of loss. After all, Uncle Blaise had died after a wintertime fall six years earlier. And Uncle Bremond had also died in 1646. Spiritual conversion in 1646 reaffirmed beliefs that there was a higher community of the faithful that no accident could truly injure, no illness kill. Blaise's Vacuum Experiments later in that same year and in the next allowed him to tie his life to his father's in yet another way. And his peculiar "sort of paralysis" in the next winter then virtually identified the imperiled son with his injured father.

Seeking treatment for his strange disorder and perhaps also an escape from the tensions that must have been inseparable from their lives as young adults under their father's direct supervision, Blaise and Jacqueline returned to Paris, where Étienne still maintained a household. They left their father and older sister together in Rouen. This was in the summer of 1647. The crisis that had begun with marriage proposals for Jacqueline then entered its last phase, as the matured but not emancipated woman, supported by Blaise, resolved on a religious vocation at Port-Royal, the convent of the Arnaulds, where spiritual life followed the counsels of Saint-Cyran. This was openly to oppose these grown children to their father.

In a letter addressed nominally to Gilberte and actually to Étienne on 1 April 1648, Blaise and Jacqueline broached the sensitive topic. Entry into a convent would have entailed withdrawal from the household, of course, but the two converts tried to convince their father that their natural ties were as nothing compared with their spiritual unity. After the grace of conversion, the family of blood relatives was now one at heart:

Our great happiness is to have been united in the latter way. We ought to come together to acknowledge this and to rejoice in it. We must confess that it is only since this time (which M. de Saint-Cyran calls the beginning of life) that we may consider ourselves as properly related. It has pleased God to join us in spirit in the other world, after having joined us in the flesh in this world.[27]

The same letter argued the case against human attachments in the strongest terms. There is pathos as well as irony in the fact that Blaise was Jacqueline's advocate in her unsuccessful efforts to discipline Étienne's attachment and so to prepare her withdrawal. The brother who was later to cling so desperately to this most dearly beloved sister, pleading with her to defer her vocation still longer, had raised the doctrine of the Two Loves against just such creaturely attachments in his earlier letter:

Scripture is full of stories of the vengeance taken by God against those guilty of [the idolatrous love of creatures in place of the Creator]. The First Commandment . . . , which includes all the others, forbids above all the adoration of images [including man, created in the image of God]. Because He is much more jealous of how we direct our affection than our esteem, it is obvious that there is no crime more offensive or more detestable than the sovereign love of creatures. . . .

Every day we think of you and of God's providential direction of our lives. He has made us not only brother and sister, one to another, but also children of the same father. You know that, so to speak, he foresaw us and conceived us with this intention [that we should be one in spirit]. And so we ought to marvel that God has given us both the figure [the Pascals' flesh and blood] and the reality [the converts' grace] of that alliance. As we have often repeated, the corporeal is only the image of the spiritual.[28]

It would be "carnal and Judaic blindness" for the flesh and blood father to mistake the figure for the reality. Étienne's children were more truly "God's children," bound to obey the Scriptural injunction, "Be ye therefore perfect, as your Father which is in heaven is perfect."[29]

In May 1648, Jacqueline's desire to leave the world for the convent was the occasion for a confrontation between father and son and for further pathos. Gilberte tells us that Étienne responded angrily and suspiciously when Blaise informed him about the vocation. Blaise was then almost twenty-five years old, Jacqueline, twenty-two:

My father was very surprised by this proposition, his mind strangely divided. On the one hand, he was glad to see that his children shared his sentiments, because he, too, was a convert to the maxims of the most pure Christianity. But on the other hand, he couldn't reconcile himself to a lasting separation, because of the tenderest affection that attached him so strongly to her. His ambivalence forced him first to answer my brother [N.B.], that "he would see," and that "he would think about it." But finally, after a period of indecision, he told him [N.B.] that he couldn't give his consent.[30]

Indeed, Étienne charged a trusted servant to maintain his paternal authority by a domestic surveillance.

After a tense year, father and daughter eventually reached an accommodation.[31] Étienne agreed to allow her to lead a religious life within the household, promising not to arrange a marriage, but he also begged her not to leave him for the convent, reassuring her, so to speak, that he could not live much longer. Jacqueline, in turn, acceded to what seems to have been his request, not quite a command, that she remain faithfully with him in the world until after his death, but she also withdrew from secular society and continued to maintain relations with Port-Royal.[32]

This resolution could hardly have pleased anyone, but the family did hold together despite further dislocations caused by the civil unrest of the Fronde. Étienne retreated from Rouen to Paris, where he rejoined his son and daughter in 1648; then, with them, he retreated again from Paris to Clermont, where they all rejoined Gilberte in 1649. There, in the Florin Périer household, for the last time the Pascals lived together, except, of course, for Antoinette Begon. After a prolonged period of refuge and reunion in their native city, Étienne, Blaise, and Jacqueline returned again to Paris in 1650. There, the old man died in 1651.

CHAPTER 6

The Crisis of 1651–53

Étienne Pascal died on 24 September 1651. Jacqueline entered Port-Royal on 4 January 1652. These events and their aftermath constitute what I call the Third Crisis. There is nothing comparable in the traditional story, where a vaguely defined Worldly Period of dissipation precedes the Second Conversion of 1654. In the First Version of Gilberte's *Vie de Monsieur Pascal,* Étienne's death comes as an aside in a paragraph on Blaise as a zealous convert. *This son* taught *his father* to embrace "a more exacting life"; Étienne thus learned "always to perfect himself by the continual practice of virtues"; then he drops from the story of Blaise's life, having died a "completely Christian death" at the end of a buried sentence.[1]

In the Second Version, Gilberte added a reference to the letter of consolation that Blaise addressed to her on 17 October 1651. In retrospect, she remembered it as "still another proof" of the "charity" with which "he loved without attachment." But this same letter provides the best evidence that he had been attached to his father, that he could not reconcile himself to his loss, and that his immediate concern was to hold his sisters in the embrace of his love. He appealed as much to Jacqueline, whose withdrawal he feared, as to Gilberte, who had already withdrawn.

Blaise's Loss of His Father and the Two Loves

Pascal's letter includes a succinct statement of the doctrine of the Two Loves. He derived its fundamental concepts from the greatest masterpieces of Augustine himself and his seventeenth-century disciple, Cornelis Jansenius:

> In order to overcome more absolutely the revulsion [that we naturally feel at death], we must carefully reconsider its origin. And to move you in just a few words, I have to tell you in general what is the source of all vices and all sins. This is what I have learned from two very great and very holy persons [probably Augustine in *The City of God,* bk. XIV, chap. 28; Jansenius in the *Augustinus,* bk. II, chap. 25].
>
> The truth that explains the mystery is that God made man with two loves, one for God, the other for himself. God's law was that man's love for Him should be infinite, that is, unbounded by any end other than God Himself, while his love for himself should be finite and relative to God. In this state [of innocence before the Fall], man loved himself without sin—and would have sinned, had he failed to love himself.
>
> Since the Fall, man has lost the first of these loves, and, his love of self having remained alone in that great soul, [which was created to be] capable of an infinite love, that self-love has expanded and overflowed into the void left by the now-lost love of God. Thus, he has come to love himself alone, and everything else for himself, that is to say, infinitely. And that's the origin of self-love.[2]

Pascal's own secular identity as a mathematician and physicist suggested new forms for the old idea of the Two Loves. The mathematician shows himself in his use of the concept of infinity, and the physicist, in his image of the vacuum. This language was particularly appropriate for his brother-in-law, Florin, who had performed the Great Experiment by carrying a mercury barometer up the puy de Dôme. Blaise himself had become a zealous convert, and he instructed Gilberte on her failings with respect to spiritually correct attitudes toward death. In "just a few words," he told his sister that *her* grief as a bereaved daughter was actually a form of self-love and, as such, "vicious," "sinful," "criminal," "immoderate," "defective," and "excessive."[3]

Blaise's letter also includes evidence of *his* grief as a bereaved son. It emerges most painfully in one remarkable sentence, here italicized, that is neither well prepared in the long discourse that precedes it nor well developed in the few short paragraphs that follow. Nevertheless, it is one of the most important testimonies on his affective life:

> Having found a basis for consolation with respect to his person [why it was not bad for Étienne himself that he had died], we ought not to fail ourselves or to disregard our future need for and benefit from his presence [the father's earthly afterlife in his children's affective unity].
>
> I am the one who is most concerned. *If I had lost him six years ago, I myself would have been lost; although I believe that I now have a less absolute need of him, I know that he would have been necessary for me ten more years and beneficial, my whole life long* [emphasis added].[4]

The reference to a past occasion of possible loss "six years ago" is of exceptional interest. Blaise can only have had in mind the serious injury that Étienne had suffered in the fall on ice in January 1646. He suggests not just that he had feared for his father's life, but also that his dependence as a twenty-three-year-old son had been so "absolute" that Étienne's death would have been tantamount to his own death. At the age of twenty-eight, he supposes that Etienne would have been "necessary" for him until, say, thirty-eight. Then he adds to that number. Ten more years of life with his father might not have been enough for the grown son, after all.

With this one italicized sentence in mind, let us look back at the rest of Pascal's remarkable letter on his father's death. There are recurrent references to his "natural sentiments," always as something to be overcome:

> I will speak here only of the consequence that I draw, which is that his end was so Christian, so happy, so holy, and so much to be desired, that, except for those persons affected by the sentiments of nature, there is no Christian who must not rejoice. . . . I will begin with a discourse most consoling for those who have sufficient strength of mind to reflect in the time of greatest grief.
>
> We must seek consolation for our ills in God, not in ourselves, other men, or anything created. . . . Uniting our will with that of God Himself, with Him, in Him, and for Him, we will the thing that He has eternally willed in us and for us. Let us consider matters in that way, and let us practice the lesson that I have learned from a great man [reference obscure] in the time of our greatest affliction. . . . [Let us regard] life as a continual sacrifice that cannot be consummated otherwise than in death.[5]

Consideration of life as well as death in terms of Christian sacrifice leads to spiritually consistent, if "unnatural," even "irrational" conclusions. Blaise instructs his sisters and his brother-in-law that they had already lost Étienne at his spiritual birth in 1588, long before his physical death in 1651.[6] Contrarily, they had not lost him even after this death. The latter point is the more important. Despite "the sentiments of corrupted and confused nature," the survivors' knowledge of the truths of religion teaches them that death, rather than being the end, is the beginning of a new life:

> Let us no longer consider the man as having ceased to live—although nature suggests it—but as having begun to live—as the Truth assures us. Let us no longer consider his soul as having perished and been reduced to nothingness, but as having been given life and unity with the living Lord. By our consideration of these same truths, let us also correct the sentiments of error that are so deeply rooted in us and the feelings of horror [at death] that are so natural to man.[7]

Only a careless reader could accuse this Pascal of not feeling grief. But along with his strong faith and profound psychology, there is a brittle rationalism. It was a matter of Pascal's Augustinian faith to repeat that man was created to love God, but that in his fallen state he naturally loves himself. It was also a brilliant psychological intuition to relate our revulsion from death to our love of self.[8] But, from the vantage point of anyone familiar with more modern studies of bereavement, it must seem only brittle rationalism for him, however powerful his mind, to have supposed that he could "correct the sentiments of error," simply accepting the unacceptable fact of loss.[9]

Perhaps he did not aspire to such perfect consolation. He likened his words to seeds and looked to God to bless their growth. He had fewer illusions about his nature than some readers have supposed, and he confessed his grief:

> It isn't that I want you to be unfeeling. The blow has been too violent, and without divine support we couldn't stand up to its impact. Therefore, it isn't just for us [to expect ourselves] to be free from grief, as if we were angels without natural feelings. But at the same time, it is no more just for us to be inconsolable, as if we were pagans without any notion of grace. Justice requires that we be afflicted and consoled as Christians and that our natural feelings yield to the consolations of Grace. . . .
>
> It is true that the death of the body is only the image of that of the soul. . . . [T]he death of the body is so terrible that it causes us great distress, and the death of the soul ought to seem still more terrible, leaving us inconsolable. In the time of our great pain, let us then appreciate the greatness of our blessings, and let the excess of our grief be measured by that of our joy.[10]

Blaise's Supplication of His Two Sisters

Gilberte remembered Blaise's letter of consolation as "a proof" that he had loved "without attachment." But she also recalled its claim that the father "lost to him on earth" had been "won for him in heaven."[11] She seems not to have recalled her brother's plea for the continued love of his two sisters.[12] These relationships, too, were problematical in the months after Étienne's death. Jacqueline had already retreated from her own family within the paternal household, and now she wanted to retreat further behind the walls of a notably strict convent.[13] Gilberte herself had already returned with her husband to distant Clermont, and there she had given birth to her fifth child on the day after her father's funeral in Paris.[14] Thus, his sisters were committed to separate lives in religion and in the world, leaving Blaise with the awful prospect of being alone, all alone, for the first time in his life.

In the guise of "charity toward the dead," Pascal expressed his own attachment to the living. The following few paragraphs merit the closest analysis; they advance no fewer than six powerful arguments for the continued love that he so desperately needed:

> At the time of our affliction, I have learned from a holy man [Antoine Singlin] that one of the most substantial and useful charities toward the dead is to do those things that they would command us to do if they were still in this world. We should practice the holy counsels that they have given us [in the past], and we should place ourselves in the situation that they wish for us at the present time.
>
> In this way, we make them live again in us, in a manner of speaking, because it is their counsel that is still living and active in us. Just as the heretics are punished in the other world for the sins of those whom they have misled and in whom their venom still circulates, so also the dead are rewarded not only for their own merits but also for the good done by those who have followed their counsel and their example.
>
> Let us then do all that is in our power to give him new life before God in ourselves. Let us console one another in the unity of our hearts, in which it seems to me that he still lives. Our reunion returns us in a manner into his presence, as the gathering of the faithful is blessed by the presence of Jesus Christ.
>
> I pray that God may create and sustain these feelings in us [meaning "you and Jacqueline"?] and that he may continue those he gives me. I feel greater affection than ever for you and for my sister, because it seems to me that the love that we had for my father ought not to be lost. We ought to

reinfuse ourselves with this love, regarding it as our principal inheritance from the affection that he showered upon us and loving one another more dearly than ever, if that is possible.

I pray that God may fortify us in these resolutions, and in this hope I beg you to agree that I give you counsel that you would have reached on your own. But I do it anyway, because, having found a basis for consolation with respect to his person, we ought not to fail ourselves or to disregard our future need for and benefit from his presence.[15]

All this leads up to Blaise's moving confession of his enduring attachment to his deceased father, which I have already emphasized. In context, this confession is a supplication. He says, in so many words: My grief is greater than yours, and my need is greater. Six years ago, this would have killed me. I still need him, and I will never wholly outgrow that need. Without him, I need you more than ever.[16] Blaise pleads for love with a masterful brief on all that is most sacred—and most affecting.

First, there is the discreet appeal to the *spiritual authority of Father Antoine Singlin,* the powerful preacher at Port-Royal, whose instruction Jacqueline, particularly, would esteem. In the two years before her entry into Port-Royal, letters from Mère Agnès Arnauld counseled the young woman, but it was to Singlin's authority that the old nun herself deferred.[17] It is especially important to Blaise's argument that Singlin was so stern a preacher against human attachments, even in the face of human losses.[18]

Second, there is Blaise's appeal to their *Christian "charity" toward their dead father.*[19] This is doubly clever, if a bit sanctimonious. It robes his plea for a human attachment in the vestments of the supposedly antagonistic principle of Christian charity, and it makes the beneficiary of this holier love not the pious pleader himself, the living brother, but the dead father. By loving Blaise in this world, Jacqueline and Gilberte could serve Étienne in Purgatory, hastening his heavenly reward.

Third, there is Blaise's appeal to their respect for *paternal authority*. It would be difficult to exaggerate an Old Regime father's rights and his children's obligations. Civil law and divine Commandment reinforced one another. No one questioned a child's duty to obey, even if this child had reached adulthood within the parental household.[20] Once again, this is an argument that was more relevant to the unmarried Jacqueline, freed from her father by his death, than to the married Gilberte, to whom the living man had given a husband. It was Jacqueline who had promised Étienne, when he had begged her not to leave his household for a religious life at Port-Royal, "that she would never give her father grounds to complain of her disobedience."[21] She had then been twenty-three years old. Spiritual counselors from within the convent, who had connived with her to maintain relations before her father's death, had told her to wait patiently, taking his paternal disapproval as "God's decree."[22]

Fourth, there is Blaise's seductively joined appeal to his sisters' sense of loss and biblical faith. They could make their *father live again,* as Singlin had taught, if they would follow his paternal precepts. More specifically, the spiritual presence of the father would bless the affective unity of his children, if they gathered in his name. After all, Jesus Christ had promised the Disciples: "Where two or three are gathered together in my name, there am I in the midst of them."[23] The reader is left to wonder what sort of gathering would be possible for the single worldling at Paris, the nun-to-be headed for the community of Port-Royal, and the wife-and-mother wedded to Florin Périer in Clermont?

Fifth and sixth, there is Blaise's more straightforward assurance that *he now loved the two of them more than ever* and his open admission that *he now needed them more than ever.* How could Gilberte have missed this when she first read the letter or later when she remembered it? And what effect, if any, did the letter have on Jacqueline, who must also have seen it before it was posted?

Jacqueline's Death to the World and Life in Religion

In the *Vie de Jacqueline Pascal,* Gilberte's account of her sister's life in the world ends with what can be considered either the unqualified pathos of a worldling's feelings of loss and abandonment or the qualified heroism of a nun's triumph over human attachments. Blaise was "deeply affected" by his father's death, but his beloved sister's presence brought him "great consolation." He thought that his human needs were so obvious and that his sister's Christian charity was so great, that she would stay with him for "at least a[nother] year." He spoke to her about it with such desperate intensity that she did not dare to communicate her true intentions, "for fear of redoubling his grief." Her plan was to remain in the world only until the settlement of the estate at the end of December. "To spare her brother," she proposed to tell him that she was only going on a "retreat."[24]

The qualification of Jacqueline's heroism is largely a matter of her failure to face her brother with the truth or even this untruth. She asked *Gilberte* to bear the bad tidings of her white lie about a temporary retreat:

He was struck to the heart, nevertheless. He retired to his chamber in a state of profound sadness, without seeing my sister, who was then in a little room where she used to say her prayers. She came out only after my brother had retired, because she was afraid that seeing him would move her to pity. On his behalf, I repeated his loving words, and then we both went to bed.[25]

Gilberte could not sleep that night, but Jacqueline herself slept like a hero, not a nun. On the morning 4 January 1652, she had to be awakened from untroubled repose at seven o'clock. Then, without risking farewells to brother or sister, whose movements within the household seem almost choreographed to avoid painful encounters, she left, never to return.

Gilberte's termination of her sister's life history at this point is appropriate. In a real sense, Jacqueline had died to the world.[26] That this had been her firm intention is evident from her meditations on the death of Jesus, composed some four months before the death of Étienne. She began with a brief recital of the doctrine of the Two Loves. She was determined to love God with an undivided heart, to live only in God, and, as she repeated again and again, to die to the world. Several passages hammer the nails into the Cross:

Jesus died, not only with respect to Himself, but also with respect to His Holy Mother, His family, and His friends, depriving them of the consolation of His presence and depriving Himself of theirs. This teaches me to die not only to myself, but also to all the interests of flesh and blood and human affection. That is, I must forget everything about my [family and] friends that doesn't concern their salvation. . . .

Jesus died on the Cross, raised above the world, with everything, even His Holy Mother, beneath His feet. This teaches me to raise my heart above everything on the earth . . . and to regard everything most grand and most lovable as beneath me. . . .

Jesus died, but He did not leave His own as orphans. He sent them His Holy Spirit, Who is His divine love, to help them and to remain with them to the end of the world. This teaches me to separate myself from my own in every way. Nevertheless, I ought to remain forever with them by love born purely of God. And I ought to help them with my prayers.[27]

Jacqueline's life at Port-Royal formalized and regularized the reorientation of her affections. She had been Étienne's daughter and Blaise's sister; she would become Christ's bride. The roles were mutually exclusive. The line between religion and the world had been drawn around Port-Royal, and, when Jacqueline withdrew behind it, Blaise had lost her. It is no wonder that, having prompted her conversion, he tried to defer her vocation. The wonder is that she should have been so successful in securing from him at least the outward signs of support for her action.

After entering the convent on 4 January 1652, Jacqueline's first known communication to Blaise came in a long and passionate letter dated 7-9 May. This is the most important evidence from her on the implications of her vocation for him. In the first paragraph came Jacqueline's adaptation of the idea, personal loss as Christian sacrifice, that he had expressed in his October letter of consolation after Étienne's death. So much for the effectiveness of his supplication. She now told him, from behind her convent walls, that he, too, should be "eternally grateful" to her letter bearer:

[H]e will help you to stifle the natural feelings that could oppose the so-happy opportunity that God now offers you to make the sacrifice of my person. . . . [H]e will be God's chosen instrument, as He finally answers the constant prayers and tears that I have offered Him for over four years. God punishes us while favoring us, and His blows are blessings. You know how it has pleased Him to lift the only legitimate obstacle to the engagement that I want to make, although I don't dare mention it [Étienne's death] for fear of mixing something sad with my joy.[28]

Jacqueline's message was ambiguous on a crucial point. Did she or did she not grant Blaise a measure of authority over her conduct? She reminded him, rightly, that her father's death had terminated all paternal authority and that she had been emancipated. However, she seemed also to acknowledge her brother's lesser claims, permitting him "a sort of mastery," if but only if he used it to add his blessing to her vocation. She suggested that she might delay the beginning of her novitiate out of deference to his wishes, but she also made it clear that she was going to put on the habit with or without his approval.[29]

Jacqueline recalled her own experience of the Pascals' particular susceptibility to "natural affection," but she seems to have supposed that, at the time of writing, only Blaise's sinful nature was affected, not her own. We may doubt that. She would hardly have written such a letter, if Blaise had not still mattered to her. But what language she used! She wrote as if what I would call his anxious attachment were neither more nor less than the fiendish tyranny of the world, the flesh, and the devil, and she likened her own situation as a beloved sister to that of the tortured martyrs.[30]

In powerful—but tortured—sentences, she rejects her brother's love while renouncing the world. In what follows, the pronoun *il* is "the world," and *elle* is "a person," but the context, the first words quoted, and the lapses into the first- and second-person leave no doubt about her meaning:

> [W]hen the world shows you some regret at no longer seeing me, be assured that this is only an illusion that would disappear in a flash, were it not a matter of opposing a good. This is because it is impossible for it truly to love a person who doesn't belong to it, who wants never to belong to it, and whose greatest desire at the present is to blot out its vision and to abandon it forever [N.B.] by her solemn vow and her commitment to a life that is utterly opposed to its maxims. . . . If it is true that it has kept some impression of the love that it showed me when I belonged to it, God grant that this may neither turn me back from leaving it nor turn you back from giving your consent.
>
> It ought to be my glory and your joy, and that of all who truly love me, to have borne witness to the power of the grace of my God. It doesn't leave me; I abandon it [N.B.]. Although its attempts to hold me back seem to be a perfectly obvious punishment for the complaisance [Étienne's word for his paternal regard for his obedient son] that I once had for it, God graciously grants me the strength to resist. All its efforts serve only to adorn the victory that He has deigned to achieve in my heart.[31]

Jacqueline's thinly veiled condemnation of Blaise's attachment and her denial that he could have truly loved her must have made excruciatingly painful reading. Her third-person pronouns hardly cushion the impact of passionate and reiterated affirmations that she had deliberately chosen to abandon him.

When Jacqueline finally reestablished the second person, addressing Blaise directly, she commanded him, in God's name, not to oppose her will. An unsympathetic reader might judge her harshly for the spiritual pride with which she denounced her brother's humanity, while likening herself to the Apostles, the angels, and even the Deity. She saved her worst, from this perspective, for the penultimate paragraph:

> I pray to God with all my heart that He may not impute against them [the third-person plural here must mean Étienne and Blaise] who opposed me for the past four years the sin that they committed in doing so. May He forgive them, for, truly, they knew not what they did [cf. Luke 23:34].

She rose to threaten her brother: "I will surely renounce you, if you don't [come to the *vêture*]. Do with good grace what you've got to do. . . . Don't displease me, because I haven't given you any reason to do so."[32]

There are good reasons for a less judgmental reading of Jacqueline's letter. Spiritually, her condemnation of her father's and brother's love is another expression of the Two Loves. Psychologically, it is best interpreted as the defensive denial of her own separations and losses. She, too, had lost her mother at a very early age; she had almost died in the course of her father's traumatic absence in 1638; she had converted after his accident in 1646 and settled upon a religious vocation after her relocation in 1647; she had left the paternal household for Port-Royal only after his death in 1651. Having finally retreated from the world of sorrows, she now feared that knowledge of her brother's desolation would be an additional burden. Indeed, she wanted a "sign of love from you more than anyone else."[33]

Blaise had been demanding that she wait two more years before beginning her novitiate. After her letter, he reduced his demand to six months. Within days, pious friends had talked him down still further, and he had finally agreed that the *vêture* might just as well take place on the date specified in her request or ultimatum: Trinity Sunday, 26 May 1652.[34] His final concession, like his stubborn opposition, is evidence of love.

A year later, on 5 June 1653, Jacqueline said her vows. She promised stability of place, amendment of manners, and obedience to the Rule.[35] She had renounced all prospect of ever returning to the world. But, again, she insisted on visible and tangible signs of Blaise's love, his presence at her profession and a substantial donation in her name to the community. He complied, grudgingly but not ungenerously.

Jacqueline's account of their differences, which nominally concerned money, was written as a testimonial to Mère Angélique's perfect charity, and Blaise's opposition to the donation was long seen as evidence of his worldly cupidity.[36] Jean Mesnard has gone far toward correcting this simplistic distribution of praise and blame in two learned papers on the vocation. But to make the money the issue is to miss the more profound problem. It was Blaise's attachment that had made him unable to accept the separation entailed by her vocation in 1652.[37] The same problem still divided the two in 1653.

Blaise and his worldly allies, the Périers, had a perfectly legitimate objection, when they represented to her that her donations to the convent would deprive her siblings of their inheritance.[38] But even they did not draw the bottom line at money. They told her that it would take a long time to share the estate equally among the three heirs, because it consisted almost exclusively of credits, not all equally good and some quite bad. If Jacqueline did want to make a large donation at the time of her profession, which was legally her civil death, she would have to defer these vows. How long? *Four years.*[39]

For Jacqueline, this was another tragic act in the same domestic drama already begun in 1648 (*just wait* until Étienne's death before entering the convent), continued in 1651 (*just wait* "at least" another year before entering the convent), further continued in 1652 (*just wait* another two years before beginning her novitiate), and now climaxed in 1653 (*just wait* still another four years before professing her vows).[40] It is no wonder that she had become a little impatient for the final curtain.

Mère Angélique provided her with a sympathetic audience. In fifty years of religious life, the matriarch of Port-Royal had witnessed many other young nuns struggling to break away from their families. What she had to say to Jacqueline is important both for her instruction in the religious life and for her analysis of the younger woman's spiritual state. Remarkably, Jacqueline's own *Relation* preserves a contemporaneous firsthand account. Angélique gave the following counsel after Jacqueline had announced her unwillingness to delay her profession:

> What, my daughter, can it be possible that you are still sad? Haven't you learned long ago that you can never trust the affection of creatures, and that the world loves only those who are the world's? Aren't you happy that God teaches this to you so clearly by the behavior of those from whom you

would least have expected it? This should answer any doubts that you might have had, before you leave the world forever. Now you can do so with a bolder heart, because your action is the more necessary. Your resolution must be unwavering, because you can now say, in a manner of speaking, that you no longer have anyone to leave behind.[41]

Mère Angélique believed that all creaturely love was vain and empty. Her timely lesson in the Two Loves taught Jacqueline that her worldly brother Blaise and brother-in-law Florin could not truly love her.

On the next day, the old Mother Superior spent a consoling hour alone with the troubled young novice. Angélique comforted Jacqueline, whose face betrayed her "extraordinary sadness":

[I]mmediately after Mass she made a sign for me to follow her. Sitting me down beside her, she held me for a whole hour with my head resting on her bosom, embracing me with the tenderness of a real mother. I can truly say that she forgot nothing that she could possibly have done to charm away my sadness.[42]

The young woman was soothed by what she called this precious milk from her spiritual mother. She had known no abiding affection in the world, but she found solace in religion.

Mère Angélique understood a great deal about Jacqueline, even if her knowledge of Blaise was distant and unsympathetic. Angélique thought that Jacqueline suffered more than she realized from a "wounded love." Her good daughter had truly loved the other members of her natural family—but they had not returned and could not have returned such love. They were worldlings, ruled by creaturely love and material self-interest: "The great riches of your family have been the love and unity which have bound you so closely and made all things common among you."[43]

There could be no future to the relationship between the sister in religion and the brother in the world. The rules pertaining to a nun's communications with the members of her family provide us with properly impersonal and quite decisive evidence on the subject. They actively discouraged and severely limited both the exchange of letters and the reception of visits.

In the Third Crisis, Blaise had lost his father and then been "abandoned" by his favored sister. He was left alone. Étienne Pascal's fatherhood had been the most important fact of Blaise's life in the years after Antoinette Begon's death. His love had helped to make good his son's loss. But that same loss of a mother in Blaise's early childhood and that same love of a father in Blaise's later childhood and youth had prepared this son for a most difficult bereavement in his adulthood. Étienne's three consequential decisions had effectively denied Blaise other attachments and bound father and son the more tightly together. His example, his lessons, his admiration, his ideas, his money, and his status had all helped to make the great Pascal one of the leading savants of his day, the heir apparent to the great Descartes as the preeminent French mathematician and physicist. Nevertheless, there was a cost to be reckoned and a price to be paid after Étienne's death. In 1651, at the age of twenty-eight, Blaise had still never lived in an independent residence, never trained for an independent professional life, never earned or enjoyed an independent income, and, apparently, never been encouraged to marry. We know of no love outside the household, nor even any intimate friendship in Paris. In these circumstances, it is hardly surprising that the young man tried to hold his unmarried sister. But he failed.

In the course of 1653, the year of Jacqueline's vows and his own thirtieth birthday, Blaise did make one close friendship, that with Artus de Roannez. This seems to have helped him considerably, although no new friendship could have replaced his old familial relationships. We owe to a member of the Roannez entourage, the Chevalier de Méré, a lesser light who preferred to shine upon himself, the first publication of following verses, which seem to have been Pascal's and to have been written in 1653. The insufferably vain Chevalier savored them as evidence of the wonderful pleasure and great profit of his society. I cite them as evidence of the terrible pain that I attribute to prior losses. Nothing in the poem refers specifically to Étienne's death or Jacqueline's vocation, but everything testifies to the poet's experience of desolation:

Quel changement subit du sort qui me conduit!
J'étais en ces climats où la neige et la glace
  Font à la terre une horrible surface
Pendant cinq ou six mois d'une profonde nuit;
Après, quand le soleil y revient à son tour,
Il se montre si bas, et si pâle et si sombre,
  Que c'est plutôt son fantôme ou son ombre

Que l'aimable Soleil qui ramène le jour.
Dans un triste silence et comme en un tombeau,
Je cherchais à me plaire où l'extrême froidure
  Ensevelit au sein de la Nature
Par un nuage épais ce qu'elle a de plus beau.[44]

This Pascal felt that he had emerged from wintertime entombment in cold and ice, darkness and sadness, without pleasure or beauty. There would be other such winters.

PART THREE

THE HEART OF THE MATTER

Whatever were the facts of Pascal's religious devotion in the years after his First Conversion (1646), the spiritual rigorists of the Two Loves were sure that he had relapsed into a sinful love of the world before his Second Conversion (1654). Mère Angélique and Sister Jacqueline de Sainte-Euphémie shared this opinion.[1] But whatever his human weaknesses with respect to the attractions of wealth, status, and learning itself, he did not love the world after his sister's religious profession.[2] He hated it. We know this from celebrated letters in which Jacqueline informed Gilberte of his renewed devotion. According to her reports, Blaise's "great contempt for the world and almost unbearable disgust with everyone in it" went back "more than a year" before the first of these letters, dated from Port-Royal on 8 December 1654.[3] That brings us back to the months following her religious vows and civil death.

In principle, the convert's turn toward a new love of God should also have been a turn away from an old love of self expressed in attachments to other persons. In fact, his stubborn love of his sister helped to ensure both his hatred of a world from which she had been lost and his embrace of the religion that she had found. She had left home for good; he pursued her into the convent parlor; there, she took him in hand and led him to the apostles of the Two Loves.

The Heart of the Matter as the title for this part 3 plays on three meanings of the word: the physical provenance of the *Mémorial* recovered from "over his chest," the psychological prepotency of familial attachments in Pascal's emotional life, and the historical centrality of the Second Conversion in his intellectual and spiritual life. These chapters are also the pivot of my analysis of his life and work, its most ambitious and original part.

In chapter 7, I consider Jacqueline's letters, Singlin's sermons, Arnauld's theology, and Port-Royalist spirituality with respect to the Two Loves. In chapters 8 and 9, I analyze the *Mémorial* from the night of 23 November 1654. This document is the crux. The text is familiar, but its meaning has remained mysterious. I believe that I have discovered a way toward a methodical analysis of *the* document on *the* experience. This way leads through the Scriptures, and so it has been closed to those opposed on philosophical or other grounds to the sympathetic study of religion. But it also requires a willingness to inquire into the incapacities of the conscious mind—and, contrarily, the capacities of the unconscious mind—and so it has also been closed to those who have been overawed by the great Pascal's intellect, those committed to a reading of the *Mémorial* as the testimony of a transcendent spirit, and those repulsed by anything that could be traced back in any form to the notorious Sigmund Freud's *Interpretation of Dreams* (1900).[4]

CHAPTER 7

Jacqueline de Sainte-Euphémie and the Second Conversion

Blaise approached Jacqueline at Port-Royal "sometime toward the end of September" 1654, opened his heart despairingly, and returned time and again in the next three months for her counsel. She explains this in letters to Gilberte that provide testimony from the most intimate person at the most crucial period. This evidence has been accepted as regulative since its first publication in the eighteenth century. However, it is potentially misleading, insofar as it directs attention away from the human relationship; Jacqueline was a strong-willed and strong-minded participant-observer whose purpose, in keeping with the Two Loves, was to redirect Blaise's affections.

Jacqueline's Letters to Gilberte

The first of these letters, which announces Blaise's Second Conversion, is dated 8 December 1654:

> It's time that you were told about God's work with the person who is so dear to us. . . . Time presses, and all that I can tell you is that, by the grace of God, he desires to give himself to Him. He still hasn't decided on a way of life, although he has felt a great contempt for the world and an almost unbearable disgust at all worldly persons for more than a year. Given his ardent nature, this could have led to great excesses, but he has been so moderate in everything that I have every reason to hope for the best. . . .

He has come around to M. S[inglin] as his choice for a director, and I hope that he will be childlike in his submission, if he [Singlin] will have him. He hasn't agreed; nevertheless, I hope that in the end he won't refuse us [note plural].

Although he [Blaise] feels more sickly than he has for a long time, that isn't stopping him in his undertaking. This proves that his former "reasons" were only rationalizations. I notice that he is humble and submissive, even to me, which is very surprising. Well, that's about all I have to say, although I should add that it's clear that it isn't his own natural spirit at work. . . . Adieu. Please, keep all of this a secret, even from him. I'm all yours.[1]

Four points about this letter seem most important. First, God is the Alpha and the Omega. At the beginning and end of her note, Jacqueline attributes the great change in her brother's life to God's action, not man's: "It's time that you were told about God's work. . . . It's clear that it isn't his own natural spirit at work." Her faith was perfectly in keeping with the Port-Royalist emphasis on grace. Saint-Cyran was the great authority from the previous generation: "If God alone can work a conversion before baptism, how much more is this true after [baptismal vows] have been broken and profaned."[2] Jacqueline's belief was spiritually correct, but it virtually precluded her notice of more mundane circumstances, first among them her own role in Blaise's life.

Second, Jacqueline uses very strong language in describing Blaise's rejection of the ways and persons of the world. Her report of his "great contempt" and "almost unbearable disgust" must be taken very seriously, even if her observations were limited by the convent walls and what Blaise would tell her within them. If his "contempt" and "disgust" really did extend to "all worldly persons," its objects must have included, however temporarily, the great man who had recently become his great friend, Artus de Roannez. Indeed, the Duke must have been not just one of the persons so rejected, but the principal one.[3]

Third, Jacqueline was determined to persuade Blaise to submit to Singlin and to persuade Singlin to direct Blaise. She had to overcome resistance from both sides, as she was to explain in her second letter. However great her own role as the beloved advocate of Port-Royalist spirituality, she redirects our attention to the elusive, unromantic, but once authoritative figure of her humble priest.

Fourth, Jacqueline reports that Blaise had been and still was quite unwell, suggesting comparison with the illness(es) of 1647. She clearly believed that ill health had not justified his relapse into worldliness in the years that had followed and that it raised no obstacle to his renewed spiritual progress in 1654. It would be reckless to reduce these poorly documented illnesses to the psyche alone, as reckless to reject such considerations out of hand. Her testimony on Blaise's violent revulsion from the world and uncharacteristic submissiveness during the autumn, when combined with her later remark on the upswing of his moods in the winter, suggests that his ill health at the time of spiritual crisis was at least in part psychological.[4]

Jacqueline began her second letter to Gilberte on the Feast of the Conversion of Saint Paul, 25 January 1655:

> I owe you an account of the whole story from the very beginning, which was a few days before I sent you the first word of it [8 December], that is, sometime toward the end of September [sic]. He came to see me and opened himself to me in the most pitiable manner.[5]
>
> On the one hand, despite all of his great activity and all of the things that should have made him love the world, he wasn't as attached to it as we might have thought. He confessed to me that he felt more detached from all this than ever before, beyond any comparison. He wanted to quit the whole works. He felt a great revulsion from the follies and amusements of the world, and his conscience troubled him continually.
>
> But on the other hand, he felt that God had completely abandoned him, so that religion didn't attract him either. Nevertheless, he was doing all that he could, although he feared that it was his own reason and spirit that drove him on and not, insofar as he could tell, any movement from God. He said that in his present detachment from everything, he could have been capable of anything, if he had been favored by God with the same feelings as those that he had formerly known. He supposed that he must then have been horribly attached to have so resisted the graces and movements of God.
>
> His confession surprised and pleased me greatly, and from that time forward I conceived hopes beyond any that I had ever known. I thought I had to tell you, so that you would pray for him. It would take a book to tell the story of every visit, because they were so frequent and so long that I seemed to have no other work to do. My only task was to follow his lead, without directing him. Little by little, I saw him make such progress that I hardly recognized him. If God continues his work, I think that you won't either, especially with respect to his humility, submissiveness, mistrust and contempt for himself, and the desire to be obliterated from others' esteem and memory. That's the present state of affairs.[6]

Jacqueline's letter goes on at some length about disagreements over the choice of a director. Blaise accepted his need but questioned her choice. He reminded her of the claims of his parish priest as his "natural pastor."[7] This difference of opinion related directly to a controversy of much more general significance. Generally, the Parisian curés were Jansenist in their sympathies and very hostile to Jesuit confessors who attracted parishioners to confessionals outside the parishes. The Jansenist side of the case, defending the integrity of the parish, had just been argued by Nicolas Mazure in his *Obligation des fidèles de se confesser à leur curé* (1653).[8] Blaise could claim to be on the side of the angels.

With a pride worthy of a Pascal, Jacqueline answered that her priest was the best priest, and that, just as for medical treatment Blaise would seek out the best doctor, so for spiritual direction he should seek out the very best "doctor of the soul."[9] With an agility worthy of a casuist, she also argued that, "lacking an establishment," Blaise was perfectly free to move from parish to parish and so from priest to priest. Given that freedom of movement, reflected in his relocation from the Right to the Left Bank at the beginning of October 1654, it seemed only reasonable that he could freely change priests again. Finally, he agreed.[10] She had won.

The task of convincing Singlin, in turn, tested even Jacqueline's powers of persuasion. For one thing, the priest was unwell, and he spent much of November at Port-Royal des Champs.[11] For another, he was characteristically troubled by a sharp sense of his social and intellectual inferiority.[12] For still another, he was an experienced director, and the combination of the eagerness shown by the newly professed nun and the reluctance shown by her worldling brother, a sometime convert but also a sometime obstacle to his sister's vocation, ought to have given him pause. In any case, on an unspecified date, Singlin wrote a "perfectly beautiful letter" in which he authorized Jacqueline to act in his stead as Blaise's director.[13]

The priest was back in Paris by the beginning of December, but he did not accept the new convert even then. On 8 December, Jacqueline confessed that she had not yet prevailed, while expressing hopes that "in the end he won't refuse us."[14] On 25 January, she reported that, "despite Singlin's great reluctance to commit himself in such affairs," she had finally won him over by a combination of "reasons" and "importunities." However, no sooner had he assumed responsibility for the delicate case, than, for whatever reasons, surely including his own ill health, he deferred to Le Maistre de Sacy, who was to be Pascal's director at Port-Royal des Champs.[15]

Jacqueline played a leading role in this drama of the Two Loves, even if she believed that the only actors in the piece were God, the Port-Royalist priest(s), and the penitent who had "rejected the world." This left for the sometime actress herself hardly so much as a supporting role. In historical retrospect, things look very different. God commanded her attention, but Blaise commands ours and Jacqueline commanded much of his. Again and again, he had come to her: "It would take a book to tell the story of every visit, because they were so frequent and so long."

In "many visits and many combats," he had resisted her urging that he submit himself to her revered priest. Why? If he had really wanted to participate in the spiritual life of his own new parish of Saint-Cosme and to submit to its Jansenist priest Nicolas de Bry as his "natural pastor," he could quite simply have done so. If he had preferred to live among the like-minded Solitaries of Port-Royal des Champs under the "incomparable" Le Maistre de Sacy, a social and intellectual equal who quickly won his delighted approval in the happy month of January, presumably he could have done that, too. Apparently, he did not really want either of these good alternatives. He wanted Jacqueline's love, even if, to restore himself to her good graces in her new life, he had to emphasize his most perfect detachment.

Paradoxically, Blaise could hope to maintain his attachment to Jacqueline only by denying it—no doubt to himself as well as to her. Jacqueline herself, her religious superiors, and her revered director would instantly have rejected the appeals of a worldly brother who merely wanted to spend so much time with his natural sister. So he returned to her on her own terms, taking comfort from her presence and her concern for his spiritual welfare. For a season, the fall of 1654, her superiors tolerated his frequent visits to her at Port-Royal, in part because of what must have been their great confidence in the strength of her vocation, in part because of their Christian charity for a suffering sinner, and in part because Singlin would not quite say "yes" and would not quite say "no."

Jacqueline's accounts of Blaise's parlor visits betray some impatience at his demands on her attention along with great joy at his spiritual progress. She was eager to cast off her role as his director and to entrust her brother to her priest. While she waited for the "apprehensive" Blaise and then the "apprehensive" Singlin to agree with her matchmaking, she must have urged the former to listen to the latter's preaching from the pulpit, an easier relationship for both men.

Singlin's Spirituality and Arnauld's Theology

Antoine Singlin's *Instructions chrétiennes,* his teachings in the whole set of sermons for the liturgical cycle, not particular bits from particular days, provide the best evidence on what Pascal would have learned indirectly from his sister and directly from the public voice of Port-Royalist spirituality. Gilberte's *Vie de Monsieur Pascal* is not helpful on the point, but her *Vie de Jacqueline Pascal* shows that her brother and sister had first approached Port-Royal specifically in order to hear Singlin's sermons. She says that his preaching was directly responsible for Jacqueline's vocation and that the prospect of his guidance drew her to Port-Royal:

> [My sister and brother] often went to hear M. Singlin. She knew that it was he who conducted the nuns of Port-Royal, and she learned that he spoke of the Christian life in a way that agreed perfectly with her own ideas. . . . She concluded that a decision to lead a religious life there would be, as she put it, reasonable. She shared this thinking with my brother, who, far from attempting to dissuade her, supported her in it, because that was his opinion, too.[16]

Even at the time of her profession, when relations between Jacqueline and Blaise were at their most strained, she realized her worldly brother's respect and affection for her priest:

> M. Singlin [is] the father both of this house and of my family, some of whom are entirely under his direction, while the others share a boundless respect for him and have an extreme affection for him.[17]

The theology of the Two Loves pervades Singlin's sermons. The Christian must love God with all his heart, all his soul, and all his mind. For Singlin, this First Great Commandment seems to engulf the Second, the love of neighbor. He warns against a divided heart; it is only for the love of God, not for themselves, that we must love family, friends, and everyone else, too. All our love is owed to the Creator, none, to creatures.[18]

Singlin offered "rules" for a Christian's love of fellow men and women. His first such rule best explains what was wrong with Blaise's natural attachments to family members:

> The first thing that we ought to observe in our examination of our love for our fellow man, in order to see whether we have received a few sparks of that divine love . . . , is to see if our charity is equal and universal, that is, if it leads us to love all our brothers alike. For if we love only a few persons [in particular] for their eminent qualities or agreeable dispositions, we demonstrate that our affection has nothing divine about it.[19]

That is, if it is to be legitimate, human love cannot be personal, particular, preferential. Thus, it cannot be an attachment, properly speaking, because attachments are specific. For the Augustinian, such creaturely love is sinful.

Singlin suggested other tests of human love in other sermons. Loss is one such test. If we are overwhelmed with sadness at a loss, that is a sure sign of sinfully misplaced love.[20] What holds true for material objects also holds true for personal objects:

> To discern the movements of our hearts properly, and to see whether in fact we use these things with attachment or detachment, we have only to examine ourselves following Saint Augustine's maxim. He instructs us that, to judge our love of a thing, we have only to consider whether or not we feel eagerness in desiring it, joy in possessing it, and pain in losing it.[21]

Augustine's psychology still pertains. Attachments are specific, enduring, and highly emotional.

Singlin's loss test and his alternative separation test clearly apply to personal relationships.[22] On an All Souls' Day, he emphasized the grief of loss as a lesson against attachment:

> Let us consider ourselves happy for understanding at least our misery and for knowing that the unhappy pleasures we take in creatures ought to be the occasion for our sighs and laments in this life, as in the next they will be the proper object of God's wrath, whether eternally, if we have so completely abandoned ourselves as to have preferred them to God, or for a time only, if our lapse has been less grave.[23]

The love of creatures is doomed. All things in this world pass away, so that the momentary pleasure of loving turns to lasting misery, and the apparent security of love becomes the desolation of loss. Yet false promises of pleasure and security lure us from the love of God. That is the human condition without God's grace and our conversion to the true love of Him alone.[24]

Singlin's sermons are a valuable source in part because of his particular influence over the Pascals, but also in part because he spoke for the entire community. Both Antoine Arnauld and Le Maistre de Sacy contributed regularly to these sermons, and, unsurprisingly, their spirituality is his.[25] Here, we need consider only Arnauld, whose massive learning, unshakable doctrine, and voluminous writing command something like awe.

The greatest of the Great Arnauld's works was the *Fréquente Communion* (1643). The Augustinian theologian refers readers back to the *City of God,* book 14, chapter 28, for a succinct statement of the Two Loves, the love of God that is the source of every good and the love of self that is the source of every bad:

> Two loves have founded two cities: the love of God is the foundation of Jerusalem; the love of self is the foundation of Babylon. The two cities are intermingled here below, but you can tell your citizenship by examining your heart and seeing what you love.[26]

There can be no compromise, no sharing. Attachment to God entails detachment from wordly objects, not just wealth, status, and power, but also all persons, especially those closest to us: "We must be truly disposed to abandon father, mother, brothers, sisters, friends. . . ." Of course, this is humanly impossible. Without grace, we are powerless; we cannot turn toward God, any more than He can turn away from the world.[27]

These fundamental principles have important consequences for the Port-Royalist theory of conversion:

> It isn't so easy to bring a soul back to God and to snatch it away from sin and the Devil. You might like to think that . . . in a moment desires formerly limited to creatures could become a wholehearted determination to serve Jesus Christ alone. You can think that, if you want. As for me, I think that it would be safer to follow the counsel of Saint Augustine and the other Fathers.[28]

Only God can know the secrets of hearts, discriminating true from false conversions; the theologian knows only the principle that an access of devotion expressed in the words of a moment means little and that penitential acts over time signify more.

Arnauld draws heavily from Saint François de Sales' *Traité de l'amour de Dieu* in his *Tradition de l'Église sur le sujet de la Pénitence* (1644), interpreting this higher love not only as God's *commandment,* obligating all men totally, but also as man's *delectation,* a human choice made for spiritual delight:

This is what God asks of us: that among our loves, the love of Him be the warmest, dominating everything else in our heart; that it be the dearest, occupying our entire soul; that it be the most pervasive, involving all our powers; that it be the most exalted, filling our entire mind; and that it be the most forceful, exercising all our strength and vigor.[29]

Ideally, the love of God is exclusive, permitting no other object. Practically, the attraction of lesser objects is such that perfect disengagement from them can be accomplished, if at all, only after long time and with divine assistance:

The true Christian may well still feel some affection for creatures, it being impossible to disengage oneself without the passage of a long time and the exercise of great perseverance in the good life and the practice of virtue. Nevertheless, he loves God with all his heart and all his thought, as all of the faithful are obligated to do by the Scriptures, and he wills to be attached only to God. He renounces all worldly attachments sincerely, combats them seriously, and does what he can to deliver himself from them.[30]

Every desire, every prayer, and every effort of the penitent must tend to detach him from all creatures so that he may unite himself the more perfectly with God.

Arnauld's *Seconde Apologie de Jansénius* (1645) provides a more systematic restatement of the same principles. "All Christian morality" is summarized in a passage on the two loves from Augustine's *On the Trinity*. Only the true love for God can be called charity, and only this love can legitimate any lesser love for any person. The false love for a human object, as such, is properly cupidity; its preference for a creature over the Creator is not only sinful but also foolish, given the transience of everything natural.[31]

Arnauld reduces this Patristic wisdom to a single maxim, "that no action is good unless it is motivated by the love of God," and then, with a logician's rigor, he deduces this maxim from three principles:

The First, that all voluntary action proceeds from love of some sort.

The Second, that all love is necessarily either the love of God or the love of the Creature.

The Third, that all that proceeds from the love of the creature is vicious and consequently (as we have undertaken to prove) that all voluntary action is sinful unless it proceeds from some love of God.[32]

This is the whole of Christian morality, the only true morality. The implications for a Pascal are unforgiving. Mathematical and scientific curiosity is sinful, even if motivated by an apparently innocent desire of knowledge "for its own sake."[33] And his attachment to other persons, his father and sisters first among them, is also sinful, even if it seems to be love given others "for their own sakes."[34]

A Perfect Nun and the Religious Community

Blaise Pascal had not yet collaborated with Antoine Arnauld in 1654, and Jacqueline could have had little or nothing to do with him. She was, however, quite close to Arnauld's two older sisters, the matriarchs of Port-Royal, especially to Mère Agnès.[35] Indeed, Jacqueline is said to have collaborated with her on the *Image d'une religieuse parfaite et d'une imparfaite,* which begins by opposing two ideal types, perfect and imperfect, with respect to their love for God.[36] The Perfect Nun knows that she belongs to Jesus Christ, and she prefers her God to all other objects. The corresponding trait of the Imperfect Nun is that her heart is divided by her love for creatures, too. She wants something else in addition to God, and she fears the loss of something other than God.[37]

Mère Agnès reiterates the lesson in her *Manuel des âmes religieuses:*

> Be like Melchisedec, who had neither father nor mother [Heb. 7:3]. Raise yourself above nature, and admit no attachment to your parents. Live as if there were no one but God and you on earth. Forget your father and your mother, and remember only your Spouse.[38]

For the love of God, the nun must renounce all love of man, even all memory of such love:

> As your Spouse gives Himself wholly to you, so give yourself wholly to Him. Like everything else, your memory belongs to Him. Never remember the world or the life that you led in it, unless it is to give thanks for the grace that has removed you from it. The world is so contagious that even the memory of it is dangerous.[39]

Mère Angélique Arnauld herself, the dominant figure within the community, offered conferences "On the detachment from creatures, even the most saintly, that we ought to maintain":

> Attachment to creatures is our greatest obstacle. . . . We must attach ourselves to God alone. Creatures come and go, but God is immutable and

remains forever. . . . When we distance ourselves from creatures, we approach God. . . . In God is every good thing, and apart from God there is nothing good. . . . This requires us to attach ourselves to Him alone, because He is the inestimable good that cannot be taken from us.[40]

The Pascals affiliated themselves with an extended spiritual community in which attachments, as such, were systematically devalued. Blaise's own Augustinianism would have discouraged any overt display of attachment behavior, quite apart from any defensive denial. This was also the case for Jacqueline, whose entry into religion at Port-Royal meant a decisive withdrawal from familial life. Finally, Gilberte as the memoirist of their edifying lives had been schooled in the same thinking, especially just after her brother's death and just before her composition of the *Vie de Monsieur Pascal*. It is no wonder that she who was so close could not see the evidence of his attachments.

Belief that human attachments are spiritually dangerous cannot be mistaken as evidence that they are psychologically weak. Quite the contrary. Consider the prepotency of familial bonds even within the innermost circle of Port-Royal. This was very much the family convent of the Arnaulds.[41] Angélique may have closed the door to her father in a celebrated scene of reformist rigor, *but* she was to open that door to her mother, who entered the convent after her husband's death, *and* to her five sisters (including Agnès), *and* to her five nieces, *and* she was also to witness the remarkable phenomenon of the "Solitaries" who clustered around the convent, among them two brothers (including Antoine) *and* four nephews (including Le Maistre de Sacy).[42] Thus, the very authorities who taught the Pascals to shun human attachments came from the same extended family and rejoined one another in the same religious community.

CHAPTER 8

The *Mémorial* I: Remembering and "Forgetting"

The direct route to the heart of the matter for Blaise Pascal in 1654 went from the Parlor at Port-Royal, where he reconciled himself with Jacqueline, through the Church of Port-Royal, where he received the Instructions of Singlin, to his chambers on the rue des Francs-Bourgeois Saint-Michel, where he experienced a mysterious ecstasy on the night of 23 November. Pascal's own record of this experience in the *Mémorial* is the centerpiece, not Jacqueline's letters, Singlin's sermons, or any other expression of Port-Royalist spirituality or theology. This document offers an almost unbearably intense view of a spiritual world apparently inhabited only by the penitent himself and his God. Indeed, he promises to "forget the world and everything else but God."

Despite the appearances and the promises, I argue that this central document on this central experience directs us to *the* evidence on the fundamental place of his parental attachments and losses in his spiritual life. Because my argument is novel in its method and radical in its conclusions, I proceed very deliberately. In this chapter, having described the dramatic discovery and presented the spectacular text, my first task is to acknowledge formally Pascal's conscious preoccupation with the properly spiritual relationship, his guilty confession of past separation from *God,* his joyous sense of present communion with *God,* and his anxious prayer that there may be no future separation from *God.* The second task is to examine systematically his scriptural citations. It has never been noticed that his fragmentary texts take us back to biblical contexts in which two themes are consistently, closely, and strongly combined. These themes are *parent* and *attachment.* The third task is to demonstrate statistically that this combination of biblical associations cannot plausibly be explained as accidental. If not chance, then design. What that means is another matter for another chapter.

At least some of the obscurity of the *Mémorial* stems from the fact that neither the experience nor the written record is so much as mentioned in other testimony from Pascal himself or his sisters. Jacqueline's silence in the two letters that report Blaise's conversion has led scholars to infer that she did not know about the Night of Fire or the *Mémorial.* Gilberte herself, who treasured the document, makes no mention of it in her *Vie de Monsieur Pascal,* apparently maintaining a spiritually correct silence about the remarkable evidence of extraordinary favors. The Périer children did later inform the priest who left this account of the discovery:

> A few days after M. Pascal's death, a servant happened to notice that one part of the lining of the dead man's doublet appeared thicker than the rest. Having pulled apart the seam ["over his chest" from the external perspective of the survivors,[1] which must have meant "over his heart" for the living Pascal]. . . , he found a little parchment, written in M. Pascal's hand and folded [by him]. Within this parchment there was a paper written in the same hand; the one [Parchment] was a faithful copy of the other [Paper]. Immediately, the two documents were brought to Mme. Périer, who showed them to several friends. All agreed that this parchment, written with such care and in such a remarkable script, was doubtlessly a sort of *Mémorial* that he had guarded very carefully in order to preserve the memory of something ever-present before his eyes and his mind.[2]

In his *Mémorial,* the convert had preserved "the memory of *something* that he wanted to keep ever-present," over his heart if not "before his eyes." But what was that something? The Périers themselves could hardly have interpreted the *Mémorial* as anything less than documentary evidence of a supernatural incursion into the natural world by the God of Abraham. The existence of Pascal's elegant parchment copy and the careful preservation of his paper original, sewn together over his heart, surely suggests that he, too, cherished such a belief. It remains powerfully attractive to other believers, and I approach this unique document with great respect. A translation of the text from Pascal's Paper follows, although neither print nor language itself can fully represent Pascal's experience. I add facsimiles both of the Paper and of the more legible Parchment.

+

i The year of Grace 1654
ii Monday 23 November day of St. Clement pope and martyr and
iii of others in the martyrology.
iv Eve of St. Chrysogonus martyr and of others.
v From about ten-thirty at night until about twelve-thirty.

1 fire
2 God of Abraham, god of Isaac, god of Jacob.
3 not of the philosophers and the learned.
4 Certainty, Certainty sentiment joy peace.
5 God of Jesus Christ.
6 My God and your god.
7 Your god will be my god.
8 Forgetfulness of the world and of all except god.
9 He is found only in the ways taught in the Gospel
10 Grandeur of the human soul
11 Just Father, the world has not known you but I have
12 known you.
13 Joy Joy Joy tears of Joy
14 I have separated myself from him. ———
15 They have forsaken me the fount of living waters.
16 My god will you leave me ———
17 Let me not be separated from him eternally.

———

18 This is the eternal life that they know you the only true
19 God and the one whom you have sent J.C.
20 Jesus Christ. ———

21 Jesus Christ. ———
22 I have separated myself. I have fled, renounced, crucified him

23 Let me never be separated from him.
24 He is kept only by the ways taught in the Gospel.
25 Renunciation total and sweet.
26 Etc.

Several parts of the text are discriminable. I shall call them the Heading (lines i–v), the Core (lines 1–20), and the First Postscript (lines 21–25). That leaves only the final "et cetera" (line 26), which must refer to the Second Postscript later added to the text on the Parchment (facsimile, 109; translation, 225).[3]

Manifest Separation and the Love of God

The *Mémorial* uses the language of attachment for the love of God. The Paper ends with lines that express Pascal's hope to "keep" the God (lines 24–25) whom he has now "found" and "known" (lines 8, 11–12, 18–20). On the Parchment, he appended lines that are best read as a promise of lifelong and "total submission to Jesus Christ and to my director" linked with hopes for an afterlife of "eternal joy" (lines 26–27). This makes perfect sense in light of the discussions on spiritual direction and the soaring mood reported in Jacqueline's letter of 25 January.

The antithetical theme of separation from God pervades lines 14–17 and 22–23 and dominates the last half of the text:

14 I have separated myself from Him.
15 They have forsaken me the fount of living waters
16 My God will you leave me
17 Let me not be separated from Him eternally.
. . .
I have fled, renounced, crucified Him
22 I have separated myself from Him./
23 Let me never be separated from Him.

In these few, short lines, Pascal used the verb *séparer* four times and the verbs *derelinquere* and *quitter* once each. In a terrible afterthought, he added a painful thesaurus in which *séparer* becomes *fuir, renoncer,* and, in a closely related usage, *crucifier*. Such repetition with variation is only the most obvious sign of preoccupation with separation. After all four instances of *séparer* and after the one instance of *quitter,*

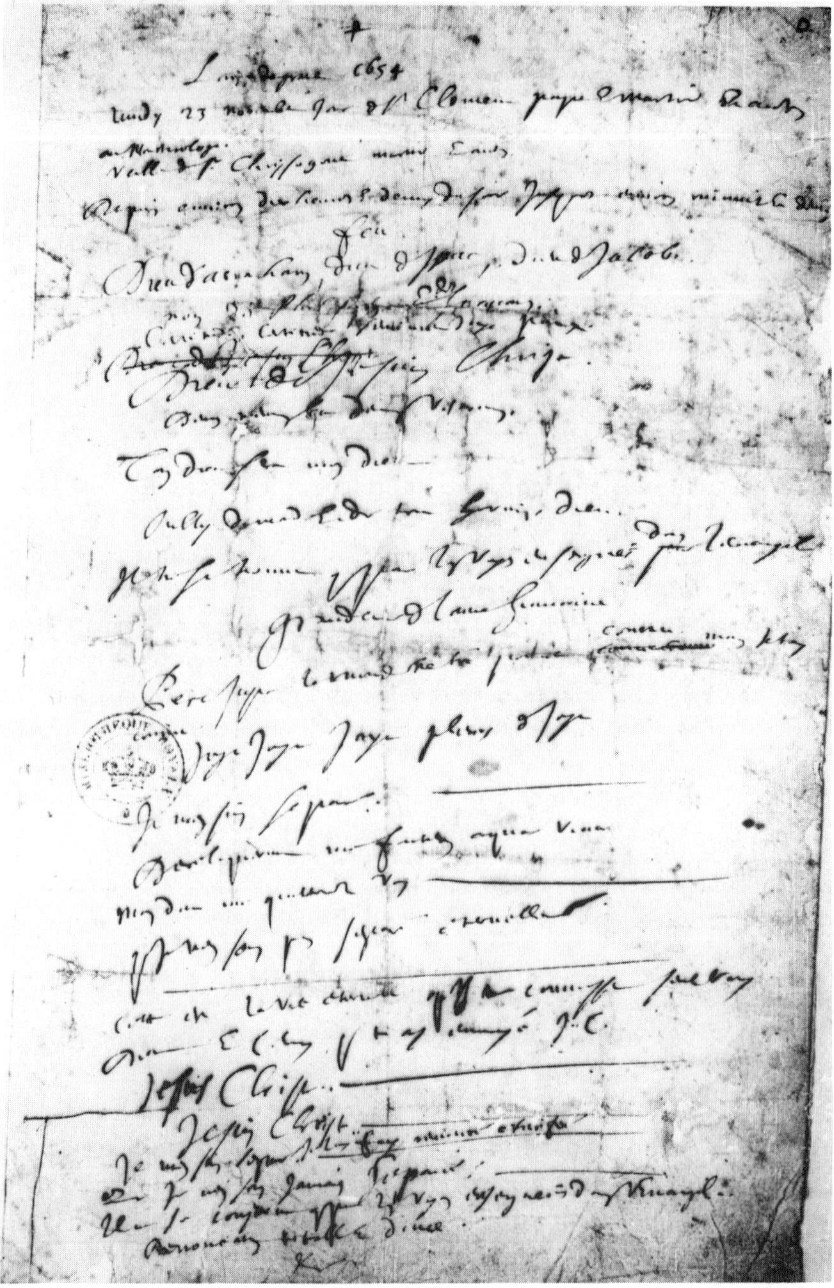

The *Mémorial*, Paper Original. Photograph © Bibliothèque Nationale de France, Paris.

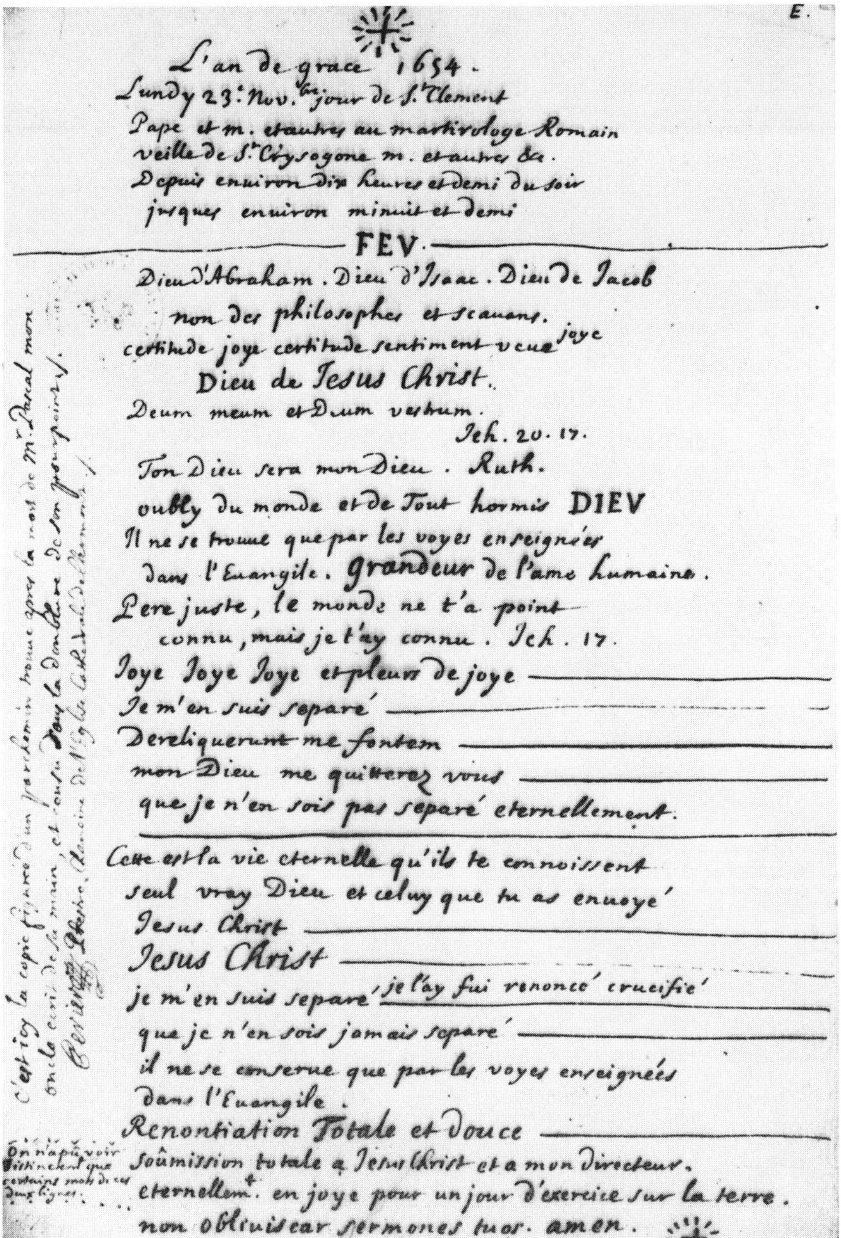

The *Mémorial*, Parchment Copy. Photograph © Bibliothèque Nationale de France, Paris.

of separation toward the right margin. Such strokes to the right are quite exceptional in his manuscripts.[4] I "read" them as both emphases and, for reasons to be explained, ellipses.

In the Core and again in the First Postscript, where lines 22 and 23 repeat lines 14 and 17, Pascal moves from a confession of his own responsibility for past separation from God ("I have separated myself . . .") to a prayer that God may not withdraw from him ("Let me not be separated . . ."). This pattern fits what we know of his spiritual life from his sisters' narratives. Prior to the Second Conversion, he had fallen away from his earlier fervor, so separating himself from his God (lines 14 and 22); in the fall of 1654, he had sought to resume a properly spiritual life, and God's renewed graces made that possible. Especially after the experience of 23 November, his spirit was one of contrition for past sins (most acute in the afterthoughts at line 22) and a penitent's hope for continued grace (lines 17 and 23). This makes good Augustinian sense.

However, these lines might also make another sort of sense, one in which the author is less a guilty subject than a forlorn object. Line 15 repeats the basic theme from line 14, but it also reverses roles: "I left him" becomes "they left me." Pascal's own first person remains in the predicate for lines 16 and 17, where he pleads, in so many words: "Don't leave me; don't leave me." For this person in this situation, this anxiety was complex and deeply rooted. Having acknowledged, even emphasized its manifest spiritual meaning, I turn to explore evidence of a latent human meaning.

Latent Attachment and the Love of Deceased Parents

Blaise Pascal had been left alone: his parents had died, and his sisters had withdrawn, one into marriage and the other into the convent. Although this was not a new fact in November 1654, it was still the most important fact of his social life. This chapter develops an argument that the *Mémorial* documents Blaise's stubborn attachment to his deceased parents, especially his father. The argument is painstakingly detailed, but its overall structure is quite simple. It consists of a preliminary identification of the scriptural texts cited in the Core of the *Mémorial,* then a systematic reexamination of the several scriptural contexts in search of a historically meaningful pattern of associated themes.

At least eight of the twenty lines that make up the Core are biblical. Probably, the count should be twelve. These lines represent eight fragmentary citations from ten or more biblical passages, some of the citations recalling more than one passage. Pascal worked from memory, not from an open book. Others have long known or suspected most of this, but I have discovered a further, most peculiar fact. *All* the biblical passages that Pascal recalled must have been selected on the basis of a definite combination of thematic associations, although *no* citation in the *Mémorial* records the combined themes. The Bible and the *Mémorial* together provide empirical evidence that he must have "forgotten" exactly what he had "remembered."

Pascal identified four lines of his *Mémorial* as biblical by the marginal references that he added to his Parchment following lines 6, 7, and 11–12. In addition, another four lines are certainly biblical, lines 2, 15, and 18–19. Finally, still another four lines have remained problematical, including lines 1, 5, 16, and 20.[5] In table 2, question marks indicate problematical citations. Asterisks signal texts for which there are alternative biblical references.[6] Subsequent discussion progresses across the columns from left to right, building an argument for citation from memory.

Line 1, like line 20, is so brief and so elemental that certainty is impossible; lines 5 and 16 also remain uncertain. Nevertheless, avail-

TABLE 2
Biblical Citations in the *Mémorial* Core

Mémorial	*Bible*	*Version*	*Variants*
line 1	? Ex. 3:2	Louvain	
2	Ex. 3:6*	Louvain	omission
	Matt. 22:32*	Louvain	omission
5	? Eph. 1:17	Louvain	omission
6	John 20:17	Vulgate	
7	Ruth 1:16	Louvain	addition; tense
11–12	John 17:25	Louvain	modernization
15	Jer. 2:13	Vulgate	word order
16	? Matt. 27:46	original	adaptation
	? Ps. 26:9*	original	adaptation
18–19	John 17:3	Louvain	modernization; abbrev.
20	? John 17:3	Louvain	repetition

able evidence suggests that lines 1–2, 5, 6, 7, 11–12, 15, 16, and 18–20 are all biblical. These scriptural texts were remembered, not read or researched. There is good external evidence that Pascal's memory was legendary and that he took particular pride in his knowledge of the Bible, which he was eventually to know virtually by heart.[7] His letter on his father's death already shows a remarkable biblicism well before the Second Conversion. The argument for dependence on memory, not an open book, can rest securely on internal evidence from the *Mémorial* of scattered, fragmentary, and imprecise citations from two different versions of the Bible.

The scattering itself is almost enough to decide the question of citation from memory. Imaginative painters of the scene represent him with John 17 in the Louvain translation open on his desk at 10:30 P.M.[8] There are indeed three citations from this Gospel (lines 6, 11–12, and 18–20). However, the three happen to come in reverse order (first, John 20:17; second, 17:25; third, 17:3). Furthermore, other known citations from other parts of the Bible are interspersed (Ruth 1:16 at line 7; Jer. 2:13 at line 15). The first citation from John comes only at line 6, only after the certain citation from Exodus 3:6 and/or the Synoptic Gospels in line 2 and the probable citation from Ephesians 1:17 in line 5. Finally, that first citation from John is from the Vulgate Latin, not the Louvain French.

Fragmentariness also provides evidence of work from memory, not an open book. Pascal's range is very impressive, as he draws in no apparent order on the Pentateuch; the historical, poetical, and prophetic books of the Old Testament; and the Synoptic Gospels, John, and the Pauline Epistles from the New Testament, all within twenty short lines. However, he quotes an entire verse only once; he often quotes only a few words; those few words often seem a bit beside the point; and only memory can have built the bridges from one fragment to another.

Imprecision also suggests memory work, not reading. Even in the two relatively long passages from John 17 (lines 11–12 and 18–20), Pascal's text departs from that of the printed page, modernizing its archaic language. Elsewhere, there are omissions (lines 1–2, 5), addition (line 7), inversion (line 15), and adaptation (line 16). Only line 6 reproduces words exactly, but, in context, even it gives us evidence of reliance on memory:

Line 6 *My God and your God* [Vulgate].

John 20:17 Jesus said unto her, Touch me not; for I am not yet ascended to my Father: but go to my brethren, and say unto them, I ascend unto my Father, and your Father, and to my God, and your God.

Line 7 *Your God will be my God* [Louvain].

Ruth 1:16 And Ruth said, Intreat me not to leave thee, or to return from following after thee: for whither thou goest, I will go; and where thou lodgest, I will lodge: thy people shall be my people, and thy God my God.

Every believer—including Pascal himself in the *Abrégé de la vie de Jésus Christ*—knows the first of these two passages by Jesus' first words: "Touch me not." Its crucial importance lies in the revelation, "I ascend unto my Father." But the Pascal of the *Mémorial* somehow chose something else, the last five words of the verse. Having written them, he was reminded of similar words from Ruth. Associatively, he progressed from verse fragment to verse fragment, book to book, Testament to Testament, version to version. Such agility, which would have been almost inconceivable for a reader, was easy for this rememberer. His memory was powerful but not perfect, and, with books spread out, any lesser reader can see the imprecision of his citation and the incompleteness of his reference: "Ruth."

As quoted, Pascal's eight biblical passages are so elliptical as to encourage merely speculative interpretation, while frustrating any critical check on historical imagination. Pascal's own words in nonbiblical lines are obviously important, but they, too, are suggestive rather than narrative or demonstrative, and, unlike the scriptural excerpts, they refer to no fuller text. It is Pascal's book that provides materials for the reconstruction of Pascal's meaning; used in conjunction with the *Mémorial,* it can grant privileged access to his memory and mental processes.

Henri Gouhier has begun the serious study of scriptural contexts as evidence for the meaning of the *Mémorial*. He infers that Pascal remembered whole "scenes" from the Bible, even if he quoted only fragmentary verses as "a sort of abridgment." He also infers that Pascal selected these "scenes" as "situations in the image of his own" and quoted those passages that concerned "most significant events." These two inferences are very suggestive.[9]

Acknowledging that Pascal *may have envisioned pictures* of Moses at the Burning Bush, Mary Magdalene at the Resurrection, and Ruth clinging to Naomi, I prefer to emphasize that in these three cases and all others he *certainly recalled words*. The simplest definition of verbal context is the whole verse along with the proximate verses, before and after. This definition is arbitrary but conservative, and it permits a systematic and objective inquiry, leading methodically to the conclusion that Pascal had in mind more of the Bible than he recorded on the Paper and empirically to the identification of what it was that he so paradoxically remembered and forgot.

Gouhier was right to infer that Pascal remembered more from the Bible than he actually quoted in the *Mémorial* and that his memory selected the passages according to his personal "situation" and significant "events," not "ideas and reasonings." The evidence for the truth of both inferences has lain hidden, even from the great historian of philosophy, in the biblical contexts as defined above, where personally relevant verbal associations remain to be discovered. Two themes regularly emerge from these contexts: *parent* is always there, defined as father or mother, either named as such or addressed directly; *attachment* is also always there, negatively defined as the denial of separation or loss, of abandonment or death.

My hypothesis is this: Pascal selected the biblical texts that appear so fragmentarily in the *Mémorial* on the basis of combined associations that can be recovered from the corresponding scriptural contexts. "Parent" and "attachment" are my terms for these associations. In what follows, this hypothesis is formulated on the basis of the first three certain citations (lines 2, 6, and 7), tested by reexamining the last three certain citations (lines 11–12, 15, and 18–19), and then applied to the suspected citations (lines 5 and 16).

Line 2 of the *Mémorial* refers in the same words to eight biblical passages, which naturally fall into two families, on the one hand, Exodus 3:6, 3:15, 3:16, and 4:5, and Acts 7:32, and on the other hand, Matthew 22:32, Mark 12:26, and Luke 20:37. All texts in each family are so nearly identical that the first can represent the rest. The referents for line 6 and for line 7 are happily simpler. In each case, here and below, the words actually written are italicized and the themes hypothetically associated are marked by capitals.

Mémorial line 2 and contextual associations:

(a) Exod. 3:5 And [God] said, Draw not nigh hither; put off thy shoes from thy feet, for the place whereon thou standest is holy ground.

3:6 Moreover, he said, I am the God of thy FATHER, the *God of Abraham,* the *God of Isaac,* and the *God of Jacob.* And Moses hid his face, for he was afraid to look upon God.
3:8 And the Lord said, I have surely seen the affliction of my people which are in Egypt, and have heard their cry by reason of their taskmasters, for I know their sorrows.

(b) Matt. 22:31 But as touching the RESURRECTION OF THE DEAD, have ye not read that which was spoken unto you by God, saying:
22:32 I am the *God of Abraham,* the *God of Isaac,* and the *God of Jacob?* GOD IS NOT THE GOD OF THE DEAD BUT OF THE LIVING.
22:33 And when the multitude heard this, they were astonished at his doctrine.

Mémorial line 6 and contextual associations:

John 20:16 Jesus saith unto her, Mary. She turned herself and saith unto him, Rabboni, which is to say, Master.
20:17 Jesus saith unto her, Touch me not, for I AM NOT YET ASCENDED TO MY FATHER: but go to my brethren, and say unto them, I ASCEND UNTO MY FATHER AND YOUR FATHER, and to *my God and your God.*
20:18 Mary Magdalene came and told the disciples that she had seen the Lord, and that he had spoken these things unto her.

Mémorial line 7 and contextual associations:

Ruth 1:15 And she [Naomi] said, Behold, thy sister-in-law is gone home unto her people, and unto her gods; return thou after thy sister-in-law.
1:16 And Ruth said, INTREAT ME NOT TO LEAVE THEE, OR TO RETURN FROM FOLLOWING AFTER THEE, FOR WHITHER THOU GOEST, I WILL GO, AND WHERE THOU LODGEST, I WILL LODGE; THY PEOPLE SHALL BE MY PEOPLE, and *thy God my God.*
1:17 WHERE THOU DIEST, WILL I DIE, AND THERE WILL I BE BURIED: the Lord do so to me, and more also, if OUGHT BUT DEATH PART THEE AND ME.

All three of these texts in the *Mémorial* (lines 2, 6, and 7) concern God. In addition, all of the contexts (Exod. 3:5–7/Matt. 22:31–33, John 20:16–18, and Ruth 1:15–17) share less obvious but potentially significant concerns with two human themes, "parent" or father/mother and "attachment" or no separation/no loss.

"Father" is the closest and strongest association imaginable for the first certain citation (line 2). It appears in the biblical context that immediately precedes the quoted text in Exodus 3:6 *and* in all of the other references that belong to this family, Exodus 3:15, 3:16, and

4:5 and Acts 7:32. The association is further strengthened by other closely related passages, Genesis 26:24, 28:13, and 32:9 and Exodus 3:13. Thus, both juxtaposition and repetition relate "father" to the "God of Abraham." These memorable passages and the patriarchal identity combine to make "father Abraham" a Christian commonplace.[10]

"Father" also stands out as an association for the second certain citation (line 6), where it is also immediate and reiterated in context (John 20:17). The impact of the Easter event and the parallelism of the language help to join the parent theme memorably with the words so enigmatically quoted: "[I ascend unto MY FATHER AND YOUR FATHER, and] *my God and your God.*"

A widowed mother-in-law serves as the heroine's parent figure in Ruth 1.15–17. My restrictive definition of biblical context happens to trim the explicit mention of this relationship in Ruth 1.14, but there can be no questioning the presence and the power of the attachment in the verse quoted and the two adjacent verses. There is no more affecting expression of such feelings in the Scriptures than Ruth's plea to Naomi, which is so reduced in Pascal's third certain citation (line 7). Thus, the parent theme appears regularly in the unquoted contexts corresponding to the first three quoted texts.

Now attachment. For the first certain citation (line 2), Exodus 3:6 has always been the preferred reference. There is no element of "attachment" as I have defined it in the Old Testament context as I have circumscribed it. But Jesus chose to use the passage as His proof text for immortality when He responded so memorably to the Sadducees. He denied death as loss not only in the immediate context of Matthew 22:32 but also in Mark 12:25–27 and Luke 20:36–38, where the attachment theme is overwhelming:

(a) Mark 12:25 For when THEY SHALL RISE FROM THE DEAD, THEY neither marry nor are given in marriage, but ARE AS THE ANGELS WHICH ARE IN HEAVEN.
12:26 And AS TOUCHING THE DEAD, THAT THEY RISE, HAVE YE NOT READ in the book of Moses, how in the bush God spake unto him, saying, I am the *God of Abraham,* and the *God of Isaac,* and the *God of Jacob?*
12:27 HE IS NOT THE GOD OF THE DEAD, BUT THE GOD OF THE LIVING; ye therefore do greatly err.

(b) Luke 20:36 NEITHER CAN THEY DIE ANY MORE, FOR THEY ARE EQUAL UNTO THE ANGELS AND ARE THE CHILDREN

> OF GOD, BEING THE CHILDREN OF THE RESURRECTION.
> 20:37 NOW THAT THE DEAD ARE RAISED, EVEN MOSES SHEWED at the bush, when he calleth the Lord the *God of Abraham,* the *God of Isaac,* and the *God of Jacob.*
> 20:38 FOR HE IS NOT A GOD OF THE DEAD, BUT OF THE LIVING, FOR ALL LIVE UNTO HIM.

Pascal's one line from the *Mémorial* thus recalls death-denied or loss-denied (attachment-affirmed) from the closest contexts in all three Synoptic Gospels as well as "father" from the closest contexts in as many passages from Exodus 3, to go no further.

"Attachment" as the denial of death or loss is also a potent theme in the biblical context (John 20:16–18) for the second certain citation (line 6). Mary Magdalene had wept for her aggravated loss, Jesus' Crucifixion followed by the apparent removal of His body from the Sepulcher: "THEY HAVE TAKEN AWAY MY LORD, and I know not where they have laid Him." Her grief turned to joy, when she found Him whom she had lost. Theologically, John 20:17 announces the Resurrection and the Ascension; having risen from the tomb of death, Christ will ascend to rejoin the Father in heaven. This second citation, like the first, recalls a theophany and helps to explain why the Périers supposed that Blaise had a vision and interpreted it according to the most orthodox theology and the purest spirituality. But the immediate biblical context here, too, provides good evidence for the same two associated themes, "father" and attachment or death-denied.

The third certain citation (line 7) recalls a biblical context (Ruth 1:15–17) that begins with the heroine's final separation from her sister-in-law and the threat of separation from her mother-in-law. Ruth responds in the moving verses that Pascal cites almost unrecognizably: she will not consent to this last separation. She will stay with Naomi, follow after Naomi, go with Naomi, lodge with Naomi, worship with Naomi, and, if necessary, die with Naomi, following her into the grave itself. Here there is no theophany, nor any theology. Here in a chapter suffused with the deaths of father-in-law, husband, and brother-in-law, there is an adamant refusal to accept separation from her mother-in-law. This reaffirms the attachment of the grown child to the parent, in this case a mother figure.

It is the regular combination of the parent theme with the attachment theme in the biblical contexts that is so remarkable, given the absence of the combined themes from the *Mémorial.* In these contexts, it is not a matter of either/or, either one theme or the other, but of both/and, both parent and attachment. Contrarily, in the first three certain citations just reviewed, it is neither/nor, neither explicit mention of the parent theme nor explicit mention of the attachment theme.

Are the combined associations that are found in the first three certain biblical contexts also consistently discoverable in all others? The hypothesis can be tested against the evidence of the contexts corresponding to the citations from John 17 (lines 11–12 and 18–20) and Jeremiah 2 (line 15). On Pascal's Paper, the indentation and the content of line 10 suggest a new heading, "Grandeur of the human soul." In the second half of the Core, the themes of parent and attachment are much closer to the surface.

Line 11 begins with the word "father," the only instance of the term in the text of the *Mémorial.* Pascal's fragmentary citation from John 17:25 does not make explicit the associated theme of attachment, but the biblical context does so. In this chapter, Jesus prays for the inseparable unity of the Father and Son, the assembled Apostles, and the community of the faithful. In the three-verse context, His moving prayer concludes:

John 17:24 FATHER, I WILL THAT THEY ALSO, WHOM THOU HAST GIVEN ME, BE WITH ME WHERE I AM; THAT THEY MAY BEHOLD MY GLORY, WHICH THOU HAST GIVEN ME, FOR THOU LOVEST ME BEFORE THE FOUNDATION OF THE WORLD.
17:25 *O righteous FATHER, the world hath not known thee, but I have known thee,* and these have known that thou hast sent me.
17:26 And I have declared unto them thy name, and will declare it, that THE LOVE WHEREWITH THOU HAST LOVED ME MAY BE IN THEM, AND I IN THEM.

Pascal's other citation from John 17 begins with the one explicit reference in the *Mémorial* to "the eternal life," death-denied, or attachment-affirmed. Here, it is the parent theme that must be recovered from the biblical context. Jesus calls to the "Father" as such in verses 1, 5, 11, 21, 24, and 25, and the immediacy of this association is guaranteed by his own prior citation of verse 25. The second three-verse context emphasizes the attachment theme in words addressed by the Son to the Father:

John 17:2 As THOU [FATHER] HAST GIVEN HIM [SON] POWER OVER ALL FLESH, THAT HE SHOULD GIVE ETERNAL LIFE TO AS MANY AS THOU HAST GIVEN HIM.
17:3 And *this is LIFE ETERNAL, that they might know thee the only true God, and Jesus Christ, whom thou hast sent.*
17:4 I have glorified thee on earth; I have finished the work which thou gavest me to do.

One certain citation from the Core of the *Mémorial* remains, Jeremiah 2:13 at line 15. Here again, as in the two citations from John 17 and in the immediately adjacent lines of the *Mémorial* (14, 16, and 17), a theme that had in earlier instances been recoverable only from hidden contexts emerges into the open text. "Separation" is antithetically related to "attachment," of course, and confessed anxiety with respect to the former is often the best evidence of the latter. But here and here only, the traces of Pascal's memory seem not to lead back to "father" or anything else parental:

Jer. 2:12 Be astonished, O ye heavens, at this ["my people have changed their glory for that which doth not profit"], and be ye horribly afraid, be ye very desolate, saith the Lord.
2:13 For my people have committed two evils; *they have forsaken me THE FOUNTAIN OF LIVING WATERS,* and hewed them out broken cisterns, that can hold no water.
2:14 Is Israel a servant? Is he a homeborn slave? Why is he spoiled?

Where is the parent theme? It is right there in the Patristic annotations of Pascal's Louvain Bible; this is the marginal gloss from Chrysostom: "The FATHER calls himself *THE FOUNTAIN* from which proceeds the Holy Spirit, which is *THE LIVING WATER.*"[11] Thus, even a mechanical application of the contextual method (adjacent verses and marginal glosses) succeeds in recovering the combined associations in all six cases of certain citation within the *Mémorial* Core. This confirms the hypothesis.

The same Pascal who would later write of associational thinking as mechanical also knew that there is more to the human mind and spirit than to any machine, even his own marvelous Arithmetic Machine.[12] In the name of methodical inquiry, regular and objective, my restrictive definition of biblical context has surely reduced what must have been much richer associations in Pascal's mind. That is nowhere clearer than in the case of Jeremiah's "fountain of living waters."

To restrict attention to literal senses is not to read Pascal's Bible in Pascal's way.[13] Jeremiah 2:13 and, more clearly, the closely related passage at Jeremiah 17:13–14 both prefigure spiritual meanings already evident for those with eyes to see and a heart to comprehend. But it is only in John 4:14 and Apocalypse 21:6 that the revelation is complete:

(a) John 4:14 But whosoever drinketh of the water that I shall give him shall never thirst; but the water that I shall give him shall be in him *A WELL (FONS) OF LIVING WATER* springing up into EVERLASTING LIFE.

(b) Apoc. 21:4 AND GOD SHALL WIPE AWAY ALL TEARS FROM THEIR EYES; AND THERE SHALL BE NO MORE DEATH, NEITHER SORROW NOR CRYING, NEITHER SHALL THERE BE ANY MORE PAIN; FOR THE FORMER THINGS ARE PASSED AWAY.
21:5 And he that sat upon the throne said, BEHOLD, I MAKE ALL THINGS NEW. . . .
21:6 And he said unto me, It is done. I am the Alpha and the Omega, the beginning and the end. I WILL GIVE UNTO HIM THAT IS ATHIRST OF *THE FOUNTAIN (FONS) OF THE WATER OF LIFE* FREELY.
21:7 HE THAT OVERCOMETH SHALL INHERIT ALL THINGS; AND I SHALL BE HIS GOD, AND HE SHALL BE MY SON.

Furthermore, to restrict Pascal's biblicism to his solitary reading of Scripture is, in effect, to isolate him from the Catholic community. As Philippe Sellier has emphasized, the *Mémorial* begins with a meticulous heading in which the date is given in liturgical form: "Monday, 23 November, day of St. Clement, Pope and martyr, and of others. . . ."[14] In the Roman Breviary, the propers for the day return insistently to the image of the "fountain of living waters." This *fons* flows through antiphons, responsories, and lessons in the offices for Vespers, the First Nocturn, the Second Nocturn, Lauds, Sext, and the Second Vespers. There are nine instances in which the "fountain" represents salvation, its "living waters," death-denied.[15]

Finally, I return to the problematical passages with a confirmed hypothesis in hand. Line 5 is a straightforward case. In Ephesians 1, Paul writes of our election by the Father and our adoption by Christ, who was raised from the dead to rejoin the Father and redeem the faithful. Two verses are quite sufficient to associate the themes of parent and attachment:

Eph. 1:17 That the *God of* our Lord *Jesus Christ* the FATHER OF GLORY may give unto you the spirit of wisdom and revelation in the knowledge of Him;

1:18 The eyes of your understanding being enlightened, that YE MAY KNOW WHAT IS THE HOPE OF HIS CALLING, AND WHAT THE RICHES OF THE GLORY OF HIS INHERITANCE IN THE SAINTS.

Line 16 is complicated by alternative possibilities. The Scriptural lament from the Son on the Cross to the Father, that He has been forsaken, does express filial attachment, as Pascal emphasizes in the *Abrégé de la vie de Jésus Christ:*

"*My God,* my God, why *HAST THOU FORSAKEN ME?*" that is, in his human nature ABANDONED to all the torments of his executioners and his enemies without consolation. And he calls to God to ask the cause for this ABANDONMENT. . . . Perhaps this appeal may even be understood as a prayer made by Jesus to the FATHER that he might remember the end for which he AFFLICTS AND ABANDONS HIM, as if he said: "*My God,* my God, why *HAST THOU FORSAKEN ME?* You know, my God, that it is for THE SALVATION OF THE WORLD. . . ." And these words are FULL OF HOPE AND NOT OF DESPAIR, for he says "*My God,* my God!" Well, GOD IS NOT THE GOD OF THE DEAD [Matt. 22:32], NOR OF THE DESPAIRING.[16]

The associated themes, "father" and death denied, provide new evidence that the traditional identification of line 16 in the *Mémorial* has been correct; it is an adaptation of Matthew 27:46.

Associative thinking knows no law of the excluded middle. To argue for Matthew 27:46 is not to argue against alternatives from the Psalms, which, of course, Jesus could recall. Only one among the several Psalms that have been suggested meets the associative criteria that I have hypothesized and tested. But that one, Psalm 26:9, speaks quite particularly to a believer with Pascal's historical experience of parental loss:

Ps. 26:8 When thou saidst, SEEK YE MY FACE; MY HEART SAID UNTO THEE, THY FACE, LORD, WILL I SEEK.
26:9 HIDE NOT THY FACE FAR FROM ME: PUT NOT THY SERVANT AWAY IN ANGER: THOU HAST BEEN MY HELP: LEAVE ME NOT, *NEITHER FORSAKE ME, O GOD* OF MY SALVATION.
26:10 WHEN MY FATHER AND MY MOTHER FORSAKE ME, THEN THE LORD WILL TAKE ME UP.

In the Vulgate, the crucial predicate in the first clause of verse 10 repeats the same verb and object in the same forms that are also seen in the snippet from Jeremiah 2:13 in the preceding line: "*Dereliquerunt me . . .*" Who forsakes whom? "MY FATHER AND MY MOTHER FORSAKE ME . . ."

All eight of the citations in the Core of the *Mémorial* point back toward biblical contexts in which the closest associations include both "parent," especially "father," and "attachment," especially death denied. *Not one* of the eight such citations as elliptically quoted in the *Mémorial* expresses these two themes together, and *not one* of the four such citations in the first part of the Core (to line 10) expresses even one of the themes in even the most oblique language. This cannot have been the result of mere chance, as is statistically demonstrable.

Scriptural Associations and Statistical Significance

The argument that "parent" and "attachment" explain the human meaning of this central experience is a radical departure from all past scholarship. That is reason enough for second thoughts. Before I can convince even myself that Pascal really had in mind what he did not set down on paper, I must establish that the combination of contextual themes cannot plausibly be explained otherwise. After all, this most elemental social relationship and the deepest psychological need must somehow inform passage after passage. And if "attachment" is taken to mean "death denied," what surprise can there be in finding the most exalted religious belief here, there, and everywhere in the Bible?

Computer-assisted sampling techniques make it possible to select biblical verses randomly for comparison with Pascal's selections. These randomly selected verses can then be expanded into three-verse contexts, defined as above, which can be searched for the themes of "parent" and "attachment," also defined as above. The results can be scored, and the scores for the randomly selected controls can then serve as the basis for a methodical calculation of statistical significance.[17]

I select a large set of controls, one hundred verses-in-context, so as to permit statistical generalization. The following contingency table (table 3) presents in each of the four cells the observed instances and, in parentheses, the statistically expected instances. I find just

TABLE 3
The Statistical Significance of the Contextual Associations (whole Bible)

	Combined associations	*No combined associations*	
Mémorial observed	8	0	8
expected	(.815)	(7.185)	
Controls observed	3	97	100
expected	(10.185)	(89.815)	
	11	97	108

degrees of freedom = 1; chi-square = 76.172; probability < .001

three instances of the combined associations in the hundred verses-in-context.

By the measure of this test, there is not so much as one chance in a thousand that the contextual associations could have been combined fortuitously. Statistical tables understate these results, because they do not calculate probabilities beyond the third decimal place. More sophisticated methods allow the calculation of a fourth place. The chance of reproducing Pascal's results from randomly selected verses is 0.0000.

This test has drawn from the entire Bible indiscriminately. Perhaps that very randomness inadvertently begs the question. Pascal emphasized "the ways taught in the Gospel" (lines 9 and 24), and five of his eight citations in the Core do indeed recall passages from just these four books of the Bible (lines 2, 6, 11–12, 16, and 18–20). However, the Gospels make up a relatively small part of the whole. It seems intuitively probable that these books include disproportionate numbers of passages affirming an afterlife or "denying death."

I repeat the statistical exercise, limiting selection of another set of one hundred verses-in-context to the Gospels. This limitation does affect the results, as anticipated (see table 4). I count eleven instances of the combined associations in these hundred verses-in-context, but the chi-square is still monstrous:

TABLE 4
The Statistical Significance of the Contextual Associations (Gospels only)

	Combined associations	*No combined associations*	
Mémorial observed	5	0	5
expected	(.762)	(4.238)	
Controls observed	11	89	100
expected	(15.238)	(84.762)	
	16	89	105

degrees of freedom = 1; chi-square = 29.199; probability < .001

This means that it is implausible to suppose that random selection *or any sort of selection other than a choice made on the basis of these combined associations* could produce the pattern so laboriously analyzed in this chapter. Even in the Gospels, there is much less than a one in a thousand chance of happening upon the combined associations consistently in a randomly chosen set of five verses-in-context. The most precise calculation of the probability is still 0.0000.

Pascal did *not* chance upon biblical citations closely associated with the combined themes of "parent" and "attachment." He *must* have chosen them on that basis. This conclusion is so intriguing because he *never* quoted together those themes that he *always* chose together. Indeed, in his first four citations (lines 1–2, 5, 6, and 7), he never recorded anything even vaguely suggestive of even one such theme. In short, he "forgot" just what he had "remembered." What can this mean?

CHAPTER 9

The *Mémorial* II: What Does It Mean?

In the literal reading of Pascal's mysterious *Mémorial,* only his soul and his God appear. In lines 1–13 of the Core, he shows his joy at having "found" the God of Abraham; in the rest of the Core and First Postscript, he also shows his desire to "keep" the God so found, complicated by guilt for past separation and anxiety about possible future separation. This literal reading of the manifest text is very important, but to go no further would be to accept subjective enthusiasm as regulative and to reject the objective evidence of a pervasive if latent preoccupation with parent, especially father, and attachment, especially death denied. This newly discovered evidence opens the way to a newly methodical interpretation of the pivotal experience in Pascal's life.

Before venturing further into the dark world of historical dream-visions, let me salute two classics in the secular study of related phenomena. First, Sigmund Freud's *Interpretation of Dreams* (1900) is still very instructive, especially for its innovative method. Freud's proudest claim was to have discovered what he took to be the secret of all dreams, wish-fulfillment, but his most enduring contribution was methodical interpretation by each dreamer's private associations.[1] As a clinician, he could not imagine the adaptation of this method for historical inquiry; as a historian, I claim to have discovered in Pascal's Bibles the functional equivalent to an awakened dreamer's associations.[2] Second, William James's *Varieties of Religious*

Experience (1902) is also still very valuable, especially for the naturalistic inquirer's exemplary respect for the personal force and pragmatic value of religious experience.[3] I want to understand my convert and his ecstasy, not to dismiss the great turning point of his life as nothing more than a backward-looking wish.

Dream-Visions and Patterns of Unconscious Thought

The earliest datable reference to the *Mémorial* comes in a well-informed letter from Louis-Henri Loménie de Brienne to Gilberte Périer, dated 7 December 1668:[4]

> They [Roannez and perhaps others] tell me that you know wonderful stories of *dreams, witches, spells, apparitions,* etc. I'm making a little collection of such material. . . . I don't include anything in my book that isn't very exact, very true, and as detailed as I can make it. If you could send me something, or if you hear of anything of the sort from reliable persons, I would be very grateful. All these things, when they are true, are great proofs of religion.
>
> With respect to this, please have a copy made for me of the document found on M. Pascal, which M. de Roannez has told me about. It's the one that is figured, with "*fire, flame, day of Saint Chrysogonus,*" etc.[5]

Loménie de Brienne's "witches" and "spells" must refer to Gilberte's Strange Story of Baby Blaise and the Old Witch. It is possible but hardly likely that she also told other such stories for which we have no other record. That leaves "dreams" and "apparitions" from this list of supernatural wonders. What dreams and apparitions? Gilberte may have told a number of such stories, for instance, that of the dream-vision received by Mère Agnès on the night before the Miracle of the Thorn that had saved her daughter.[6] Nevertheless, in a letter that asks specifically for the *Mémorial,* nothing else, it seems inescapable that "dream" or "apparition" is his category (perhaps from Roannez?) for Pascal's experience on the Night of Fire.

Gilberte's longest-lived son, Louis Périer, provides the one commentary on the *Mémorial* from within the family.[7] His term was "vision," not "dream," and he thought in terms of theological abstractions, sacred history, and spiritual development:

> At Pascal's death, the Paper copied here was found, written in his hand, wrapped in a Parchment, and sewn under his doublet over his chest. His family believed that it was a vision, the record of which he wanted to keep because of the vivid impression that it had made on his mind. The same

words were written on the Parchment, which had radiating crosses at its beginning and end.

These few words and what we know of Pascal's last years suggest that the vision must have represented to him in a vivid way the Sovereign Majesty of God, His Holiness, His Goodness, and the mystery of the Redemption. He never separated Jesus Christ from God, and one can see in his *Pensées* that the knowledge of God without Jesus Christ is the lot of philosophers and not the saving truth of Christians. The fragmentary words of the text reflect the various impressions made on M. Pascal by the vision of divine Majesty, which were almost like those made on Moses by God's appearance in the Burning Bush: "Certainty, joy," etc.

The radiating cross shows the impression of compunction, love, and renunciation that Jesus Christ made on Pascal's heart; he couldn't forgive himself for having been somewhat dissipated in the world.[8]

Both Brienne and Périer seem to have regarded the provenance of the *Mémorial* and the existence of a figured copy as remarkable. This alone is enough to suggest that Pascal himself was not simply following a pious custom when he made his Parchment copy and sewed Paper and Parchment within his clothing.[9] Other cases cited in modern scholarship are not truly similar.[10] The facts are that Pascal made the elegant copy, kept the scrawled original, sewed the package into his doublet, and wore it over his heart. Such extraordinary efforts to record, ornament, preserve, enfold, and embrace the textual record surely imply that on the night of 23 November 1654 he had experienced something that he regarded as extraordinary.

Brienne and Périer apparently shared the belief that this was a theophany and, as such, "a great proof of religion," something comparable to "the vision of divine majesty" that Moses experienced at the Burning Bush. This belief must reflect opinions of the persons closest to Pascal at the time of his death, his friend Roannez (Brienne's informant) and his sister Gilberte (Périer's informant). In seventeenth-century terms, it hardly mattered whether such a nighttime event was called a "dream" or a "vision." Dreams were not categorically dismissed as evanescent fantasies, and even the most worldly experts on dream life accepted the possibility of heaven-sent visions in the form of dreams.[11] Furthermore, visions were not necessarily confined to periods of wakefulness, and, however reluctant were the Port-Royalists to encourage spiritual pride, they, too, accepted the possibility of extraordinary graces.[12]

The great Pascal himself was quite ready to credit dream-visions as supernatural phenomena. Shortly after his Night of Fire, apparently in December 1654, he drafted a meditation on the admirable humility of the great modern visionary, Saint Theresa (Pensée 928, tentatively datable by other fragments on the same manuscript page, which refer to Singlin's inability to speak or to direct him). Other fragments, presumably later, show that he retained a particular interest in her (Pensées 598, 721, and 920). Pascal also paid close attention to the biblical Daniel as an inspired dreamer and dream diviner (Pensée 485). He eventually went so far as to argue that popular credulity with respect to the many false dream-visions is sufficient evidence that some few are truly divine (Pensées 734–735).

All this is historical prelude to the following psychological observation. The formal relationship between the "manifest" biblical texts that Pascal incorporated into his *Mémorial* and the "latent" scriptural contexts that he recalled from memory but did not record is strikingly like the formal relationship between elements from "manifest" dream reports and the corresponding "latent" dream thoughts recovered by free association. Freud first introduced three concepts for the processes by which latent thoughts are unconsciously transformed into manifest dreams.[13] David Foulkes has updated them for a later generation that has been informed by the empirical research of sleep laboratories and has become skeptical of many orthodox psychoanalytical doctrines.[14] The three transformative processes are *condensation, displacement,* and *pictorial representation.*

First, condensation. This is an unconscious process inferred by Freud to account for the fact that the associations he elicited for the several dream elements, which alone enabled him and his patients to make sense of their dreams, were so consistently so much more ample than the narrative reports themselves. He supposed that this thought must have been latent within the mind before the dream, which "condensed" it. Foulkes still theorizes that some parts of the latent thought simply disappear from the manifest report, and sometimes two or more latent thoughts are combined into a single dream element. Figuratively speaking, the content of dreams is "condensed."[15]

Second, displacement. This correlative process, also unconscious, was first inferred by Freud to account for the related fact that associations called up from his patients so regularly suggested a meaningful latent thought that was not just "more ample" than the seemingly meaningless manifest report, but also "differently centered." Foulkes agrees that what is most important in dreamers' associations is not also most important in the corresponding narratives, and vice versa. Figuratively, the focal point is "displaced."[16]

Third, pictorial representation. This concept is fundamentally even simpler, although, as Foulkes notes, Freud's relevant discussion is not as clear. Dream reports and free associations are necessarily verbal, but dream experience is primarily visual. It is a form of thinking in pictures. Latent thoughts are "pictorially represented."[17]

Now back to the long-familiar *Mémorial* from Pascal's Night of Fire and the newly discovered pattern of combined associations for his fragmentary citations. Lines 1–2, reread in light of the several scriptural contexts, provide a wonderful illustration of the workings of condensation, displacement, and pictorial representation. Conversely, these psychological concepts make good sense of the otherwise puzzling discrepancy between the expansive meanings observably "latent" in Exodus 3 and Matthew 22, to go no further, and the few "manifest" words recorded in the first lines of the *Mémorial*. From Exodus 3, there is the "fire" of the Burning Bush, the appearance of the Lord, and His declaration as "the God of thy father, the God of Abraham. . . ." Then comes God's promise to deliver His people from affliction and sorrows, God's call to Moses as His appointed leader, and God's pledge of support: "I will be with thee; . . . I have sent thee; . . . ye shall serve God upon this mountain."

Who would dare to circumscribe the reach of Blaise Pascal's memory in the two hours on the night of 23 November 1654? The further boundaries are indistinct, but one close reminiscence is virtually certain. Because the closely associated and emphatically reiterated "father" (Exod. 3:6, 15, 16; Exod. 4:5; Acts 7:32) also appears so regularly in various guises in the other contexts for Pascal's other citations, this association is as certain as such things can possibly be. Furthermore, because the association is missing from the text itself in this first part of the Core (to line 10), it was probably unconscious.

The same first words from Pascal's Core take us further into the Scriptures (see chapter 8). From Matthew 22 (and Mark 12 and Luke 20), there is Jesus' repetition of the memorable "God of Abraham" in the context of *the* proof text on the afterlife (Matt. 22:32). Verses 23–32 are all very closely associated, with the Sadducees' challenge by the hypothetical case of the wife with seven successive husbands, all of whom die. These deaths are not incidental; they raise the crucial question for Jesus as for Blaise. Christ has the answer: "I am the God of Abraham . . . ; not the God of the dead, but of the living."

Again, who can say where to draw the line around Pascal's memory? At verses 34–40, a Pharisee lawyer takes up the challenge after it is dropped by the Sadducees, and Jesus takes the occasion to summarize the Law in the Two Great Commandments, the basis for the theology of the Two Loves. Who can draw the line? Still in the same chapter, at verses 41–46, Jesus finally silences His challengers with a question of His own: "What think ye of Christ? Whose son . . . ?"

It is impossible to limit Pascal's memory but quite possible to specify one more highly significant and hitherto unknown part of its contents. Because the reiterated denial of death as loss *does* appear so prominently in the immediate contexts of Matthew 22.32, Mark 12:26, Luke 20:37, *and* Pascal's other citations, but *does not* appear, in any form, in any of the biblical texts as recorded before lines 18–20 ("This is the eternal life . . ."), I conclude that this association, too, is as certain as such things can be—and that it was unconscious when Pascal recorded the *Mémorial*.

The "God of Abraham" from the Burning Bush is most immediately and powerfully associated with "father" and "not dead." Knowing this from the Scriptures and the patterns of citation in this document, we can look in other Pascalian texts for the symbol of fire in conjunction with "father" and "not-dead." His most powerful spiritual writing from the period between conversions was his letter of consolation after his father's death; "fire" appears in this passage: "And God resurrected Him and sent Him to His glory, represented formerly by the fire of heaven that fell on victims, to burn and consume the body and to give eternal life and the life of glory to the spirit. That is what Jesus Christ has done for us. . . ."[18]

"Fire" is so elemental that its verbal associations are literally endless, its pictorial representations so commonplace as to defy enumeration. Many associations and representations were quintessentially spiritual. Fire-from-heaven, seen at the first Pentecost in Acts 2:1–4, represented the grace of the Holy Spirit in all sorts of devout literature, engravings, and so on.[19] There is, for instance, a profusely illustrated contemporaneous translation of the *Imitation de Jésus-Christ* (Paris, 1654). The translator was Pierre Corneille, the eminent poet who so honored Jacqueline's early religious verse. The *Imitation* was one of the devotional works most highly recommended at Port-Royal, and it is a possible source of inspiration for one of the lines in Pascal's brief Second Postscript.[20]

In Thomas à Kempis's book 3, "The Inward Speaking of Christ to a Faithful Soul," fire represents not only God's grace but also man's love in return, a reciprocal giving rather awkwardly depicted in an engraving that was to ornament de Sacy's later translation (1662). A fleshy cherub with a tiny vessel pours down a thin stream from the heavens above, while a grander brazier roars with flames leaping up from the earth below: "This fire descends from heaven and ascends once again to its source."[21] The style of the engraving is dated, but the language of the text is timeless in its celebration of the spirituality of the Two Loves:

> Love will always have a man's mind raised to God and not occupied with the things of the world. Love will also be free from all worldly affection, so that the inward sight of the soul is not darkened or hindered, and a man's affection toward heavenly things is not banished from his free will by an inordinate winning or losing of worldly things. Nothing, therefore, is sweeter than love, nothing higher, nothing stronger, nothing larger, nothing more joyful, nothing fuller, nothing better, in heaven or on earth, for love descends from God and may not finally rest in anything lower than God. . . .
>
> Love wakes much and sleeps little, and, in sleeping, does not sleep. It faints and is not weary; it is restricted in its liberty and is in great freedom. It sees reasons to fear and does not fear, but, like an ember or a spark of fire, flames always upward, by the fervor of its love, toward God, and through the special help of grace is delivered from all perils and dangers.[22]

Having said this much about the spiritual associations of fire, I add a briefer word about a Frenchman's "feu." The word also means "late" or "deceased," as in the phrase, "le feu Messire Étienne Pascal." It is a dictum of the most orthodox dream theory that "words are treated as though they were concrete things." Otherwise stated, instead of the word of discourse being a sign for the things of concrete reality, the picture in a dream may be interpreted as a sign for the words that give it meaning. In this case, pictorial fire represents the word "feu" and its many associations, including "the deceased."

What does it mean? Traditional believers like the abbé Périer in the seventeenth century have looked for proofs of faith and come well schooled in sacred history and theological abstractions. To them, the *Mémorial* has meant that the fiery God of Abraham appeared to Blaise Pascal at a given place and time, namely, in his quarters on the rue des Francs-Bourgeois Saint-Michel in Paris at about 10:30 P.M. on 23 November 1654. *This* meaning has seemed to leap from the *document itself,* although it is telling that Périer appeals to his knowledge of Pascal's *later* life and *later* thought to support his interpretation.

That Pascal himself believed that he had been the recipient of a heaven-sent vision is a perfectly valid inference from the remarkable form, content, and provenance of his record. This belief presumably did help to inspire his later life and work. He had been specially favored, graced, called. But can even his subjective enthusiasm decide the matter? What does it mean?

Aggressive unbelievers like the psychiatrist Dr. Louis François Lélut in the nineteenth century have come to the record with contrary convictions and, unsurprisingly, seen evidence of an earthbound reality. The *Mémorial* documents not the presence of the "God of Abraham" but the delusions of Blaise Pascal. In their efforts to explain how so brilliant a mathematician and scientist could have gone so wrong at the time of his conversion, they have supposed mental illness. The "vision" becomes a "hallucination," and a sign of grace becomes a symptom of psychopathology.[23]

For all their differences, these two sorts of interpreters have shared presumptions and limitations. Both have presumed from the remarkable fact of this documentation, whether it is taken as a sign of more-than-human blessedness or less-than-sane craziness, that something truly extraordinary must have occurred. Both have also been limited, insofar as they have virtually ignored history as a discipline. They have looked *forward* in time to Pascal's later life, that of a saintly exemplar, but not *backward* in time to his earlier life, back through and beyond the fall of 1654. So, they have not seen the potential relevance of Blaise's personal history as Étienne's son. It is a further limitation that both have ignored the psychology of ordinary dreams. Not thinking to look systematically beyond the *Mémorial* text to the relevant scriptural contexts, they have missed the opportunity to recover Pascal's associations from the book of Pascal's memory.

What does it mean? Associative thinking obeys no law of the

excluded middle; the rule is both/and, not neither/nor. It *is* certain that Pascal focused his conscious mind on the God of Abraham, and it is also inconceivable that he would not have offered much more spiritually significant material, if asked to "free associate" on "the God of Abraham" and the rest. It is *also* as certain as such things can be that Pascal's unconscious thinking concerned his human attachment to his worldly father. The "attachments" scripturally associated with the certain citations in the first part of the Core (lines 1–2, 6, 7) are not "purely spiritual," not simply those of a devout Christian to the divine Father.[24] Even those corresponding to line 6 (Mary Magdalene's encounter with the risen Christ from John 20:17) are "psychological," familial, those of father-son.

Pascal did believe guiltily that he had "separated himself" from his God, as he wrote in the *second* part of the Core and repeated in the First Postscript (lines 14, 22). This alone would have been enough to explain his sense of overflowing "joy" at having been approached by this merciful God (lines 13, 25). But there was much more. In the contexts for the scriptural passages that came in the *first* part of the Core, the separation that the enthusiast seems most anxious to repair is not his own spiritual straying, as a sinful man, from the love of God into worldly indifference but rather his experience of death itself, that most painful and final form of loss.

Pascal's first expression of "joy" (line 4) follows his quotation of words from *the* proof text for immortality (line 2). The "God of Abraham," first announced in the Book of Exodus, also recalls Jesus' promise of an afterlife in the Gospels:

(a) Matt. 22:31 But as touching the resurrection of the dead . . .
32 . . . not the God of the dead, but of the living.
(b) Mark 12:26 As touching the dead, that they rise . . .
27 not the God of the dead, but . . . of the living.
(c) Luke 20:35 . . . the resurrection from the dead . . .
36 Neither can they die any more . . .
37 Now that the dead are raised . . .
38 For he is not a God of the dead, but of the living.

The progression in the *Mémorial* is from a biblical citation with psychologically powerful associations to lines in Pascal's own words that fully justify spiritual interpretation (lines 3–4).

Pascal's verbal recollection of the Gospel record of the Easter

Morning encounter between Mary Magdalene and her risen Lord takes us back to a context in which she who had lamented meets the living Christ. This is spiritually meaningful for all later sinners, who are also sorrowful, but also given hope. More immediately, in the verse partially quoted (John 20:17), the Son announces His Ascension to rejoin his Father. This was historically and psychologically significant for the bereaved Pascal: "I am not yet ascended to my Father . . . ; I ascend unto my Father and your Father. . . ." Thus, there is filial attachment as well as spiritual devotion in the same biblical context.

Nowhere is the strictly psychological force of the attachment more evident than in the context for the words that Pascal quoted from the Book of Ruth:

> Ruth 1:16 Intreat me not to leave thee or to return from following after thee, for whither thou goest, I will go; and where thou lodgest, I will lodge . . .
> 17 Where thou diest, will I die, and there will I be buried: the Lord do so to me, and more also, if ought but death part thee and me.

Here, there is a cry of the heart from person to person, grown child to parent, not man to God. In the following lines of the *Mémorial,* after his fragmentary citation, Pascal does conclude this first part of the Core with a spiritual pledge and a reaffirmation of faith (lines 8–9).

What it all means seems clear enough, even if exactly what happened at about 10:30 P.M. on the night in question must remain obscure. It means one thing, looking backward historically from the occasion: the undying love of Blaise for the deceased *Étienne.* It expresses a "hope" that might also be called a "wish," the promise of an afterlife that would be shared. Christian doctrine, of course, emphasizes hope. Psychoanalytical doctrine alerts interpreters to wish-fulfillment. I do not mean to reduce the former to the latter or to dismiss the experience as a "dream" in pejorative senses. I do want to confront a pattern of evidence consistent with dreamlike thinking. The most economical explanation of this evidence is that Pascal *wished* that he had not lost his beloved mother and father. There is nothing shameful in this, everything human. In his own terms, he was a man, not an angel or an animal (Pensée 678).

The *Mémorial* means another thing, looking forward to later years: the unprompted love of God for Pascal, which inspired a more fervent love of Pascal for *God.* The love of man preceded the love of God, underlay the other, and served the other.

What happened? I infer historically from the season, the time of night, others' daily schedules for bedtime, and Pascal's illness that he had probably fallen asleep before this time.[25] I know from psychophysiological research in sleep laboratories that everyone dreams several times every night, normally for the first time within about ninety minutes after the loss of consciousness, and, in cases of depression, significantly sooner.[26] The evidence suggests that Pascal awakened from a powerful dream, which on the latent if not manifest level probably concerned his father or his father's death. This is, in Freud's words, "the most important event, the most poignant loss, of a man's life."[27]

At least in part, this latent dream thought may have taken the manifest pictorial form of the Burning Bush. The first nine lines of the Core, quoted above, reflect a believer's awakened excitement, not critical reflection, historical reconstruction, or psychological analysis. The rest of the Core, although highly emotional, seems less strictly ecstatic and more properly spiritual. Here Pascal reconsiders his own relationship to his God.

It may be that I am mistaken to infer sleep and dreaming before 10:30 p.m. A long and lonely waking vigil could have been quite as effective as sleep itself in inducing a hallucinatory experience. If so, a waking hallucination, experienced as a vision, could have had exactly the same impact.[28]

The psychological literature on bereavement is relevant, even though Pascal's most recent familial loss, strictly speaking, was his father's death on 24 September 1651. A sense of the continued presence of the dead person is very common for the closest surviving relatives. There is nothing intrinsically pathological about it. In cases of chronic or delayed grieving, there may be an intellectual "acceptance" of the fact of the loss, together with seemingly contradictory feelings that the dead person is recoverable or even still present.[29]

Augustine himself understood "that dead men have at times appeared to the living either in dreams or in some other way." While allowing for "human infirmity" in the interpretation of such dreams and for madness in "other visions of persons awake," he attributed true dreams or visions of the dead to "angelical operations":

Similar to this is also that condition when persons, with their senses more profoundly in abeyance than is the case in sleep, are occupied with the like visions. For to them also appear images of quick and dead; but then, when they return to their senses, whatever dead they say they have seen are thought to have been verily with them.[30]

Circumstances That Favored Preoccupation with Loss

Among the paradoxes of this subject, one of the most striking is that it is the devotional life of the community that provides the best evidence on what passed through Pascal's mind before he fell asleep, alone in the world, on the night of Monday, 23 November 1654. In comparison, it is merely curious that it is not any child of modern psychology but Herodotus, the father of history, who should first have published the opinion that the stuff of dreams is made up of real-life memories of the most recent past, not heaven-sent prophecies of the distant future.[31]

The Night of Fire was a *Monday,* as Pascal noted in the Heading of his *Mémorial.* Port-Royalist penitents were expected to pray for the repose of the souls of the dead on Mondays, and, for Blaise in 1654, that would have meant prayers for his mother and father. The evidence for this practice comes in Antoine Arnauld's *Fréquente Communion* (1643), which is addressed to "persons who think seriously about conversion." It is the one of the great theologian's books that is most likely to have been most familiar and most useful to Pascal as a convert.[32] Arnauld incorporated the Penitential Canons renewed by Saint Charles Borromeo and the Council of Trent. He instructed readers on "the tests of a true conversion"; the pertinent test concerns prayer: "pray daily, at least every evening and every morning; pray for the dead every Monday."[33]

This Monday was "*23 November, day of St. Clement* pope and martyr *and* of *others* in the martyrology." The Pascal who wrote this was no novice. He was closely familiar with the liturgy.[34] Jacqueline's letter of 25 January 1655 shows him reading the offices, and Gilberte's little memoir stresses the great love that he later showed for the offices, especially the Little Hours.[35] While it would be anachronistic to take this testimony on later practice during the January retreat as necessarily valid for 23 November 1654, it would be a worse mistake historically to think of the Second Conversion as a sudden flash, unprepared by devotional life before that night. Line 15 of the *Mémorial* on "the fount of living waters" is itself powerful if indirect internal evidence that Pascal had read the offices for that day, which repeatedly recalled the "spring" or "fount" as a symbol of eternal life.

Following Sellier and going further, I note that the Nocturns for the Feast of Saint Clement retell the story of just one other saint, Felicity. She mothered seven sons and gave them all as martyrs before her own martyrdom:

> That blessed woman Felicity . . . had as much dread of leaving her seven sons living after her in the flesh, as have carnal-minded mothers of seeing them go dead before them. When she was taken up in the strong pains of persecution, she braced up the hearts of her children by bidding them cleave to the Fatherland above, and became their mother for the spiritual, as she had aforetime been for the fleshly life, bringing them forth for God by her exhortation, as she had brought them forth for the world by her body. And shall I not call this woman a martyr? Nay, more than a martyr. The seven whom she trusted to God were seven children sent before her to death. She trusted first and triumphed last.[36]

Here was a mother who gave her sons before giving her own life to God. So doing, she witnessed their martyrdoms—and spared them the sight of her own death.

"The fount of living waters" expresses a powerful faith. But in the context of a dreamlike experience in which there are other signs of preoccupation with deceased parents, it may also symbolize a nursing mother, while its abandonment suggests weaning. This suggestion is reinforced by the immediate biblical context of "broken cisterns that can hold no water" and the immediate *Mémorial* context so burdened with guilt and anxiety concerning separation (lines 14–17). For Pascal to have *forgotten* just two words, the "living waters," when he copied this line onto his otherwise more-than-meticulous Parchment suggests a Freudian slip related to the Strange Story of Baby Blaise, his weaning, his separation, and his infantile outrage. The water! The damn water!

There is more, of a more conventionally historical nature, to explain why Pascal should have been particularly concerned with father and mother, separation and loss, on 23 November 1654. Blaise had come to Jacqueline, sorrowfully and submissively. He had moved his residence to the Left Bank, closer to Port-Royal, and visited her at the convent again and again. In his visits, she had begun to press the case that the best director for his spiritual life would be her priest, Père Singlin.[37] But Singlin was reluctant, himself unwell, and, on 23 November, he was still at Port-Royal des Champs, not in Paris.[38] He would survive, and he would return, but at the time the whole community was anxious about him, and his ill health and separation must have, to say the least, frustrated her on what had become the principal point of open disagreement between brother and sister.[39]

Blaise would have been acutely sensitive to all of this. For him to follow her counsel would have been for him to agree to submit himself to this other person as his spiritual father. Whatever else was wrong with this resolution at deeper or higher levels, there was the simple fact that committing himself to this new relationship would also be discontinuing the exceptional series of frequent and long visits with the beloved Jacqueline, which were justifiable only by her service as his temporary director. But, if he resisted her on the point that seemed most important to her . . . That he considered this situation to be relevant to the experience of the *Mémorial* is clear from the beginning of the brief Second Postscript: "Complete submission to Jesus Christ and to my director."

Jacqueline's religious community was also in crisis, or very close to it, with respect to its leadership. Mère Angélique (1591–1661) had been given Port-Royal in 1602 when she herself was a mere child, but she matured quickly, reformed the convent, and obtained royal approval for a new regime of triennial elections. Her sister Agnès was elected as Abbess for two successive terms in 1636 and 1639, and Angélique herself then served for another four successive terms, from October 1642 to November 1654.[40] Angélique felt old and unwell by the end of her last term, and she was determined to relieve herself of the burdens of office and to retire to Port-Royal des Champs after the election of 26 November, as in fact she did.[41]

The nuns were understandably anxious about her impending departure and the beginning of a new regime under a new superior.[42] Mère Angélique had become Abbess fifty-two years earlier under an old regime, and she and her sister had dominated the community even after the introduction of the triennial elections; it was almost impossible to imagine new leadership. Marie des Anges Suireau was the designated successor, but she dreaded her election, feeling inadequate as well as old and infirm in her own right.[43] From other nuns, there were so many rumblings about the insufficiency of this humble successor that Mère Angélique supposed that the demon was actively at work; she exhorted and she admonished, trying to convince them to trust in God and not to surrender to human affections.[44]

Thus, on 23 November 1654, Jacqueline's spiritual mother was preparing to leave for the duration at the very time that her spiritual father was also away. These circumstances surely contributed to her brother's preoccupation with familial, especially parental separations and losses.

Finally, there were also other contemporaneous separations and losses in Pascal's worldly relationships, including those with strongly paternal associations. First, as Blaise approached his sister and the religious community of Port-Royal, he broke from the company of Paris savants into which his father had brought him. This separation was followed by loss. His father's closest surviving friend, Jacques Le Pailleur, died on 4 November.[45] Le Pailleur was the patron of the Academy among whom the younger Pascal had been "raised," as Blaise told them earlier that year in the course of reporting his ambitious plans for further work in mathematics and the sciences.[46]

Second, Pascal's own closest friend, Artus de Roannez, had spent most of the summer and all of the fall away from Paris in Poitou, as Mesnard has remarked pertinently.[47] It is no wonder, then, that themes of separation and loss should have preoccupied him on 23 November.

The Écrit sur la conversion du pécheur

This opuscule provides the best evidence on the Pascals' understanding of conversion as such.[48] Mesnard has emphasized its interest as evidence on the Second Conversion.[49] This is not to lend to the text an intimacy at all comparable to the *Mémorial* or to take from it formal similarities to the thought of Augustine's *Confessions*.[50] It is to relate the author's generalities to Jacqueline's testimony on her brother's state of mind in the fall of 1654.

What I find most striking is the insistent emphasis on the painful experience of loss, which can be broadened as a truth for Everyman or sharpened as a truth for the children of Antoinette Begon and Étienne Pascal. It is the loss of human objects that "pushes" the soul to seek a divine object. The *Écrit* offers this analysis of a soul on the verge of conversion:

It considers perishable things as dying and even as already dead. Considering the certain annihilation of all that it loves, it takes fright. Every instant tears away enjoyment of its objects. Every moment, all that is dearest flows away. It sees that, finally, a day will come when it will be deprived of everything. In this way, it comes to understand perfectly that the heart that has been attached only to fragile and empty things will find itself alone and abandoned. . . .

It begins to consider as naught all that must return to nothingness, such as the earth and sky, the body and mind, relatives and friends. . . . In short, [it concludes that] all that cannot endure as long as the soul is incapable of satisfying its earnest desire to establish itself in a felicity as enduring as itself.

It begins to wonder at its own former blindness, recognizing the certain truth that the soul, being immortal, cannot find its felicity among perishable things, which are taken from it at death if not sooner. This . . . leads to a very salutary distress. . . .

[H]owever many persons there are who seek their felicity in the world, it is certain that, even if worldly things bring some real pleasure (which isn't at all the case, as countless experiences teach us, so painfully and so continually), it is inevitable that we will lose these things or that death will take them from us.[51]

Thus, temporal goods and transient objects can offer only a fleeting happiness. The soul must seek an object that can "endure as long as the soul itself and can't be taken away without its consent." There follows a powerful restatement of the Two Loves by someone who knew the grief of loss. The author rejoices in having found God, an eternal object who cannot be taken away, a Creator more worthy of love than any creature. The goal is "to attach oneself to Him and to cling to Him forever."[52]

The *Écrit* documents in a different way the linkage between the Two Loves that has been the subject of the last three chapters. Its very generality may have permitted the author a more nearly unblinking confrontation with the real pains of human losses than was possible in more personal writings. The Pascals' experience had been exceptional for the uniquely attentive and retentive love of father Étienne. But Jacqueline's and Blaise's experience was also subject to the same harsh laws of human love that then ruled and still rule all of us. Étienne had died, as all men die, leaving his children, already devout, in need of a more lasting attachment to a more perfect object. Thus, Pascal's love of man, theologically the alternative to the love of God, historically served the latter.

PART FOUR

EXALTATION

After the Second Conversion, Pascal's life was exalted spiritually, intellectually, and emotionally. Spiritually, he had been favored by a vision of the God of Abraham, which aroused powerful and joyful emotions. In addition to the *Mémorial,* the *Mystère de Jésus* and Pensées 927–929 also document his mystical sense of communion with God. He also appended the Second Postscript to his Parchment *Mémorial,* ending with a sort of vow from Psalm 118: "I will not forget thy word."[1] The new convert did remember and serve the Word.

Intellectually, Pascal turned against prior mathematical and scientific interests. He terminated a very productive correspondence on mathematical probability with Pierre de Fermat.[2] He abandoned plans to perfect and promote the Arithmetic Machine.[3] He set aside manuscripts on the vacuum, although they were "all ready to print."[4] Still more remarkably, he withheld from distribution the *Traité du triangle arithmétique,* although he had already seen it into print![5] He never returned to these projects or published another word of mathematics or natural science under his own name.

In the following three chapters, I consider the enduring products of his redirected creative energies: the so-called *Entretien* with Sacy, the polemical campaign of the *Provinciales,* the contemporaneous *Écrits sur la grâce,* and the letters of spiritual counsel addressed to Charlotte de Roannez. In all of this, I look for the man in his work, the man understood as something more, not less, than spirit and intellect alone.

Emotionally, Pascal was elated. Jacqueline emphasizes Blaise's high spirits in her first letter after his conversion:

> I rejoice as much to find you cheerful in your solitude as I was pained when you were cheerful in the world. But I really don't know how M. de Sacy can deal with a penitent in such good spirits. . . .[6]

Jacqueline's lines may have been artful, but her testimony on Blaise's elevated mood is invaluable. The woman who had so pitied her downcast brother four months earlier now teased him for feeling a bit too happy and blessed his rereading of the philosophers in light of his religious beliefs.

What follows departs from prior scholarship most radically in the suggestion that much of what we so admire in Pascal's written work reflects more than the exceptional qualities of his reason and his faith alone. Consider the following hypomanic traits, which are associated with exceptional creativity in the modern world, where closer observation and more systematic research are possible: elevated, expansive, and irritable moods; increased energy and productivity; decreased need for sleep; inflated self-esteem; risk taking; and "sharpened and unusually creative thinking."[7] Pascal's exceptional creativity does not qualify him as hypomanic, but hypomania could have favored his sort of creativity. We cannot diagnose; we can inquire.

CHAPTER 10

The *Entretien de M. Pascal et de M. de Sacy:* The Illustrious Penitent and His Forgotten Director

Nicolas Fontaine composed *Mémoires,* which included the *Entretien de M. Pascal et de M. de Sacy,* sometime between 1696 and 1700. This was long after the deaths of Pascal (1662) and Sacy (1684), whom Fontaine had long served as a secretary.[1] The memoirist purports to record a historical conversation between the illustrious penitent and his revered priest, dating it by Pascal's definitive conversion and subsequent retreat to Port-Royal des Champs. Within Fontaine's dialogue, Pascal's references to resolutions and beginnings (par. 13) and Sacy's references both to Augustine's model conversion and to his interlocutor's own change of heart (par. 24–25) provide internal evidence for this date. In her letter of 19 January 1655, Jacqueline seems to refer to some such project as that sketched by Pascal in the *Entretien* and so to provide external evidence.

Fontaine's dialogue is made up of five speeches, which he himself would not have had the intelligence, imagination, or learning to invent:

1. Pascal: For and against Epictetus; for Montaigne (Mesnard par. 11–22)

2. Sacy: Against Montaigne; admonition on readings (par. 23–26)
3. Pascal: Against Montaigne; comparison of philosophers (par. 27–35)
4. Sacy: Apparent partial concession on usefulness (par. 36)
5. Pascal: Usefulness of combined and directed readings (par. 37–38)

Fontaine's uncritical adulation of the great genius, whose authorship of the anonymous *Provinciales* and the posthumous *Pensées* was well known by the end of the century, has helped to turn this little part of the world upside down. Most readers now approach the *Entretien* as one of Pascal's own works, important especially for its anticipation of certain aspect of the *Pensées*. Sacy's more modest responses seem much less significant. In modern memory, the priest attends, while the penitent instructs. Pascal triumphs over the world by worldly means, opposing two philosophers, one a pagan and the other a humanist (par. 15–22 and 27–29). He contrasts their partial truths, exposes their fundamental errors, and so serves the greater glory of the one true Faith (par. 30–35 and 37–38).

As for Sacy, it is too easy to forget that he has quietly but firmly objected to the whole enterprise in his "first speech." Explicitly, he condemns only Montaigne's writing, but implicitly he counsels Pascal against all such readings (par. 23–25). The otherwise respectful memoirist cuts him short, turning attention back to Pascal: "M. de Sacy said much more in the same vein, whereupon M. Pascal told him . . ." Give or take a few mere courtesies best interpreted as Fontaine's handiwork (par. 26, 32, 33, and 35), Pascal then develops his own argument as if he had not heard Sacy and did not need to respond, much less to submit. For a "second speech," Sacy gets only a bit of indirect discourse in which he expresses his admiration and at least partially retracts his objections (par. 36). Then Pascal gets the last word.[2]

This cannot be right, but the material is promising enough to justify another attempt to get it right. Taken as literary evidence on the new convert's state of mind and spirit, the *Entretien* is unique. The critical reader must strip the memoirist's nominal dialogue of its suspect trappings, reassemble Pascal's three "speeches" into one coherent exposition, *and* allow his director, Sacy, the last word.[3] That leaves a rather impenitent penitent, much too confident in his limited learning and limitless intelligence, and a firm if gentle director who reminded him that Augustine himself had experienced similar intellectual temptations before his own conversion and then pronounced against them thereafter.

Before the Second Conversion, Pascal had been an enthusiastic reader of Epictetus and Montaigne, if not a disciplined student of philosophy as such. Very soon afterward, he boldly redirected these worldly diversions toward Christian apologetics. There's the rub. The new convert should have been looking inward and upward, not outward and downward. His first obligation was to concern himself with his own spiritual life, not to create little marvels of philosophical or rhetorical invention, even in hopes of serving others' spiritual well-being.[4] He himself had to fear the temptations of pride, especially intellectual pride.[5] His use of secular materials, susceptible to misuse, increased the spiritual danger.[6]

Pascal As a Reader of Epictetus

Consider briefly Pascal's claims to have found truths if not the Truth in the works of the philosophers. He recommends Epictetus highly as a teacher of "man's duties" (par. 11–14). In so doing, he effectively rewrites the philosophical text that he purports to read. Although neither his nominal auditor nor later scholars have objected, this rewriting is fundamental. In paragraph 11, Pascal adapts Epictetus' Stoicism to the dictates of an Augustinian Christianity. The Greek philosopher (and his French translator) had made piety a matter of right "opinion," an affair of the head and not the heart. Pascal's adaptation substitutes the crucial term "object," making the heart and not the head capital, so to speak. What matters most is not our pitiful judgment on the wisdom of divine Providence in the disposition of human affairs; what matters is our choice between the Two Loves.[7]

Having so baptized the pagan philosopher, Pascal quickly adapted passages from his Epictetus concerning just three moral duties. The first duty, the "philosophical" acceptance of loss, is particularly interesting to the historian of Pascal's affective life. In the brief *Manual,* Epictetus had returned to this theme repeatedly, in chapters 3, 7, 11,

14, 15, 16, 18, and 26. Perhaps for the scriptural resonance of its language, Pascal selected and adapted a passage from Epictetus' chapter 11:[8]

> Never say, "I lost it." Rather, say, "I gave it back. My child is dead; I gave him back. My wife is dead; I gave her back." And so with respect to property and everything else . . . While he allows you to use it, care for it as for something belonging to someone else, behaving like a traveler at an inn. (par. 11)

This first duty, which prohibits grieving after losses or even love with attachment, relates directly to Pascal's loss of his father and separation from his beloved sister. This, in turn, suggests that either the *Entretien* was intentionally self-referential or Pascal unintentionally generalized his own recent experience as a lesson for others.

The second duty, the philosophical acceptance of death, is relatively uncomplicated in the saying if not the living. Pascal followed his philosophical source very closely (*Entretien,* par. 12; *Manual,* chap. 17 and 21). Life is a comedy; we must play our parts; the curtain will fall. Pascal's determination to accept his own mortality makes particularly good historical sense. His illness was already one of the great facts of his life. In early December, Jacqueline had reported to Gilberte that his health was "worse than it had been for a long time." In mid-January, she exhorted him in a paragraph on the "great advantage" of his ill health, which was still bad enough to suggest a form of penance imposed by God Himself.[9]

The third duty, a philosophical modesty in the guise of a more properly spiritual humility, again shows Pascal's adaptation of Stoic thought to meet the very different standards imposed by Christian belief. Where the pagan had wanted the admiration of men, the Christian wants humility before God. Rather than reading Epictetus, Pascal reads *into* Epictetus.[10] This third duty, too, reflects his past experience and present situation. As a savant, he had displayed a penchant for the spectacular: Thinking Machines of brass, ivory, and ebony exhibited before the prince de Condé, dedicated to Chancellor Séguier, and donated to Queen Christina; Vacuum Experiments performed in public with mercury-filled glass tubes twelve and even fifteen feet long, wine-filled glass tubes a scarcely credible forty-six feet long, more conventional tubes most unconventionally carried up the puy de Dôme, and so on.[11] As a new convert, he now guarded his "secret." He folded up, wrapped up, and sewed up his *Mémorial,* apparently without telling even Jacqueline; he withheld even the humbler facts of his conversion from even Gilberte; he retreated from even his closest friend into the desert of the Solitaries; and, of course, he turned away from other mathematicians and scientists.[12]

He turned to his God and his director. It is important that the Pascal who finds lessons on humility in his reading of the *Manual* also faults Epictetus for his pride in the *Discourses* (par. 14, 32–34, and 38). Nevertheless, from Sacy's perspective, Pascal's qualification could hardly have redeemed the pagan philosopher as a teacher of man's duties. It is a peculiarity of Fontaine's "conversation" that his Sacy does not comment on his Pascal's partially Christianized Stoicism, as such. As it happens, Epictetus was not the only ancient author of a *Manual* or *Enchiridion;* Augustine had written another. A detailed inventory of Sacy's great library survives, and it shows that the former was missing from his shelves: no Epictetus in Greek, Latin, or French, no modern exposition or adaptation. But Augustine . . . Sacy had at hand not only the Latin *Opera* in great folios, set after handsome set, but also a bilingual *Manuel* in a more convenient octavo, recently published by the great theologian of Port-Royal, Sacy's Little Uncle, Antoine Arnauld.[13] These learned neo-Augustinians, for whom neo-Stoicism was a closed book or none at all, knew that man's duties must depend on principles of Faith, Hope, and Charity.[14]

Even as translated by Jean Goulu, popularized by Guillaume Du Vair, and adapted by Pascal, Epictetus' alternative one-two-three is premised on erroneous notions of man without the history of the Fall and God without the promise of Redemption. The theology taught in *the Manual,* Augustine's, requires a displacement of self for the love of God, while the philosophy taught in the other *Manual,* Epictetus', serves pride without allowing for this higher love. Pascal papered over this all-important difference when he converted the pagan philosopher's proud boast to raise his head as "a friend of God" into a quasi-Christianized claim to be able "to love God" (par. 14).[15]

Why did Pascal lay his Epictetus on Sacy's table? Even if we were to accept Fontaine's dubious explanation, that this priest invited this "philosopher" to talk philosophy, we would have to account for Pascal's choice of this author. It is tempting to speculate that his appreciation of the once modish neo-Stoic philosophy along with his copy of Epictetus in Goulu's rather dated translation (first published in 1609 and last reprinted in 1630) had come to him, along with almost everything else, from his late father. The best-known Christian popularizer of Epictetus, Du Vair, had been another son of Clermont and another magistrate, whose great vogue had coincided with Étienne's adult life.[16] In any case, Epictetus was a high-minded moralist with useful lessons to teach, first among them, the acceptance of loss.

Pascal As a Reader of Montaigne

Even older contemporaries like the Chevalier de Méré considered Du Vair's work to be passé, and they faulted Pascal for not knowing any better than to admire its style and substance.[17] In their opinion, the work from the 1580s and 1590s that still merited attention was Montaigne's *Essais*. They seem to have had little trouble in making a convert; Pascal was to make this book his own.[18] His sympathetic summation of Montaigne's skepticism in the *Entretien* is familiar and generally unproblematical. In Fontaine's text, he refers to specific passages and general themes from various Essays, including especially the "Apologie de Raimond Sebond" (bk. II, chap. 12) and "De l'expérience" (bk. III, chap. 13).[19] It is easy enough to explain the particular appeal of the long essay in which Montaigne attacks the pretensions of human reason and so serves his Catholic faith. In the *Entretien,* Pascal renews this attack on the same enemy for the same high-minded purpose. But there may be more to it.

Pascal's exposition of the case that a Christian could make for Montaigne (par. 15–22 and 27) relates to his own emotional life in several ways. First, its review of the Essayist's Pyrrhonism is remarkably joyous and very aggressive:

> I confess that I can't restrain my joy in this author, when I see proud reason so badly bruised by the irresistible blows of its own arms, the bloody conflict of man against man precipitating him from the company of God into which he would raise himself by his ["philosophical"] maxims, [and debasing him] to natural level of the beasts. (par. 27)

Pascal *rejoices.* Why? His Montaigne *bruises* proud reason when his philosophical skepticism denounces philosophical dogmatism, and he *fells* it when he shows thinkers of all sorts opposing one another, philosopher against philosopher, school against school. This is a "great vengeance" and "useful humiliation" (par. 27).

Second, Pascal's appropriation of Montaigne, like his appropriation of Epictetus, left him with a very personal and at least implicitly self-referential reading.[20] Pascal had been acclaimed as a mathematician and savant, if not as a philosopher, properly speaking, and he was then a new convert submitting himself as well as his thinking and writing to the priest who was responsible to God for his spiritual direction. What was wanted? Penitence and not vengeance, humility and not humiliation.

By 1655, it should have been perfectly clear to Pascal that Montaigne had failed to consider adequately the potential of mathematical and scientific knowledge.[21] Nevertheless, the young savant manfully turned his own arms against the sort of intellectual endeavor with which he had been most closely identified, explicitly exaggerating the humanist's profundity and implicitly limiting his former self to mathematical shallows. Montaigne's whole argument for the uncertainty of that most certain science, geometry, consists of his very brief report that a friend had said that he could demonstrate that two lines could not intersect, no matter how far extended, although the eye could see that they would do so. For the purposes of the *Entretien,* Pascal retraced and extended this "line of argument," claiming that the Essayist had "demonstrated" the uncertainty even of the very axioms of geometry—and almost everything else.[22] The Pascal who read, remembered, and appropriated Montaigne in this way at this time was more the penitent than the philosopher or proto-apologist. This text stops well short of confession or contrition, but it does represent a turning away from the mathematics in which he had taken such pride.

Third, in his review of Montaigne's attack on proud reason, Pascal did not follow every meander of his source. He did recall particularly good material from the Essayist's wonderful carnival of animals and from his more serious exposition of Pyrrhonism. However, he made no reference to the substantial and overtly religious pages between these two sections of the "Apologie," pages arguing that man's intelligence and learning cannot make him happy. That is, even while hitting thinkers over their heads again and again for their pretension and their ignorance, the Pascal of the *Entretien* missed an opportunity to batter them with the body blows of their unhappiness. In the elevated season after his Second Conversion, his Montaigne taught men to doubt their dignity and their intelligence, not to lament their misery.

Indeed, in 1655 his Montaigne was cheerful to a fault. Having praised the humanist as a Pyrrhonian, Pascal turned against him as an Epicurean:

> There isn't anything extravagant in his conduct; he behaves just like anyone else, and all that others do in the foolish conviction that they are following the true good, he does following another principle, namely, that the probabilities are about the same one way or the other. . . . Therefore, he follows the ways of his country, custom carrying him along. . . . Therefore, he utterly rejects that stoic virtue that others portray with a severe countenance and an unsociable look. . . . His [demeanor is contrarily] easy, informal, pleasant, cheerful, even sportive. He goes the way that seems more enjoyable and chats casually about events, good and bad. He relaxes on the soft bosom of a tranquil indolence, showing others who take so many pains to seek felicity that it can be found where it rests and that ignorance and incuriosity are two pillows for a well made head. (par. 28–29)[23]

Taken on its own merits, this would be a very poor reading of the *Essais*—aggressive, reductionistic, and willfully blind to Montaigne's moral preoccupations.[24] Pascal read Epictetus and Montaigne in his own way and passed summary judgment on their partial truths (moral duties and intellectual doubt) and countervailing errors (intellectual pride and amoral laxity). Then he explained to Sacy how he could serve religious purposes by reading the two philosophers together. It is for this bold juxtaposition that the *Entretien* is justly celebrated. Something very similar was to be fundamental to the *Pensées*.

The great antinomy of *grandeur/misère* that Pascal was later to develop more fully in Pensée 149 first appears in the *Entretien:*

> It seems to me that the source of the errors of these two sects is not to have known that the human condition at present differs from that at its creation. Thus, one [Epictetus], noticing some signs of *man's first grandeur* but ignoring his corruption, has regarded human nature as healthy and in no need of redemption, which has led him to the summits of pride. The other [Montaigne], experiencing *his present misery* but ignoring his first dignity, has regarded human nature as necessarily infirm and irredeemable, which precipitates him into despair at ever achieving the true good and leaves him in an extreme abasement. (par. 32; emphasis mine)

Pascal goes on to say that the two philosophies are mutually destructive rather than complementary. Christianity alone can teach the Truth about human nature, created good but fallen into sin. And Christianity alone preaches the God-man who is proper for such creatures of *grandeur* and *misère*.

Grandeur/misère, introduced in the *Entretien* but used only once in that text, was to have a great future in the *Pensées,* but in 1655 Pascal had not settled upon any one formulation of his antinomy. *Grandeur/foiblesse* seems to be an equivalent, used three times in rapid succession (par. 33–35), and it lacks the affective overtones of the alternative. "Weakness" also fits Pascal's more detailed exposition of Epictetus and Montaigne in a way that "misery," in its primary psychological meaning, does not. Montaigne as read by Pascal in 1655 *is a weakling,* good in that he knows his own and others' ignorance but bad in that he is morally lax and seemingly unperturbed by his sinfulness. He *is not unhappy,* a sufferer. Quite the contrary: he has found felicity, resting his well-made head on pillows of ignorance and incuriosity (par. 29).

Sacy As a Reader of Augustine

Pascal had submitted a coherent exposition, offering *his* case for a Christian rereading of Epictetus and Montaigne *together.* It would not have been novel or remarkable for an early- or even mid-seventeenth-century Frenchman to have found reinforcement, even spiritual reinforcement, from either the *Manual* or the "Apologie" read separately. Epictetus had been baptized, so to speak, by two worthies, Guillaume Du Vair and Jean Goulu. Du Vair is now forgotten, but even in his youth he had published other pious works, including *Méditations sur les Psaumes de la Pénitance,* and he had ended his life as the Bishop of Lisieux and one of the great dignitaries of the Kingdom. As for Goulu and the Epictetus on Pascal's table, Saint François de Sales had offered recommendation enough:

> Above all, I admire that poor but good man Epictetus, whose *Discourses* and *Manual* make such good reading in the recent translation from the learned and graceful hand of the Reverend Father Dom Jean de Saint-François [Goulu], Provincial of the Feuillants of France. . . . One would take him for a Christian.[25]

Montaigne interests Pascal's readers more, as he interested Pascal more. His orthodoxy had yet to be questioned. Pope Gregory XIII had literally blessed him not once but six times, the customary three times as he approached the Papal throne and three times as he withdrew from a private audience. Gregory's Master of the Sacred Palace, Sisto Fabri, then a professor of theology at the University of Rome and later General of the Dominicans, had supervised an exhaustive examination of the *Essais* before adding his figurative blessing on the book.[26] At the height of the Counter-Reformation and in the center of Christendom, the Roman theologians found absolutely nothing to question in the Pyrrhonian "Apologie" that Pascal recommended to Sacy. It was only later that Pascal himself would turn decisively against Montaigne and attempt to convince others that the *Essais* were dangerous reading.[27]

At Port-Royal in 1655, Pascal's own spiritual state was the prior question, not the effects, good or bad, of worldly readings. This penitent was already particularly suspect as prideful even before he submitted his exposition to his director.[28] Perhaps this is the place to remark that in his magnificent thousand-volume library, the priest did not possess a copy of Montaigne's *Essais* any more than Epictetus' *Manual* or, for that matter, the other works to which Pascal incidentally and perhaps accidentally alludes, Descartes's *Meditations* and Charron's *Sagesse*.[29]

Pascal argued that he had discovered a novel way to benefit (other) worldlings by the "regulated" or, perhaps more properly, *directed* readings of the philosophers (par. 38). Of course, the new convert was not a director; he had come to be directed. Historically and spiritually, the last word on his contributions to the *Entretien* belongs neither to the penitent himself (par. 37–38) nor to the uncritical memoirist (par. 39–40) but to Sacy and his spiritual authorities, especially Augustine. We could easily add Thomas à Kempis and the abbé de Saint-Cyran.

Sacy's abbreviated "first speech" and Augustine's *Confessions* together provide the best evidence on the historical Sacy's "last word." Pascal may have wanted to talk about his reading of Epictetus and Montaigne; Sacy responded with *his* reading of *Augustine*. He had nothing to say about philosophical works that he did not possess; he gives no sign of having read them or wanting to read them. Rather, he challenged the still proud intellectual with a greater teacher of a higher wisdom. His part in this pseudoconversation was to discuss his reading of *Pascal* in the light of his reading of *Augustine*. The problem at hand was not book learning or abstract philosophy or Christian apologetics; it was the immortal soul of a particular penitent.

The exact form of Sacy's written response to Pascal's exposition is unknown, but the content is recoverable. Courcelle's researches have identified the passages from Augustine that his disciple brought to bear on the particular case. The task now is to consider the significance of Sacy's selections for Pascal in January 1655. The numbering of the following reminiscences is Courcelle's; unbracketed material in block form is Sacy's from Fontaine; bracketed words summarize or quote extended passages from Augustine, which are often more telling than the abbreviated paraphrases in Fontaine (par. 23–24) and always well within the reach of Sacy's memory:

1. *Confessions,* V, 4, recalled in *Entretien,* par. 23.
   [The young Augustine had remembered his philosophical studies and, with mathematics and observation, used them to refute erroneous teachings of Manes.] But, Lord God of truth, do those who know these subtleties of reasoning please you the more on that account?
2. *Confessions,* IV, 16, recalled in *Entretien,* par. 23.
   [The young Augustine had by himself read and understood Aristotle's *Categories* and then, proudly, tried to use them to categorize the God of Abraham. "My thoughts of you were falsehood and not truth, fictions of my misery and not realities of your blessedness."]
3. *Letters,* 231, 6, recalled in *Entretien,* par. 24.
   [The old Augustine has been praised in a letter from Darius, a celebrity whom he has not met. He welcomes the friendship of a believer but refers all praise to God. With the words quoted, he sends the *Confessions,* wherein Darius may] contemplate and see [his sins.]
4. *Confessions,* VII, 20, recalled in *Entretien,* par. 24.
   ["After reading these books of the Platonists . . . I talked away as if I were a finished scholar, but, if I had not sought the way to you in Christ our Saviour, it is my soul that would have been finished. For I had begun to want the reputation of a wise man . . . ; I was merely puffed up with my knowledge. Where was the charity that builds from] the foundation of humility and piety? [. . . Humility was not a subject which those books would ever have taught me. . . . Later, tamed by your books, . . . I saw clearly what the difference is between presumption and confession."]

Sacy was very intelligent and deeply learned, especially in the works of Augustine, whose *Confessions* he carried in his pocket, contemplated in his mind, and cherished in his heart. Singlin must have informed him of Pascal's spiritual progress and continued needs. The more bookish—and equally humble—Sacy hit upon a brilliant strategy as the surrogate director of this rather headstrong new convert. He cited a series of passages in which he implicitly compared Pascal *after* what we call the Second Conversion to Augustine *before* that true Saint's more perfect conversion. There could have been no more inspiring example, no more authoritative teacher.

Sacy's Augustinian lesson concerned the fact of intellectual pride and the ideal of spiritual humility. The illustrious Pascal *had* shown himself in his expositions of Epictetus and Montaigne to be perfectly capable of formally correct attitudes about the range and power of the human mind. He had censured Epictetus' philosophical presumptions and praised Montaigne's philosophical Pyrrhonism. All of this was at least implicitly self-referential and self-critical. But, judging from Fontaine's materials, Pascal *had not* shown any awareness that his own elegant little exercise of philosophical rereadings was itself intellectually prideful in its sweeping reduction of all past thought to two "sects" and, for that matter, its dubious representation of Montaigne as a sectarian agnostic (par. 30). Worse, Pascal *had not* shown any awareness that his recommendation of combined readings of the opposed philosophies for apologetic purposes was spiritually prideful (par. 37–38). What Jacqueline quite carefully called his "*more* permissible jeux d'esprit" *were not* perfectly innocent or spiritually desirable for a penitent whose own salvation was not assured.[30]

Sacy's message was severe, but his manner was gentle. He referred Pascal to Augustine, leaving it to the convert to see the personal relevance of what the Father had said about his own enthusiasm for the philosophical skepticism of the Academy before his own conversion. It applied not just to Montaigne as a sometime enthusiast for the skepticism of Pyrrho but also to Pascal himself, who shows such an interest in the skepticism of Montaigne even after his Second Conversion (Mesnard's notes to par. 24; Courcelle's parallels 5–7). In the following passage from Fontaine's abbreviated "first speech," which alone mentions "conversion," the "et cetera" is especially intriguing. Was it Fontaine's or Sacy's own? In either case, Pascal was summoned "to take and read":

> I don't condemn that author's intelligence, which is a great gift of God, but he could have made a better use of it and sacrificed it to God rather than the Devil. What's the use of a good when we use it so badly? *Quid proderat* etc., as the saintly Father said about it before his conversion. (*Entretien,* par. 24)

> [*Confessions,* IV, 16: *What good* did it do me that . . . I read and understood for myself every book? . . . I had my back to the light and my face to the things on which the light shone. . . . Without an instructor, I could quite easily understand every book on rhetoric or logic, geometry, music, and arithmetic. . . . But I did not use these gifts by sacrificing them to you. And so it all turned more to my destruction than to my profit. . . ."]

Sacy then recalled passages from the *Confessions* on the last obstacles to Augustine's conversion, the "vanities" that he had yet to sacrifice (*Entretien,* par. 25). Then he pulled down from the shelves of the great library in his mind *the* Book for a pertinent citation:

> Col. 2:8 Beware lest any man spoil you through philosophy and vain deceit, after the tradition of men, after the rudiments of the world, and not after Christ.

How hollow, after this, are Fontaine's assurances of a happy agreement between Sacy and Pascal on the spiritual usefulness of philosophical readings (par. 36 and 39)! How unfaithful it was for the priest's former secretary not to realize that his Paul, his Augustine, his Thomas à Kempis, and his Saint-Cyran had already passed judgment on Pascal's brilliant but spiritually unfortunate exercise![31] How simplistic and anachronistic it still is for us to suppose that Pascal's life had swung at the Second Conversion as if on a hinge, closing him off from sin and opening his way to save others!

Whatever Fontaine's assertions to the contrary, Pascal had already read widely in the works of Sacy's master, Augustine.[32] Why, then, did he venture this rereading of Epictetus and Montaigne, and why did he thrust it at his spiritual director?[33] One possibility is that the Old Adam still lurked deep within the new convert. Another is that, also deep within, the energy, volubility, self-confidence, aggressiveness, and something like risk taking represented by the exercise submitted to Sacy were related to the exceptionally gay, cheerful, and joyous spirits that so struck Jacqueline.[34]

CHAPTER II

The *Provinciales* I

Shrewd critics warn against a facile identification of Blaise Pascal with any of the personages invented for the *Provinciales,* even "Louis de Montalte."[1] A literary discourse called Montalte into his pseudobeing as a pseudonym.[2] The true author did not properly sign the eighteen pamphlets with any name, true or false. "Montalte" first appeared in print on the title page of the first edition of the collected letters—in the good company of an imaginary addressee and an imaginary printer.[3] Nevertheless, there was a man behind this extraordinary work, and his discourse expresses his "nature." Pascal knew this and, in the privacy of his chambers, proclaimed it (Pensées 675 and 745).[4]

E.A.A.B.P.A.F.D.E.P. and the Arnauld Affair

Pascal did sign his Third Letter in his own way, with a wonderful string of ten initials: "E.A.A.B.P.A.F.D.E.P."[5] The success of this disguise depended in part on the very length of the string, which has a comic effect in its own right, compared, say, to the soberly restrained signature on his earlier printed work: "le sieur B.P."[6] Success also depended on first arousing and then frustrating the curiosity of seventeenth-century readers who expected a man to qualify himself by his rank, estates, and corporate affiliations, which might totally eclipse both given name and family name, as in the case of

Antoine Gombaud, who presented himself for his own and others' admiration as the chevalier de Méré and who referred in print to Artus Gouffier, le duc de Roannez, as "L.D.D.R." or "D.D.R."[7] In this world of artifice, Pascal confounded the curious by initialing his own name, his true homeland, and his actual filial identity: "Blaise Pascal auvergnat, fils d'Étienne Pascal."[8]

Finally, success depended on the first three initials, "E.A.A." The most respected recent editors have preferred the reading "et ancien ami," taken as an exceptional extension of the conventional complimentary closing, "your very humble and very obedient servant," which is itself almost a joke at the end of a clandestine pamphlet in which anyone but a partisan might have seen proud defiance of the Pope, the Chancellor, and the Faculty of Theology.[9] I prefer an alternative reading, which also has seventeenth-century support: "et Antoine Arnauld."[10] Pascal and Arnauld lodged together at the beginning of their polemical campaign, and the most authoritative source on the collaboration says that the Doctor "planned, reviewed, and polished" all of the Letters.[11] Pascal made especially heavy use of Arnauld's prior writings in the Third, which is devoted to his censure.[12] The last trick of the disguise so interpreted would be the inversion of "Pascal-and-Arnauld" so as to leave "and-Arnauld-Pascal."[13]

"B.P.A.F.D.E.P." must come first. The shadowy figure of Étienne Pascal lurks behind Blaise's anti-Jesuit polemics, even as he also preceded his son's mathematics and physics. Gilberte reports that her father taught his children one maxim on the subject of religion: "All that is the object of faith cannot be the object of reason."[14] Étienne himself probably first understood this as a corollary of Cartesian rationalism. Descartes's *Discourse* (1637) carefully set aside the Faith as something beyond his reason, then as carefully distinguished God and the soul from the material objects of scientific inquiry. In the years after Galileo's trial, he was probably more concerned to protect savants from Churchmen than to guard religious truths from rational doubts. After their conversions, the Pascals reversed this; now, the danger was that proud reasoners within the Church would doubt away the traditional truths of Augustinian theology and corrupt the Christian values of a scriptural morality.

Even before the conversions of 1646, Étienne may have opposed the Jesuits. We do know that his closest brother Blaise was one of the most aggressive defenders of local interests in 1630–31, when the Edict of Union ordered the closing of the municipal *collège* in Clermont and authorized in its stead the foundation of a Jesuit *collège* in Montferrand.[15] We know that the new *collège* was to have been housed in the old *palais* of Étienne's Cour des Aides and that the city renovated the building at great cost before a delegation of Jesuits including François Annat pronounced it unsatisfactory and demanded other quarters at much greater cost.[16] And we know that, unlike other fathers of his class who entrusted their sons to the Jesuits, Étienne schooled his son at home even in Paris, an extraordinary decision that may reflect in part a temper hardened and sharpened in the politics of his native Clermont.[17]

Etienne's most important known writing is a scathing attack on a Jesuit, the Rector of the Collège de Clermont in Paris, Étienne Noël. This vehemence of his attack is as interesting as the correctness of his defense of his own theories and his son's Vacuum Experiments.[18] Somewhat similarly, father and son were allied against the Jesuits after a Montferrand thesis hostile to Blaise's work on the vacuum had been dedicated to the *premier président* of Étienne's old court by Jean-Paul Médaille, S.J. The dedicatee clearly assumed that Étienne and not Blaise was the prime mover in the ensuing controversy, and Blaise in response acknowledged his father's participation if not initiative (1651).[19] All of this suggests a paternal precedent for the antipathy to Jesuits later shown by the younger Pascal.

Now "E.A.A." Pascal's Letters 1–4 concern the theology of grace. They were occasioned by the Arnauld Affair, itself an episode in the sad history of the controversies surrounding Cornelius Jansenius's *Augustinus* (1640). Very briefly, French opponents of this posthumous work considered that its doctrine of grace, reduced to five summary propositions, was heretical.[20] They submitted the Five Propositions to Rome for judgment, and in the Bull *Cum occasione* (1653), Innocent X condemned them, forbidding Christians to believe them or teach them.[21]

Unfortunately, this Constitution left unresolved what became known as the Question of Fact and left undefined even the heresy that it condemned, let alone the orthodoxy that it reaffirmed, raising the Question of Right. With respect to the Fact, it merely implied that the Five Propositions were derived from Jansenius's *Augustinus;*

it did not state this unequivocally, much less cite specific passages. This allowed Jansenists to defend the *Augustinus* even while formally submitting to the Pope. With respect to the Right, the Bull merely restated the Propositions without explanation other than the briefest possible statement of the "sense" in which the last was heretical. This had the unintended effect of encouraging self-styled "Friends of the Truth" to defend the Propositions in other senses as orthodox.[22]

The obstinacy of the Jansenists outraged their opponents, who moved against Antoine Arnauld in the course of 1655. In his *Seconde Lettre à un Duc et Pair,* they managed to find another five propositions, which also involved questions of fact and right. In the first four offending passages, Arnauld publicly and repeatedly questioned *the* Fact, defending Jansenius by denying that the original Five Propositions had been drawn from the *Augustinus.*[23] In the fifth, Arnauld counterattacked courageously but perhaps foolishly, arguing that the Holy Father was fallible.[24]

In November 1655, the Sorbonne began a formal investigation. Louis XIV was still in his teens and not much concerned with the recriminations of the Doctors, and even Mazarin was uninterested in the theological questions, as such. However, for reasons of state, the Cardinal was determined to please the Pope.[25] Furthermore, the Queen Mother was outspokenly hostile to the Jansenists, and Chancellor Séguier was also a very powerful and determined opponent, to the extent that he irregularly intervened to chair sessions of the Faculty.[26] For the occasion, the membership was packed and freedom of expression was curtailed. Rather than appearing before his enemies on the terms that they offered, Arnauld went into hiding. In these circumstances, a majority condemned him with respect to the Question of Fact (14 January 1656) and proceeded to debate the Question of Right (18 January), tending inexorably toward the eventual condemnation on that issue (29 January).[27]

Letters 1–4 and the Écrits sur la grâce

Enter Pascal. Pierre Nicole left an authoritative account of his "entrance" late in the debate on the Question of Right:

> Someone [Nicole himself?] said that the thing to do was to publish a sort of pamphlet to explain that these disputes didn't concern anything important

> or serious; it was a question of mere words and pure chicanery, concerning nothing but equivocal terms that they didn't care to explain. Everyone agreed that this was the best plan, but no one volunteered to carry it out.
>
> Then Montalte, who hadn't yet written much of anything and who had no idea how successful he would be, said that he had a good idea how to put together such a pamphlet but that he could only promise a draft for someone else to polish and prepare for publication. And that's how it all began. . . . As promised, he set to work the next day, but instead of a draft, he dashed off the First Letter itself, just as we have it. He showed it to a friend [Arnauld?] who judged it fit to print right away, and that's what was done.[28]

Pascal's First Letter was dated 23 January, and it appeared in print four days later. It was a great success with laymen as well as theologians. Pascal had discovered an unsuspected talent to arouse, amuse, and instruct the worldly. The Second (dated 29 January), Third (9 February), and Fourth (25 February) followed "almost as quickly," to be met with ever greater applause.

Nicole's preface for the *Provinciales,* Pascal's Pensées on Montalte's "natural style," and the tone of the Letters themselves could lull readers into the false impression that, just as "the disputes didn't concern anything important or serious," so, too, the Letters did not require much more than a gifted hand with a light touch—and others' knowledge and ideas. However, Mesnard's thorough reconsideration of the opuscule *De l'esprit géométrique* and fundamental reconstruction of the *Écrits sur la grâce* now make it clear how much thought Pascal himself had already given to relevant issues of style and substance, too. His success was not borrowed and did not just happen.

With respect to content, it is especially impressive that within the year after he had been gently chided for having represented Epictetus and Montaigne to the priest Sacy, *he* was prepared to represent *Augustine* to other laymen confused by the controversies of the theologians. Pascal's *Lettre sur la possibilité des commandements* (the first of his *Écrits sur la grâce*) was drafted in the fall of 1655.[29] His working library included recent technical literature as well as various relevant books from the time of his earlier fervor.[30]

The problems of grace were personal as well as theoretical; they concerned not only the intended reader of the first *Écrit,* apparently the duc de Roannez, but also Pascal himself. One question in particular struck home, that of whether the Just could obey the Commandments. The First of the Five Propositions condemned in 1653 concerned the power of the believer *to persevere* and the contrary willingness of God *to withdraw*. Pascal's question for himself was this: Do I have the power truly to pray for God's grace? To continue to pray for continued graces? If so, asking, I shall receive, as promised in the Scriptures. But if not, if I lack this power and if, unasked, God leaves me unaided, I will not pray and He will abandon me.

Pascal was the convert of 1646 who had relapsed, then reconverted in 1654. In the drafts of the *Écrits* from 1655, he seems obsessed by the problems of man's impotence to persevere and God's "double *délaissement*." In so many words, here radically reduced and personalized, he says: "He withdraws from me, so I quit Him, and He abandons me."[31] Pascal appears guilty about his past infidelity and anxious about his future capacity to persevere. Jacqueline's great letter of 25 January 1655 emphasizes the pitiful state in which he had approached her in the autumn with this confession of God's withdrawal:

> [Blaise] felt that God had so completely abandoned him that He no longer attracted him. Although he was making every effort within the limits of his powers, he realized that it was more his reason and his own spirit that was moving him to do what was best, not any movement from God [attracting him by grace].[32]

Pascal's personal investment in the issue of man's powerlessness and the theology of the double *délaissement* also makes sense in a way that is historically prior and psychologically deeper. This has to do with his experience of separation and loss, which profoundly affected his spiritual life, as argued above: "They leave me, and I am powerless to keep them." There was also a double delectation after the double *délaissement:* "They loved me in the ways of the flesh and love me still, more truly and more securely, in the ways of the spirit."

The ways of the Two Loves are mysterious, but Blaise's love of Jacqueline as well as of God is active in the *Provinciales*. It had been she who had directed him at Port-Royal toward his Second Conversion. She was the one who had referred him to Singlin and, in turn, de Sacy and apparently Arnauld, too. And her convent as well as Arnauld's theology was under attack in 1656. "Montalte" never mentions her in the Letters, of course, and his defense of Port-Royal is explicit only in Letters 16–17. Nevertheless, Pascal fought the entire campaign for his sister, her community, and its truths.[33]

To suggest affective resonance is not to deny literary intelligence or theological substance. Pascal was ready to answer the claimants of man's "proximate power" and "sufficient grace" in Letters 1–2. He was ready philosophically and rhetorically, because his *De l'esprit géométrique* had led him to reflect systematically on the need for rigorous definition and calculated pleasing.[34] He was ready theologically, too, because his preparations for the *Écrits* had led him steadily toward a rejection of these notions.[35] His Letters failed to save Arnauld in the Sorbonne, but they did succeed in the world by presenting his opponents as partisans who abused the language as well as the Faith by their willful ambiguities, powerless "powers," and insufficient "sufficiency."

In Letter 3, Pascal's bon mot on the Question of Right is justly celebrated: "The heresy isn't a matter of M. Arnauld's opinions; it's his person. This is a personal heresy."[36] This seems true enough, with the significant qualification that the "heretic" was not truly autonomous or historically solitary. Antoine Arnauld the Doctor was the son of Antoine Arnauld the Advocate, who had argued passionately on behalf of the University of Paris and against the Society of Jesus in a celebrated *Plaidoyer* (1594).[37] The Jesuits had been expelled from the Kingdom later that year. Wits called the Advocate's diatribe "the original sin of the Arnaulds." The elder Antoine (1560–1619) died when the younger (1612–94), the twentieth of twenty children, was still a boy, but this boy imbibed partisan fervor from his mother and her family, too; on her deathbed at Port-Royal in 1641, Catherine de Sainte-Félicité Arnauld, née Marion, exhorted him to remember his whole life long that he had sworn "to defend the Truth, if necessary with his life's blood."[38] She need not have worried.

Somewhat similarly, Pascal's faith was a "personal faith." He shared it with his sisters and his brother-in-law and defended it with his own passion. Letters 1–4 required a measure of theological competence and great persuasive powers. After a year of reading and reflection, Pascal could offer both. The *Provinciales* also required other qualities that are not strictly intellectual or even spiritual. I count these five:

1. irrepressibly high spirits in desperate circumstances;
2. a capacity for anger and a taste for combat;
3. wholly exceptional energy;
4. boundless self-confidence;
5. a reckless willingness to take risks.

These combined qualities, all strengths for the pamphleteer, suggest the hypomanic syndrome.[39] Pascal had not always been so spirited, so angry, so energetic, so self-confident, and so reckless in earlier years and would not be so in later years.

The Persecution of 1656 and the Miracle of the Thorn

Pascal's redirection of the *Provinciales* from a desperate defense to an aggressive attack was fateful; Nicole provides testimony that the decision was his own, not his collaborators'. But circumstances do help to explain it. I reconsider the situation in the late winter of 1656 from the perspectives of the Arnaulds, Antoine the Doctor, and Angélique the Mother Superior.

As the Sorbonne was concluding its deliberations and voting on the censure, Antoine went into hiding with a modest Parisian family. The Doctor's "extraordinary gaiety," reported on the day of the second censure, must have been tempered by the firm belief that men's errors had triumphed at least momentarily over God's Truths. The Censure had "opened the door to every imaginable persecution." The *Journal* of the sieur de Saint-Gilles, apparently commissioned by Arnauld himself, rumbles ominously and continuously with the expectation of "all sorts of distressing events" and "new acts of violence" and "fearful persecutions" and "terrible storms."[40]

At the Sorbonne, Arnauld's name was struck from the ranks of the Faculty, and other members had to subscribe to the censure on pain of expulsion. Most did so, a painful fact, and those who did not suffered the consequences.[41] Printing shops known to be sympathetic and suspected of work on the clandestine *Provinciales* were raided with all the arbitrariness and ineffectiveness of the Old Regime. In the most startling incident, the printer Savreux, two assistants, *and* his wife were arrested, imprisoned, and interrogated. Spies were thought to be everywhere.[42] And behind the rigors of the Faculty and the *Librairie* loomed the figure of the Chancellor. Séguier, the one-time patron of the Pascals, was now so enraged at the Letters that he had to be bled seven times in five or six days, or so they said. Such news might have been satisfying; it was also alarming.[43]

There was worse. Port-Royalist intelligence indicated that Pope Alexander VII was determined to disperse the remaining Solitaries and that Cardinal Mazarin was ready oblige him. By the beginning of March, Church and State seemed to contest perversely for the honor of repressing the Friends of the Truth. On the one hand, the Pope was reported to be so hostile that "there was every reason to fear, none to hope"; on the other hand, the Cardinal was so eager to please him that he offered "to destroy the Jansenists, particularly those of Port-Royal."[44]

> And so the persecution of this holy community and those who defend the Truth approaches, day by day. . . . I do believe that Demons conspire with men to bring great suffering down upon those persons who have found refuge in and around the two houses [of Port-Royal].[45]

Rumors added the municipality of Paris and the Assembly of the Clergy to the list of enemies.[46] The Queen was hostile, even violent; she was reported to have told two Jesuits:

> [I]t was the strength of their cause [and not her support] that had won the victory [in the Sorbonne]. They added that it was up to her to complete what she had so well begun and that it was intolerable after the celebrated censure that such strange sorts should be tolerated at Port-Royal des Champs. She answered that it was as good as done, and that nothing would be left but the walls.

The pious courtier who had presented the two priests responded that Port-Royal was infected and should be burned.[47]

In mid-March, the remaining Jansenist priests on the staff of Saint-Merri, the old family parish of the Arnaulds and the Pascals, were forbidden to perform clerical functions; the two most prominent were forced into exile. Then emissaries from the Queen informed Arnauld d'Andilly, an old client, that the Solitaries could avoid the humiliation of being driven away by armed force only if they would leave voluntarily—and immediately. They complied. Refugees told pitiful tales of the exodus, emphasizing the pathos for the children of the Little Schools. The date was 20 March, the date also given Pascal's Fifth Letter; it was only on 30 March that the collaborators decided to circulate it, being forced to act by a raid on the shop of the printer Langlois.[48] Thus, to the little band of refugees in hiding with Arnauld the Doctor, things looked darkest just when Pascal began his most brilliant letters.

Mère Angélique's correspondence shows how the guiding spirit of the community proper saw the situation. First, persecution: Angélique acknowledged the threat. On 10 March, she reported rumors that enemies wanted to disperse the nuns, too. She would have liked to discount them, but even she spread the rumors with pungent commentary: "They are progressing nicely with preparations for our persecution, dredging up water and muck from the bottom of the Tiber under which to submerge us."[49] In the next few weeks, she expressed particular concern for the vulnerable confessors and *pensionnaires*. There was the terrible prospect that the community itself might be destroyed, its buildings taken for others' use and its own members exiled to other convents.[50] For her, the persecution was real, its spirit demonic, its power great, and its end unknown.

Second, the Faith: Angélique lived the Faith that her brother argued. She trusted in God, knowing there would be suffering in this world and accepting it as part of a providential scheme beyond her power fully to comprehend, much less to control. Her sins merited something worse: "None of us is free from sin, and the least of our sins merits a greater punishment than the world can inflict."[51] She counseled that the proper attitude was one of humble submission, patient endurance, and penitential silence. Just as Pascal ("and Antoine Arnauld"?) extended their polemic beyond the Censure, she wrote:

> Our [nuns] never see any of the writings [in the ongoing theological dispute]. We are content to know only that we can do nothing without God's grace, and we pray for this gift. We want to experience an ever-present need for His divine assistance, so that we will pray for it never-endingly. The impending persecution shows us our need, and so it is fortunate. If we have now to defend ourselves against other men, we have always much more to resist our own cupidity, which puts us at the edge of the precipice and of sin. . . .[52]
>
> Our greatest temptation is to amuse ourselves with our own vain reasonings. At the bottom of our hearts, we know that these thoughts come from nothing but the self love that is our greatest enemy. So scorn them! Consider them ridiculous, which they are. Adore instead the thoughts and plans of Our Lord Jesus Christ. Let us die to everything else and to ourselves and live only for Him who died for us.[53]

Marie des Anges Suireau proved to be a worthy successor to Mère Angélique as Abbess. On Monday, 20 March, the very day of the evacuation of the Solitaries and the pupils from Port-Royal des Champs, she received reliable word that lists had been prepared for an imminent dispersal of the nuns from Port-Royal in Paris. Mère Marie des Anges responded appropriately:

> We must drop everything else and devote ourselves exclusively to beseeching God's Mercies, because the House is lost if He doesn't take pity on us. They're about to meet in Council to decide on our dispersal, but that's a foregone conclusion. We must implore God's mercies night and day to deflect this evil. Therefore, I shall begin three days and three nights of continual prayers . . . before the Holy Sacrament.

And so she prayed for three days and three nights, from Tuesday, 21 March, to Friday, 24 March.[54]

On the last night of Mère Marie des Anges's vigil, the old and sick Mère Agnès dreamed a dream. Jacqueline de Sainte-Euphémie later reported the heaven-sent vision in verse, after its meaning had been revealed by the events of the following day:

> Avant ce grand miracle, au milieu du sommeil,
> [Elle] pensait voir dans l'église un superbe appareil,
> Sans savoir le sujet de sa magnificence,
> Et qu'un peuple dévot, avec empressement,
> Cherchait mille moyens, quoique inutilement,
> De témoigner son zèle et sa reconnaissance.[55]

As for Blaise Pascal, he shared the perspectives of the Arnaulds, and he also had personal reason for anxiety. He was Antoine's collaborator, almost his ghostwriter, and the campaign of the *Provinciales* was at once very risky and very uncertain. He was Étienne Périer's uncle, and he would have had to receive the young man into his household had he been separated finally from the Solitaries charged with the Little Schools. He was also the uncle of the Périer girls, Jacqueline (eleven years old) and Marguerite (almost ten), both then pensioned at Port-Royal; he would have had to receive them, too, had the impending dispersal taken place. This was potentially a much greater problem, given their gender, age, and health. Finally, of course, he was Jacqueline de Sainte-Euphémie's brother, strictly limited in his access to her but unlimited in his devotion.

For Blaise as the Parisian head of the family, there would have been quite heavy responsibilities this winter even without the hurried composition of the *Provinciales* and the apparent continuation of the *Écrits sur la grâce.* The most affecting problem was the "lachrymal fistula" with which his younger niece, a godchild, had been afflicted for several years. In search of a cure, Gilberte had brought little Margot (born 5 April 1646) to Paris in December 1653. In the course of the next two years, they had tried repeated irrigations as a gentle remedy.

Nevertheless, the infection had progressed, with noisome effects apparent and worse consequences foreseen.[56] Already, Margot was badly disfigured; she ran a fever, and she lost her appetite and sense of smell; she could not sleep or tolerate grooming; the stench revulsed the other children and appalled adult caregivers, as fetid matter ran not only from her eye but also from her nose and down her throat.[57] Without an operation, doctors and surgeons warned, "her nose would fall" or she would die. Even with it, they feared that her malady might be incurable or that an operation would kill her.[58]

The prescription was for a surgical incision and the application of the *cautère aegilopique,* a fiendish-looking iron hook designed to be heated to red-hot temperatures and plunged into the decaying tissues beneath the interior angle of the infected eye.[59] Her father weighed the options—certain horrors and possible death without the operation, certain horrors and possible death with it—and for months and years he temporized. In early March 1656, Blaise wrote that the time had come for the surgical application of the red-hot iron or, more simply and more terribly, "the fire."[60] On 24 March, Jacqueline summoned her brother-in-law with greater urgency.

Twenty March is the date on Pascal's celebrated Fifth Letter, but the pamphlet had not yet appeared, and his more radical and more aggressive redirection of the polemic had not won the wholehearted support even of his collaborators, Arnauld and Nicole.[61] Then came the Miracle of the Thorn.

On the Lenten Friday of Jacqueline's letter, 24 March 1656, the religious community venerated a reliquary containing a spine from the Crown of Thorns. The relic was placed momentarily on Margot's eye, and afterward it no longer troubled her. She had been cured. There would be no need for "the fire." Jacqueline heard the Good News and saw her niece the next day, and Blaise learned of the miracle when he visited five days later, on 29 March. Leaving

Clermont on that very day, Florin Périer traveled rapidly and arrived in Paris on 4 April, where the astonishing news and, another day later, the welcome sight awaited him.[62]

The Miracle was one of the great events of Pascal's life. Gilberte says that he tended to appropriate it as his own:

VMP, 39. My brother was very touched by this act of grace, which he regarded as done to himself. After all, this was a person who was his close relative by birth [*his* niece] and his spiritual daughter by baptism [*his* Godchild]. He was greatly consoled to see that God was manifesting himself so clearly at a time when faith seemed to be extinguished in most hearts.

Gilberte does not relate the Miracle to the contemporaneous *Provinciales,* but Blaise must have done so.[63] Anxieties and uncertainties about the radical shift from the defensive to an offensive would have been inevitable, given the nature of the opposition and the division of opinion among the collaborators. In this context, God offered a sign of His love for Margot; it was a very short hop-skip-and-jump to the notion that He so signified extraordinary support for the beleaguered convent, its contested truths, and the pamphlet-warrior himself.

A later biographer passed on an additional anecdote, which is unverifiable but plausible. According to this report, "a few days beforehand" an acquaintance had pointed to the escalating attacks on the defenseless Friends of the Truth as an argument against a superintending Providence:

If God meddles in human affairs, if religion is his work par excellence, and if the Church is the Kingdom of Truth, how can it be that it is the few theological defenders of the Truth who are oppressed and excommunicated by man and left unsupported by the silent God?[64]

Pascal is said to have responded without hesitation "that miracles were necessary and that God would perform them right away." After the Miracle of the Thorn became known,

[h]e remained in a state of wonderment for a long time, having reason to be still more closely touched than others. For it seemed that God had granted the Miracle not only to the prayers and needs of Port-Royal, but also to his faith. . . . Seeing that the Lord had interested Himself, if it's permissible to speak in this way, in the word that he had pronounced [Pascal's prediction or prophecy of the Miracle], his joy was so great that it permeated his very being.[65]

Whatever the historicity of this tradition, Pascal did adopt as his cachet a luminous cloud, surrounded by a Crown of Thorns and inscribed with these words from II Timothy 1:12: "I know [Him in] whom I have believed."[66] Like Paul, Pascal was an author of epistles who knew that he had been called:[67]

II Tim. 1:11 I am appointed a preacher, and an apostle, and a teacher of the Gentiles.
12 For the which cause I also suffer these things. Nevertheless I am not ashamed, for *I know whom I have believed,* and am persuaded that He is able to keep that which I have committed unto Him against that day.

"Montalte" may be related to the emblems of this cachet. The pseudonym first appeared in print on the title page of the collected *Provinciales* (probably July 1657), but it may go back to the previous year.[68] This name has never been explained satisfactorily.[69] The luminous cloud from the cachet is also properly obscure, but the symbol of Christ's Passion and the words of Paul's vocation both had identifiable personal meaning for Pascal at this time. Images of the "high mountain" and the luminous cloud and the conviction of a special revelation and a special commissioning come together in the Gospel story of the Transfiguration (Matt. 17). Jesus, Peter, James, and John go "up into an high mountain apart," where they see visions of Moses and Elias and hear God's voice from a "bright cloud," saying:[70] "This is my beloved Son, in whom I am well pleased; hear ye Him."

Pascal had a reputation for enthusiasm in pejorative senses. This was the opinion not just of worldly friends but also of others from within the innermost circles of Port-Royal, where shrewd directors and counselors knew the spiritual pride so often encouraged by extraordinary graces.[71] Even the Miracle of the Thorn could be a snare for the members of the very community that benefited from it.[72] Martin de Barcos, Saint-Cyran's nephew and successor, was most critical of Pascal. The anecdote that informs us gives the last word to his defenders:

M. Barcos said that Pascal had been struck down by God like a pygmy. It was none of his business [as a layman] to write about religion. M. Lombert rejoined that M. Pascal was more intelligent than he was, and that his book is very useful.[73]

CHAPTER 12

The *Provinciales* II

With his Fifth Letter, Pascal began a set of pamphlets on the moral laxism of the Jesuits in which the "good friend" and stern Jansenist of Letters 2–4 yields to the "good Father" and accommodating Jesuit of Letters 5–10. This fictional casuist naively cites surreal opinions on real problems from real works by real Jesuits, and so the Society seems to damn itself.

Did the passionately engaged author "damn himself," too, in the process of attacking others?[1] Of course, Pascal's Jesuit antagonists thought so—and noisily said so.[2] More surprisingly, some of his Jansenist allies tended to think so—and quietly said so. Angélique Arnauld, that "Mère de l'Église," advocated silence as the Christian response to persecution. When pressed for an opinion on the Fifth Letter, she did confess a certain satisfaction, somewhat guiltily, but on principle she rejected artful amusements in favor of penitential tears.[3] Even Nicole, Pascal's collaborator, betrayed considerable defensiveness about "Montalte's" shift of subject matter and rhetorical tone in the Fifth Letter. Nicole himself and apparently Arnauld, too, would have preferred further consideration of grace in a more restrained manner; Pascal was the mastermind of the brilliant counterattack.[4]

Letters 5–10

I return to the five characteristics quickly sketched in the previous chapter.

I. Irrepressibly high spirits in desperate circumstances. The context of persecution and the horrors of Margot's ailment in the winter of 1656 make Pascal's sprightliness in the earlier letters of the polemic the more remarkable. No one could suppose that the author of the *Pensées* just happens to have been a lighthearted fellow. Nor could any informed person suppose that Arnauld or even Nicole contributed this tone to the earlier *Provinciales*. Pascal was relatively worldly and relatively unburdened by excess learning, and these factors do help to explain his ability to compose letters in the manner of "Montalte." Furthermore, the Miracle of the Thorn was naturally as well as supernaturally elevating; the sudden cure and the subsequent relenting of the persecution cheered Blaise.

Yet Pascal's high spirits had been manifest *before* the Miracle in the desperate circumstances of mounting persecution. And his very intelligence, deep spirituality, layman's knowledge, *and* willing collaboration must mean that he *cannot* have been ignorant of *his allies'* reproaches for his playful manner. In Letters 1–4, I note his punning on Molinist "pouvoir prochain" and the Second Great Commandment ("j'aime trop mon prochain," cf. Matt. 22:39) and the sarcastic application to poor Étienne Bauny, S.J., of John the Baptist's salutation of Jesus Christ ("Ecce qui tollit peccata mundi," John 1:29).[5] Letters 5–10 more deeply offended many contemporaries, as Arnauld later admitted. The problem was not this or that unfortunate sally, but the general tone of derision:

> As soon as the Letters turned to morality and began to attack the Jesuits in so trenchant a style, we heard from every side nothing but murmuring and complaints from pious men and women, even our best friends, who thought that such writing wasn't Christian, that it wasn't charitable, that it was inappropriate to treat sacred things jokingly, and that right-thinking people were scandalized. I can't tell you how much M. Singlin tormented us on all of this.[6]

In modern clinical settings where closer observation is possible, "inappropriate laughing, joking, punning" can be considered one symptom of a hypomanic disorder.[7]

The most general criterion for such a diagnosis is an "elevated, expansive, or irritable mood."[8] We lack direct testimony on Pascal's moods at the time of the *Provinciales,* but some Letters are suggestive. In the Ninth, he struck back at Pierre Le Moyne, S.J., who had caricatured Jansenists as melancholy-mad in their association of Christian life with "sorrows and travails."[9] Pascal was particularly irked by passages like this:

> I don't deny that there are *dévots* who are pale and melancholy in their temperaments, who love silence and solitude, and who have nothing but phlegm in their veins and clay on their faces. But there are lots of others whose disposition is happier and who have in abundance that sweet and warm humor and that genial and refined blood that makes us joyous.[10]

Pascal had known low moods, as evidenced by his poetry from the "worldly period" and Jacqueline's letters on the Second Conversion, but at the time of this Ninth Letter he was in no mood to accept the caricature.

II. A capacity for anger and a taste for combat. The circumstances of the anti-Jansenist persecution seem at first glance to explain anything and everything angry in the *Provinciales.* Pascal and his friends were under siege; enemies were mounting repeated attacks on all sides; the defenders fought back with some of the righteous wrath that has characterized so many disputants over faith and practice. Well and good. But two aspects of Pascal's wrath distinguish the *Provinciales* from most other polemical writings: the *commingled wit* and the apparently *increasing anger* just when the storms of persecution were lifting and gentler seasons were returning.

At the beginning of the campaign, Pascal left his own household and chose winter quarters strategically located directly opposite the Jesuit Collège de Clermont, in an aptly named inn, the King David.[11] There, he readied his smooth stones. In his continuation of the polemic after the censure announced in the Third Letter, he attacked the Jesuits more and more directly, more and more personally. Nicole offers formal testimony of his particular responsibility for the two most important escalations, those that followed the Fourth and Tenth Letters. Apparently, his collaborators would have preferred to continue on the subject of grace at the former juncture and to call a halt at the latter.[12]

Pascal redirected the campaign after the Fourth Letter, resumed writing and dropped fictional disguises after the Tenth, and directly addressed the old enemy Annat after the Sixteenth (to say nothing of writing the Eighteenth after seventeen had seemed to suffice, beginning a Nineteenth, or contributing as a layman to the *Écrits des curés*).[13] Is it too much to conclude that he must have *liked* this sort of warfare? That his triumph means that he must have been "naturally gifted" *as a polemicist?*

The angriest of the letters under consideration is certainly the Tenth (2 August); this is also the one from which Nicole took the greatest care to distance himself. It had been *Montalte's* letter and *Montalte's* anger, a righteous anger, to be sure, but anger, nevertheless. Its Truth (the Two Loves) and the corresponding deviation (a "Jesuitical" indulgence of self-love) certainly helped to inspire the irate author. But the great controversialist, speaking through the Jansenist character of the Fourth Letter, had already expressed a profound insight that he may not have turned back upon himself:

> Who can doubt that he often falls into sins of surprise without being aware of it? . . . [Even the saints fall unwittingly, even Augustine (*Confessions,* bk. 10, chap. 31).] How common it is to see the most zealous be carried away by movements of anger on their own behalf in the course of debate, without their conscience telling them, at the time, anything other than that they are being moved solely by concern for the Truth. Sometimes, they aren't even aware of it until long afterward![14]

Long afterward, Pascal was asked whether he repented the vigor of the *Provinciales.* He answered that he had nothing to repent, but that he did have a related regret; if he were to do them all over again, he would make them "still stronger."[15]

There is suggestive testimony that Pascal, who seemed so submissive to Gilberte in 1647, to Jacqueline in 1654, and to his confessor in 1662, was also much of the time notably angry, not necessarily at anything in particular, just angry. It is a Jansenist cleric from a family allied to the Pascals' oldest and dearest friends, François Arnoul de Saint-Victor, who serves as authority for this intriguing anecdote on Pascal's temper:

> M. Pascal took great pains to hide his virtue, particularly in the presence of ordinary sorts, to such an extent that someone once told M. Arnoul that it seemed that M. Pascal was always angry and ready to curse. (This story

is amusing [for anyone privy to the secret], but it wouldn't be good to record it.)[16]

Can Christian humility have inclined the converted Pascal to *feign* a vulgar, violent temper? That cannot be right. But the observation of an "always angry" Pascal here reported—and here rejected—may have been true to the facts of certain periods.

Pascal was often combative. As a savant, he engaged in controversies over his Vacuum Experiments. As a convert, he was notably aggressive in the Forton Affair (1647), in the polemical *Provinciales* (1656), and in the "civil wars" over the Formulary in which he turned against former allies (1661).[17] Gilberte herself acknowledged her brother's irritability:

VMP, 74. The extraordinary quickness of his mind sometimes made him so impatient that you could hardly please him. But when you pointed it out to him or he noticed that he had irritated someone by signs of impatience, he made it up right away.[18]

It is remarkable that Gilberte should have come so close to condemning his angry temper. For the bereaved and charitable sister, Blaise's genius suggests an explanation and an excuse.

Pascal had "good reason" to be angry much of the time, and he was not angry all of the time. Nevertheless, it is worth wondering how he can have been so very good at being angry in the *Provinciales*. One explanation would be a subclinical mood disorder: irritability is as much a symptom of hypomania as elevation or expansiveness of moods. The most recent and authoritative work on affective disorders follows Emil Kraepelin in placing the "irritable temperament" in the spectrum of manic-depression that ranges from normality to pathology. According to Kraepelin's classic description, the ideal type of this temperament is brilliant, artistic, charming, versatile, good natured, and so on, but also better at planning than completing, restless, capricious, emotionally unstable, easily offended and hot-tempered.[19] Pascal's behavior in the *Provinciales* does seem to fit this model. In any case, high spirits and irritability both contributed to his success as a polemicist.

III. Wholly exceptional energy. This quality was obviously most important for Letters 1–3, in which the pace of events in the Sorbonne and the tardiness of the defensive effort required very fast work. However, the demands of later letters, too, were great, in some ways greater. In Letters 1–4, Pascal treated a subject on which he had read and written, but in Letters 5–18 he turned to a new subject with a technical literature that he had never read. So, although his pace in the later letters does not look so fast, and he did have Arnauld's expert counsel and prior writings to assist him, his progress is very impressive.[20] He researched, wrote, and published not just three but eighteen pamphlets in 1656 and early 1657, as indicated in table 5.

In the first winter, 1656, Pascal was apparently also making substantial progress on his *Écrits sur la grâce.* While the impact of the Miracle of the Thorn was still at its strongest, he also reportedly first conceived a project for an Apology.[21] This means that he not only produced a series of polemical pamphlets of the rarest originality under exceptionally difficult circumstances, but *also* concurrently continued *and* initiated other projects of even greater scope. This was

TABLE 5
The Chronology of the *Provinciales*

Letter Number	*Dated*	*Published*
1	23 January 56	27 January
2	29 January	5 February
3	9 February	12 February
4	25 February	?
5	20 March	after 30 March
6	10 April	?
7	25 April	?
8	28 May	15 June
9	3 July	9 July
10	2 August	?
11	18 August	?
12	9 September	by 15 September
13	30 September	?
14	23 October	?
15	25 November	12 December (?)
16	4 December	16 December
17	23 January 57	mid-February
18	24 March	early May

Further detail and references in Mesnard, *OC,* III, 447–66.

the same Pascal who fell into such a prolonged lassitude early in 1659 and who left incomplete so many projects begun in a relatively few bursts of varied creativity (1647, 1654, 1658).[22] Or was he the same?

"Louis de Montalte" was different from "Salomon de Tultie," an anagrammatical derivative of the earlier pseudonym that Pascal later adopted at a moment of playfulness and self-congratulation (Pensée 745). There is no greater difference between the author of the *Provinciales* and the author of the *Pensées* than the energy that kept the one going and the *langueur* that stopped the other. The former, as he represents himself especially in the First Letter, was out and about, going restlessly from person to person and shifting quickly from topic to topic. As for the latter, in most celebrated ruminations (e.g., Pensée 136), he seems contrarily reclusive and brooding. The one energetically completed and published pamphlet after pamphlet; the other is said to have been unable to do any work at all for the last four years of his life.[23] At the extremes of creative energy are the First Letter, which he composed in a day or two (cf. the *Second écrit des curés,* "done in a day")[24] and the Apology, for which he never completed so much as the draft of a chapter. In his discouraged assessment from a gloomy period, the latter was a project that would have taken "ten years," painful and sinful years, at that, and all for a work doomed to fail (1670 Preface and Pensée 153).

IV. Boundless self-confidence. This is another of Montalte's characteristics that is too easy to take for granted. Although Pascal was a layman with negligible experience as an author and no formal training in theology, he volunteered to expose the inconsequence of the deliberations in the Sorbonne and the elementary errors made by the Faculty. Then, against the judgment of technically trained and battle-hardened collaborators, he advocated shifting ground from something on which he was at least relatively well informed (the theology of grace) to something of which he was quite ignorant (the ethical principles governing moral counsel in the confessional). This required extraordinary confidence. Pascal's youthful triumphs as a savant cannot explain his forwardness in so different an endeavor, requiring such different knowledge and skills.

Marguerite Périer much later recorded remarks that express his assurance well enough. He thought that he was the equal of any right-thinking theologian and that he could judge the works of wrong-thinking theologians without systematic study:

> I'm asked why I adopted an agreeable, witty, amusing style. I answer that if I had written in a dogmatic style, only the learned would have read my work, and they didn't need to, knowing as much as I do. . . .
>
> I'm asked if I myself read all the works that I cited. I answer, certainly not. To have done so, I would have had to pass my life reading very bad books. But I have read through all of Escobar [*Liber theologiae moralis* (1644)] twice; as for the rest, my friends read them for me, but I never cited a single passage without having reviewed it in context.[25]

Jesuit opponents exaggerated Pascal's theological incompetence, of course. René Rapin wrote scathingly: "not a trace of the scholastic theology on which he decided like a doctor, . . . no notion of morals, no familiarity with the Fathers, no knowledge of the canons and the councils, all essential materials for anyone who would speak with any assurance."[26] More surprisingly, fellow Port-Royalists with better credentials as theologians were also critical. Barcos: "It was none of his business to write on religion."[27] Nicole: "He was a *ramasseur de coquilles,*" that is, a beachcomber, an amateur.[28]

Qualified scholars have faulted Pascal for theological misrepresentations attributable to ignorance and overconfidence as well as zeal and haste. He is particularly open to criticism for his treatment of the French Dominican Jean Nicolaï in the First and Second Letters and the Spanish Cistercian Juan Caramuel y Lobkovitz in the Seventh Letter. In the former case, he errs badly on the crucial matter of "sufficient grace," apparently misled by Nicole's prior writings. In this context, he boasts rather too much of his own perfect independence, which he proudly contrasts with the Dominicans' supposed submission to the dictates of their superiors.[29] In the latter case, he errs at least as badly on the equally crucial matter of "justifiable" homicide, tearing words from context and reversing meanings; again, his collaborators probably share the responsibility.[30]

The mere fact of such misrepresentation in pamphlet-warfare is unsurprising, especially given Pascal's lack of training and reliance on others' learning. However, when he reconsiders the campaign in the Seventeenth Letter, he affirms his individual responsibility: "I declare loudly and clearly that no one else is to answer for my Letters."[31] What is "good" and what is "bad" alike depended absolutely on the self-confidence with which this sometime mathematician-physicist pronounced judgment on matters that were beyond his formal competence.

This is not to chide Pascal for bad morals or deficient learning. It is to emphasize the fact of his "boundless self-confidence" and to suggest it was a condition for his success as a pamphleteer. That confidence did not come from the Miracle—quite the opposite. It reassured him that his cause was True and that God would intervene to confirm its Truth. It enabled him to appropriate the Miracle, while the spiritual leaders of Port-Royal fretted about pridefulness. They were right to worry, but no worrier could have written the *Provinciales.*

V. A reckless willingness to take risks. Pascal's clandestine campaign against the Jesuits may not have placed him in grave jeopardy of harsh punishment by the agents of the state, but it did risk his condemnation by the Church and his censure by otherwise sympathetic churchmen. The Crown was determined to reduce the Jansenists, but it was the printers who bore the brunt of police action against the *Provinciales.* There seem to have been no comparable efforts to identify, intimidate, interrogate, or incarcerate suspected authors. And even this repression, ineffective as it was, eased in the summer of 1656, just as the Letters were becoming stronger. According to the manuscript *Journal* of Taignier, by mid-June Séguier had washed his hands of the matter; he referred inquirers to Mazarin, who was reported to be enjoying the Letters too much to tolerate any interruption.[32] According to Saint-Gilles, on 18 August:

> For the past three months or so, I've been personally responsible for having printed the last four *Lettres au provincial,* that is, the Seventh, Eighth, Ninth, and Tenth. At first, it was dangerous and we had to maintain the greatest secrecy, but for the past two months everyone, magistrates included, has taken such great pleasure in these witty pieces . . . that it hasn't been dangerous and we've been able to take greater liberties.[33]

Having said so much by way of minimizing Pascal's actual danger, I should hasten to add that the arbitrary arrests and long imprisonments of the first Abbé de Saint-Cyran (1638–43) and the Cardinal de Retz (1652–54) did suggest that lesser lights identified with "Jansenism" and suspected of "conspiracy" had reason to fear even before the Great Persecution of the 1660s. Arnauld had gone into hiding, evading his theological judges. In this situation, Pascal's most reckless act may have been the defiant flourish at the end of the Third Letter: "E.A.A.B.P.A.F.D.E.P." He himself may not yet have been a prime suspect, but his principal collaborator certainly was, and for him to tease his readers with Antoine Arnauld's initials and his own, whatever alternative meaning he may have had in mind for "E.A.A.," was to take a needless risk at a time of mounting persecution.[34]

Pascal's status as a layman would have made him immune from most sorts of ecclesiastical discipline, even had he been stripped of his thin disguise. However, by challenging the commonsense reading of a Papal Bull and ridiculing the verdict against Arnauld in the Sorbonne, he opened himself to censure by the Church as well as the state. The Parlement of Aix condemned the *Provinciales* for troubling public order and defaming the Sorbonne, the Dominicans, and the Jesuits; on 9 February 1657, the judges sentenced Letters 1–16 to be burned by the Hangman (reportedly keeping their own copies of the offending pamphlets and putting the torch to an unwanted almanac).[35] Not every cardinal enjoyed the *Provinciales* as much as Mazarin and these lay judges seem to have done, and on 6 September 1657 the General Congregation of the Roman Inquisition placed Montalte's collection on the Index.[36] Finally, on 23 September 1660, the conseil d'État in Paris formally sentenced Wendrock's Latin version to be lacerated and burned, forbidding all subjects to print, sell, purchase, or even retain the book in any form.[37]

Pascal remained defiant: "If my Letters are condemned in Rome, what I condemn in them is condemned in Heaven."[38] Perhaps so, but what of the author himself, whose confessor so opposed his sort of pamphleteering? Pascal's greatest recklessness may have been his readiness to risk his immortal soul.

Letters 11–18

In the Eleventh Letter, Pascal began to address the Jesuits directly and to defend earlier letters. Drawing from Arnauld's prior writings, he formulated four rules for Christian controversialists:[39] first, to speak the truth; second, to speak with discretion; third, to ridicule only errors, not holy things; fourth, to love one's opponents, hoping and praying for their salvation. These standards do seem just, even if

Pascal could not have judged himself impartially and the preeminent specialist prudently refrains from passing judgment.[40]

With respect to the first rule, veracity, Pascal's Jesuit opponents initially tried to defend their own authors by accusing their attacker of misrepresenting their works. This tactic failed. In fact, their Antoine Escobar and his "four and twenty elders" provided Pascal with material that he did not need to misrepresent. Escobar's *Liber theologiae moralis* (1644) was far and away his most frequent reference, the one Jesuit work which he claimed to have read and reread from cover to cover. Old allegations of "impostures" in this most important instance were long ago rebutted.[41] Outright errors in other cases, such as his treatment of Nicolaï and Caramuel, are best regarded as unintentional. Given the situation and the genre, Pascal's relative scrupulousness is very impressive.[42]

The second rule, discretion, raises more delicate questions. Pascal borrowed from Arnauld an authoritative citation from Augustine, which states the principle; the Christian controversialist must cut with a surgeon's precision and restraint, not a slasher's indiscriminate violence.[43] The difficulty is that Pascal took great care in the Fifth, Ninth, Thirteenth, and Seventeenth Letters to establish the collective responsibility of the entire Society for any publication by any Jesuit.[44] This, in turn, means that in his every "surgical" incision, he slashes not just the passage or the book on the table but also the thousands of Jesuits who had nothing to do with it.

L. W. B. Brockliss has emphasized that Étienne Bauny, S.J., whose work had already been censured in both Rome (1640) and Paris (1641), was the only *French* casuist whose published work Pascal attacked. There was no epidemic of laxist casuistry spread by Jesuit publications in France or by Jesuit teaching in French *collèges*.[45] Thus, by his own standards, Pascal was "indiscreet" when he lashed out against "Jesuitism," which was in some ways as much a creature of the controversy as "Jansenism." And yet, he did restrain himself from sensationalistic exposés of Jesuit teachings on the most inflammatory topics, regicide and sexuality, and he refrained from attacking the personal foibles or moral failings of flesh-and-blood members of the Society.

The third rule, to limit ridicule to error, not "holy things," sets a higher standard than Pascal may have realized. He did drop his tone of raillery after having defended it in the Eleventh Letter, but he had by then effectively mocked the commonsense reading of a Papal Bull *(Cum occasione),* the debates and decisions of the Faculty of Theology, and the moral teachings and sacramental practices of the Society of Jesus. The deadly serious tone of the last letters addressed to Annat may have been even more wounding to traditional religion in the long run, insofar as Pascal presupposes that the solitary layman can discriminate between questions of "fact" and questions of "faith" and decide the former to his own satisfaction even against the dictates of a more explicit Papal Bull *(Ad sacram).*[46] On the other hand, Pascal does seem to have been perfectly justified in saying that there was nothing sacred about the contractual practice of the Mohatra or the crime of Jean d'Alba and that there was a great deal of ridiculousness in Bauny's teachings on barn burning, Cellot's on restitution-manqué, and so on.[47] His attacks helped to spur the Church to subsequent condemnations of laxist opinions.[48]

The fourth rule, the love of one's enemies, raises a Christlike standard to which the most perfect Augustinian could only have aspired. Pascal's most evident love was for the nuns of his sister's convent.[49] In the Sixteenth Letter, he defends them and then strikes out at their calumniators in a way that seems anything but charitable. The Jesuits who dare to call them crypto-Calvinists despite their truly Catholic veneration of the Holy Sacrament are themselves corrupt celebrants who deliver Christ's Body and Blood to fouled mouths with their own soiled hands. Jesus Christ hears the prayers of Port-Royal and will call the faithful to Him; he thunders at the detractors of the convent in the Miracle of the Thorn, "that holy and terrible voice that astonishes nature and consoles the Church."[50]

Although Pascal returns in Letters 17–18 to the subject matter of Letters 1–3, namely, the Five Propositions and the theology of grace, it is in a very different spirit. Gone is the lightheartedness that had characterized his writing even in the seemingly dismal circumstances of the winter of 1656. A year later, even before the reception of Alexander VII's hostile Bull, he was more subdued and apparently disheartened. In the Seventeenth Letter, dated 23 January, Jean Mesnard has noted "a new Pascal, full of anxiety, . . . almost sorrowful."[51] This Pascal had the greatest difficulty in satisfying himself with the Eighteenth Letter, dated two months and a day later, the first anniversary of the Miracle; he wrote and rewrote it thirteen times over a period of months, a striking contrast with his composition of the First Letter, which satisfied everyone in what seems to have been a first draft and final copy all in one, produced "right away."[52]

The Lettres à Mlle. de Roannez

From September 1656 to February 1657, Pascal addressed nine letters to Charlotte de Roannez.[53] Only copies of undated excerpts survive, and they have been variously interpreted.[54] I argue that they show the darkening of his perspective in this period, when he also wrote the last nine *Provinciales*. Mesnard has called attention to signs of discouragement in the last two letters to Charlotte (January and February 1657) and the last two *Provinciales* (23 January and 24 March 1657). These signs point to something far more significant than the tone of a few passages in few letters.[55]

Before Pascal's first letter to Charlotte (perhaps 10 or 17 September 1656), Charlotte herself had established a somber mood. The known facts about her situation suggest an explanation: she had been pushed toward a marriage that she did not want and prevented from finding the refuge in religion that she did want.[56] Blaise's response was Apocalyptic. Charlotte's "beginnings of sorrow" remind him of Mark 13:8, and he devotes more than half of the surviving letter to commentary on that chapter of the Gospel. His grand theme is that, just as the Second Coming of Jesus Christ will entail the destruction of the world itself, so her second birth as a new convert now requires a frightful combat, the destruction of the old woman, and the rejection of her worldly family. Charlotte must break her attachments to the world; she must reconsider whether she has the requisite "vocation" to remain in a house that is metaphorically infested with plague and engulfed in flames. Blaise concludes with reassurance that "God never abandons his own" and the counsel that death is not only necessary but also desirable.[57]

Letter 2 (24 September): Charlotte must have been torn by the opposition of her brother and mother to her religious vocation. On the fifth anniversary of his father's death, Blaise responds with a heartfelt maxim that makes good psychological sense: "No one ever detaches himself without sorrow." He rationalizes this sorrow as a product of violent tensions between the body that holds us back and the spirit that struggles to advance. The letter ends with an explicit death wish.[58]

Letter 3 (mid-October): In the context of the ongoing theological controversy, the most interesting part of this letter is Blaise's "profession of faith." He begins with a defiant rejection of an unspecified "condemnation."[59] Then he turns quickly to the God who does not abandon His Elect, the Church that is our mother, and the Pope who is its rightful head: "I shall never separate myself from communion with him."[60] Pascal's profession, surely sincere, must reflect his anxiety that Montalte's campaign was setting him against the Church headed by the anti-Jansenist Alexander VII.

Letter 4 (perhaps 29 October): Blaise reports the final verification of the Miracle of the Thorn and exhorts Charlotte as the beneficiary of a lesser miracle that recipients of such favors know God certainly and must serve Him ardently. In this context, he introduces the easily misunderstood theme of the Hidden God. For Blaise, Charlotte, and other favored Catholics, God is *known*. His handiwork is evident in miracles; His truths are revealed in Scripture; His Body and Blood are received in the Mass. In a bad world, true Christians know the Good News.[61]

Letter 5 (5 November): As part of an evident effort to encourage Charlotte, Blaise professes "certainty" that graces in this life prefigure glory in the next. He envisions her as one of the Elect, enthroned beside Jesus Christ, passing judgment on the world. Having said so much, he warns her that she might yet fall. When judged, she, too, might be found wanting. Contrarily envisioning her "in that state of eternal misery," he recoils, praying that God may not "abandon weak creatures." In the letter as we have it, the last word is "fear."[62]

Letter 6 (early December): Apparently responding to the needs of a troubled correspondent, Blaise discusses the relationship between joy and sadness. From Tertullian, he takes the important idea of a double delectation, which opposes the greater delights of God to the lesser pleasures of the world:

> We mustn't believe that the life of a Christian is a life of sadness. One never turns away from pleasures unless it is for something greater. Saint Paul tells us to give thanks always and to rejoice always [I Thess. 5:16]. It is the joy of having found God that provokes sadness at having offended Him. . . .
>
> Jesus Christ Himself says that the worldly do not share the joy that "the

world can neither give nor take away" [John 14:27 and 16:22]. The blessed experience this joy without sadness; the worldly have their sadness without this joy; Christians have this joy mingled with the sadness of having followed other pleasures and with the fear of losing it by the attraction of other pleasures that unceasingly tempt us.[63]

Some sadness is inevitable; the right sort of fear is desirable; the good Christian must not succumb to a hopeless prostration.

Letter 7 (24 December): Blaise's Christmas letter makes arresting use of the image of the Mother and Child:

["The person," surely Charlotte herself, should] remember that her worries don't come from her good beginnings [as a convert], but from the bad that remains. . . . She must respond like an infant who is snatched by robbers from the arms of a mother who won't surrender him. He blames the criminal robbers for the violence that he suffers, not the mother who clasps him lovingly.[64]

Pascal likens the new convert to an infant assaulted by the kidnappers who would snatch it from its mother. The image of maternal violence in opposition to criminal abductors was wholly inappropriate for Charlotte, whose mother was just then clinging to her grown daughter with a desperate intensity—and thereby resisting her daughter's vocation at Port-Royal, not wicked kidnappers. It is Pascal's own experience as a child torn from his mother's arms that gives his image its arresting force.[65]

Letter 8 (January 1657) is the first of those in which Mesnard has discerned Pascal's own discouragement: "We always have reason to fear . . .; [in case of future disappointment in an unspecified "affair," perhaps the vocation itself,] I would fear the bad sadness that Saint Paul says 'worketh death' . . . [II Cor. 7:10]." In any case, Pascal evidently does fear "prostration" or "depression" *(abattement)*, and his melancholy predictions of future "sorrows" (*peines*) explicitly concern himself and others as well as Charlotte. In this context, having recalled a saying of Jesus (Matt. 6:34) and an essay of Montaigne (bk. 1, chap. 3), he anticipates his own more profoundly depressive Pensée 47 on our flight from the hurtful present.[66]

Letter 9 (February 1657) ends the series with the author's manful (and faithful) attempts to keep hopes alive: "I try as hard as I can not to be distressed by anything and to take everything for the best." But then comes the truly dismal reflection that persecutory forces mount their attacks against the Truth itself, not just persons: "I won't deceive you: God is truly abandoned."[67]

In March 1657 the Papal nuncio finally delivered Alexander VII's *Ad sacram*. The *Provinciales* then finally ground to a halt in the draft beginnings of a never-completed Nineteenth Letter, where we find the Jesuits blamed for "anguish" and "affliction" and "deepest sorrow." There are confessions of "self-distrust," of "fear," and of "regret" and more anticipations of the Day of Judgment.[68] This Pascal was no longer the man who had begun the series of pamphlets so quickly, easily, even lightheartedly; this Pascal looks forward to the *Pensées* and "the misery of man."

PART FIVE

MISERY

Pascal fell more seriously ill in mid-1658 (Gilberte) or early 1659 (Carcavy) and never fully recovered before his death in 1662.[1] Gilberte would have been immediately informed, having come to Paris in 1658, probably late in the year, and remained through the following winter, but it is Carcavy who gives the earliest written report. It may be relevant that Louise Delfault, the longtime servant who "raised" the Pascal children after 1631, died that same winter sometime soon after naming Blaise as her executor (11–12 December).[2]

In the orthodox tradition, his illness has been considered important for only two reasons, one intellectual and the other spiritual. Intellectually, it incapacitated the thinker, preventing the completion of the Apology that he left in the now familiar form of fragmentary *Pensées*. Spiritually, it graced the penitent, figuring in his diseased body the natural state of his sinful soul and forcing him finally to devote himself completely to the one thing necessary (Luke 10:42). In neither respect does the nature of this illness matter much.

Strictly speaking, it is unknown, even unknowable, because no one who then observed or examined him could have claimed a medical science worthy of the name and no one who now has the requisite medical credentials can observe or examine him. But ignorance, theirs as well as ours, is relative, not absolute. Competent physicians have reviewed surviving medical records, including an autopsy, and they have concluded that what killed the great man was a cancer. The course of the terminal illness, as reconstructed, was this: stomach ulcers led to stomach cancer, which metastasized, leading to cerebral complications and death.[3]

This reconstruction raises new questions about Pascal's earlier prostration. The cancer that killed him in 1662 could hardly have been the problem in 1647, 1654, or even 1658–59. Étienne Périer, who was being schooled nearby in 1658 and who came to live with his uncle in Paris in March 1660, reports reliably on the last years that, for all Pascal's incapacitation intellectually, the "illness of *langueur* and weakness" did not confine him to his bed or his chambers physically.[4] Indeed, the great man looked reasonably well.[5]

Curiously, the senior attending physician attributed even the final illness to "a melancholic humor." The Périers' family doctor, Noël Vallant, was quite junior, still in his twenties; he called in François Guénault, a worldly-wise septuagenarian and the Queen Mother's doctor. Vallant is our informant:

> According to M. Guénault, M. Pascal suffers from an intestinal obstruction caused by a melancholy humor. As it ferments, this humor emits vapors that produce diverse symptoms, which vary with the parts that they touch. It ferments because it is boiling, and a great heat causes this boiling.[6]

Are we to laugh or to cry? Molière used Guénault as the real-life model for his comic Macroton, and this humoral medicine now seems ludicrous. But these doctors were experienced observers who saw the man whom we remember only as mind and spirit. However ignorant of modern medicine, they knew the case history when they diagnosed "a melancholy humor."

Voltaire would have read Étienne Périer's preface along with the *Pensées,* but he could never have had access to Vallant's papers. Although he was quite scrupulous in his citations of Pascal's own work, he misrepresented Leibniz when he attributed to him the assessment that the great man had been afflicted by *mélancholie.*[7] This was Voltaire's own opinion, inseparable from his indignant protest against the great author's *misère.* The question remains whether the opinion based on literary criticism and philosophical differences can be upheld. My approach is historical and psychological. For better or for worse, it has led me toward conclusions anticipated in the great philosophe's Anti-Pascal. This is for the better, if it makes my work of some use to students of Voltaire. It is very much for the worse, if it wrongly suggests a Voltairean attack on Christianity. My purpose is to understand Pascal, the man and his work.

Chapter 13 reconsiders Pascal's distinctive emphasis on "misery" as the essence of human nature, relating affective meanings to the Apologist's intended argument. Chapter 14 examines particularly expressive and explicitly self-referential fragments, looking for evidence on the author's affective life. Chapter 15 turns from the work to the man, as such, and the available evidence on his last four years of illness, which I take to be depressive.

CHAPTER 13

The *Pensées* I: The Misery of Man

With this chapter, I begin the argument that the *Pensées* provide historically invaluable testimony on Pascal's affective life—and that an analytical understanding of that life can add new depth to the interpretation of a masterpiece of pieces that was significantly shaped, colored, and informed by his emotions. My first section reconsiders the theme of man's "Greatness and Wretchedness," *grandeur/misère,* as developed in Pensée 149, an extensive draft, not properly a fragment, that was apparently prepared for an oral exposition of his apologetic argument to friends "at Port-Royal," hence the manuscript heading, "A.P.R."[1] My second section focuses on "the misery of man" in Pensées 13–148, most of them much scrappier but all sorted into ordered dossiers prepared for the First Part of the two-part plan that is sketched in Pensée 6. My third section reconsiders the human condition as represented in Pensées 150–382, fragments sorted into dossiers ordered by the three-stage scheme of Pensée 12.

Pol Ernst's *Géologie et stratigraphie des Pensées de Pascal* will make fundamental contributions to our understanding of the chronology of composition, but important questions of Pascal's planning remain unanswered and perhaps unanswerable by even the most meticulous studies of the various papers in the *Recueil original*. The paper on which Pascal drafted Pensée 6 is still "unidentified," and the paper of Pensée 12 seems to be otherwise unexampled. Yet more frustratingly, we have no autographic original and so no Pascalian paper for the table of contents; this most crucial text is known only from posthumous copies, so that Ernst's methods are strictly inapplicable.[2]

I suggest that Pensée 6 and the plan that it represents followed Pensée 12 and its rather different scheme. Pascal's "First Part" structurally came last chronologically. "The last thing that one discovers in writing a book is what to put first." The plan of Pensée 6 was much more original, more subtle, and potentially more forceful than that of Pensée 12, which would have had him begin with the old threats of death and damnation ("Commencement," Pensées 150–166).[3] Apparently, he came to think that he could better persuade worldly readers to seek the Redeemer God, if he initially avoided such flashes of hellfire, appeals to the authority of revelation, and all potentially off-putting God-talk. He hoped to direct readers' self-examination, but, however unintentionally, he also represented what he had seen within himself. He was confident that others would see what he had "seen" introspectively, the necessary failure of any merely human search for happiness.

I challenge what I take to be a hyperrationalism that goes all the way back to Gilberte Périer and her son Étienne.[4] They write as if the mind and the spirit were the essence of the man. Their Pascal was a thinker whose great genius would have allowed him finally to refute "the reasoning of the atheists," had the accident of ill health not raised insuperable physical obstacles. This venerable tradition emphasizes the orderliness of his planning despite the apparent disorder of his manuscripts and makes the exposition of his fragments in light of one supposedly coherent plan the primary critical task.[5] Voltaire and Condorcet supposed contrarily that Pascal's ill health was psychological and that his fragments were the cries of a brilliant but troubled man, requiring editorial selection and critical responses.

I believe that Pascal's writing is most remarkable for its capacity to move persons emotionally, not to establish truths rationally. Paradoxically, the obscure illness that prevented the completion of the projected Apology was also a condition for the accomplishment of his powerful *Pensées*. Thus, Pascal's complex personality helped him posthumously to achieve his apologetic ends, even as it prevented him from completing the "grand design" for which others had such very high expectations.

Grandeur/Misère: *The Great Thinker's Unhappy Ambiguity*

Étienne Périer and Nicolas Filleau de La Chaise report that there was one particularly memorable occasion when, on the urging of "many very important persons among his friends," Pascal presented an oral exposition of his projected Apology for the Christian religion. Périer says that he spoke extemporaneously for two or three hours, in the course of which he sketched "the plan of his entire work." Filleau speaks more guardedly about this "plan" but, if anything, more enthusiastically about the work in progress, "the greatest work that man could accomplish." The two agree that Pascal intended to begin with "a portrait of man" as an "astonishing contradiction" of "greatness and baseness" (Périer) or a "monstrous combination of incompatible parts" (Filleau).[6] His goal was to inspire in readers a sort of introspection that would be spiritually beneficial.

Neither informant specifies "the very important persons," the date, or the place for the memorable conference. Nevertheless, it is an easy inference that the persons must have included Pascal's great friend and admirer, Artus de Roannez.[7] The date was probably before de Roannez urged him to promote his work in progress indirectly by sponsoring, entering, and winning a mathematical competition; Pascal announced this competition at the end of June 1658. It was certainly before the onset of his incapacitating illness in mid-1658 or early 1659.[8] Finally, the place must have been Port-Royal, as scholars have inferred from the draft headed "A.P.R." (Pensée 149).[9] Subheadings strongly suggest written preparations for a conference presentation there: "A.P.R. for tomorrow" and "A.P.R. for tomorrow 2."[10]

"A.P.R." begins with the incomprehensible *grandeur* and *misère* of man, much as reported by Périer and Filleau. This "greatness" clearly refers backward to Adam's Creation in the image of God and forward to sinners' Redemption by the grace of God. This "wretchedness" refers to Everyman's condition after the Fall. That is the concern of this chapter.

Pascal's particular alertness to the dangers of ambiguity and his rigorous insistence on precise definition, which is so prominent in the *De l'art de persuader* and the *Provinciales,* suggest a careful reconsideration of seventeenth-century meanings for the term that he used to characterize human nature.[11] According to him, man is *misérable,* a creature marked by *misère*. Although it is Pascal's somewhat earlier and personally distinctive usage that concerns us, we turn to the great lexicographer Antoine Furetière for the admirable definitions of the adjective in his *Dictionnaire universel* (1690):

1. *MISÉRABLE.* He who is in pain, sorrow, poverty, affliction, or oppression. Job was reduced to the most *misérable* state. A sufferer from the gout is *misérable* during an attack. This man is *misérable;* he has no bread. That one is *misérable* for having lost his wife. A *misérable* lover languishes in his chains. He is a *misérable,* abandoned without the support of man or God.

2. *MISÉRABLE* also means wicked, sinful. One has to be *misérable* indeed to kill one's father or one's prince. A sinner is *misérable* indeed to attack his Creator. Lord, have mercy on a *misérable* who repents his wrong-doing.

3. *MISÉRABLE* is also used to express exaggerated scorn. Adam fell from grace for having eaten a *misérable* apple. A *misérable* peasant who is righteous in the eyes of God will stand before princes. We slit one another's throats for *misérable* honors.

According to Furetière, *misère* denotes a pain or sorrow explained by the lack of something or someone particularly needed or valued. Primarily, the word designates the emotional effects of the greatest losses, namely, those of a wife, a lover, a friend, or God. This is timeless. Then come secondary and tertiary meanings that presuppose the established Church and the social hierarchy of the Old Regime. Furetière's *misère*-I is profound unhappiness, *misère*-II is sinfulness, and *misère*-III is contemptibleness. In ordinary usage the several meanings shadowed one another, but analytically they relate to quite different categories of thought. The first is psychological, the second theological, and the third sociological.

Pascal's Augustinian convictions and apologetic purposes require us to begin with *misère*-II, sinfulness. In its final draft, his "A.P.R." formally commenced with this "Beginning":

The *grandeurs* and *misères* of man are so evident that the true religion must necessarily teach them to us. There must be some grand principle of man's greatness and some grand principle of *misère*.

It [the true religion] must also make sense of these astonishing contradictions. To make man happy, it must show him that there is a God, that we are obliged to love Him, that our true felicity is to be with Him and our one malady to be separated from Him, and that it acknowledges that we are full of a darkness which prevents us from knowing Him and loving Him. Thus, our duty obliges us to love God, while our concupiscence [self-love] turns us away from Him.

The familiar theology of the Two Loves provides the conceptual basis for this passage. God commands us to love Him; we prefer to love ourselves.

In succeeding paragraphs, Pascal's references to the Fall and original sin are unmistakable: man's "presumption" tempts him to equate himself to God. He becomes a creature of "pride" and "concupiscence." Lest there be any doubt, the Apologist gives voice to "the Wisdom of God" in an extended Prosopopoeia:

> I am He who formed you, and I alone can teach you who you are. But you are no longer in the condition in which I formed you. I created man to be holy, innocent, and perfect; I filled him with light and intelligence; and I communicated to him My glory and My wonders. The eye of man then witnessed the majesty of God. He was not yet blinded by darkness or afflicted by death and *misères*.
>
> But he could not endure such glory without succumbing to presumption. He willed to center himself on himself and to make himself independent of my support. He withdrew from my dominion, equaling himself to me in the desire of finding his felicity in himself. I abandoned him and raised the lower creatures against him. . . . [Today,] man has become like the beasts, far removed from me. . . . Every creature either afflicts him or tempts him, dominating him either by forcibly overcoming him or by sweetly seducing him, a form of domination that is more terrible and harmful.
>
> That's the human condition. There remains only a feeble impression of the happiness of their first nature. They have plunged into the *misères* of their blindness, which has become their second nature.

Pascal argues for Furetière's *misère*-II, sinfulness, as the defining characteristic of human nature after the Fall, but he does not attempt to use the word with a lexicographer's precision.[12] Rather, he takes full advantage of the rhetorical possibilities offered by the other meanings of the term. In his initial opposition of *grandeur* to *misère* and in his heavy emphasis on the base creatureliness of fallen man, he evidently means to convey *misère*-III, contemptibleness. And in his initial emphasis on the happiness and felicity of man with God before the Fall, as in his yet more emphatic lesson in God's voice that fallen man cannot by himself recapture happiness and felicity, he associates *misère*-I, profound unhappiness.

There is good reason to fear that the thinker who does not more clearly distinguish among the several meanings of this protean term may weaken the logical force of his apologetic argument. A skeptic need not be persuaded that theological *misère*-II is the sole or best explanation for psychological *misère*-I or sociological *misère*-III. Even good evidence of profound unhappiness or contemptible baseness need not be accepted as a valid argument for the doctrine of original sin.

Rhetorically, the boldest aspect of "A.P.R." would also be most problematical in a publication intended for a worldly readership. This is the Prosopopoeia. Would this audience have heard Pascal's words, had he taken voice as "the wisdom of God"? The too heavy burden of this inspired rhetoric is the old story of the Fall, Adam's disobedience and God's punishment.

To be sure, the devout auditors at Port-Royal in 1658 were ready to respond favorably to an oral presentation in the manner of Pensée 149. Before Pascal spoke, they *knew* the truth of the doctrine, and they also *knew* his reputation as a thinker. After he had spoken, they admired the beauty, forcefulness, and emotional intensity of his words, that is, his wonderful capacity to draw from and appeal to the heart as well as the head.

Left-Column Misery: The Appropriation of Montaigne

Pensée 6 neatly presents Pascal's concept of his projected Apology. It sketches a two-part plan in which human "misery" without God is opposed to "felicity" with God. These two affective states, to call them that, are given a religious explanation. We are wretched without God and blissful with Him, damned by our sins and saved by His grace:

1. Part. Misery of
   man without God.
2. Part. Felicity of
   man with God.

Otherwise
1. Part. That [human] nature is corrupt,
   from [the evidence of] nature itself.
2. Part. That there is a Redeemer,
   from [the evidence of] Scripture.

The truly distinctive—and brilliant—feature of this plan is Pascal's intentional avoidance of overtly religious language or argumentation in the First Part. This is particularly true in dossiers prepared for the chapters with which he would have begun, conventionally numbered 2–5: "Vanité," "Misère," "Ennui," and "Raisons des Effets." In the dossiers "Grandeur" and "Contrariétés," numbered 6–7, he filed several fragmentary variants on the theme of *grandeur/misère* in which the Fall and original sin are implied but not quite specified. Pensées 113–114, written in order on the same sheet under a single heading, link the celebrated "thinking reed" (with first-person pronouns) to the more fundamental antinomy of *grandeur/misère* (in the third person). Here, the thought that dignifies us is not physical science but a self-awareness that is loosely "sociological," knowledge of where we fit in the great chain of being, and "psychological," consciousness of our wretchedness:

Thinking Reed

It is not in space that I must seek my dignity but in the government of my thought. It will do me no good to own land. In space, the universe includes me and engulfs me like a point. In thought, I embrace it.

Grandeur of man. He is *grand* because he knows that he is *misérable*. A tree doesn't know its own *misère*.

Thus, it is to be *misérable* to know one's *misère*, but it is also to be *grand* to know one's *misère*.

Pensées 116–124 develop similar themes, coming closer to an explicit presentation of the Fall but never mentioning "sin" or "corruption." Pensée 131 is the great exception; here and here alone in fragments filed in dossiers prepared for the First Part, the reader finds a coherent development of explicitly theological ideas—sin, corruption, and grace, as such. Here and here alone, the consummate biblicist appeals formally to the authority of Scripture, concluding with a set of specific citations. Pascal had evidently concluded that anything obviously theological in the First Part might alienate the very readers whom he wanted to attract. He would make his case about "the misery of man" by arguing "from nature."

The Apologist's goal in this First Part was to encourage and direct readers' confrontations with themselves. In this way, perhaps, he could help them to see and to feel the essential truth, their corruption and so their need for redemption. This would make them more receptive intellectually to the overtly religious argumentation of the Second Part and, more importantly, it could impel them toward spiritual conversion and a life of Christian penitence.

Two unclassified pensées suggest this strategy more clearly than anything filed away in the planning *liasse* (Pensées 1–12). Pensée 620 lays down as a quasi-Cartesian first certainty that "man is made to think," then affirms that "the proper order is to begin by thinking of ourselves and our author and our end." This may not be clear and distinct, but it suggests that a reasoner's reflection on the self properly comes first and logically leads to further reflection on God. Pensée 780 is more explicit with respect to self-knowledge as the proper starting point and to the works of the Christian humanists as reference points:

> Preface to the First Part.
>
> Talk about those who have treated self-knowledge. Charron's boring and depressing divisions. Montaigne's confusion and confessed lack of a regular method; he avoided it [self-knowledge?] by jumping from topic to topic, always trying to look good. His foolish project of self-portraiture, not accidentally or despite himself, but as his primary intention. It's a common enough failing to talk nonsense by chance or weakness, but to do so by design! That's intolerable, and such nonsense as his!

So much for this preface, which got no further than the dyspeptic draftlet, and so much, apparently, for Charron and Montaigne. But in his First Part, Pascal did adopt "divisions" from the much-maligned Charron and fill these borrowed forms with substance that owed a great deal to the much-maligned Montaigne.[13]

Mesnard has suggested that the "misery" of the *Pensées* was learned from Montaigne, who "has his defined place at the beginning of a sound Apology. . . . He clearly sees man's misery. . . . Montaigne profoundly inspired the first chapters of the Apology."[14] Did Montaigne "clearly see man's misery"—in the primary sense? And did he "profoundly inspire the first chapters of the Apology"—in this respect? As a latter-day skeptic, I doubt it. Reconsideration of Pascal's appropriation of materials from Montaigne in preparations for the First Part of his Apology shows that his *misère*-I was his own, that he avoided explicit discussion of *misère*-II, and that Montaigne was most influential with respect to *misère*-III. Psychological misery most concerns us.

Bernard Croquette has published as full a catalog of Pascal's reminiscences of Montaigne's *Essais* as is ever likely to be truly useful. Many of the most celebrated "fragments" are actually mosaics in which even smaller bits and pieces of prose remembered from this reading are rearranged into new patterns. In the dossier "Vanité," for instance, Croquette tabulates thirty-five reminiscences in twelve pensées.[15] Only three of these fragments concern *misère*-I.

In Pensée 43, Pascal recalls Montaigne's "De la diversion," twisting the Essayist's lines into a knot that is wholly his own. Montaigne considers bereavement and recommends the therapeutic strategy of attempting to distract the grieving person rather than to deny the legitimacy of grief. This is to divert passions that are too strong to block. At the heart of the essay is his reflection on his own overpowering grief after the death of his great friend and soul mate, Étienne de La Boétie. Before the passage adapted by Pascal, Montaigne refers to the loss; afterward, he refers to roughly comparable losses—a daughter, a ruler, a master, a friend, and a father. He describes Plutarch's mourning for his daughter and her little games, then his own confrontation with the prospect of death and the loss of life's little pleasures—a dog, a horse, a book, a glass.[16] And Pascal? Reminiscences in Pensée 43 allow us to follow his memory back to pages on the most profound grief and how to live with it: "It doesn't take much to console us, because it doesn't take much to afflict us." What happened to Montaigne's preoccupation with significant loss? Where are his "little pleasures"? *Trifles* are enough to *distress* us? *This* dark thought was Pascal's own.[17]

Pascal's Pensée 44, headed "Imagination," skims from the edges of Montaigne's "De la force de l'imagination" and draws deeply from several other essays.[18] Pascal considers misery-unhappiness in two brief passages. Only the first depends in any way on anything from Montaigne. It is a complicated case in which Pascal telescopes two reminiscences into a single dark thought.[19] In one, Montaigne's point is that fortune is quite enough to make a man successful, if not wise.[20] Pascal sharpens the point and turns it against thinkers like himself: "Imagination" or the irrational mind "can't make fools wise, but it does make them happy, quite unlike reason, which can only make its friends miserable [*misérable*-I]."

In the other passage here recalled, Montaigne confesses his vexation at the self-satisfaction of opinionated fools and a ruefulness that self-criticism should seem so much wiser. This is very far from the Pascalian conclusion that the only reasonable state of mind is to be miserable. Indeed, Montaigne followed his passage on foolish self-satisfaction and wise self-criticism with a prompt acknowledgment of "my natural gaiety."[21] Given the choice between Democritus' disdain for human follies and Heraclitus' pity for human miseries, he did not hesitate: "I do not think that there is so much unhappiness in us as vanity, not so much malice as stupidity. We are not so full of evil as of inanity, not so *misérable* as we are worthless."[22]

Pensée 47 is the last fragment from the dossier "Vanité" to include both affective substance in Pascal's thought and verbal tracers to Montaigne's *Essais.* The humanist had emphasized the "vanity" of anyone who would claim continued potency for a lifeless corpse and so deny the finality of death. He had then generalized and qualified the idea: All of us anticipate the future, living beyond ourselves and the present, but this is natural and not simply foolish. Pascal made the ideas and words his own in a brilliant but very dark fragment. His view—not Montaigne's—was that Everyman's present life is "wounding" and "afflicting." He concluded—as Montaigne had not—that we will "*never*" be happy. This "never" is emphatic; he wrote it and then struck it, wrote it again and then struck it again, wrote simply that we are not happy and then struck that, too, before finally satisfying himself: "It is inevitable that we will never be happy."[23]

Pensée 56 is the one fragment from the dossier "Misère" that carried affective burdens in words that Pascal seems to have borrowed in part from Montaigne:

> We are so unhappy that we can only find pleasure from something that would pain us if it turned out badly, which could happen in a thousand ways and does happen all the time. The secret would be to find a way of enjoying good things without getting upset by the corresponding bad, [but no one has discovered how to do that]. It's like perpetual motion.

The Essayist had contrarily defended the pursuit of pleasure, as such, while debating the pros and cons of heavy drinking. Does alcohol befuddle the sage? Perhaps so, but he can be confused "in a thousand ways." If Pascal recalled the essay in question, he transformed another's reflections on a simple pleasure into his own thought that there is no such thing.[24]

Pascal's eighth dossier, "Divertissement," is certainly the one in which his transformations of Montaigne's meanings are most significant. Pensées 133, 136, and 139 concern us. With respect to the first, Montaigne had asked his readers, the philosophical few, to keep death ever present in their thoughts. Pascal began Pensée 133 with a false start on our desperate search for happiness, and then, with no exemption for an intellectual aristocracy, he added *misère* and ignorance to death:[25] "Being unable to cure death, misery, and ignorance, but wanting to be happy, men have decided not to think about them." In a marginal afterthought (Pensée 134), Pascal returned to the desperate search for happiness: "Despite these miseries, he wants to be happy. He wants nothing other than to be happy. And he can't fail to want this. . . . [So he doesn't think about death.]"

The common scholarly presumption is that Pascal filed the several papers in the *liasses* in an "inverse" order, first knotting his thread beneath the "last" paper as copied after his death and then running it through one paper after another as he added to the pile. If so, the paper filed just before this raises the horrific prospect of "my" mother's death before "my" birth (Pensée 135):

> I feel that I might never have existed, because my self is my thought. Therefore, I who think would not have existed if my mother had been killed before my birth. Therefore, I am not a necessary being.

This combines the hyperrationalism of Descartes's cogito with an hyperbolical anxiety that is Pascal's own. His pensée links an imagined *prenatal* "loss" of mother to the loss of selfhood; especially in the literary context of other fragments on our common tendency to "divert" attention from painful thoughts of death, this recalls his particular bereavement as a young child and suggests deeply repressed grief. Montaigne left nothing remotely comparable to this.[26]

Pensée 136 as first drafted begins as a meditation on "The Misery of Man" in which man's *misère* is clearly psychological. There is one "effective reason" for our "unhappiness," our incapacity for "pleasure," our "unsupportable discomfort," and our "painful sufferings." That "reason" is "the unhappiness of our condition." *All men* are "so miserable," and therefore *we* are "so miserable."[27] When Pascal developed this deep and dark "thought," he did so with materials from Montaigne, but the depth and darkness of Pensée 136 remained his own, as in lines on miserable monarchs. Montaigne's king, closely observed, is discovered to be mean-spirited, *misérable*-III, "perhaps baser than the least of his subjects"; Pascal's is rather unhappy, *misérable*-I, "unhappier than the least of his subjects."[28]

Pascal continued the theme of the miserable monarch in Pensée 136, and his first draft includes yet another passage in which his reminiscence from Montaigne betrays his own deeper and darker perspective. For Montaigne, the fact was that the richest king cannot be assured of the greatest pleasure; paradoxically, a poorer subject, knowing fewer pleasures better, may enjoy greater happiness. It looks as if the apologist first rebuked the Essayist for "foolish philosophizing." For Pascal, the Truth was that this world's goods can offer no one happiness.[29]

Montaigne did have his melancholy moments, as he freely confessed. In another passage from Pensée 136, Pascal adapts this confession to serve his very different claim that *everyone* is *always* miserable, actually or potentially: "We are preoccupied with miseries, those that we experience and those that we fear." Thus, according to Pascal but not Montaigne, our condition is such that we despair even when things are going well.[30]

Pensée 136 includes one more reminiscence of the same sort. In it, Pascal recalls generally relevant themes and words from Montaigne, but he also expresses an ennui, unhappiness, and misery that have no warrant from this source of his literary and philosophical inspiration. Both great minds consider self-deception, but it is only *Pascal* who focuses sharply on *misère*-I. His imaginary antihero is the deluded gambler who seeks a false "happiness" and flees a true "misery," for which there is no specific cause. Contrarily, *Montaigne* offers the sorry spectacle of individuals who suffer from particular illnesses, injuries, and losses. He has no interest in how worldly men try to escape from a generalized misery.[31]

Pensée 139 is the last of those in Pascal's First Part that concern *misère*-I and recall identifiable passages from the *Essais*. As in the previous parallel, the context recalled does include close reference to the experience or threat of loss, but Pascal and not Montaigne is responsible for the implication that the common search for happiness is commonly frustrated.[32]

Verbal reminiscences have suggested that Pascal borrowed his *misère*-I from Montaigne, but a systematic comparison demonstrates just the opposite. Pascal *never* simply *borrowed* his unhappiness. He did recall many words from many *Essais,* and he had learned much from the substance and style of this wonderful book. But there is no instance in which his "misery of man" simply reflects Montaigne's prior introspection, observation, or book learning. In the fragments that we have reviewed, he *always darkened* the substance, *never light-*

ening it. How did Pascal put it in Pensée 689? "It's not in Montaigne that I find everything I see there, but in myself."[33]

This argument affects more than pedantic questions and problematical answers concerning the literary sources of particular passages. The logical validity of Pascal's Apologetic conception is at stake. From Pensée 6, it seems clear that he planned to make the case for human "corruption" by adducing evidence drawn from human "nature." That is, he was to have demonstrated man's sinfulness and need for redemption by his "misery." But to argue in this way is to play on two or three quite different meanings of the word *misère,* to use *misère*-I and -III as evidence of *misère*-II, that is, misery-unhappiness and -contemptibleness as evidence of misery-sinfulness. This is invalid.

On the other hand, logical validity is not the summum bonum. The Pascal who wanted to persuade readers to seek God knew that formal proof is rarely as persuasive as rhetorical appeal. He also believed that the truths of religion are "infinitely far above nature," instilled in man by God alone in his own way. That way leads through the heart to mind, not vice versa.[34]

In the last "fragment" filed under left-column titles (for left and right columns, see the text of table 6 and the facsimile that follows), a single sheet filled on both sides (Pensée 148), Pascal concludes the First Part and, in his heading, announces the Second Part. He says that all men without exception seek happiness, but that no man, without faith, has ever found it. Others' experience—*and our own*—should be instructive, but it is not, as *we* lurch "from unhappiness to unhappiness," unsatisfied but unpersuaded that we will not find the happiness we seek:

> This yearning and this impotence cry out to us [sic]. Once, there must have been a true happiness for man. There remains only a mark, a trace. Ineffectually, he [sic] tries to fill the void with all that surrounds him, seeking from things that are absent the help he cannot get from things that are present. Nothing will do, because this infinite gulf can be filled only with an infinite and immutable object, that is, God Himself.

Once, "he" enjoyed that satisfying object, but "he" left it and so lost it. Now, to fill the void within, the right-thinking man must seek a "true good" that can be "possessed without loss and [shared] without jealousy," an object that "cannot be taken from him against his will."

Pascal supposed that all persons unhappily experience the persistent ache that he describes so movingly. Sacred history and Christian theology explain it. There was a primal paradise for all mankind; in the Garden, our common ancestors knew and loved God, the one true object. Then came their Fall and our great loss, followed by our perverted love for transient creatures. They cannot satisfy; they cannot last; they are taken from us against our will. Neither the nature of the problem, "misère," nor the appeal of this explanation, the Fall, can have been simple or simply personal. But, knowing what we do about a more proximate history, that of the Pascal family, it is hard to resist the conclusion that the mature Apologist drew deeply on the affective experience of the child and young man.

Right-Column Misery: The Appeal to Reasonable Sinners

Working copies of the *Pensées* made soon after Pascal's death provide the best evidence on the partial order that he had established for Pensées 1–382. Each copy begins with an identical table of contents in which the titles of dossiers being prepared for chapters are listed in two columns, ten titles on the left (from "Ordre" to "Souverain Bien") and eighteen on the right (from "A.P.R." to "Conclusion"). Although the *Recueil original* does not include this table in Pascal's own hand (see table 6), scholars have established the authenticity of the surviving copies.[35] The two columns suggest the two-part plan known from Pensée 6. However, there are problems with this reconstruction.

A reader who seeks the light of human happiness in right-column dossiers read as a "Second Part" finds only occasional glimmers. In Pensée 149, there is the profession of faith that "our true bliss is to be with Him"; in Pensée 160, there is the assertion that only the faithful are "reasonable and happy"; in Pensée 243, there is the opinion that Old Testament saints display admirable "morals and happiness"; finally, in Pensée 357, there is the simple declaration: "No one is as happy as a true Christian, or as reasonable, virtuous, and worthy of love." But that's about it. There is literally neither "joy" nor "rejoicing" in any of the 234 fragments filed under the titles of the right column.[36] Nor do these titles by themselves suggest a plan in which "felicity" is the governing principle. Pascal did not have this argument in mind when he composed these fragments and conceived this sequence of dossiers.

TABLE 6
The Two-Column Table of Dossiers for the Two-Part Apology

Ordre	A.P.R.
	Commencenment
Vanité	Soumission et usage de la raison
Misère	Excellence
	Transition
Ennui	—La nature est corrompue
~~Opinions du peuple saines~~	Fausseté des autres religions
Raisons des effets	Religion aimable
	Fondement
Grandeur	Loi figurative
	Rabbinage
Contrariétés	Perpetuité
	Preuvres de Moise
Divertissement	Preuves de J.C.
	Prophetie
Philosophes	Figures
	Morale chrétienne
Le souverain bien	Conclusion

See Mesnard, *Les Pensées de Pascal,* 27 and note 4.

The right-column titles and corresponding dossiers develop the three-stage scheme of Pensée 12:

Order

Men have contempt for religion. They hate it, fearing that it might be true. To remedy that, [Stage I] one must begin by showing that religion isn't irrational, [but rather] venerable and worthy of respect.

[Stage II] Then make it attractive; make good men wish that it were true, and [Stage III] then show that it is true. Venerable because it knows man truly. Attractive because it promises his true good.

"A.P.R.," conventionally read as a chapter 11, is in almost every way exceptional, a case apart. Its place on the Table at the head of the right column is roughly comparable to that of the dossier "Ordre" at the head of the left; neither would have prefaced or introduced a finished Apology.

"Commencement," which is nonsensical as the title for a chapter

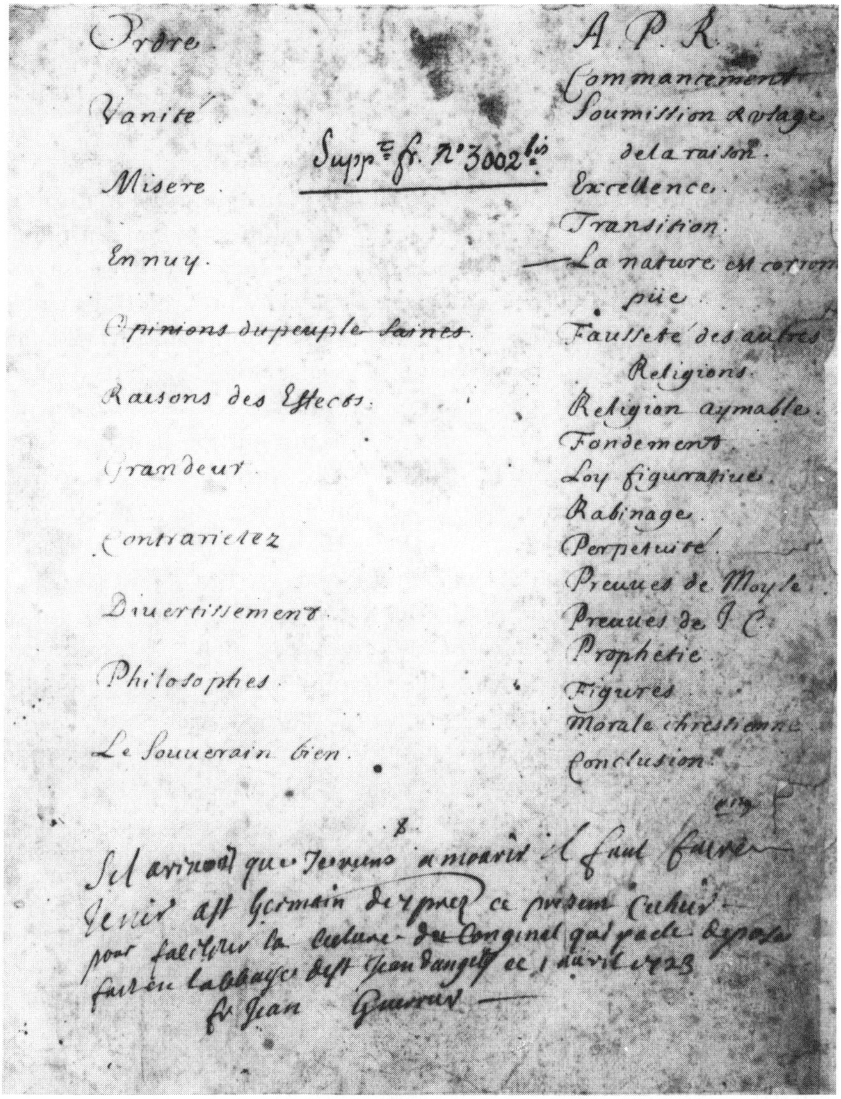

Ordre.
Vanité.
Misere.
Ennuy.
~~Opinions du peuple saines~~
Raisons des Effects.
Grandeur.
Contrarietez.
Divertissement.
Philosophes.
Le Souuerain bien.

Supp^t fr. n° 3002 bis

A.P.R.
Commancement
Soumission et usage de la raison.
Excellence.
Transition.
La nature est corrompue.
Fausseté des autres Religions.
Religion aymable.
Fondement.
Loy figurative.
Rabinage.
Perpetuité.
Preuues de Moyse.
Preuues de J.C.
Prophetie.
Figures.
Morale chrestienne.
Conclusion.

S'il arrivoit que je vins a mourir il faut faire tenir a st Germain des prez ce present cahier pour faciliter la lecture de l'original qui y a esté deposé fait en labbaye de st Jean dangely ce 1 avril 1723
fr Jean Guerrier

The Two-Column Table from the First Copy. Photograph © Bibliothèque Nationale de France, Paris.

12, properly begins Stage I as envisioned in Pensée 12. "Soumission et usage de la raison," conventionally chapter 13, seems superfluous when read after left-column materials but fits neatly into a scheme without them. "Excellence [de cette manière de prouver dieu]," conventionally chapter 14, establishes the divinity of Jesus by the old argument from prophecy, then makes a case for the *misère* of man, a surprising exercise after the naturalistic First Part but quite in keeping with the more overtly religious scheme of Pensée 12. "Transition [de la conaissance de l'homme à dieu]," conventionally chapter 15, is very awkward so far into a Second Part but unproblematical if reconsidered without the First Part. "La nature est corrompue," conventionally chapter 15b, has been yet more awkward, because *this* dossier is empty, there being no correspondingly ordered fragments. Indeed, no chapter on original sin in this position could have been part of a coherent two-column plan.[37] Pascal's Stage I with its dossier on sinfulness, as such, seems to have exploded into a Part One with its more artful evocation of *misère*. But the author had not fully assimilated materials filed according to the prior scheme into the dossiers of the new plan or finally accommodated his two conceptions.

Stages II and III of the three-stage scheme are less relevant to our concerns, however important for the Apology. They fit much more neatly into the Second Part of the two-part plan. "Fausseté des autres religions," and "[Rendre la] religion aimable," conventionally chapters 16–17, perform the functions outlined in Pensée 12 for Stage II. Finally, the nine dossiers, from "Fondations" to "Morale chrétienne" (conventionally chapters 18–26) present formal arguments for the truth of the Christian religion as envisioned in Pensée 12 for Stage III. This all supports the "Conclusion" (conventionally chapter 27).

In right-column dossiers, Pascal was not setting out to make a case for the happiness of Christians. Rather, he began by trying to show that the Christian religion is "venerable," even "reasonable," insofar as its theological conception of man's sinfulness (*misère*-II) accords with the experiential facts of the matter (*misère*-I). In Pensées 149, 192, 208, 352, 354, and 360, the Christian is he who *knows* his own *misère* as well as God's redemption. Of course, this *misère* and that of Pensées 189, 190, 222, 239, and 260 is theological. Yet it is also psychological, denoting unhappiness.

Many of the classified fragments that follow Pascal's announcement of a Second Part in Pensée 148 seem ominous with respect to his emotional life, although any biographical interpretation is complicated by known apologetic intentions and unknown inventions of voice and persona. The most haunting fragments are those from the dossier "Transition." Pensées 198-200, all headed with an enigmatic "H.," seem to have been retained from an earlier draft "on man." The first of these merits a careful rereading:

> Seeing the blindness and misery of man, regarding the silent universe and man left in the dark, abandoned and alone, as if lost in this corner of the universe without knowing who put him there, what he is to do, or what is to become of him after death, incapable of understanding anything, I become terrified, like a man carried off in his sleep to a frightful, desolate island who awakens without understanding how he has gotten there or how to get off.
>
> Then I marvel that a situation that's so miserable doesn't drive men to despair. I see other persons of my own kind around me, and I ask them if they are any better informed. They say they aren't. Then these lost and miserable creatures, having looked around and seen attractive objects, commit themselves and form attachments. As for me, I couldn't become attached here. Considering how much more likely it is that there's more to existence than I can see, I've tried to find some evidence of God.
>
> I see many different religions, all but one false. Each commands belief on its own authority, and each threatens unbelievers. Therefore, I can't accept any of them on that basis. . . . But in the Christian religion I find [true] prophecies, and that's not something that just anyone can do.

Who speaks in Pensée 198? About whom? The answers cannot be simple. At the beginning of the first nightmarish sentence, the speaker, apparently a detached observer, contemplates the misery of isolated "man." By the end of the sentence, he himself recoils in terror, as if he, too, has been spirited away to a place of utter desolation, "like a man. . . ." He tries to engage other men in dialogue. What do *they* know? Why don't *they* despair? How can *they* form attachments? They don't know, can't say. Then, once again, the first-person asserts itself: *I*'m different; *I* can't form attachments; *I* seek a divine object and find scriptural evidence.

Who speaks?[38] About whom? It would be comforting to distantiate Pascal from this voice and from the "man" of Pensée 198, and there is some reason to do so. Pensée 427 puts somewhat similar sentiments into the mouth of the foolish atheist who acknowledges ignorance, suffers miseries, and yet awaits death unconcernedly. Surely, nothing about Pensée 198 is intentionally autobiographical. Yet there are also disturbing indicators of deeply personal meanings. *Pascal had been "abandoned"* by both parents and both sisters. After the loss of Étienne and separation from Jacqueline, for at least a time *he had despaired.* At his Second Conversion, *he had renounced attachments* (*Mémorial, Écrit sur la conversion,* Pensées 373, 396, 597, 617–618, 688).

The two texts that follow in the Copies have always been admired as distinctively Pascalian. In Pensée 199, the man suspended between the two abysses finds self-knowledge painful. In Pensée 200, while asserting his dignity as a "thinking reed," the man-and-author emphasizes human vulnerability to microcosmic as well as macrocosmic forces:

> Man is only a reed, the weakest in nature, but he is a thinking reed. It isn't necessary for the whole universe to arm itself against him to crush him; a vapor or a drop of water is enough to kill him. But even if the universe were to crush him, man would be still nobler than his killer, because he knows that he is dying and the advantage of the universe over him. The universe knows nothing.

Pascal did ennoble himself by his thought, literally in 1645 and figuratively in 1670. Better than anyone else of his time, he understood that even the greatest thinker is ridiculously weak and that all perceptions of nature, including human nature, are in part subjective. This is as true for himself as for anyone else. He states the case admirably in Pensée 199: "Rather than simply receiving ideas of things as they are, we mark them with our qualities and stamp every simple object that we contemplate with our complex being."

CHAPTER 14

The *Pensées* II: The Misery of This Man

When his heirs discovered only partially ordered bits and pieces among Pascal's papers, not the long-anticipated Apology, they might well have discarded everything. Instead, they kept everything *and* made meticulous copies, not only of the written materials that he had classified in service of his Grand Design (Pensées 1–382) but also of many other papers with expressive and self-referential texts, most of which would have been too intimate for a published Apology. This chapter reconsiders this exceptional evidence on the man's feelings, intentionally subordinating the author's thinking.

Two and a half centuries after Voltaire, I argue more methodically that Pascal himself was a man of exceptional unhappiness, *misère*-I. The philosophe did not notice that his antagonist cryptically identified himself as a veritable man of misery. He did intuit that Pascal's fragments express melancholy moods. I suspect from this and from other evidence to be discussed in chapter 15 that the great man was what we would call a depressive.[1] The Périers, who were closest to him, had a different terminology but not a wholly different understanding; Gilberte, Florin, and Étienne all said that after 1658 Pascal had suffered from a "*langueur.*"[2] The term is vague, but it denotes depressed moods. It is another word for *chagrin, malheur, mélancholie,* or *tristesse*.[3]

Depressed Mood in Expressive Fragments

Pascal chose cryptic signatures and pseudonyms that expressed truths about himself. He really did collaborate with "Antoine Arnauld," and he really was "Blaise Pascal, Auvergnat, son of Étienne Pascal," hence "E.A.A.B.P.A.F.D.E.P." Somewhat similarly, after the Night of Fire and the Miracle of the Thorn, he really had seen from the "high mountain" and heard the voice from a "bright cloud," and so, metaphorically, he was "Montalte." We cannot say how he would have named himself on the title page of a completed Apology, but he provides a clue in Pensée 745, showing himself behind the double veil of an anagrammatical variant on his earlier pseudonym:

> The style of Epictetus, Montaigne, and *Salomon de Tultie* is the most familiar and most persuasive. It remains longest in memory and is most often cited, because it is composed entirely of thoughts deriving from ordinary conversation. For instance, when people talk about the common error that the moon is the cause of everything, they never fail to remark that *Salomon de Tultie* said that it is good for there to be a common error when the truth is unknown.

On the opposite side of this sheet, Pascal had in fact advocated humble acquiescence in error as preferable to a vain curiosity, using the supposed effects of the moon as his example. Here, in the last sentence, the devout author seems to undercut too proud a reference to his own literary gifts by a consciously ironic report on the popular reception of a book that was still so far from publication. His choice of a pseudonymous identity remains very intriguing.

Why *Salomon* de Tultie? Biblical associations of royalty and wisdom must have been pleasing, but there was something far more important. Solomon was thought to have been the author of the Book of Ecclesiastes, which memorably addresses human vanities. This Book emphasizes the transience of things human, the hollowness of worldly pleasures, and the mortality even of the wisest man. It is a book opposed to bookmaking, the book of vanity and vexation, grief and sorrow, death and mourning.

Pensée 403 couples Solomon with that more familiar figure of human misery, Job. A secretary recorded this reflection in a fine, even elegant, hand. Pascal then added and heavily retraced his own heading, "Misère," in a huge, dark scrawl.[4] Thought bows beneath the weight of feeling:

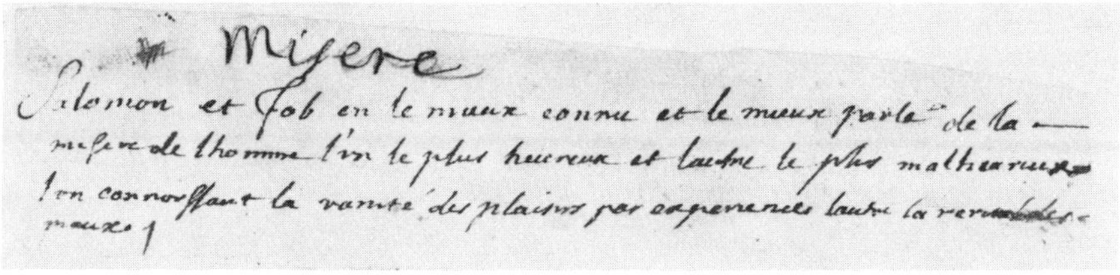
Misere
Salomon et Job ont le mieux connu et le mieux parlé de la misere de l'homme l'un le plus heureux et l'autre le plus malheureux l'un connoissant la vanité des plaisirs par experience l'autre la realité des maux.

Pascal's Autograph of Pensée 403. Photograph © Bibliothèque Nationale de France, Paris.

Misery

Solomon and Job best knew and best expressed the misery of man, one the happiest and the other the unhappiest of men. One knew the vanity of pleasures from experience, and the other, the reality of pains.

In the dossier "Misère," Solomon appears three times as a teacher of the subject. Pensée 75, which was apparently the first fragment filed under this title, cites Ecclesiastes as an authority for our "inevitable unhappiness" and states the theme of Pascal's First Part, "the misery of man without God":

> Ecclesiastes shows that man without God is in a condition of absolute ignorance and inevitable unhappiness, for it is to be unhappy to want something without being able to get it. Well, he wants to be happy and to be assured of some truth. And yet he can neither know nor fail to want to know. He can't even doubt.

So much for ignorance. What of unhappiness? Pensées 69 and 74 also couple Solomon with Job, in the first instance under the single-word heading "Misère" and in the second under a sentence on "concupiscence." The great interest of the Solomon-pseudonym together with the Solomon-pensées is that they establish Pascal as a figure of misery *in his own mind*.

Pensée 622, all in Pascal's hand, provides further evidence that is also arresting visually. No edited text can represent the combined effect of the hesitations, the telling strikeouts (here bracketed, following Tourneur's typographical conventions), the emphatic reiterations, the "central" afterthought (here conventionally italicized), and the darkly drawn heading, apparently added and "centered" after the afterthought (and so also italicized).[5] I provide a facsimile and a printed text in the apparent order of composition: first, the block of text from the left, second, the afterthought from the right, and third, the heading from above.

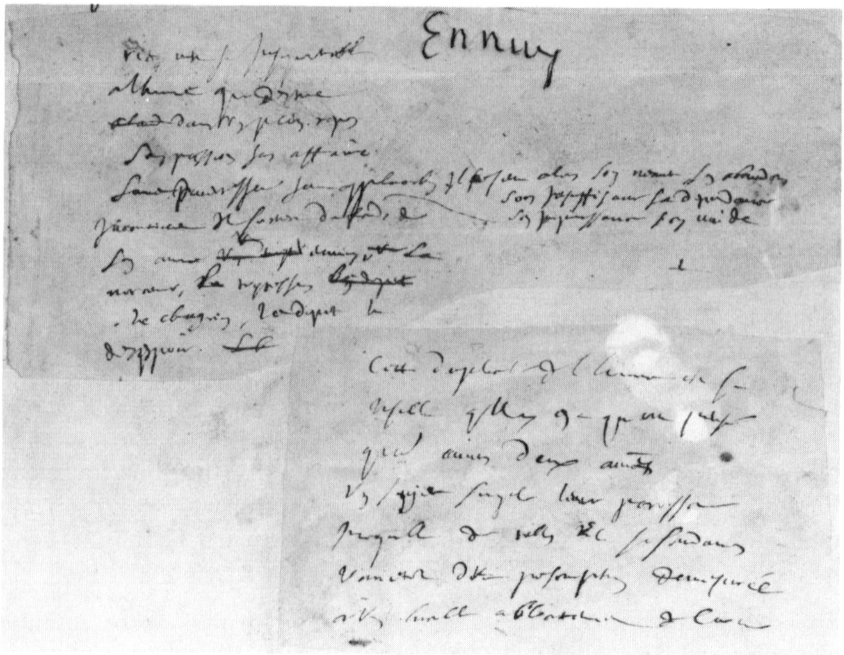

Pascal's Autograph of Pensées 622 and 629. Photograph © Bibliothèque Nationale de France, Paris.

Rien n'est si insupportable à l'homme que d'être [aband] dans un plein repos, sans passions, sans affaires, sans [p] divertissement, sans application. Incontinent il sortira du fonds de son âme [une trist [un]] l'ennui, [une] la noirceur, [une] la tristesse, [un [le dépit]], la chagrin, le désespoir. [L'h] *Il se sent alors son néant, son abandon, son insuffisance, sa dépendance, son impuissance, son vide.* ***ENNUI***

"Nothing is so unbearable as for man to be [aband[oned]], at rest, without passions, occupations, [p[leasures?]], diversions, or work. Feelings well up from the depths of his soul, [sad[ness]], anxiety, gloom, sadness, [melancholy], depression, despair. *Then he feels his nothingness, his abandonment, his inadequacy, his dependence, his impotence, his emptiness.* ***ENNUI."***[6]

"Ennui" is Pascal's word for the greatest anguish, not mere boredom. He used the term in the *Mystère,* for instance, for the agony of Jesus about to be betrayed by Judas and abandoned even by the other

Disciples. Pensée 622 is not properly a "thought," nor can it be read as the draft of a part of an apologetic argument being prepared for publication by a dispassionate genius. It is the cry of a desperately unhappy man, someone who felt "abandoned" and was "depressed."

It would betray my own ignorance of medical science, as well as a lack of historical judgment, were I to affix a single scrap of paper, even this paper, to the dead man's image, as if it were a diagnostic label and he were a psychiatric patient. Nevertheless, in light of such extraordinary documentation, so suggestive of deeply depressed moods, I do question the contrary presumption of mental health. I do affirm the relevance of modern studies of affective disorders. And I do challenge explanations limited to abstract thought.

Pascal *began* Pensée 622 by tripping over what may have been the most painful word of all: "Nothing is so unbearable for man as to be *aband* . . ." He *ended* the text with the italicized afterthought, that is, with another reference to *"abandonment"* and the associated feelings of "insufficiency, dependence, weakness, and emptiness." This makes psychological sense in light of his historical experience: his loss of his mother in early childhood after an anxious attachment, his loss of his father in early adulthood after a uniquely dependent upbringing, and separations from the beloved sisters who found other loves.

In the *Recueil original,* Pascal's heirs mounted Pensée 622 with Pensée 629 (reproduced in the lower right of the facsimile and discussed more fully below). On this other paper, the author reflects on "man's doubleness," his sudden mood swings "from unbounded presumption to horrible, heartfelt despondency."

Depressed Mood in Self-Referential Fragments

Scattered evidence on Pascal's moods, which certainly varied, can be found in a few other self-referential fragments that were never intended for an Apology. Pensée 931 in particular has long been accepted as a true representation, and it provides whatever caution is needed against a simplistic linking of Pascal's devotion with Pascal's misery. Gilberte, who knew him best, called it his "self-portrait on a little paper."[7] Although Pascal condemned public self-portraiture in the manner of Montaigne, his own profession of faith, intended for his private use, can serve us in this way:

I love all men like brothers, because they are all redeemed. I love poverty, because He loved it, and I love property, because it gives me the means with which to assist the poor. I keep faith with everyone, not repaying in kind those who wrong me, but wishing for them a condition like mine, which is beyond men's harm or men's help.

I try to be just, truthful, sincere, and faithful to all men, and I have tender feelings for those with whom God has united me more closely. And whether I am alone or within the sight of others, my every action is chosen with regard for the eye of God, who judges all and to whom I have consecrated all. These are my sentiments.

And I bless my Redeemer every day of my life for having given them to me. I was a man bound by weakness, *misère,* concupiscence, pride, and ambition, and He has freed me from these evils by the power of His grace, to which all glory is due, there being nothing of my own but *misère* and error.[8]

Pascal confesses that he once was a creature of *misère* and other failings that are quite clearly sins. He also says that he *still is* essentially a creature of "*misère* and error." What sort of *misère* is this? The context, a prayer of thanksgiving for God's redemptive love, requires us to read this instance, too, as *misère*-II, a term for human sinfulness. There was no contradiction for Pascal to claim both that he was now redeemed, having been a sinner, and that his redemption was the gift of God's grace, he being naturally a sinner. The term as used here need not imply *misère*-I.

This confessed sinner seems almost angelic in his superiority to human attachments. He imagines himself to be a creature beyond the reach of others' harm or help, while professing a universal love for all men and promising charitable assistance to the poor. He withdraws even in the long afterthought in which he expresses particular affection for "those with whom God has united me more closely" (presumably Jacqueline, Gilberte, and the Périers); they may see him, but he looks to God alone. Of course, austere Port-Royalists preached withdrawal and detachment. What seems distinctive about Pascal's situation as portrayed here is that the devout convert, an unmarried layperson, chose to remain in the world while withdrawing from the worldly.

On the same manuscript page, Pensée 932 concerns the propriety of a sort of apparent mockery that Pascal defends as the expression his actual pity;[9] this suggests a date when the author was struggling to reconcile his aggressive *Provinciales* with his Christian principles.

So Pensée 931 may portray not the author of the *Pensées* or the invalid of the last four years but the author of the *Provinciales* in healthier years. The detachment that I take to be implicit in the self-portrait was explicit in the last of the Letters, which is securely datable to the winter of 1657: "I have no attachment on this earth . . . , being unattached to any community or individual . . . , being free, without commitments, without an attachment, without a tie, without a relationship."[10] The discouragement of this same Letter has already been documented.

On the other side of the manuscript sheet, there is more important material.[11] In Pensée 792, Pascal effectively denies the possibility of true friendship. In Pensée 793, he peremptorily rejects false religions and reaffirms the true. The apparent end of the latter fragment is actually the beginning of the self-portrait. Before the more familiar lines that Gilberte incorporated into her memoir, he wrote:

Thus, *I hold up my arms* to my Liberator, who, having been prophesied for four thousand years, came to suffer and die for me on earth at just the time and in just the way that had been predicted. By His grace, *I peacefully await death,* hoping to be united with Him forever. Nevertheless, *I live joyfully,* whether among the [bad] good things that it pleases Him to give me or among the bad that he sends me for my good and that he teaches me to endure by His example [emphases added].

Peace and joy characterize the man here portrayed. That is very important. Nevertheless, the one physical image, upraised arms, suggests a deeper vulnerability. These arms are those of a grown man who had used the gesture repeatedly in his early childhood. "Pick me up! Hold me!" This child, who yearned to be picked up and held, lived on in the mature thinker. We expect an author, and we find a man, in the words of Pensée 675. And in the man, there is a child, as he wrote in Pensée 779:

. . . How can someone who is so weak as a child be really strong as an adult? . . . All that was once weak can never be absolutely strong. It's only talk to say that "he has grown" or "he has changed." He's still the same.

The same man presents an unposed portrait in Pensée 545, where the context for the upraised arms seems much more threatening. The fragment is undatable:

Libido sentiendi, libido sciendi, libido dominandi. Woe to the accursed world that these three rivers of fire engulf without watering! *Happy are they who remain* beside these rivers, not plunged in, not carried away, but motionless and secure beside these rivers, *not standing up, but sitting down, in a low and safe position!* They do not rise up before dawn, but after a peaceful night, *they hold out their arms to Him who will raise them up* to set them on the porches of Jerusalem, where they can stand upright and steady. There, pride can no longer attack them and knock them down. *Nevertheless, they cry, not to see that the torrents have swept away everything perishable, but to remember the dear fatherland* of the heavenly Jerusalem, . . . kept alive in memory throughout their long exile [emphases added].

Pascal here recalls I John 2:16 and perhaps also Jansenius's exegesis. The verse as fragmentarily quoted could have suggested useful, even profound ideas, especially the pervasiveness of human sinfulness in the orders of body, mind, and spirit.[12] But John had developed no such philosophical theology; in the text that inspired Pascal there is no idea more profound than the insecurity of man's love for mortal objects:

I John 2:15 *Love not the world, neither the things that are in the world.* If any man love the world, the love of the Father is not in him.
16 *For all that is in the world, the lust of the flesh, and the lust of the eyes, and the pride of life,* is not of the Father, but is of the world.
17 And *the world passeth away,* and the lust thereof; but he that doeth the will of God abideth forever.

Pascal also recalled Psalm 136 (Vulgate) with Augustine's commentary:[13]

Ps. 136:1 By the rivers of Babylon, there we sat down, yea, we wept, when we remembered Zion.
2 We hanged our harps upon the willows in the midst thereof.
3 For there they that carried us away captive required of us a song; and they that wasted us required of us mirth, saying, sing us one of the songs of Zion.

"How shall we sing?" How shall we be mirthful? Augustine had taught that "the 'rivers of Babylon' are all those things that are loved and pass away."[14] For Blaise Pascal, these included his mother and father. The child's arms in Pensée 545, upraised to his parents, are his own, not John's or Jansenius's, not David's or Augustine's. How was he to sing? How was he to be mirthful?

Pensée 687 is more certainly self-referential, even autobiographical, and more certainly unhappy:

I spent a long time in the study of the abstract sciences, before the little communication that was possible led me to quit them in disgust. When I began the study of man, I saw that the abstract sciences are not proper to man and that, as I advanced in them, I strayed further from my condition than did those who remained ignorant of them. I forgave them for their lack of knowledge, but I thought that I would at least find many companions in the study of man, which is his true and proper study. I was mistaken. Even fewer pursue this than geometry. It's [not?] only because they don't know how to go about this study that they seek other subjects. Isn't it [rather] because even *this is not the science that a man ought to know and because it is better for him to remain ignorant about himself in order to be happy* [emphasis added].

There is much more here than the faint echo of an abstract idea, Pascalian diversion.

First, Pensée 687 provides Pascal's private explanation for his abandonment of mathematics and natural science in 1654.[15] The devout convert says that the worldly genius had suffered from a lack of companions with whom to share his work and its results—this at just the time when he had broken off his very productive correspondence with Fermat! But it all makes sense. The problem, I believe, was that mathematics and science had been a part of Blaise's life with his father and his father's friends, and the joy of these studies was lost for him when they died, Étienne Pascal on 24 September 1651 and Jacques Le Pailleur on 4 November 1654.[16] These deaths decapitated the scientific household and the scientific Academy among whose members the younger Pascal had been, as he put it, "raised."[17]

Second, Pensée 687 is of exceptional interest for Pascal's related recollection that he had found still less companionship "in the study of man." It is unsurprising that he had little fellow feeling for the likes of the Chevalier de Méré or Damien Mitton. It is more interesting that he was also dissatisfied by the more profound Christian humanists whom he had met in books. He dismissed Montaigne as "confused" and "foolish" and Charron as "wearisome and depressing." Descartes seemed "useless and uncertain."[18] Along with his memory of even less "communication" in this study than in geometry, this suggests an even greater "disgust." It also recalls Jacqueline's remarks on her brother's misery, his sense of abandonment, and his "almost unbearable disgust at the world and everyone in it."[19]

Third, Pensée 687 brings home the presupposition about man that underlies the Pascalian notion of diversion. Here, it is clearly Pascal himself who is the lonely student of self, and what he has found must be his own unhappiness. Are the vain Méré and the worldly Mitton happier? If so, Pascal supposes, it is only because they are ignorant of what he knows so much better, man's unhappiness.

Pensée 688 is the first of several other self-referential fragments that follow closely in the order of the First Copy and that seem to have been at least loosely grouped by the author. "What is the self?" Pascal's response to his own question strips all attractions of the body and of the mind from the "self" and so denies the very possibility of human love, not just for Everyman, but for himself. "If someone loves me for my judgment [shades of Montaigne!] or my memory [the legendary memory of which Pascal was so proud, in sharpest contrast to Montaigne], does that person love *me?* No . . ." Does *anyone* ever really love *anyone* else, another self, rather than another's accidental qualities? Not according to Pascal's pensée.[20]

This may be the best place to confront the fragmentary evidence that Pascal was almost as skeptical about the prospects for friendship. On the same sheet with his celebrated self-portrait, he remarks matter of factly that almost everyone disdains almost everyone else, even nominal friends, so that what passes for friendship requires mutual deception: "[I]n fact, if everyone knew what others said about him, there wouldn't be four friends in the world."[21]

The last of the self-referential fragments to be studied in this section of this chapter is Pensée 552, which concerns the weather, good and bad, and the author's moods, good and bad. Pascal knew that sunny days commonly make for sunny spirits, but he also knew that this commonplace relationship between the weather and moods did not hold true for him:

> *Lustravit lampade terras.* The weather and my moods have little to do with one another. I have my fogs and my clear skies within me. Even my successes and failures don't have much effect on me. I sometimes rise on my own against [bad] fortune, and the glory of overcoming it makes me do so in high spirits. Yet I am sometimes downcast in [spite of] good fortune.

The manuscript shows that the man-and-author twice began to say that the weather had "nothing" to do with his moods before correcting himself to say "little." He also slipped slightly before *le bien et le mal de mes affaires,* here translated as "my successes and failures," and again before *dégoûté,* here rendered, perhaps inadequately, as "downcast."[22]

Knowledge of the remarkable literary history of the Latin tag quoted in Pascal's first words helps to establish Pensée 552 as a virtual confession of melancholy, this man's melancholy. Some of this is a prehistory that he could not have known and would not have cared much about. That prehistory begins with Homer's *Odyssey* bk. 18, lines 136–37. Unknown Stoics in lost works later cited the passage in the course of forgotten arguments about Fate. Cicero still later translated and commented upon the verses in the course of discussing these philosophical opinions, but the work in which he did so has also been lost, and Pascal could not have gotten his "Homer" from Cicero, either.

Augustine incorporated the Ciceronian adaptation in *The City of God* (bk. V, chap. 8), which Pascal did know and revere. Montaigne recalled this passage in two essays, "De l'inconstance de nos actions" and the "Apologie de Raymond Sebond," and he knew these parts of this book, too, exceptionally well. Finally, Charron duly entered it in a prominent section of his *De la sagesse* (bk. I, chap. 40), which he also knew and used.[23]

Thus, when Pascal joined the procession, he followed illustrious predecessors. Homer's Odysseus heads it. He prophesies that the evil-doing Suitors will suffer retribution; the gods bring down lawless men. According to Cicero, Stoics used these verses as a proof text on the power of Fate. Cicero's Latin version is known only from Augustine, who interpreted the Stoic Fate as the Christian God:

> Tales sunt hominum mentes, quali pater ipse
> Iuppiter auctiferas lustravit lumine terras.

"Such are the minds of men, as is the daylight with which the Father, Jupiter himself, has illuminated the bountiful earth." Theological sunlight has poured into what had been epic gloom.

Montaigne and Charron then used the same Homeric verses as ornamental evidence on the instability of human judgment. They seem to have forgotten all about the ancient lesson that Fate or God could or would reverse the fortunes of haughty wrongdoers. Their point was that our minds are as changeable as the weather and perhaps so unstable because of the very instability of the weather. This was a psychological generalization based unsystematically on a broad application of humoral theories, a shrewd emphasis on the relationship of behavior to circumstances, and a commonsense recognition that fair weather naturally makes most people feel good and foul weather not so good.

Montaigne used the text twice, first to ornament his case for our intellectual and mental stability in "De l'inconstance":[24]

> Normally, we follow the lead of our appetite, which inclines us to the left or the right, uphill or down, carrying us along with the winds of circumstance. . . . The plan that we now make, we soon change, then change again, inconsistently swaying. . . . Every day a new fancy, as our humors change with the weather:
>
> Tales sunt hominum mentes, quali pater ipse
> Juppiter auctifero *lustravit lumine terras.*
>
> We float between different opinions, wanting nothing freely, nothing absolutely, nothing consistently.[25]

It is Montaigne's second citation of the Homeric text that gives Pascal's exact wording. It comes in the "Apologie," from a set of pages that Pascal also recalled in Pensées 27, 44, 136, and 530.[26] Here, the Essayist's point is the natural dependence of moods and judgments on the changeable weather:

> It is certain that our perception, our judgment, and in general the faculties of our soul suffer according to the movements and alterations of the body, which are continual. . . . Don't joy and gaiety lend things quite a different appearance than grief and melancholy? . . . The very air and the serenity of the sky bring us some change, as stated in this Greek verse from Cicero:
>
> Tales sunt hominum mentes, quali pater ipse
> Juppiter auctifera *lustravit lampade terras.*
>
> It isn't only fevers, potions, and great accidents that upset our judgment; the slightest things in the world spin it around. . . .[27]

Men enjoy good moods when God's sun shines. And when Michel de Montaigne as an individual has enjoyed a good meal, good health, and a good day, he says, he is quite an agreeable fellow.[28]

Not so, Blaise Pascal? In Pensée 552, *he* adapts the old verse fragment to his brief discussion of the variability of *his* moods and only his moods, not men's external fortunes (in the manner of Homer, the Stoics, Cicero, and Augustine) or mental operations more generally (in the manner of Montaigne and Charron). He says that sunny days do not bring him sunny moods.

Pascal does allow for the private experience of "beautiful weather within me," but even the upside of the pensée suggests something other than contentedness. He proclaims "the glory" of struggling against adversity "in high spirits." Together with the downside, the "fogs within" during periods of good weather and the "disgust" when everything would seem to be going well, these fierce "high spirits" give a properly Pascalian overcast to a fragment that was provoked by his disagreement with the humanists—and his own self-awareness.

In two other passages, Montaigne, too, had claimed a personal independence from any law regulating mood swings by weather changes. A passage from "De l'expérience" represents his mature philosophical outlook: "I pass the time when the weather is bad and inclement; when it is good, I don't want to let it go, and I hold it and savor it. We must run through the bad and settle into the good."[29] The other passage, from "De la vanité," concerns travel. Montaigne boasts that no weather can stop him or spoil his enjoyment on the road. If it is too hot for summertime travel under the burning sun, he sleeps though the heat of the day and rides through the cool of the night. Even if it is cold and wet, he will not let that bother him; he professes "to love the rains and the mud like a duck."[30]

It is tempting to conclude that Montaigne did not mind even bad weather—and that Pascal did not enjoy even good weather. This would not be a happy thought, nor would it be quite true. Pensée 552 reflects Pascal's experience of mood swings, up as well as down, independent of circumstances.

Pensée 629 is in many respects similar, although it is not clearly self-referential. It, too, has an evident literary inspiration in Montaigne's "De l'inconstance." The Essayist emphasizes that we are so "inconsistent," heroes one day but cowards the next, that we seem to have "two souls." He was concerned with moral conduct and its mental basis:

> These supple variations and contradictions that are seen in us have made some imagine that we have two souls and others, that two powers accompany us and drive us, each in its own way, one toward good and the other

toward evil. For such sudden diversity cannot well be reconciled with a simple subject.[31]

In Pensée 629, Pascal retains Montaigne's interest in inconstancy and his language of duplicity/simplicity but somehow transforms the moralist's preoccupation with good/*evil* and courage/*cowardice* into a more psychological observation on presumption/*despondency:*

The doubleness of man is so evident that there are those who have said we have two souls. A single subject would seem incapable of such [extreme] and sudden variation, from unbounded presumption to a horrible and heartfelt despondency.

Anxious Convert, Unhappy Uncle, and Joyful Christian

An obvious—and substantial—objection to my emphasis on the lasting emotional effects of earlier familial separations and losses is that the convert enjoyed exceptional spiritual favors, the Night of Fire and the Miracle of the Thorn, which were powerfully exalting. This is true, but his state of mind even in periods soon after these two great events was hardly the simple felicity of the blessed. Our documentation on the former is superior.

In addition to the *Mémorial,* the *Mystère de Jésus* and Pensées 927–929 also provide fragmentary but powerful evidence from the winter of 1654–55. The *Mystère* (Pensée 919) offers the most intimate expression of human anguish yielding to divine consolation. Although the manuscript is undated, incidental references to particular circumstances place it in this season. The *Mystère* begins with Pascal's powerful meditation in the present tense on the night in Gethsemane when Christ suffered, in his thesaurus, "torment, agony, pain, sorrow, sadness, distress, and abandonment." Jesus has been forsaken even by the sleeping Disciples. Pascal must be vigilant, not just for part of a night or a whole night or even a series of nights, but until the end of the world, never yielding to sleep:

He suffers this pain and this abandonment in the horror of the night.

I think that this is the only time that Jesus ever complains. But then He cries out as if He couldn't contain His excessive grief: "My soul is sorrowful even unto death." [Matt. 26:38]

Just this once in His entire life, it seems to me, Jesus seeks companionship and consolation from men, but he doesn't get any, because His Disciples sleep.

Jesus will be in agony until the end of the world. Until then, we mustn't sleep.

Like Jesus, Pascal would have to separate himself from the persons closest to him, including his sisters, especially Jacqueline, and his friends, particularly Artus de Roannez:[32]

Jesus tears Himself away from His disciples at the beginning of His Passion. We must imitate Him, tearing ourselves away from our nearest and dearest. . . .

If God gives us masters with His own hand, oh, how willingly we must obey them! Necessity and events are what they must be.

The God-given "masters" of this paragraph apparently refer to Singlin and de Sacy, Jacqueline's preferred director and the substitute made necessary by his illness.[33] Pascal's submissiveness here recalls the Second Postscript from the Parchment *Mémorial:* "Total submission to Jesus Christ and my director. An eternity of joy for a day of exercise on earth. I will not forget Thy Word."

At this point, the text of the *Mystère* shifts from meditation in Pascal's own voice to consolation in Jesus' voice:

Be consoled. You wouldn't seek Me, if you didn't possess Me.

I thought of you in My agony. I shed such blood for you!

It's more to tempt Me than to test yourself, [for you] to suppose that if only circumstances were different you would have done the right thing. I'll do it for you, if it comes to that.

Let yourself be guided by My rules [cf. *Mémorial,* lines 24–25 and Second Postscript]. You know how well I guided the Virgin and the other saints who let me act in them. . . .

These words recall Pascal's autumnal despair that he had cut himself off from God (*Mémorial,* lines 14–15, 22), even that God had already abandoned him or might yet abandon him (Jacqueline's letter of 25 January 1655; cf. *Mémorial,* lines 16–17, 23). They also testify to the subsequent advent of his newfound confidence that God specially favored him, even that he now "possessed God." Jesus Himself would direct him.

Pensées 927–929 are less celebrated than the *Mémorial* or the *Mystère* but from the same period and in some respects similar. These numbered fragments are part of a complex whole on one manuscript sheet headed by three elliptical lines. Signs of wear along folds strongly suggest that at least for a time Pascal carried this paper, too, on his person:[34]

What good would it do me.
Abominations.
Singlin.

The first of these lines echoes Augustine's reflections, which de Sacy brought particularly to Pascal's attention, on the uselessness of his exceptional philosophical intelligence (as a reader of Aristotle).[35] Here, the dispirited penitent reflects on problems that run deeper than his great pride as a critical reader of Montaigne and Epictetus. His "exterior works" of devotion like fasting are not necessarily good, because they can foster spiritual pride.[36] In this context, Pascal also reflects that interior graces like Saint Theresa's have the same potential for evil, so that anyone who sets out to imitate her without her humility may actually be disserving himself. "What good would it do me to remember it [cf. *Mémorial,* Second Postscript], if it could as easily hurt me as help me?"

Pensées 927–929 apparently come from very late in the season when Pascal had haunted Port-Royal and his cloistered sister. The new convert had been extraordinarily favored by his vision of the God of Abraham and had vowed a "total renunciation" and "total submission," only to find that Père Singlin first would not and then, after the loss of his voice, could not take upon himself his direction.[37] In this historical situation, on the same manuscript page, his God took voice reassuringly:

Don't compare yourself to others, but to Me. If you don't find Me in those to whom you compare yourself, you are comparing yourself to something abominable. If you do find Me in them, compare yourself to Me. But what will you be comparing? Will it be yourself or Me in you? If it's yourself, that's something abominable. If it's Me, that's to compare Me to Myself. Well, I'm God in everything.

I often take voice and counsel you, because your director can't speak and I don't want you to lack a director. Perhaps I do it in answer to his prayers, and so he directs you without your knowledge.

You wouldn't seek Me, if you didn't already possess Me. Therefore, be not anxious.

Nothing is simple: in Pensées 927–929, as in the *Mémorial* itself and the *Mystère,* there is good evidence of personal anxiety as well as spiritual comfort. Pascal believed that, whatever his intellectual genius and penitential exercises, he could not help himself and might harm himself. He might turn even God's favors against himself:

"What good would it do me?" All persons, including the devout and, of course, himself, were "abominations." And when he thought of his spiritual journey, he was frustrated by the fact that, after he had yielded to Jacqueline, her priest could or would not direct him: "Singlin."

Some two years later, the Miracle of the Thorn inspired a brief but important expression of apparently uncomplicated happiness. Pascal did feel a renewed sense of God's love. The ideals of faith, hope, and charity had combined to arouse extraordinary expectations of extraordinary assistance, and these expectations were not disappointed. In Pensée 922, he prays for the additional grace necessary for true thanksgiving: "On the miracle. As God has made no family happier, let Him make none more grateful."

Pensée 923 follows, with 924 on the other side of the same sheet.[38] The former concerns the insufficiency of penitential works and the necessity for contrition; the latter concerns the inner war between our sinful nature and God's redemptive grace. It anticipates (or echoes) the remarkable passage from the letter to Charlotte de Roannez of 24 December 1656 in which Pascal compares the convert's soul to an infant caught in the violent struggle between kidnappers and the mother who grasps her child.[39] God brings just such a war between nature and grace, not peace, still less contentment. The "familial happiness" of Pensée 922 must be interpreted accordingly.

According to Gilberte, Pascal's gratitude for the Miracle inspired the earliest conception of an Apology, which was to have been based on miracles.[40] Pensées 830–912 suggest instead that in the fall and winter of 1656–57 Blaise first intended to compose another polemic against the Jesuits, although there are also signs of a broadening of this conception in which the antagonists would have been "atheists" and "skeptics," that is, disciples of Montaigne and Descartes. Thus, polemical *Provinciales* evolved into apologetic *Pensées*.[41] Pascal never developed projects for a work of either sort based on miracles, and Pensées 830–912 have not attracted much scholarly interest.

Significant introspective passages within the set are among those that have been neglected. Consider Pensées 885–891, all from one manuscript page.[42] Pensée 885 justifies the vigor of his *Provinciales* by the persecutions of Port-Royal. Pensées 886 and 887 censure philosophical skeptics, particularly Montaigne, and the doctrinaire rationalist, Descartes; this criticism of the antithetical philosophies recalls the *Entretien*. Pensée 888 "wagers" that whoever put the title on the *Provinciales* was not from the provinces. Pensée 891 distinguishes between divine miracles and demonic pseudomiracles, a matter of great concern for a year or more after 24 March 1656, when the meaning of the Miracle of the Thorn was debated by the rival parties.

Pensées 889 and 890 are separated only by one of the author's customary traits. I bracket his strikeouts, which are very suggestive:

> Pensées.
>
> *In omnibus requiem quaesivi.* If our condition were truly happy, we would not have to divert ourselves from thinking about it [to cheer *(réjouir)*] [to che *(réjou)*] to make ourselves happy.
>
> ---
>
> All occupations of men are undertaken in pursuit of their own interest, but they lack the title for legitimate possession or the strength for secure possession. It's the same for knowledge and pleasure; we don't have either the truth or the reality.

According to Pascal, "we" are not happy; "we" have no right to pleasure and no way of securing it.

The term "Pensées," which is centered at the head of fragment 889, is properly read as the author's informal reference to his own projected Apology (cf. Pensées 532, 542, 696, 745). The Périers, too, are quite consistent in their earliest posthumous references, which seems to confirm that the term had Pascalian authority.[43] Furthermore, the same manuscript page also includes autobiographical reflections on other writing. Thus, Pensée 889 must be autobiographical.

But how different were the perspectives of the author manqué himself and his heirs! The Périers later preferred to imagine the "great work" that the illustrious thinker had not been given healthy years enough to complete, but Pascal himself wrote of his fragmentary thoughts as if the work nominally in progress were an escape, his own diversion from his own unhappiness: "Pensées. 'In all these I sought rest.' " It was *his* condition that was not truly happy; *he* diverted *himself* from thinking about it to make *himself,* if not truly happy, then at least less unhappy.

Within the somewhat artificial bounds editorially assigned to Pensée 889, the first-person singular subject occurs only in the fragmentary citation from Ecclesiasticus 24:7. This passage resonated in Pascal's mind, associating God, Wisdom, and the Chosen People. But there is no scriptural basis for his seemingly discordant expression of unhappiness or for what was later to be developed as one of his most profound ideas, that of "diversion." In the fall of 1656 and winter of 1657, his exalted feeling of being specially chosen as a defender of Truth slid into the depressed mood that betrays itself in the last *Provinciales* and the last *Lettres à Mlle. de Roannez.*

Pascal's spirits were to rebound, then to fall back again. 1658 was a year of exceptional productivity for the mathematician and the Apologist alike. Despite this, available evidence suggests that his acute sense of "the misery of man" antedated the composition of "A.P.R." with its antinomy of *grandeur/misère,* the conception of the three-stage Apology with its first stage on fallen man, and the conception of the two-part Apology defined by the opposition of the misery of man without God and the felicity of man with God. Whatever his sense of having been saved and called and whatever his conviction that *he knew* God, he had been and would be again a miserable man.

Pascal believed that there was a promised "felicity" or supreme happiness for the Christian, but he reserved it for the afterlife and contrasted it with miseries here below. Consider Pensée 427, which provided the Port-Royal editors with most of their first chapter:[44]

It requires no great spiritual elevation to comprehend that there is no true and lasting satisfaction here below, that our pleasures are only vanity, that our ills are infinite, and finally that death, which threatens us at every moment, must necessarily confront us in a few years with the horrible alternative of being annihilated or wretched throughout eternity. Nothing could be more real or more terrible. . . .

In the *Lettres philosophiques,* Voltaire somehow let this pass without particular objection, but in the year of his own death—and worldly triumph—he made good the lapse.[45] Even the Port-Royal editors, who knew Pascal and shared his Augustinian faith and apologetic purposes, excised this part of his continuation, presumably because even they judged it to be unpersuasive:

Let anyone think about this. Let him then say whether it isn't incontestable that there is no good in this life other than the hope of another life, that one is happy only insofar as he approaches it, and that, just as there will be no more unhappiness for those who have perfect confidence in eternity, so also there is no happiness for those who have no knowledge of it.

Had they not made the excision, Voltaire would have found another occasion for another remark on another statement of the same simple falsehood.

I stand back from my own work far enough to acknowledge expressions of the "joy, trust, and love" that his faith brought to Blaise Pascal. Here is one such expression, from Pensée 449, chosen for its significant reference to "the God of Abraham":

> The God of Abraham, the God of Isaac, and the God of Jacob, the God of the Christians, is a God of love and consolation. He fills the heart and soul of those whom he possesses. He is a God who makes them feel both their misery and his infinite mercy; who unites himself with them in the depths of their soul; who fills it with humility, joy, trust, and love; and who makes them incapable of having any other end but him.

Abstractly, here is the theology of the Two Loves, yet again. Here is the champion of opposed truths, corruption and redemption, yet again. And, I believe, here is a man of misery, unhappy as well as sinful, yet again. His religion was his consolation.

CHAPTER 15

Other Depressive Traits in Pascal's Last Years

In his last years, Pascal exhibited not only depressed spirits but also other symptoms of what would now be considered a mood disorder. What follows draws from Pascal himself and other informants not primarily concerned with his illness. Generally, their testimony is anecdotal and neither precise chronologically nor sophisticated medically. Such scattered reports cannot make good our lack of a medical case history, properly speaking, and I do not attempt a pseudoclinical diagnosis. I do look for a significant pattern in the available historical evidence, and I do argue that modern psychiatric manuals provide such a pattern.

In the most respected diagnostic system, depression is conceived as a syndrome involving at least five of the following nine symptoms, including at least one of the first two:

1. depressed mood
2. diminished interest or pleasure in usual activities
3. decrease in appetite
4. insomnia
5. psychomotor retardation
6. fatigue or loss of energy
7. feelings of worthlessness or excessive or inappropriate guilt

8. diminished ability to think, concentrate, or decide
9. recurrent thoughts of death.[1]

Having interpreted various fragments as evidence of depressed moods even before the last four years of Pascal's illness, I turn to this period of relative incapacitation in search of historical evidence of these other psychiatric symptoms.[2] The historical and cross-cultural applicability of this modern American diagnostic system is discussed briefly appendix 2.

Diminished Interest or Pleasure in Usual Activities

"Loss of interest or pleasure is probably always present in a major depressive episode. . . ."[3] Of course, seventeenth-century priests warned against the very "interests and pleasures" that would seem healthiest to twentieth-century psychiatrists.

Pascal's most important known interests and pleasures before his conversion were mathematical and scientific. Afterward, that is, after 1654, there was to be *no* further development of the Arithmetic Machine, despite previously announced intentions; *no* further publication related to the Vacuum Experiments, despite the fact that the *Traités* of 1663 had been "all ready to print more than twelve years ago"; and, astonishingly, *no* distribution of the *Traité du triangle arithmétique,* despite the fact that it had already been printed in 1654 before the author "entirely quit this sort of study."[4]

Pascal's only mathematical work after conversion concerned the *roulette* or cycloid. Gilberte later claimed that this had been a brief and wholly exceptional episode, begun accidentally in nights made sleepless by an acute toothache and ended after "eighteen days" of precipitous work, all dedicated to the greater glory of God.[5] Her evident defensiveness about his return to secular concerns probably echoes his own; the more important point is that from late 1654 to mid-1658 and then again from early 1659 to his death in 1662, he showed no interest in mathematics.[6] Nor need we rely on an argument from silence.

Florin Périer's testimony is explicit and authoritative. He was uniquely qualified by intimate familiarity, spiritual sympathy, and scientific interest. He was a blood relative who had allied himself more closely by marriage in 1641, another Jansenist whose devotion was evident to supporters and opponents alike after the conversions of 1646–47, and the scientist who actually performed and reported the Great Experiment on the puy de Dôme in 1648 and published Pascal's posthumous *Traités* in 1663. We have to take him at his word when he writes:

> [M]ore than ten years before his death [1662], he had come to know the vanity and nothingness of these sorts of knowledge. He had conceived such a disgust for them that he could hardly tolerate that intelligent persons should pursue them or talk seriously about them. . . .
>
> [It was "more than twelve years ago," counting backward from 1663,] that Monsieur Pascal devoted himself entirely to more serious studies. They so disgusted him with mathematics and physics that he abandoned them absolutely.[7]

Alternative calculations establish the same date for Pascal's rejection of mathematics and the sciences. It must have been in late 1651, when the Périers came to Paris for the division of Étienne's estate, that Florin first observed not just Blaise's "abandonment" of these pursuits, but something stronger, his "disgust."[8] Apparently, he had not observed anything comparable in 1649–50, when the Pascals, father and son, had spent about a year and a half in his household in Clermont. This chronology does not conform to that of the celebrated spiritual conversions, in that the rejection of the sciences came well after the First Conversion and well before the Second. Yet it does make perfect sense, given Blaise's close association of these interests with Étienne during his father's lifetime and his desolation after his death. Otherwise documentable bursts of such activity in later years, 1654 and 1658, which Périer was in no position to observe, qualify without wholly discrediting his report. He did spend extended periods with his brother-in-law in 1656, 1660, and 1661–62, and Pascal cannot have pursued the earlier interests in these periods.

Jean Mesnard has argued that applied sciences and technological development were spiritually acceptable and that, even after the Second Conversion, Pascal pursued such interests. Mesnard discusses swamp drainings, steam power, flying machines, and public transportation. We reconsider the evidence.

First, swamp drainings.[9] The duc de Roannez surely had a great interest in this work, and Pascal did invest in his friend's projects. However, his commitment of funds preceded the Conversion and was made at a time of exceptional energy and optimism (March 1654); his financial stake was very modest (one-third of a one-forty-eighth share, representing a capital of some 350–400 *livres*), and he liquidated this investment within about three years (by June 1657, perhaps in the preceding winter of discontent, discouragement, and discontinued projects).[10] Furthermore, there is no good evidence that he ever visited the sites of the work in Poitou.[11] His own writings include no word on swamp drainings or land reclamation, and intimates and others alike make no mention of such interests.

Second and third, steam power and flying machines. Christian Huygens is our informant in a single, tantalizing journal entry, dated 13 December 1660:

> Saw Chapelain, Conrart, Roberval. Didn't find Carcavy. . . . The duc de Roannez came to see me, and Pascal later. Talked about the force of steam in their cannon and about flying. I showed them my telescopes.[12]

What was "their cannon"? A pump? And who did the talking? Roannez himself? Huygens's other entries on the "cannon," without reference to Pascal, show that Roannez took the initiative in the absence of his friend (3, 27, 30 December). Pascal's degree of interest is unknown.[13] The Duke had actually fitted out at least one musket barrel with a piston, but we are left to speculate about its purpose, design, and operation.[14]

Huygens's reference to flight in the same journal entry is even more mysterious. The single-word notation on 13 December cannot tell us much. There is an earlier "description" of a flying machine with the address "Chez Monsr. Pascal rue Brisemiche," but the *Étienne* Pascals had left this address in *1648,* and there is no other evidence of *Blaise*'s later interest in relevant physical phenomena or technological innovation.[15]

Huygens's *Journal* is more telling for what it does not say than for what it does say about Pascal's interests in this period. The great Dutch scientist visited Paris from October 1660 to March 1661, and he was very curious about his French counterpart, but he encountered him only twice.[16] Significantly, he never found him at the regular Tuesday gatherings of the Montmort Academy, which was later to become the royal Académie des Sciences. On 5 December 1660, he did see him at the Roannez mansion, but he did not hear anything about Pascal's current interests that he considered worth recording. The 13 December entry, discussed above, is a very faint echo.

Fourth among suspected interests, there is urban public transportation. Since the publication of an *on dit* in Henri Sauval's *Histoire et recherches des antiquités de la ville de Paris* (1724), Pascal has been honored for the conception of the unprecedented system of carriages following fixed routes on city streets according to a regular schedule. *On dit.* Who says? None of the Périers in the familial memoirs and prefaces, despite the fact that Gilberte, Florin, Étienne, Marguerite were all in Paris when the *carrosses à cinq sols* began to roll down the city streets, none of the savants who so admired Pascal's earlier work, nor anyone else in anything published within two generations after the great man's death.[17]

Nevertheless, a notarial record discovered by Mesnard proves that Pascal did share in the first conception of the transportation system as early as 1658, a year of wonderful energy and varied creativity, including his contributions to the *Écrits des curés de Paris,* his Conference on the projected Apology, and his triumph in his own mathematical competition.[18] Then the project languished for several years, as Pascal also languished in these years. Louis de Montalte (Pascal the polemicist), Salomon de Tultie (Pascal the apologist), and Amos Dettonville (Pascal the mathematician) all fell silent.

Progress toward implementation came in late 1661, when an agreement was reached among three great noblemen, including Roannez but not Pascal. It was only in the winter and spring of 1662 that the organization of the new enterprise was completed and carriages moved. Pascal played no documented role.[19]

There is evidence that other interests and pleasures also suffered in Pascal's years of illness. His former enjoyment of Montaigne, which is explicit in the *Entretien* and implicit throughout the *Pensées,* is especially important. He was so imbued with the whole of the *Essais* that he repeated his predecessor's words frequently and probably inadvertently, even when his own thought was quite different and his copy of the *Essais* was closed.[20] Pascal's absorption of so much shows that he must have been very interested in the author and pleased with his book at some earlier date—but most explicit references to Montaigne in the *Pensées* betray extreme impatience, displeasure, even intolerance (Pensées 89, 525, 577, 649, 680, 689, 780, 863, 872). Pensée 745, with its praise for Montaigne's style, is exceptional.

Otherwise, where once he had found both instruction and enjoyment, now he professed to find less than nothing.

Of course, after the Second Conversion, there were other interests, especially the attack on theological error and the defense of religious truth. But the *Écrits sur la Grâce* are now dated to 1655–56; the last of the *Provinciales* was dated 24 March 1657; the *Sixième écrit des curés de Paris* was dated 24 July 1658; the best qualified scholar dates most of the *Pensées* to 1657–58, the celebrated Conference at Port-Royal to May 1658, and "the great classification" of fragments to the fall of that same year.[21] What was left to be written after 1658? Only some fragmentary and disorganized pensées and few brief *opuscules* that cannot be dated with confidence or precision?[22]

There are indications that Pascal lost interest and pleasure even in work on the projected Apology. Gilberte says that he could not accomplish anything in his last four years, although there is some evidence of late fragments, including some in her own hand as his secretary.[23] However, her report does justify the conclusion that he no longer showed continued interest in the project and no longer derived any pleasure from its pursuit. Does chronic "ill health" provide explanation enough? Her son Étienne put it this way:

> These *Pensées* are only the slight beginnings and the feeble drafts, never revised or retouched, of a sick person who set them down only for his own reference, so that he could keep in mind thoughts that he was afraid of forgetting. . . . He often said that it would have taken him ten years of health to complete his book.[24]

Pascal himself used his "ill health" as an excuse for his suspension of work on the project, but the matter cannot have been simple. The "ten years" of his spoken lament complements a written expression of what is at best ambivalence about his great project. This is Pensée 153:

> What would be the extent of the commitment you seek? Ten years are at stake, what's worse, ten years of self-love and of really trying to please without succeeding, not to mention the inevitable pains.

The penitent evidently feared the pride of authorship, *and* that even a completed Apology would fail to convince unbelievers, *and* that it would all be a lot of trouble and sorrow. So much for late mental "interests and pleasures," even those directed toward spiritual ends.

The quest for late social "interests and pleasures" is as unrewarding. We have already seen that he withdrew—in "disgust" (Pensée 687)—from the learned company of the savants of Paris. He wrote as disparagingly of friendship (Pensées 139, 606, 731, 792, 978) as of romantic love (Pensées 46, 197, 413). Having rejected wordly society and all its various "diversions" (Pensées 136–137, etc.), he did not then join the devout Solitaires at Port-Royal des Champs. Nor, in his chamber, did he welcome the visits even from those seekers-of-God who valued his counsel. Indeed, he armed himself against them with a studded belt worn discreetly under his clothing, so that its sharp points, driven into his flanks by pressure from his elbows, could instantly punish any vanity or pleasure.[25]

It is far harder even to imagine this Pascal enjoying physical "interests and pleasures" of any sort. Gilberte says repeatedly that his "*two principal maxims*" were "*to renounce all pleasures and all superfluity.*"[26] In this context, she claims that "he always acted on principle in everything."[27] It seems clear that the late Pascal could not enjoy simple pleasures, but equally clear that Gilberte's hyperrationalism is incredible. Ascetic principles alone cannot fully explain Blaise's behavior, as is clear from the cases of eating and sleeping.

Decreased Appetite

Within his own household, Pascal's meals were very private. After 1652, he lived with only servants for "family," and, after 1654, he reduced even this household and avoided companionship. Indeed, he carried his own food to his own room, where even servants could not have observed his eating. It is unclear whether his nephews, Louis after 1658 and Étienne after 1660, normally shared a common table with him.[28]

Outside this household, as in his sister's residences at Clermont and Paris in 1660 and 1661–62, Pascal ate in others' company. He did not eat well. Gilberte documents "his frequent loss of appetite" during these years of chronic illness. Her efforts to arouse this appetite show her concern for her brother's health and her assumption that eating better might help to strengthen him. This must mean that she did not take at face value his protestations of a spiritual rationale for his table behavior. She could observe that he maintained "constant vigilance over his senses, refusing absolutely everything pleasurable," but there is a tension in her account between implicitly medical and explicitly spiritual explanations:[29]

For example, his constant ill health required him to eat daintily, but he took very great pains not to savor anything that he consumed. We noticed that, whatever trouble we took to find him something tasty to eat because of *his frequent loss of appetite,* he never said: "That's good!"[30]

Any assessment of this testimony must take into account that Gilberte was fully aware of Blaise's spiritual values, that she herself and her husband had been converted, and that she insisted upon the strictest standards of conduct for her own family.[31] Even from her perspective, Blaise's behavior was quite exceptional. When he was asked after a meal whether he had enjoyed a particular dish, he would not answer. When he heard others remark on their enjoyment, he would rebuke them:

Even when we served him something different and fresh, and asked him . . . whether he had found it tasty, he would simply say: "You've got to warn me ahead of time. I don't remember, and . . . I really didn't notice." And when anyone remarked favorably on a dish in his presence, he couldn't bear it, and he called it being sensual, even when it was only a matter of the simplest foods. This was because he said that it was a sign of eating to please the taste, which was always an evil.

To avoid falling, he wanted to forbid us to make him any sauces or ragouts, even with oranges or sour grapes or anything else that might have aroused his appetite, although he naturally loved them all. And so, to keep himself within regular bounds, from the beginning of his retreat he had been careful to satisfy the needs of his stomach. Since then he had regulated his eating so that, however great his appetite, he never ate more, and, however great his revulsion, he never failed to eat. When we asked him why he so constrained himself, he answered that the stomach had to be satisfied—but not the appetite.[32]

Pascal seemed to the closest observer to be prone to *dégoûts,* and his refusals to acknowledge the simple pleasures of eating—or to tolerate any such acknowledgment by others—went rather beyond the pious behavior of other devout converts, beyond even the spiritual counsel of the most austere authorities. In his most influential penitential tract, Jansenius himself had endorsed Augustine's rule: the Christian must not seek out pleasure as the purpose of eating but may enjoy pleasures that are incidental to meeting bodily needs.[33]

Insomnia

Patterns of sleep are even more private than patterns of eating and so even more difficult to document. Furthermore, the wakefulness of a devout person need not mean insomnia. In the *Mystère de Jésus,* an agonizingly personal document, Pascal states the case for Christian vigilance in the most extreme terms imaginable: "Jesus will be in agony until the world's end. We must not sleep until then. . . ."[34]

Gilberte knew that vigils and fasts are pious mortifications of elementary appetites—and yet, even in her work of Christian edification, she does not represent her brother's sleeplessness as an act of devotion. She provides instructive testimony on insomnia as such in a casual aside in the second version of her story about his work on the *roulette:*

> This aggravation of my brother's illnesses began with a toothache so severe that he couldn't get any sleep. But how could a mind like his be awake and not be thinking of anything? That's why, even *in his sleepless nights, which were, by the way, so frequent and so exhausting,* there came to him a few thoughts on the *roulette.* The first was followed by a second, and the second by a third.[35]

Quite apart from this occasion of dental torment and mathematical excitement, Pascal had notable difficulty sleeping. Gilberte's aside on his frequent insomnia is undated, but it must pertain to periods when she observed him, 1658–59, 1660, and 1661–62.

Psychomotor Retardation

"Psychomotor retardation" refers to a dramatic slowing of movement that is symptomatic of depression.[36] Clinicians are especially alert to retardation in conversation. They listen for a slowed pace, frequent pauses, low monotones, and simply a decreased amount of talking. The depressed person is apt to start sentences without completing them. There are pauses, hesitations, and awkward lapses into silence, often on particularly painful subjects.[37]

Reports that Pascal had trouble talking or that he avoided talking altogether are too widely separated in time and too summary to serve as evidence of his behavior in the years that interest us most.[38]

But we can still see his hand at work in the manuscripts of the *Pensées,* and I suggest that, for all their flashes of brilliance, they also provide evidence of retardation.

The more intriguing but less understood aspect of Pascal's incompletion is what might be called the micro-level of individual fragments as opposed to the macro-level of the Apology as a whole. Jean Mesnard suggests that Pascal composed in stages, so that fragments "grew," as if organically. According to this hypothesis, the great author regularly began with verbal "kernels," which he "progressively enlarged" from the littlest "fragments" into the biggest "wholes." Mesnard implies that, if Pascal had been healthy enough for long enough, he would somehow have produced a coherent work from these lesser drafts.[39] I remain skeptical.

From among the hundreds and hundreds of fragmentary bits and pieces, Mesnard singles out two as "particularly finished." They are Pensées 44 and 199.[40] It is important to acknowledge that Pascal occasionally expounded at some length (a few pages), but he left even these exceptional pieces incomplete. Even here, he paused, hesitated, broke off, and lapsed into silence.

Pensée 44, "Imagination," is a little essay reminiscent of Montaigne in subject matter, attitude, and language. It comes to a conclusion of sorts on "imagination" that trails off in these words: "Such, more or less, are the effects of this deceptive faculty. . . ." Then it continues in a sketchy and loosely bound addendum on other principles of error, but even this addendum has no proper end. The author seems to promise his readers that he will count the many such principles: "Let us see how many there are." But the promise turns out to have been a penultimate sentence. As his last word, he mentions just one principle: "But the most ridiculous cause of his errors is the war between the senses and reason." And then, so abruptly, he breaks off.

Pensée 199, "Disproportion de l'homme," is the other that Mesnard has singled out as "particularly finished." Even this most nearly complete piece is properly fragmentary, insofar as that term does not presuppose a whole that was ever in any sense complete. Pascal begins with a wonderful vision of the human body suspended between telescopic and microscopic infinities. This leads into a related discussion of the human mind and its remoteness from opposed extremes. But the parallelism breaks down, and, after a rather disappointing paragraph or two, the author seems ready to conclude well before he actually does so: "Such is our true state . . ." Does he ever really conclude? He resumes with loosely bound reflections on human ignorance ("If man were to study himself . . ."), then sends up verbal signal after verbal signal that he really does intend to conclude: "Finally, to complete the proof of our weakness, I will finish with these two considerations. . . ." Finally? Complete? Finish? Pascal never continued, let alone concluded this pensée, which ends with these words before trailing off in this ellipsis.

Neither physical illness nor spiritual devotion can possibly explain the peculiar form of incompletion observable in Pascal's fragments. However, the retardation of depression could provide a sufficient explanation for much of what is most characteristic about the fragmentariness of the *Pensées:* "[P]atients may start sentences but not complete them. . . . There may be pauses, hesitations, evasion, breaking-off, and brevity." [41]

Fatigue or Loss of Energy

Modern clinicians give this brief description of depressive fatigue: "A decrease in energy level is almost invariably present, . . . experienced as sustained fatigue even in the absence of physical exertion. The smallest task may seem difficult or impossible to accomplish." [42] This aspect of the disorder may be perceived by the patient as a purely physical phenomenon, while the clinician may be unable to discriminate it from losses of motivation or satisfaction. Rest and sleep do not help; indeed, the physically rested depressive is apt to feel most tired upon awakening in the morning. [43]

From Pascal himself, there are only vague statements of incapacity for mental and physical exertion in his letters to Huygens (6 January 1659) and Fermat (10 August 1660). [44] In the second paragraph of his *Prière pour le bon usage des maladies* (perhaps fall 1660), he does represent "some vigor" as the principal characteristic of his former physical health and incapacitating weakness as the contrary sign of his illness. [45]

Observers emphasized that the valetudinarian genius could not do anything at all, as Carcavy and Gilberte report, or anything much, as Florin and Étienne say. Carcavy reports his condition from February to August 1659: "The illness consists in a sort of prostration and complete loss of strength. . . ."[46] His term, *abattement,* has psychological as well as physical connotations, denoting a loss of "mental" or "moral strength" associated with *tristesse, mélancholie, découragement,* and the like. Gilberte generalizes on the "unrelieved *langueur*" of the four-year period, 1658–62: "It was his ill health that prevented work on his great project. . . . His maladies returned so overwhelmingly that he couldn't do anything more in the last four years of his life, if it can be called living to endure so pitiable a *langueur.*"[47] Her uses of *accablant* and *accablement* in this context also have psychological connotations associated with *désespoir, douleur, malheur, misère,* and so on.

The Périer men qualify Pascal's supposed incapacitation, doing so in prefaces where their editorial justification of his failure to complete work would have invited exaggeration. Florin on 1647–62: "His continual illnesses and incommodities left him scarcely two or three years . . . of a more bearable *langueur.* From time to time, he wasn't entirely incapable of working."[48] Étienne on 1658–62: "An illness of weakness and *langueur* left him so unwell that he was virtually incapable of any [mental] effort whatsoever—although he didn't look sick and didn't have to stay in bed or remain in his room."[49]

Feelings of Worthlessness or Excessive or Inappropriate Guilt

The most widely respected diagnostic manual defines the depressive's symptomatic "feelings of worthlessness" in this way:

> The sense of worthlessness varies from feelings of inadequacy to completely unrealistic negative evaluations of one's worth. The individual may reproach himself or herself for minor failings that are exaggerated and search the environment for cues confirming the negative self-evaluation. Guilt may be expressed as an excessive reaction to current or past failings or as exaggerated responsibility for some untoward or tragic event. The sense of worthlessness or guilt may be of delusional proportions.[50]

The cultural relativity of modern psychiatry is nowhere more evident than in this criterion for the diagnosis of a depressive disorder. What *guilt* was excessive or inappropriate for *Pascal?*

Pascal's conception of human nature emphasizes opposed qualities. Greatness and misery are complementary principles, and to deny either would be to falsify his fundamental antinomy. In Pensée 450, he concludes that we deserve our own self-esteem *and* self-contempt, self-love *and* self-hatred. But in other pensées, self-hatred obliterates self-love:

220 No other religion has proposed that we should hate ourselves. Therefore, no other religion can please those who do hate themselves. . . .
271 Jesus Christ didn't do anything else other than to teach men that they loved themselves and . . . would have to hate themselves and follow Him. . . .
373 We must love God alone and hate ourselves alone. . . . Every member must be willing to perish for the sake of the body. . . .
381 [Christians] want to love God alone and hate themselves alone. . . . [I]n our religion, we must love God alone and hate ourselves alone. . . .
564 Thus, the one true virtue is to hate ourselves, because our concupiscence makes us hateful, and to seek a Being truly worthy of love. . . .

It is unsurprising that Pascal's emphasis on self-hatred as Christ's unique truth and unique good later aroused the indignant protests of Voltaireans. It is more surprising that the same emphasis was already unacceptable to the most sympathetic Jansenists.[51] The devout compilers of the Port-Royal *Pensées* recoiled from the self-contempt in Pensée 597: "The self is hateful." They added a qualifying note:

The word "self" *(le moi)* that the author uses in the following pensée signifies only self-love *(l'amour-propre)*. This was a term that he customarily used with certain of his friends.[52]

Pensée 617 does provide a textual basis for this more restrictive reading, hatred only of a sort of self-love that displaces God in our hearts. Pensée 618, like all of the others just reviewed, then requires an extensive conception of the hateful self; Pascal argues that we are all concupiscent in our human attachments, that this love of creatures always distracts us from the love of God, and, *therefore,* that our attachments are always "wrong," and, "*therefore,* [that] we are full of evil," and "*therefore* [that] we ought to hate ourselves."[53]

These pensées express in general terms a viewpoint that was painfully personal to the reclusive Pascal. That is, the Apologist's theme of self-hatred seems to reflect self-loathing. In the *Prière* on his illness, Pascal speaks only for himself, to his God. Matter of factly, he confesses sins that justify his suffering as divine punishment. He says that the greatest of his illnesses is his utter insensitivity to his own sinfulness, his perfect unconsciousness of "his own miseries." He laments "the total uselessness of my actions and my thoughts, the complete waste of the time that you have given me." His guilt goes far beyond sins of omission to sins of commission: "I have always opposed you." Pascal was convinced that he had offended God by a contemptuous indifference to religion and a contrary devotion to the world. "All that I am is odious. . . ."[54]

No contemporary seems to have shared the harshness of Pascal's own judgment on himself, however rigorous the spiritual standards or great the partisan enmities. When the time came for a final reckoning on the worldling in whose life and work even a friend might discern both pride and anger, the spiritual leaders of Port-Royal pronounced their final blessings.[55]

Pascal's partisan enemies saw matters quite differently, of course, but even the bitterest, least inhibited by standards of fairness and veracity, never equaled Pascal's own self-condemnation. René Rapin, for instance, was willing to accuse him of the foulest crimes, even of having invoked the Devil. With somewhat more justification, the Jesuit polemicist also condemned the Jansenist polemicist for his prideful and contentious spirit in the *Provinciales*. But this same antagonist also acknowledged Pascal's mathematical genius, his sense of honor, and even his morals.[56] What is so striking about the comparison of Rapin-on-Pascal with Pascal-on-Pascal is that the former accused his fallen opponent of particular offenses, while the latter accused himself of the most general odiousness.

Nothing is simple. Blaise Pascal was not always equally self-reproachful, just as he was not always equally miserable. Several self-referential fragments do express quite favorable judgments (Pensées 916, 919, 929, 931). The limited evidence suggests that the first three of these self-approving pensées antedated the medical crisis of 1658–60 and that the last one postdated the serious illness of 1659. Thus, the best explanation for this man's opposed judgments on himself is that they come from different periods.

Diminished Ability to Think, Concentrate, or Decide

Who would dare to suggest that *Blaise Pascal*, the man who invented a *thinking machine* and the author who conceived *the Pensées*, ever suffered from a "diminished ability *to think*"? How perverse! But, perversely or not, Pascal himself said so, and his adoring sister said so, and his admiring brother-in-law said so, and his respectful nephew said so.

Pascal's own first words of intellectual incapacity in his last four years, 1658–62, come in his letter to Huygens on 6 January 1659: "I would really like to have something [of my own] to send you, but *I'm really incapable. . . .*"[57] The letter writer offers no explanation for his professed incapacity, saying nothing about either debilitating illness or religious scruples. We might doubt the fact, were it not for the concordant testimony of others, beginning with Carcavy's letter of 7 February 1659, which reports incapacity and explains it by ill health.[58] From Carcavy's report on Pascal's health in his letter of 14 August 1659, the relevant fact is the *anéantissement* and *abattement* that had left the invalid unable to accomplish anything requiring "even the slightest concentration."[59]

Gilberte says that Blaise "couldn't read or write" or accomplish anything at all "in the last period of his life." This chronology is very vague, but the context shows clearly that she means the four years from June 1658 to June 1662, when he *could* still go out for occasional walks and for devotional purposes.[60] What was he unable to do? He could not work on the *Pensées*. In short, when he was ill, he could not think.

Florin Périer does not make the point so emphatically. Nevertheless, this loyal brother-in-law did state that chronic illnesses after 1647 left Pascal only brief periods of relative health "in which he wasn't entirely incapable of working." This necessarily implies longer periods of utter incapacity. Pascal's proper work had been to think, whether it was the lesser thoughts of mathematics and the physical sciences or the greater thoughts of religion.[61] In short, when he was ill, he could not think.

Étienne Périer reached a similar conclusion by a different route. He claimed that when Uncle Blaise of the marvelous memory was feeling well, he did not need a written record of his good thinking. But then, after the onset of his illness affected his memory enough to make working papers necessary, it also affected his intellectual energy and his powers of concentration enough to make a finished composition impossible.[62] In short, when he was ill, he could not think well.

Pascal himself implied as much in his frequent remark during these years of illness that "he would have needed ten healthy years to finish" the Apology.[63] In Pensée 29, the little lesson in human incapacity that he headed "Faiblesse," he wrote, "It [our weakness] is the same with respect to knowledge. For illness deprives us of it." In Pensée 44, a longer lesson focused somewhat more narrowly on intellectual incapacity, he added, "We have another principle of error in illnesses. They spoil [both] our judgment and our senses." That is, Pascal thought that illnesses efface memories, cloud judgments, and darken perceptions.

Pascal's brilliance shines through the wreckage of his projected Apology. But that wreckage is a fact, and what we see within it reflects indecisiveness, which is a hallmark of a disorder that affects cognition and volition as well as mood.[64] The healthy person makes all sorts of easy decisions without giving them much thought, and the healthy genius makes difficult decisions after thought, however much or little. When healthier, Pascal had shown a remarkable capacity to define and pursue objectives, as in the Vacuum Experiments or the *Provinciales*. But when he became ill, he seems to have drifted toward the indecision and vacillation that plagued his work on the Apology.

The editorial revolution associated with the work of Louis Lafuma has led to an exaggeration of the orderliness of the fragments in the First Copy. Moderns can claim to have recovered a partial order, but it has been an abuse of the evidence to rationalize this order as if it were *the* final plan or even *a* single plan. Pensées 383–993 as a set still seem virtually planless, and even Pensées 830–912 on miracles are, at best, thematically grouped. Had Pascal decided what to do with them? I doubt it. Had he even decided just how to accommodate his plans and his preparations for the three-stage Apology sketched in Pensée 12 so as to assimilate the First Part of the two-part Apology sketched in Pensée 6? I doubt it. Had he then *finally* decided that there could be no order and so no Apology? Despite the suggestiveness of Pensées 532 and 694, I doubt that, too.

Even where Pascal's filing scheme requires decisiveness, there is indecision. The *liasse* "Ordre" is itself one fragmented monument to disorder. Had he decided to write letters (Pensées 4, 5, 7, 9, and 11), dialogue (Pensée 2), epistolary dialogue (as in the *Provinciales*), or a more straightforward exposition (almost all of what he actually wrote)? Had he decided to follow the plan of Pensée 12 (with *after*-thoughts *before* its "Commencement") or that of Pensée 6 (with its alternative formulations)? And how in the world had he reached the decision to classify Pensées 1, 9, and 10 in the planning dossier? And so on. My second-guesses are unimportant, but the implications of his evident indecision are potentially quite important.

Recurrent Thoughts of Death

"Recurrent thoughts of death" is the last of the depressive symptoms to be considered: "There may be fear of dying, the belief that the individual or others would be better off dead, wishes to die, or suicidal plans or attempts."[65]

Many pensées concern death, but, even when they imply fear, it is hard to tell whether he was voicing his own anxieties or "only" trying to arouse readers' anxieties as an apologetic tactic. Some element of the former could have strengthened the latter. The *liasse* "Commencement" includes several fragments that may be self-referential: almost certainly Pensée 153, probably Pensée 159, and possibly Pensées 151 and 166. The most pathetic of these is surely Pensée 151, in which a "miserable and helpless" man confronts a solitary death and urges others to reject all human comfort.

Pensée 154 is the work of a man preoccupied with death as an hourly prospect, and strikeouts and second thoughts betray strong feelings. I translate the first and most orderly draft:

> Choices
>
> We must live in the world according to [one of] these different propositions:
>
> 1. It is certain that we shall be here forever.
> 2. It is uncertain whether or not we shall be here forever.
> 3. It is certain that we shall not be here forever, but it is also certain that we shall be here for a long time.
> 4. It is certain that we shall not be here forever, and it is uncertain whether or not we shall be here for a long time.
> 5. It is certain that we shall not be here for a long time, and it is uncertain whether or not we shall be here for one hour.
>
> This last proposition is ours.[66]

What a "beginning"! And what "choices"! The fourth proposition, not the fifth, states the hard truth. It might seem difficult enough for healthy readers to accept the great fact of mortality, so presented, but the author will not leave it at this.

After having written these propositions, Pascal began to strike them. He rewrote the first so as to emphasize uncertainty: "If we could be here forever . . ." He cut the second, eliminating the words "It is uncertain. . . ." He curtailed the third with a yet more vigorous stroke, striking the clause ". . . but it is certain that we shall be here for a long time." He slashed the fourth and so the very possibility of a significantly longer life. He superimposed on these more optimistic assessments of our lot a bold "FALSE" as his emphatic rejection and then cut through the propositions that he had already stricken and already falsified with dismissive strokes. That left only the fifth:

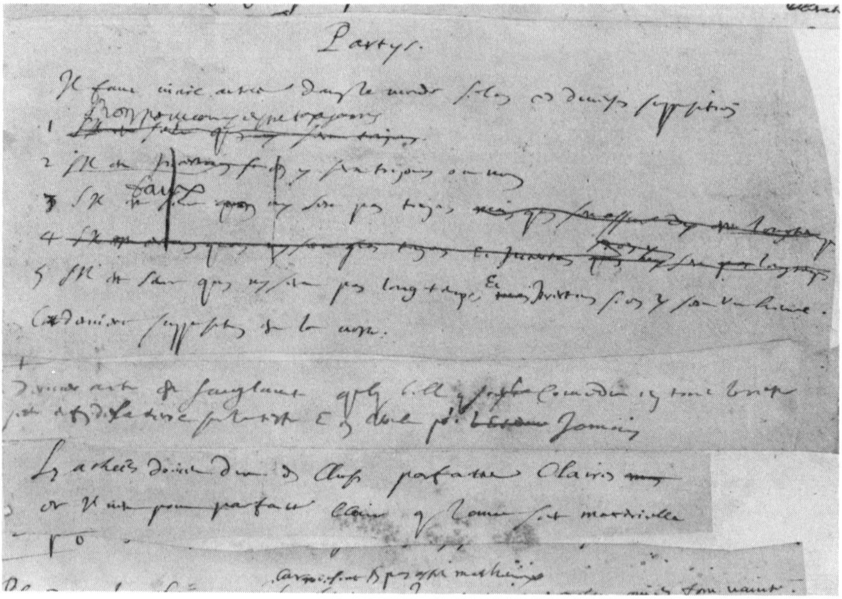

Pascal's Autograph of Pensée 154, mounted by heirs with Pensées 165, 161, and 156. Photograph © Bibliothèque Nationale de France, Paris.

"Beliefs that the individual or others would be better off dead" are now considered pathological by secular psychiatrists. But who among Pascal's devout contemporaries did not at least profess similar beliefs, especially after someone else's death? Such beliefs expressed about oneself before death are rather different, spiritually as well as psychologically. They may approach "wishes to die." Gilberte later recalled Blaise's letter on their father's death, with its idea of life itself as a sacrifice accomplished only in death, then added this remarkable report on her brother's attitudes at the end of his own life:

He told us that death is horrible without Jesus Christ, but that in Him it is adorable, holy, and the joy of the faithful. He said that if we were truly innocent, . . . it would be just to hate [death], because it would separate a holy soul from a pure body. However, in our present state, it is just to love it, because it separates a holy soul from an impure body.[67]

Gilberte's paragraph on Blaise's attitudes to his own illness in its final stages is more familiar, even notorious. He expressed fears of recovery, not illness or death:[68]

Don't pity me! Illness is the Christian's natural state. We all ought always to be like the sick man, suffering from the privation of every good and of all sensual pleasures, exempt from every passion . . ., without ambition or greed, constantly awaiting [or in some manuscript copies, "thinking of"] death. Isn't this how Christians ought to spend their lives? And isn't it a great good fortune to find ourselves forced to be just what we ought to be . . . ? That's why I ask you only for your prayers that God may grant me this grace [my illness, not my recovery].[69]

Gilberte looked and saw saintliness in his suffering. The senior physician looked and saw the effects of a melancholy humor.

The perspectives of the devout and of the doctors come together in a late report of bizarre behavior. The published correspondence of the abbé Jean-Jacques Boileau includes the following anecdote, which gives us a distant glimpse of Pascal himself "blocking the view," in the words of Pensée 166, as he rushed toward the abyss:[70]

This great genius always thought that he saw an abyss at his left side, and he would have a chair placed there to reassure himself. I have this on good authority. His friends, his confessor, and his director tried in vain to tell him that there was nothing to fear and that his anxiety was only the alarm of an imagination exhausted by abstract and metaphysical studies. He would agree, . . . and then, within a quarter of an hour, he would have dug for himself the terrifying precipice all over again.[71]

Boileau's claim of "good authority" is probably justifiable. He was later a member of the household of the duc de Luynes, Pascal's host at Port-Royal des Champs in 1655, and also an intimate of Le Maistre de Sacy, Pascal's director at this time.[72]

Supposing Boileau's report to be historically reliable, what is the significance of Pascal's Abyss?[73] Voltaire wanted to believe that he was so "mad" that his life as a convert and his religious writings have no meaning.[74] Condorcet wanted to believe that a terrifying event drove him over the edge.[75] They wrote, as Montesquieu said, for their convent. If Pascal hallucinated the chasm, unaware that what he alone "saw" as an Abyss was actually only a product of his imagination, that would indeed be evidence of a psychotic disorder. Alternatively, if he was aware, the behavior would be obsessional but not psychotic. "Obsessions are common in depressive states and vice versa. . . . Obsessions and depression occur together so commonly that discriminating symptom from illness may be difficult."[76]

An obsession of an abyss or precipice would be very rare in modern clinical practice, but, as a spiritual metaphor, the image was a Jansenist commonplace. Saint-Cyran, Singlin, and Sacy (Boileau's probable informant), all used it for the sinfulness that threatens to doom us all to the depths of Hell.[77] Boileau's theme in the crucial letter as a whole is his penitent's unreasonableness: "Where they see only a continuous roadway, you see frightful precipices. This reminds me of M. Pascal. . . ." Boileau uses the "way" as one of the oldest and most familiar of all images for spiritual progress. The "continuous roadway" and the "frightful precipices" that lead into the Pascal anecdote are metaphorical, not literal.

From one end of the Bible to the other, Genesis (1:2, 7:11, and 8:2) to Revelation (9:1, 2, 11, 11:7, 17:8, and 20:1–2), the "abyss" has the deepest and darkest spiritual connotations. At the beginning, it signifies the primal chaos and the Great Flood and, at the end, the Bottomless Pit into which is cast "the dragon, that old serpent, which is the Devil and Satan." It is the sphere of the dead and the place of imprisonment for rebellious spirits. In other letters, Boileau uses the word in these old senses for the domain of the Demon, Hell.[78]

Pascal himself uses the powerful but imprecise image in several celebrated fragments: a *précipice* appears in Pensées 44 ("Imagination") and 149 ("A.P.R.") as well as in Pensée 166; *abîmes* open up in Pensées 131, 199 ("Deux infinis"), and 919 ("Le mystère de Jésus"); and a *gouffre* yawns in Pensée 148 ("Seconde Partie"). The image is associated with acrophobic terrors (Pensée 44; cf. 101), profound melancholy (148), cosmic anxiety (199), and the ineradicable guilt of original sin (131, 149, 919). No wonder, as Pascal wrote, "we" want to block the view.

Boileau's letter is now edited and read only for what it can tell us about the great Pascal. But that good doctor-of-souls did not set out to tell *us* anything, much less everything; his only purpose was to reassure his troubled *penitent*. She was a manic-depressive. This confident assertion rests on other passages from the same letter that do not report on Pascal and are not commonly read by his students:

> Sometimes she was excessively elated; at other times she was immeasurably sad. . . . And when the [black] bile and the melancholy fermented a bit more than usual, she had impulses and visions so bizarre that, when she had recovered, she herself and her friends would laugh about them. . . . Sometimes when she suffered most from the [black] bile or melancholy, she would blame men, saints, and God.[79]

We have no such straightforward report on pathological mood swings in the case of Pascal. I doubt that he was as severely disordered. Nevertheless, the case of the manic-depressive nun who was Boileau's charge brought to his mind what he had heard on good authority about the case of the Pascal who had been de Sacy's charge. This suggests that he, too, was remembered by the devout as what we would call a manic-depressive.

Pascal's Abyss may have been culturally conditioned, but it was not remembered as "normal" or desirable by those who had been closest to him and were most sympathetic with his spirituality. Even the pious de Sacy, apparently, and his disciple Boileau, certainly, recognized that there was something very odd about this behavior. A penitent had not only to condemn the self and to fear Judgment, but also to have faith in God and hope for salvation.

CONCLUSION

The Good Uses of This Illness

Scholars have supplemented, qualified, and corrected Gilberte Périer's *Vie de Monsieur Pascal,* but even the most critical have not discredited her conception or, more importantly, formulated an alternative that would be superior in terms of overall coherence and of the human sciences as now understood. The grieving sister raised a monument to her illustrious brother's genius, conversion, and saintliness. It still stands.[1]

I have not attempted to topple this monument, which is enduringly true to the faith of the author and her subject. Gilberte's work is remarkable not just for the quality of its information but also for its dignity, restraint, and simplicity. However, from my distant perspective as a secular historian, I would emphasize certain limitations. Gilberte's conception of the life is teleological, providential, and uncritical in its idealization for purposes of edification. Furthermore, quite apart from *conceptions,* her situation as the most afflicted mourner aroused powerful *emotions.* She wrote to memorialize even more than to edify.

Instead of focusing on the end of Pascal's life, I have refocused on his childhood and youth. Instead of explaining the midlife conversions as interventions by an all-powerful God, I have reconsidered them as the behavior of a vulnerable man. Instead of monumentalizing the prodigious genius, exalted convert, and solitary saint, I have tried to return the man to his social context and to reintegrate "lower" with "higher" orders of his mental life, emotions and affects with intellect and spirit. All this has led to a new conception of the life in terms of attachments, separations and losses, and depression. And this, in turn, has significant implications for the critical understanding of his greatest works, the *Provinciales* and the *Pensées*. To paraphrase Pensée 675, when we open these books, we find a man, not an author, still less a monument.

First, I have emphasized Pascal's particular, enduring, and highly emotional love for his mother, father, and sisters. Parts 1 and 2 on these familial attachments are sure to be less controversial than parts 3, 4, and 5, which reconsider his Second Conversion, his edifying Christian life, and his now-classic literary works. Yet the revisionism of my work starts here. For attachment theory, see appendix 1.

Gilberte's canonical account of her brother's life and Jean Mesnard's modern classic on the life and works are similarly limited in this respect. In the orthodox tradition, Antoinette Begon's short life has no apparent significance; Étienne is the gifted teacher of a more gifted pupil; and Jacqueline is the spiritual director at the time of his decisive conversion.[2] The death of the first is barely noted; the death of the second is the occasion for Blaise's instruction on the Two Loves; and the death of the third serves principally to show his exemplary detachment.[3] All this underestimates his attachments and his exceptional susceptibility to the pains of separation and loss after his mother's early death and his father's uniquely close embrace. Étienne's eventual death and Jacqueline's subsequent withdrawal left him alone in the household.[4]

The best modern scholarship has actually deflected attention from Blaise's relationships with the other Pascals. Mesnard's *Pascal et les Roannez* deliberately attempts "to detach Pascal as much as possible from his family" and replace him within the entourage of his friend.[5] However, no new friend could have taken the places of his father and sister, and, by definition, the friends of the friend were at best peripheral. It was probably after Jacqueline's death that Blaise set down thoughts on attachment and mortality in Pensée 396, the Separate Little Paper that he carried on his person and repeatedly consulted in Gilberte's presence. After his own death, she appropriated and particularly treasured it, as the First Copyist specified in a unique annotation: "Mme. Périer has the original of this note." She incorporated it in her memoir as his expression of wisdom "given by God for the perfection of his Christian life."[6] Mesnard accepts it as evidence of "*saintliness.*"[7]

When we reconsider Pascal's life from its beginning, not its end, the great truth becomes his particular love for the members of his immediate family. This was eventually to become an uncomfortable truth for him as a believer in the doctrine of the Two Loves, which commanded the love of God and condemned the love of man, as such. When Pascal wrote to Charlotte de Roannez that "we can be sure that we cannot detach ourselves without pain," he knew what he was talking about; his letter was written on the fifth anniversary of his father's death.[8] When, late in life, he knelt in the *Prière* to ask for forgiveness and the redirection of affections, he was confessing his human incapacity to obey the great commandment to love God with all his heart, all his mind, and all his soul.[9]

Of course, Voltaire and the philosophes understood God's law and man's nature differently. In his Anti-Pascal, Voltaire decries the ideals of the Two Loves, particularly in Remarks 10 (on Pensée 618), 11 (on Pensée 421), and 20 (on Pensée 453). Somewhat similarly, Condorcet objects strenuously to the "unworthy" thought that, as he put it, "Pascal had arrived at such a point of perfection that he didn't love anyone and didn't want anyone to love him."[10] But neither Voltaire nor his philosophical disciple tried to understand the troubled history of Pascal's loves.[11]

Why study the affective life of a man better remembered for his intellect and spirit? Because the study of Pascal's loves can vivify the monument and reintegrate a life that has been conceptually divided at its midpoint. Although psychological approaches have been suspect as being reductionistic, overly theoretical, and insufficiently attentive to the rules of evidence, in this case they help us to make sense of the great man's intellectual achievements and spiritual qualities. Psychology and psychiatry enable us to make better use of historical evidence that has resisted other approaches, and attachment theory allows us to enlarge our conceptions, to appreciate Pascal's complexity, and to understand the nature of his achievement and his qualities.

The mathematician and scientist who followed in his father's footsteps was a creature of emotion as well as intelligence. Love spun the wheels of the Arithmetic Machine and filled the mind that conceived the Vacuum Experiments. When death took the object of this love, the wheels stopped turning, so to speak: his work on the Machine ceased, and his experiments ended.

Second, I have approached the central problem of Pascal's conversions from this study of familial attachments. The precondition for his reorientation toward a divine object in 1646 was the threat of separation and loss (the marriage project for Jacqueline and the accidental injury to Étienne). Étienne's eventual death and Jacqueline's withdrawal then made Blaise painfully aware of the transience of human objects.

The Pascals as converts firmly believed with Saint-Cyran that only God could turn the heart and make it "new."[12] None of them could possibly have undertaken to explain the reorientation of their lives in terms of human experience and relationships. Gilberte emphasizes a providential occasion for her brother's pious reading, which transformed the young savant. Mesnard remains faithful to this tradition, whatever his criticisms of her account of an abandonment of the sciences at this point.[13]

The conversion of 1654 is better documented. Blaise's *Mémorial* and Jacqueline's letters could have sustained a detailed narrative or a deeper analysis. For Gilberte, they did not. She based her few relevant sentences as much on what she and others around her believed about conversion more generally as on what she remembered from the letters about particular events. In her narrative, Jacqueline speaks but it is God who calls; Blaise heeds the call.[14] Mesnard complicates this simple story without questioning its premises. In his modern version of the orthodox tradition, the *Mémorial* documents God's words to Pascal; Jacqueline's letters provide an authoritative narrative of the conversion; and the *Écrit sur la conversion du pécheur* defines the terms of an analysis.[15]

In the eighteenth century, neither Voltaire nor Condorcet made any historical use of these materials. A nineteenth-century disciple, the doctor Louis-François Lélut, did study the *Mémorial* as the product of a "morbid imagination," but he failed to provide a viable alternative to the orthodox tradition.[16] Other like-minded psychiatrists followed Dr. Lélut, particularly Charles Binet-Sanglé, but their papers are now buried under the dust of a dated medical science, an uncritical history, and a doctrinaire hostility to religion.[17] My purpose is to understand the Pascal whose life changed so dramatically and so consequentially. One consequence, perhaps the most important, is that he became the great modern apologist for the Christian Faith and so the philosophes' great antagonist.

The forces at work on and in Pascal in 1646 and 1654 must have been complex, and much is hidden. Yet simple facts are ascertainable about even the First Conversion: Jacqueline, not Blaise, was the Pascal who first showed the signs of devotion; her continued presence in the household was then jeopardized by marriage projects; and a severe injury to the aging Étienne was the precipitating incident for his children's conversions. With respect to the Second Conversion, in the text of the *Mémorial* we can still *see* Pascal's manifest preoccupation with separation and, in the contexts for his biblical citations, *see* the latent force of his undying attachment to his deceased parents, especially his father. In Jacqueline's letters, we can *see* good evidence of his sense of abandonment and despair in the world and of his dependence on his cloistered sister. And, in the *Écrit,* we can *see* an acute sensitivity to personal loss and the great attraction of an eternal object. Thus, the Two Loves were not simply antagonistic; Pascal's love for mortal objects preceded and supported his love for the eternal God.

Third, I have ventured historical analyses of the relationship between affects and authorship in Pascal's mature work and of the illness that incapacitated him some four years before his death. For Gilberte, this obscure illness was both an insuperable obstacle to further thinking and writing and a providential condition for further spiritual development.[18] Mesnard seems to accept the orthodox tradition in both respects, but he has also recently predicted that a psychiatric study of Pascal's illness is "one of the secrets of the future"; he has remarked that almost a century of relative neglect has left this field "wide open"; and he has acknowledged that psychological inquiry, cautiously conducted, "could render invaluable services."[19]

Voltaire and Condorcet thought of Pascal's mature life and work in terms of *misère* and *mélancholie,* understood vaguely and intended dismissively. Dr. Lélut remembered Voltaire's celebrated reference to Pascal as the "sublime misanthrope" and recast it as "sublime melancholic," and Dr. Binet-Sanglé wrote with greater restraint about Pascal as an "unbalanced genius" whose mature religion was inseparable from depressive "neurasthenia."[20] Given this philosophical tradition, it is unsurprising that more sympathetic specialists have been wary of anything "too psychological" and steadfast in their opposition to any inquiry that threatens to reduce intellectual and spiritual greatness to mere "madness."

Nevertheless, the great philosophes were shrewd critics. I believe that they hit upon the innermost vulnerability of the man as well as the fundamental logical weakness of his attempt to use the fact of some human misery as evidence of the truth of universal sinfulness. Yet affective disorder need not mean psychotic madness (see appendix 2). Contrarily, recent scholarship supports the paradoxical conclusion that some degree of psychiatric disorder may favor literary and artistic creativity (see appendix 3).

There is no good reason to accept the orthodox assumption that Pascal's illness was simply an alien obstacle to the work of his mind. A systematic review of the surviving evidence suggests that, quite apart from the cancer that eventually killed him, Pascal suffered from a mood disorder that first took a milder form and then became more severe, at least intermittently reaching the level of major depression. This illness was an integral part of a life otherwise distinctive not only for genius and saintliness, but also for a particularly painful experience of separations and losses. A substantial clinical, epidemiological, and theoretical literature argues that there is a relationship between early parental loss and later depression (see appendix 1). Illness is not the most important fact about Pascal, but it directly affected what is most important, namely, intellectual achievement and spiritual identity. Paradoxically, his "useful illness" served his development in both respects.

Mesnard suggests that Pascal's *Prière pour demander à Dieu le bon usage des maladies* be read as "a sort of spiritual testament."[21] The prayerful penitent accepts his illness as just punishment. He then confesses his sinfulness by the standard of the Two Loves; his great fault has been his attachment to lesser objects, creatures and not the Creator. Thus, his mature spirituality points backward historically toward his prior experience of loss:

> III. O God, . . . who causes the death of our body and who, at the hour of death, detaches our soul from all worldly objects of love! O God, who will tear me away at the last moment of my life from everyone to whom I have been attached, to whom I have given my heart! O God, who will destroy

> the earth, the heavens, and all creatures on the Last Day, so as to show men that only You endure, that nothing is worthy of love but You because You alone are a lasting object! . . .
> IV. . . . [M]y heart is so hardened and so full of worldly ideas, cares, anxieties, and attachments, that, unless You grant the extraordinary assistance of Your grace, nothing can even begin my conversion.

Only God is "firm and lasting"; other objects must perish. Only He can "reunite the Just in a common glory," closely, perfectly, and imperishably.[22] Pascal's acute sense of the transience of things human reflects his distinctive personal experience of separations and losses, and his fervent faith in a shared afterlife proclaims his continued attachments.

Having professed this faith, Pascal again confesses that his heart has been attracted by his fellow creatures and foul self. In this spirit, he distinguishes "internal pain" from "external ills." Baring his soul, he shows himself to be a man of *misère, douleur,* and *tristesse.*[23] And he prays that his illness may be salutary and that he may share Christ's sufferings and sorrows:

> X. If my body has this in common with yours, that it suffers for my offenses, let my soul also have this in common with yours, that it is saddened by these same offenses. Let me suffer with you and like you. . . .
> XII. Don't permit me to stray so far from you that I consider your spirit saddened unto death and your body laid low in death for my own sins without rejoicing in the sufferings of both my body and my spirit. . . .
> XIII. [T]ake from me the sadness that my self-love might feel for my own sufferings . . . , but grant me a sadness like yours. . . . May my sufferings appease your wrath . . . and occasion my salvation.[24]

Pascal's depression served Pascal's religion. If the essence of Christianity is conversion from the self-love and worldly interests and pleasures that an Augustinian would consider natural but sinful, then depression must serve spiritually desirable ends better than any physical illness. This follows logically from the very definition of the syndrome.

Conversely, Pascal's religion served him in his affliction. Faith, hope, and charity are salutary even from a mundane and therapeutic perspective. If the greatest of Pascal's afflictions was the loss of his parents, especially his father, then there really was something wonderful in the consoling faith that Christ had triumphed over death. If his greatest temptation in periods of depression was a slide into hopelessness, despair, and exaggerated guilt, then the hope, consolation, and forgiveness offered by religion really did serve him even during his lifetime. Although he experienced the vicissitudes of an affective life in which human objects were fleeting, he also experienced the joy of loving God and being loved by God.

Pascal's affective disorder also made possible his greatest works, the *Provinciales* and the *Pensées*. As I suggested in part 4, the unschooled layman who set out to answer the Faculty of Theology was served by an exaltation that may have been hypomanic. His brilliant success as a pamphleteer reflected not only his intelligence and his faith but also his high spirits, ready anger, exceptional energy, boundless self-confidence, and reckless risk taking.

This way of thinking about Pascal offers even more to students of the *Pensées*. As I discussed in part 5, his last, most original, and most powerful plan for the Apology was to begin with an appeal to introspection in a First Part on "the misery of man" as the essence of selfhood. In drafts on the subject, he appeals to feelings that we have all shared at some level and to some degree. He had experienced them profoundly and acutely. That is the secret of his power. As Mesnard puts it in his *Pascal:* "The work was born from Pascal's very life. . . . It is the author's powerful personality that makes the *Pensées* most profoundly original."[25] He makes the case for historical inquiry most eloquently at the head of his *Pascal et les Roannez:*

> While a writer's work offers the best means of access to the understanding of his personality, there are many cases in which biography has repercussions on the interpretation of that work. Pascal's writings would lose their profundity and their pertinence, if they did not reflect his experience and represent his witness. The meaning of the experience and the nature of the witness can only be analyzed insofar as we understand the life, which gives us the key.[26]

Pascal did think of himself as a witness, but he did not characteristically celebrate the joy or community of the faithful. Consider the testimony of his very first pensée in the order of the First Copy, here translated and typeset so as to indicate the disposition of the words on the autograph manuscript in the *Recueil original;* Pascal moves from Psalm-singing to misery and loneliness:

Psalms sung
everywhere on earth.
    Who bears witness
to Mohammed? Himself.

Jesus wants His own
testimony to be nothing.
The quality of witnesses
is such that they must be
always and everywhere and [sic]
miserable. He [sic] is alone.

This miserable and lonely "he" cannot be Mohammed or Jesus; it is Blaise Pascal himself.

And consider the last reported words of this witness—spoken in the house of his sister—as he received the last rites of the Church: "May God never abandon me!"[27]

APPENDIX I

Parental Loss and Attachment Theory

Students of Pascal's life *inevitably* "psychologize" on the subject of his experience of loss. The only question is how, not whether to do so. Our embarrassment is most acute with respect to his mother's death and its possible significance. Antoinette Begon's early death is a historical fact but so, too, is the silence of the sources on any immediate or deferred psychological effects on her young children. In chapter 1, I have compared our situation to that of Pascal's wagerer. We can choose to mention the fact and maintain the silence, but this is tantamount to denying the significance of the event. Of course, this is a psychological judgment, however uninformed. Alternatively, we can choose to mention the fact and fill at least some of the awkward silence with a layperson's modest references to medical science. This could lead to amateurish errors of judgment. The risks are contrary but unequal: on the one hand, prideful overvaluation of our own intuition and, on the other, mistaken application of others' science.

My choice has been to leave the historical discussion of chapter 1 relatively uncomplicated by speculation on the possible impact of Antoinette Begon's death, then to add this appendix on the relevant psychology and psychiatry, as such. Here, I review the most respected clinical studies and theoretical generalizations about childhood bereavement.

Erna Furman and thirteen coworkers at the Cleveland Center for

Research in Child Development have produced the best work based on clinical experience: *A Child's Parent Dies* (1974). Individually, they report twenty-three diverse cases in some detail and, collectively, they offer sober generalizations, combining psychiatric sophistication with evident human compassion.[1]

I summarize the clinical experience of the Cleveland Center in five points. First, young children are capable of deeply felt grief. Second, they tend to cling irrationally to the parent lost so irrevocably. Third, they feel some anger at the "abandoning" parent. Fourth, they experience a correlative guilt. Fifth, they are particularly vulnerable to varied, often long-deferred psychopathology. These points do not depend on elaborate theorizing, and Pascal's students cannot blithely ignore them.[2]

The psychiatric vulnerability of the surviving child after parental loss is a virtual first premise of the Cleveland studies. These twenty-three children were all in treatment for various problems, most of them arising some time after the parental death and not, on presentation, obviously related to this loss.[3] Erna Furman emphasizes their vulnerability:

> When a parent dies, a child finds himself in a unique situation because of the special nature of his ties to the deceased. An adult distributes his love among several meaningful relationships—his spouse, parents, children, friends, colleagues—as well as in his work and his hobbies. The child, by contrast, invests almost all his feelings in his parents. Except in very unusual circumstances, this single relationship is therefore incomparably rich and intense. . . . Only in childhood can death deprive an individual of so much opportunity to love and be loved and face him with so difficult a task of adaptation.[4]

Here is the crux with respect to historical applicability to the case at hand. Was the Pascal household in seventeenth-century Clermont socially so much larger, more varied, and more open than the diverse households of twentieth-century Cleveland that Blaise would not have invested his feelings comparably in his relationships with his parents? The Strange Story does show us other persons, coming and going, but it also shows this child's anxious attachment to his own mother before her death.

Given the vulnerability even of adults after other familial losses, it should not be surprising that young children suffer from parental losses:[5]

> The death of a parent engenders a longing of incomparable amount, intensity, and longevity. . . . Whenever we merely say "his parent died," we leave out the inevitable horror and tragedy. . . . Frequently, an object loss in adulthood revives earlier, particularly infantile, losses, and intensifies the mourning.[6]

This last observation helps to explain the crushing impact of Blaise Pascal's loss of his father in his young adulthood. It may also be relevant to the timing of his later collapse in the winter of 1659, when he succumbed to the illness analyzed in part 5, that the long-time family retainer Louise Delfault, who had "raised" the younger Pascal children after 1631, died sometime at the end of 1658 or beginning of 1659, having appointed Blaise to be her executor.

The most fully developed body of theory on these matters is known as *attachment theory*. John Bowlby is the internationally recognized authority. His work at the Tavistock Clinic and Tavistock Institute of Human Relations, London, culminated in the three-volume *Attachment and Loss* (1969–80). He also presented summaries of his theory in *The American Handbook of Psychiatry* (1975) and in the Fiftieth Maudsley Lecture (1976), subsequently published in an expanded version in the *British Journal of Psychiatry* (1977).[7] Bowlby's theory remains potentially useful for working historians because it concerns overt behavior, not obscure intrapsychic conflicts.

"Attachment behaviour is conceived as any form of behaviour that results in a person attaining or retaining proximity to some other differentiated and preferred individual."[8] For Bowlby, attachment is at least as significant as feeding or sexuality but distinguishable from either. In the natural course of human development, it leads to the formation of affectional bonds. Bowlby's work has always emphasized the mother-child dyad, which may at first have been largely a function of his "third-generation Freudianism," following the psychoanalytical theory of the first generation (Sigmund Freud) and clinical work with orphaned children in the second generation (Anna Freud). Bowlby's own mature theory depends much more on ethological observations and on a very wide range of empirical studies of human behavior in quite diverse societies and cultures. Furthermore, he recognizes that the "mother figure" need not be the biological mother or even a woman, that the needs of the parent(s) must be considered in any explanation of the relationship, that the development of the child is an ongoing process, and that an understanding of adult-adult bonds requires knowledge of particular histories.[9]

The young child displays his attachment to his mother or another attachment figure in various routine behaviors, most commonly an untroubled touching or, more distantly, looking, smiling, or calling, but also very frequently clinging, following, crying, and so on, all of which serve to maintain proximity and to elicit caregiving. Strange situations, fatigue or illnesses, and the unavailability or unresponsiveness of the preferred attachment figure(s) all serve to arouse attachment behavior.[10] Although this behavior is most obvious in the early years of a child-mother relationship, it is of the greatest importance for this theory that the bonds formed, usually within the first year, are specific, enduring, and highly emotional.[11]

Specificity means that there is a preferred individual who matters most in affective relationships. Bowlby's earliest formulations focused exclusively on the mother's central role in the child's emotional life and on what he called the "monotropy" of the child's attachment. His later work still maintains that a child's preference for one individual over other caretakers can be observed as early as the fifth week of life and that in most societies this individual is most commonly the natural mother. Even when the child shows lesser attachments to others in the household (e.g., the father or siblings), those others are few, specifically differentiated, and clearly ranked in an order of preference.[12]

Duration means that the attachments formed in the earliest years tend to endure "for a large part of the life cycle." Maternal, paternal, or other familial bonds may become weaker in later years, but old bonds are not broken even by the formation of new relationships outside the household. Because the needs met are not simply related to feeding (or sexuality), the developmental termination of any such infantile dependency cannot of itself end the attachment. "Early attachments are not easily abandoned, and they commonly persist."[13] Attachment behavior in the most mature can be prompted by the sorts of conditions that prompt it in the very young (strange situations, fatigue or illnesses, and the unavailability or unresponsiveness of preferred persons).

The engagement of emotion ranks as a third essential characteristic of attachments, after specificity and duration:

> Many of the most intense emotions arise during the formation, the maintenance, the disruption, and the renewal of attachment relationships. . . . [T]hreat of loss arouses anxiety, and actual loss gives rise to sorrow, while each of these situations is likely to arouse anger. The unchallenged maintenance of a bond is experienced as a source of security and the renewal of a bond as a source of joy.[14]

Much of this may seem to be little more than common sense writ large. That may be a way of acknowledging its measure of truth.

Because attachments are specific, a separation from or the loss of the primary attachment figure, most often the mother, cannot simply be made good by other providers of care, even loving care. Because attachments are enduring, the vulnerability of the child to separation or loss extends well beyond the period of the greatest physical dependence on the primary caregiver. Finally, because attachments arouse the most intense emotions, separation or loss is potentially pathogenic. In *Loss: Sadness and Depression* (1980), Bowlby paid particular attention to the relationship between the experience of loss, especially in childhood, and illness in later years, especially depression.

Bowlby would be the first to acknowledge that there is no necessary and sufficient causal relationship between early parental loss and later depression. He would also be the first to encourage scholarly attention to ongoing research on the hypothesized relationship between the two.[15]

APPENDIX 2

Affective Disorders and Diagnostic Criteria

I have used with permission the *Diagnostic and Statistical Manual of Mental Disorders* of the American Psychiatric Association in the Third (DSM-III, 1980) and Fourth Editions (DSM-IV, 1994).[1] Most laypersons have a vague sense that psychiatric diagnosis has been unreliable, that is, that clinicians have often disagreed. This is true. There are many lesser sources of disagreement: *subject variance,* meaning that the same patient may suffer different conditions at different times; *occasion variance,* meaning that the patient may be observed at different times and so at different stages of the same condition; *information variance,* meaning that different clinicians may work from different evidence and so reach different diagnoses; *observation variance,* meaning that different observers can perceive the same clinical evidence differently.

Criterion variance has been by far the greatest source of unreliability.[2] In the 1970s, American psychiatry made great strides toward the establishment of a system of classification and diagnosis that could promise greater reliability than had been possible previously. The objective was to standardize diagnoses by making them descriptive and atheoretical. After important preliminary steps by smaller groups, that goal seems to have been reached in the collaborative DSM-III (1980), DSM-III-R (1987), and DSM-IV (1994).[3]

Historians are bystanders to the development of psychiatric

thought, but they have been given a diagnostic tool that ought to be doubly welcome for its attentiveness to observable behavior and avoidance of theoretical constructs. The criteria specified below from DSM-IV are truly operational, although, of course, the deficiencies of even the best seventeenth-century sources mean that a historical assessment must be tentative. We cannot hope to find records of daily or weekly observations of moods, table behavior, sleeping patterns, or the other relevant behavior. We can look for patterns in such evidence as does exist.

Is it to give modern psychiatry more than its due, even to attempt to apply its standards to premodern history? I ought not to beg the question, presuming universality for affective disorders as understood by my compatriots and contemporaries. Similarly, others ought not to beg it contrarily, presuming a cultural, social, or historical particularity that would preclude general applicability of any one diagnostic system.

Psychiatrists and anthropologists have devoted considerable attention to cross-cultural studies of depression.[4] The most important finding, obviously of the greatest interest for students of Pascal, is that depressives in many cultures do not exhibit the sort of guilt and self-deprecation regarded as pathognomonic by the APA. Contrarily, somatic manifestations of depression are more prevalent in many alien cultures. However, these studies tend to oppose Western and non-Western cultures, and there are important cultural continuities in Western experience, especially religious.

There has been little work directly comparing French and American psychiatry, but there has been an important recent World Health Organization (WHO) project involving broader comparisons.[5] The Collaborative Study on the Assessment of Depressive Disorders systematically evaluated 573 patients in four nations, the same instrument of assessment being used by experienced investigators from within each cultural community: French Canada, Switzerland, Iran, and Japan.[6] The most important finding is the "existence of a 'common core' of depressive symptomatology":

> Such a "core" was undoubtedly present in all centres, and included sadness, joylessness, anxiety, tension, lack of energy, loss of interest, loss of ability to concentrate, and ideas of insufficiency, inadequacy, and worthlessness. . . . It is of interest to note that anxiety and tension appear among the most common symptoms of depression in all centres.[7]

Across cultures in the modern world, then, there is an impressive degree of commonality in the symptoms of depression.

The degree of continuity in this disorder from premodern to modern times cannot be studied so systematically. However, technically qualified students of the subject are impressed by the continuity of medical thinking on the subject. A. Jablenski and coauthors, reporting the WHO Collaborative Study: "There is hardly another syndrome of mental disorder which has been described so unequivocally at all times."[8] Stanley W. Jackson, introducing his magisterial *Melancholia and Depression* (1986):

> It is the clinical description that is essential—the symptoms and the signs, the observations that could be attested to by the sufferer or noted by another person. Accounts of this clinical description have been traced in approximately two and a half millenia of medical writings. . . . [T]here have been both a remarkable consistency and a remarkable coherence in the basic cluster of symptoms.[9]

Frederick Goodwin and Kay Jamison, in their monumental *Manic-Depressive Illness* (1990):

> Medical conceptions of mania and depression are as old as secular medicine itself. From ancient times to the present, an extraordinary consistency characterizes these conditions. Few maladies in medical history have been represented with such unvarying language. Although the essential features are recognizable in the medical literature through the centuries, the boundaries that define mania and depression and the relationship between them have changed. . . . Not surprisingly, the evolution of the concept has gone from a broader to a narrower definition.[10]

I conclude with the modesty proper for a layman that the DSM criteria are historically applicable, acknowledging always that diagnosis across place and time must be tentative.

The DSM-IV mood disorders that I take to be relevant to the historical case are *major depression* and *cyclothemic disorder,* a less severe bipolar disorder with depressive and hypomanic phases.[11] It is important to note that "a full depressive syndrome frequently is a normal reaction" to the death of a loved person; however "frequent" and "normal" the reaction, there are limits of severity and duration for a "bereavement," as such. A bereavement that is very severe or prolonged may warrant the diagnosis of a major depression.[12] The following pages present the diagnostic criteria from DSM-IV for a

Major Depressive Episode, Cyclothemic Disorder, and a Hypomanic Episode.

DSM-IV Criteria: Major Depressive Episode

A. Five (or more) of the following symptoms have been present during the same two-week period and represent a change from previous functioning; at least one of the symptoms is either (1) depressed mood or (2) loss of interest or pleasure.
   (1) depressed mood most of the day, nearly every day, as indicated by either subjective report (e.g., feels sad or empty) or observation (e.g., appears tearful)
   (2) markedly diminished interest or pleasure in all or almost all activities most of the day, nearly every day (as indicated by either subjective account or observation made by others)
   (3) significant weight loss or weight gain . . . or decrease or increase in appetite nearly every day
   (4) insomnia or hypersomnia nearly every day
   (5) psychomotor agitation or retardation nearly every day (observable by others, not merely subjective feelings of restlessness or being slowed down)
   (6) fatigue or loss of energy nearly every day
   (7) feelings of worthlessness or excessive or inappropriate guilt (which may be delusional) nearly every day (not merely self-reproach or guilt about being sick)
   (8) diminished ability to think or concentrate, or indecisiveness, nearly every day (either by subjective account or as observed by others)
   (9) recurrent thoughts of death (not just fear of dying), recurrent suicidal ideation without a specific plan or a suicide attempt or a specific plan for committing suicide. . . .

C. The symptoms cause clinically significant distress or impairment in social, occupational, or other important areas of functioning.

D. Not due to the direct physiological effects of a substance (e.g., of a drug of abuse, a medication) or a general medical condition (e.g., hypothyroidism).

E. The symptoms are not better accounted for by Bereavement, i.e., after the loss of a loved one, the symptoms persist for longer than two months or are characterized by a marked functional impairment, morbid preoccupation with worthlessness, suicidal ideation, psychotic symptoms, or psychomotor retardation.[13]

DSM-IV Criteria: Cyclothemic Disorder

A. For at least two years, presence of numerous periods with hypomanic symptoms and numerous periods with depressive symptoms that do not meet criteria for a major depressive episode.
B. During the above two-year period, the person has not been without the symptoms of Criterion A for more than two months at a time.
C. No Major Depressive Episode, Manic Episode, or Mixed Episode has been present during the first two years of the disturbance. . . .
F. The symptoms cause clinically significant distress or impairment in social, occupational, or other important areas of functioning.[14]

DSM-IV Criteria: Hypomanic Episode

A. A distinct period of persistently elevated, expansive, or irritable mood, lasting throughout at least four days, that is clearly different from the usual nondepressed mood.
B. During the period of the mood disturbance, three (or more) of the following symptoms have persisted (four if the mood is only irritable) and have been present to a significant degree:
   (1) inflated self-esteem or grandiosity
   (2) decreased need for sleep (e.g., feels rested after only three hours of sleep)
   (3) more talkative than usual or pressure to keep talking
   (4) flight of ideas or subjective experience that thoughts are racing
   (5) distractability (attention too easily drawn to unimportant or irrelevant external stimuli)

(6) increase in goal-directed activity . . . or psychomotor agitation

(7) excessive involvement in pleasurable activities that have a high potential for painful consequences . . .

C. The episode is associated with an unequivocal change in functioning that is uncharacteristic of the person when not symptomatic.

D. The disturbance in mood and the change in functioning are observable by others.

E. The episode is not severe enough to cause marked impairment in social or occupational functioning, or to necessitate hospitalization, and there are no psychotic features.[15]

APPENDIX 3

Affective Disorders and Exceptional Creativity

Among the ancient opinions on depressive states for which modern psychiatry has offered qualified scientific support is the pseudo-Aristotelian presumption that notable philosophers and poets "are clearly melancholics, and some of them to such an extent as to be affected by diseases caused by black bile."[1] "Aristotle" offered Heracles as his first case of the supposed relationship between intellectual eminence and melancholy, then named Empedocles, Socrates, and Plato, and finally threw in "most of the poets." This ancient opinion was revived in the Renaissance.[2] Pascal would have known it from a prominent passage in Montaigne's *Essais* (bk. II, chap. 8):

> It was a melancholy humor, and consequently a humor very much opposed to my natural temperament, produced by the gloom of the solitude into which I had cast myself some years ago, that first put into my head this fantasy of meddling with writing.[3]

The best medical science and the most devout literature of his day accepted the general proposition as an established truth, witness André Du Laurens's *Des maladies mélancholiques* (1613) and Jean-François Senault's *L'homme criminel* (1644).[4]

Despite the wisdom of "Aristotle," Du Laurens, Senault, and others and the examples of everyone from Heracles to Montaigne, any assertion of a correlation between creative achievement and depressive states as now defined must strain credibility. Nevertheless, there is good evidence that disproportionate numbers of the most creative people, particularly writers, do suffer from affective disorders and that disproportionate numbers among patient populations are at least moderately creative. And this does make sense. Setting aside the symptoms of depressive lows, reconsider those of manic highs: decreased need for sleep, more energy than usual, inflated self-esteem, increased productivity, sharpened and unusually creative thinking. What happiness for the creative person! Subjectively, subclinical hypomania seems like healthy productivity, not an affective disorder, and objectively, too, it may have quite tangible positive effects.

In the recent past, psychiatrists have begun to pay more systematic attention to the milder affective disorders, which do not require institutionalization and often do not come to clinical attention. Increasingly, researchers regard affective disorders as constituting a continuum from severe to moderate to mild, rather than as being catastrophic illnesses to which the only alternative is perfect health.[5] This means that subclinical manifestations can be expected in general populations, even when the subject's social and intellectual functioning seems generally satisfactory. In one set of studies, Richard Depue and coworkers at the State University of Buffalo undertook systematic testing of 850 unselected subjects drawn from among American undergraduates and found affective disorders of at least cyclothemic severity in some 8 to 10 percent.[6]

In another important study of broadly comparable European subjects with broadly comparable epidemiological findings, Jules Angst and coworkers from the Psychiatric University Hospital in Zurich selected 300 nineteen-year-old males from conscription lists and 300 twenty-year-old females from the general population of the Canton of Zurich. On a continuum, distinctions between the pathological and the normal, "cases" and "non-cases," would have to be somewhat arbitrary, especially given the importance of a minimum duration and the insidiousness of onset, and so it would be nonsensical to exaggerate the epidemiological significance of prevalence rates following any of the most respected definitions of affective disorders. Nevertheless, this Swiss study, using American diagnostic criteria, offers the strongest support for the existence of a continuum and an annual prevalence of as much as 7 percent.[7] Thus, although bipolar disorders in full syndromal forms are relatively uncommon if not rare in general populations as opposed to patient populations, on the order of 1 percent lifetime prevalence, cyclothemic disorder, diagnosed or not, seems to be relatively common—and not absolutely incapacitating.

Hagop Akiskal of the University of Tennessee and the Mood Disorders Program at the Charter Lakeside Hospital has been the leading American authority on cyclothemic disorder. He has contributed many papers on the subject to psychiatric journals and at least two significant review essays for recent handbooks.[8] He has also intensively studied a group of writers, painters, and musicians at the Salpetrière Hospital in Paris. Reflecting on this research, he asks himself how bipolarity could contribute to creativity:

> The simplest answer is that depression could provide insights into the human condition, which, however, require hypomania to be translated into the artistic oeuvre. A more profound interpretation would suggest that [the] repeated self-doubt that comes with recurrent depression is an important ingredient of creativity, but because original ideas or artistic forms are often initially rejected, the self-confidence that comes with repeated bouts of hypomania can help in rehearsing these ideas or artistic forms until they are either perfected or accepted by society.[9]

Of course, Blaise Pascal was not just another American undergraduate, Swiss conscript, or French patient. He was a mathematical and scientific genius, a saintly Christian, and one of the very greatest writers. It would be impossible to find an appropriate reference group from more recent times that has been studied with the requisite psychiatric sophistication. Nevertheless, I suggest that two empirical studies of modern writers have independently reached virtually the same conclusion about the positive correlation between creativity and bipolarity.

The first is Nancy Andreasen's study of writers at the Iowa Writers' Workshop, the oldest and most widely recognized creative writing program in the United States, with which writers of the stature of Philip Roth, Kurt Vonnegut Jr., John Irving, Robert Lowell, Flannery O'Connor, and John Cheever have been associated. Dr. Andreasen's initial study (1974) involved fifteen writers and fifteen paired controls. Both the writers themselves (ten of fifteen) and their primary relatives (parents and siblings) showed a statistically significant incidence of affective disorders compared with the controls (two of fifteen) and their primary relatives. The sample is necessarily small, but the results are striking.[10]

Dr. Andreasen has expanded this database in later years and published a fuller report (1987) on thirty writers and thirty controls with even more striking results: twenty-four of thirty writers had at some time suffered from some affective disorder; nine of thirty controls had so suffered. The latter proportion (30 percent lifetime prevalence) is very high for the general population, which may reflect the more general phenomenon of an association between bipolar disorder and any occupational achievement, high-achieving controls having been matched with the high-achieving writers. Nevertheless, even with this distinctive control group, the extraordinary lifetime prevalence of affective disorders for these writers (80 percent) is significant at the .001 level.[11]

The second study of creative writers and affective disorder is reported in Kay Redfield Jamison's paper on prize-winning British poets, playwrights, and novelists (1989). This study, too, restricted attention to creative persons who have been recognized by peers for notable achievement. It further restricted the "patient" count to those who had actually received psychiatric treatment for affective disorders (hospitalization, antidepressant drugs, or psychotherapy), without attempting to diagnose further "cases" for the purposes of the study. Of the eight playwrights, five had been treated for such illnesses (62.5 percent); of the eighteen poets, ten had been treated (55.2 percent); of the eight novelists, two had been treated (25 percent). It is notable that the biographers and artists who were also studied as part of the same project showed less such illness.[12] Again, the numbers are small, but the careful design of Professor Jamison's study and her authority as coauthor of the monumental *Manic-Depressive Illness* (1990) make it very important. To her substantial chapter on the general phenomenon in this book she has now added a book-length study intended for laypersons: *Touched with Fire: Manic-Depressive Illness and the Artistic Temperament* (1993). In the latter, she responds to the major objections that lay skeptics have raised; this would be a logical starting point for any cautious reader.[13]

There have been many important papers and one substantial monograph on the apparent relationship between creativity and bipolarity that approach its study from the other direction, beginning with patient populations and looking for significant creativity. Both

Dr. Andreasen and Professor Jamison have considered the question from this side, too, and Ruth Richards has made particularly significant contributions, including a coauthored study of Danish subjects.[14] Thus, the ancient "Aristotelian" presumption of a relationship between creativity and melancholy has been verified in rigorous modern studies of Europeans as well as Americans.

Notes

NOTES TO INTRODUCTION

1. For the best scholarly introduction, see Jean Mesnard's preface in his edition of Pascal, *Oeuvres complètes,* 4 vols. to date (Paris: Desclée de Brouwer, 1964–), I, 537–70. Following convention, I shall cite this edition as the *OC*. For the two versions of the *Vie de Monsieur Pascal,* see *OC,* I, 571–642. To simplify references and to make them as precise as possible, I shall cite the First Version as the *VMP,* with the paragraph number, not page number, and the Second as *VMP,* Second Version, also with paragraph number. I have also made extensive use of two earlier editions of the complete works. The scholarly standard for most of this century has been the Grands Écrivains edition of Léon Brunschvicg, Pierre Boutroux, and Félix Gazier, 14 vols. (Paris: Hachette, 1904–14); I shall cite it as the *Oeuvres.* For the *VMP* and some preliminary documentation not yet published by Mesnard, see *Oeuvres,* I, 29–114. The best one-volume edition is the *Oeuvres complètes,* ed. Louis Lafuma (Paris: Seuil, 1963); I shall cite it as the Intégrale. For the *Pensées,* I have used the Lafuma numeration from this edition.
2. The Second Version heads the multivolume Brunschvicg-Boutroux-Gazier *Oeuvres,* I, 50–114, and Brunschvicg's one-volume *Pensées,* 1 ff. Lafuma presents the same version in the Intégrale *Oeuvres complètes,* 17–33. Sellier includes the First Version with critical commentary in the new Classiques Garnier edition of the *Pensées* (1991), 103–45.
3. This conceptual trinity is my own: for Youthful Genius, *VMP* 1–21; for Midlife Conversions, *VMP* 22–34; for Mature Saintliness, *VMP* 35–88. In addition to Jean Mesnard's prefaces in *OC,* the most important scholarly assessments of her work, especially in its more or less hagio-

graphical aspects, are the following: Pontien Pohlman, O.F.M., "La biographie de Blaise Pascal par Gilberte Périer," *Revue d'histoire ecclésiastique* 45 (1950): 95–135; Jean Pommier, *La Vie de Pascal par Gilberte Périer: étude critique et littéraire,* vol. 57 of the *Archives des lettres modernes* (Paris, 1964); Philippe Sellier, "Pour un poétique de la légende: *La vie de Monsieur Pascal,*" *Chroniques de Port-Royal* 31 (1982): 51–68.

4. Freud, *The Interpretation of Dreams,* trans. James Strachey (New York, 1965), 647. For historical applicability, see chap. 9, and John Cole, *The Olympian Dreams and Youthful Rebellion of René Descartes* (Urbana, Ill., 1992).
5. *Interpretation of Dreams,* chap. 6, "The Dream Work."
6. For the several texts that make up Voltaire's Anti-Pascal, see his *Oeuvres complètes,* ed. Moland (Paris, 1877–82), XXII, 27–61; XXXI, 1–40. The convenient term "Anti-Pascal" was first used by J. R. Carré, *Réflexions sur l'anti-Pascal de Voltaire* (Paris, 1935). The most respected brief commentaries in general studies are probably those of René Pomeau, *La religion de Voltaire* (Paris, 1956), 226–45, and Ira O. Wade, *The Intellectual Development of Voltaire* (Princeton, 1969), 216–19, 577–88. For an exhaustive monographic study of the philosophical and literary background, with full and current bibliography, see Antony McKenna, *De Pascal à Voltaire: le rôle des Pensées de Pascal dans l'histoire des idées entre 1670 et 1734,* 2 vols., in *Studies on Voltaire and the Eighteenth Century,* vols. 276–77 (Oxford, 1990), esp. II, 837–910.

   For Condorcet, see his *Oeuvres complètes,* ed. Arago, 12 vols. (Paris, 1847–49), III, 567–662; IV, 291–95 and 559. Richard A. Brooks, "Condorcet and Pascal," *Studies on Voltaire and the Eighteenth Century* 55 (1967): 297–307.
7. I cite the fifth edition, *Pascal* (Paris, 1967), 2–5, 200.
8. *OC,* I, 539, 569; cf. 537, 656–57.
9. *VMP,* 1–21.
10. *VMP,* 22–88.
11. See Jean du Vergier de Hauranne, abbé de Saint-Cyran, *Oeuvres chrétiennes et spirituelles,* vol. IV of *Lettres chrétiennes et spirituelles* (Lyon, 1674–79), 71–88. For more on this spirituality and the Pascals' conversions, see chap. 5.
12. *VMP,* 22.
13. *VMP,* 34.
14. Jacqueline to Gilberte, 8 December 1654 and 25 January 1655, *OC,* III, 67–68, 70–75.
15. *OC,* III, 19–53. This very recent edition (1991) is much the best; it includes a full commentary and a current bibliography. For a translation and facsimilies, see chap. 8, and Louis Lafuma's handsome *Manuscrit des Pensées de Pascal* (Paris, 1962), 303–5. For material aspects of the Paper and Parchment, see Zachaire Tourneur's *Pensées de Blaise Pascal, édition paléographique* (Paris, 1942), 7–11. For historical commentary, see Henri Gouhier, *Blaise Pascal commentaires* (Paris, 1984), 11–65 and 367–87.

16. *OC,* III, 35–41.
17. Nicole to Saint-Calais, 3 September 1662, in *Oeuvres,* X, 331.
18. Brienne to Gilberte Périer, 16 November and 7 December 1668, in *Oeuvres,* XII, cxlvii. The first of these passages may echo Gilberte's own words. See also *Oeuvres,* XII, cl. The last word in Mesnard's Pascal is literally "saintliness."
19. *VMP,* First Version, 59–64; Second Version, 59, 69–78. For scholarly acceptance, see Mesnard, *Pascal,* 120–21.
20. See appendix 1 and references there, especially Erna Furman and others, *A Child's Parent Dies* (New Haven, 1974).
21. *VMP,* First Version, 30 and 60; Second Version, 19 and 71. For the letter, Blaise to Gilberte, 17 October 1651, *OC,* II, 845–63; theological commentary in Sellier, *Pascal et Saint-Augustin* (Paris, 1970), numerous passages indexed on 641.
22. *VMP,* 59–60.
23. See the classic paper by Helene Deutsch, "Absence of grief," *Psychoanalytical Quarterly* 6 (1937): 12–22.
24. *VMP,* 18, 20.
25. *VMP,* Second Version, 75–77; compare First Version, 60–64.
26. *VMP,* First Version, 64.
27. *Pensées de M. Pascal sur la réligion et sur quelques autres sujets* (Paris, 1670), 268–69. Victor Cousin was the first to call attention to this deformation of the text in his "Rapport à l'Académie française" (1842). See the relevant passages in his *Oeuvres,* 4th ser. (Paris, 1849), I, 174–75.
28. *Pascal et Saint Augustin,* 152–63 and n. 26 on 157. *Pensées: Nouvelle édition établie pour la première fois d'après la copie de référence de Gilberte Pascal* (Paris, 1976), 31 n. 3; in this numeration, now adopted in the Classiques Garnier (1991), Lafuma's Pensée 396 becomes Sellier's Pensée 15.
29. The fifth, revised edition of *Pascal: l'homme et l'oeuvre,* which I cite, dropped the subtitle *Pascal* (Paris, 1967), 120–21. *Les Pensées de Pascal* (Paris, 1976), 118.
30. *Pascal et les Roannez,* 2 vols. (Paris, 1965), I, 11.
31. *Pascal et les Roannez,* I, 169, 174.
32. *Pascal et les Roannez,* I, 15.
33. See appendix 1.
34. I have relied particularly on the work of Erna Furman and colleagues for clinical reports on bereaved children, John Birtchnell for retrospective epidemiological studies of adult patients, and John Bowlby for the construction of a coherent theory. For bibliographical references, see chap. 1, note 44. Although this theory can be simplified for presentation (see appendix 1), the issues it raises are complex, and the hypothesis of a causal relationship between early loss and later depression has been debated.
35. *VMP,* First Version, 81; Second Version, 94. *OC,* IV, 964–1012.
36. It may not be merely incidental that the first abbé de Saint-Cyran, the

great spiritual authority for this generation of Jansenists, was regarded by some contemporaries as distinctly melancholy. The eminent student of the abbé's life and Jansenist spirituality, Jean Orcibal, still regards a pathological depression as a defining aspect of his mature personality. See his *Jean Duvergier de Hauranne, abbé de Saint-Cyran, et son temps,* vols. II–III of *Les origines du jansénisme* (Louvain and Paris, 1947), II, 640–48. In this context, Orcibal notes the early deaths of Saint-Cyran's father, three brothers, and a sister. He states the case more popularly in *Saint-Cyran et le jansénisme* (Paris, 1961), 114–17. See also Henri Brémond, *Histoire littéraire du sentiment religieux en France* (Paris, 1932), IV, 67, n. 1.

NOTES TO PART ONE

1. *VMP,* 2.

NOTES TO CHAPTER ONE

1. *OC,* I, 506–8; 1090–93.
2. *OC,* IV, 937, 939, 1093 and n. 3. A minor variant in the two versions of the Strange Story neatly discriminates the provincial's version from a Parisian version. Marguerite says that "*en chartre*" is the term used for such infantile illnesses "at Paris." The Ménil recorder, presuming Parisian usages, did not so qualify the term. Cf. *OC,* I, 507 and 1091. And see Pensée 888.
3. *OC,* I, 748; Christian Huygens to J. Chapelain, 2 September 1660, in Huygens, *Oeuvres complètes* (The Hague, 1890), III, 120. Huygens, *Journal de Voyage à Paris et à Londres,* ed. H.-L. Brugmans (Paris, 1935), 132, 136, 137, 138, 140, 141, and so on.
4. *OC,* I, 506–7.
5. *OC,* I, 507. The inadequacies of seventeenth-century medicine are so evident that twentieth-century historians may underestimate the significance of the fact that the doctors in this case were ready to pronounce the little boy dead.
6. Pierre Richelet, *Dictionnaire françois contenant les mots et les choses* (Geneva, 1679), s.v. "chartre."
7. Antoine Furetière, *Le dictionnaire universel* (The Hague, 1690), s.v. "chartre."
8. M. W. Beaver, "Population, infant mortality, and milk," *Population Studies* 27 (1973): 243–54.
9. Abel Poitrineau, *La vie rurale en Basse-Auvergne au XVIIIe siècle* (Paris, 1965), I, 87, 93, 101–7, 214, 291–94, 436.
10. Maurice Aymard, "Toward the History of Nutrition: Some Methodological Remarks," in R. Forster and O. Ranum, *Food and Drink in History* (Baltimore, 1978), 1–16.

11. Nevin S. Scrimshaw, "The Effect of the Interaction of Nutrition and Infection on the Pre-School Child," in *Pre-School Child Malnutrition,* Publication 1282 of the National Academy of Sciences and the National Research Council (Washington, D.C., 1966), 63–71. John R. K. Robeson et al., *Malnutrition: Its Causes and Control, with Special Reference to Protein-Calorie Malnutrition* (New York, 1972), I, 110–15.
12. François Lebrun, *La vie conjugale sous l'ancien régime* (Paris, 1975), 133. Jean-Louis Flandrin, *Families in Former Times: Kinship, Household, and Sexuality in Early Modern France* (Cambridge, 1979), 201, 208.
13. Simon de Vallambert, *De la manière de nourrir et gouverner les enfants des leur naissance* (Poitiers, 1565), 141–45. See David Hunt, *Parents and Children in History: the Psychology of Family Life in Early Modern France* (New York, 1970), 115–17.
14. *OC,* I, 507, 1091.
15. See Jean Mesnard's prefatory remarks, *OC,* I, 645.
16. See "Growth of the Skull," in George H. Lowrey, *Growth and Development of Children,* 6th ed. (Chicago, 1973), 193–94.
17. *OC,* I, 646.
18. For the diagnosis, see M. E. Ledoux, "A propos de Pascal malade," *Académie des sciences, Belles-Lettres, et Arts de Besançon* (1923): 188–219; P. Wertheimer and A. Bouchet, "Les maladies et la mort de Blaise Pascal," in *Comptes rendus du 88e congrès national des sociétés savantes: Section des sciences* (Clermont-Ferrand, 1963), III, 19; T. Rabinowicz, commentary on P. Rentchnick, "Pathographies (71): Blaise Pascal," in *Médecine et hygiène* 41 (1983): 4536.
19. David Holvey, ed., *The Merck Manual of Diagnosis and Therapy,* 12th ed. (Rahway, N.J., 1974), 1044.
20. Stanley M. Garn, "Malnutrition and Skeletal Development in the Pre-School Child," in *Pre-School Child Malnutrition,* 57.
21. Lowrey, *Growth and Development,* 194.
22. *OC,* I, 507, 1091.
23. *OC,* I, 507, 1091.
24. See the dictionaries of Furetière, Richelet, and the Académie, s.v. "sevrer."
25. Benjamin Spock can represent modern pediatric wisdom: *Baby and Child Care,* 40th anniversary edition (New York, 1985), 105 ff., esp. 141–46 and 198–202; there is a whole section of tips on "helping your baby to like the cup." See also T. Berry Brazelton, *Infants and Mothers,* rev. ed. (New York, 1983).
26. *OC,* I, 507, 1091.
27. *OC,* II, 39–40.
28. Étienne and Francine van de Walle, "Allaitement, stérilité, et contraception: les opinions jusqu'au XIXe siècle," *Population* 27 (1972): 685–701. Lebrun, *La vie conjugale,* 125–26.
29. Roger Mercier, *L'enfant dans la société du XVIIIe siècle avant l'Émile*

(Dakar, 1961), 11–18, 81–85; Yves Castan, *Honnêteté et relations sociales en Languedoc, 1715–1780* (Paris, 1974), 211–14; Flandrin, *Families in Former Times,* 204–5.

30. *OC,* II, 40.
31. *OC,* I, 507, 1093.
32. Erik Erikson, *Childhood and Society,* 2d ed. (New York, 1963), 251–54.
33. Burton White, *The First Three Years of Life,* rev. ed. (New York, 1985) 152, 156–57, 165–67, 173–75. See also Florence L. Goodenough, *Anger in Young Children* (Westport, Conn., 1975), 71–72; Erikson, *Childhood and Society,* 80–85; Lowrey, *Growth and Development of the Child,* 154–55.
34. The Ménil Version gives evidence of the physical blow; Marguerite's Version adds that she was knocked down stairs: *OC,* I, 507, 1093.
35. Henri IV to Madame de Montglat, *Recueil des lettres missives de Henri IV,* ed. Berger de Xivrey (Paris, 1843), VII, 385. The whippings of the Dauphin began at the end of his second year; see the *Journal de Jean Héroard sur l'enfance et la jeunesse de Louis XIII (1601–1628),* ed. Soulié and Barthélemy (Paris, 1868), I, 31–34, 55, 95 ff.
36. Jacqueline to Gilberte, 25 April 1655, *Oeuvres,* IV, 70–73.
37. Bowlby, *Separation,* passim.
38. Furetière, *Dictionnaire universel,* s.v. "*sevrer.*"
39. Such care caused many deaths. See Paul Galiano, "La mortalité infantile (indigenes et nourrissons) dans la banlieue sud de Paris à la fin du XVIIIe siècle," *Annales de démographie historique* (1966), 173–74; Marcel Lachiver, *La population de Meulan* (Paris, 1969), 128.
40. Thomas, *Religion and the Decline of Magic* (New York, 1971), 433–583, esp. 512, 520–23, 533, 535, 546, 561.
41. *OC,* I, 1092–93; cf. 507–8.
42. *OC,* I, 1093.
43. Charles Baudouin has speculated in a nonscholarly essay that the mother's early death was a lifelong trauma for the son. See *Blaise Pascal ou l'ordre du coeur* (Paris, 1962), 7–17.
44. Erna and Robert Furman are the ranking authorities on parentally bereaved young children. See Erna Furman and others, *A Child's Parent Dies* (New Haven, 1974). Robert Furman, "Death and the young child, some preliminary considerations," *Psychoanalytic Study of the Child* 19 (1964): 321–33; "The Child's Reaction to Death in the Family," in *Loss and Grief: Psychological Management in Medical Practice,* ed. B. Schoenberg et al. (New York, 1970), 70–86; "A Child's Capacity for Mourning," in *The Child in His Family: The Impact of Disease and Death,* ed. E. J. Anthony and C. Koupernik (New York, 1973), II, 225–31.

    John Bowlby is the great authority on the human experience of attachments, separations, and losses. The grand opus: *Attachment and Loss,* 3 vols. (New York, 1969–80). More concise summaries: "Attachment Theory, Separation Anxiety, and Mourning," in the *American Handbook of Psychiatry,* 2d ed., ed. S. Arieti (New York, 1975): VI, 292–

309; "The making and breaking of affectional bonds," *British Journal of Psychiatry* 130 (1977): 201–10 and 421–31.

Robert Birtchnell has done particularly impressive research on the incidence of early parental loss among populations of adult psychiatric patients. The relevant papers, in chronological order: "The possible consequences of early parent death," *British Journal of Medical Psychology* 42 (1969): 1–12; "Early parent death and mental illness," *British Journal of Psychiatry* 116 (1970): 281–88; "Recent parent death and mental illness," *British Journal of Psychiatry* 116 (1970): 289–97; "Depression in relation to early and recent parent death," *British Journal of Psychiatry* 116 (1970): 299–306; "Early parent death in relation to size and constitution of sibship in psychiatric patients and general population controls," *Acta Psychiatrica Scandinavica* 17 (1971): 250–70; "Early parent death and psychiatric diagnosis," *Social Psychiatry* 7 (1972): 202–10; "The personality characteristics of early-bereaved psychiatric patients," *Social Psychiatry* 10 (1975): 97–103; "Psychiatric breakdown following recent parent death," *British Journal of Medical Psychology,* 48 (1975): 379–90; "Early parent death and the clinical scales of the MMPI," *British Journal of Psychiatry* 132 (1978): 574–79.

NOTES TO CHAPTER TWO

1. Cf. *VMP,* 2.
2. *OC,* II, 23, 41; a date after 19 June 1626 for Antoinette's death is required by Blaise's age, known from *VMP,* 2.
3. G. Cabourdin, "Le remariage en France sous L'Ancien Régime (seizième—dix-huitième siècles)," in *Marriage and Remarriage in Populations of the Past,* ed. J. Dupaquier et al. (London, 1981), 274–75. See also Micheline Baulant, "The Scattered Family: Another Aspect of Seventeenth-Century Demography," in *Family and Society: Selections from the Annales,* ed. R. Forster and O. Ranum (Baltimore, 1976), 104–16; Peter Laslett, "Parental Deprivation in the Past," in his *Family Life and Illicit Love in Earlier Generations* (Cambridge, 1977), 160–73.
4. Cabourdin, "Le remariage en France," 277–78, 280–81.
5. *OC,* I, 721.
6. Anna Freud and Dorothy Burlingham, *Infants without Families* (New York, 1944); Marion Barnes, "Reactions to the death of a mother," *Psychoanalytic Study of the Child* 19 (1964): 334–37.
7. Cf. *VMP,* 35, 77.
8. *OC,* I, 667.
9. Alexandre Féron devoted a brief monograph to her: *Louise Delfault: servante des Pascal* (Rouen, 1926).
10. Philippe Ariès, *Centuries of Childhood: A Social History of Family Life,* trans. R. Baldick (New York, 1962), 66–67, 196–97.
11. *VMP,* 3. Marguerite Périer was only the first to follow her mother's lead to the dubious conclusion that Étienne had retired to Paris "in order

to attend to the education of his children, especially Blaise Pascal." See *OC,* I, 1077. Note that Étienne did not begin formal language instruction before Blaise was twelve (1635) and that he intended to postpone mathematics even longer.

12. *VMP,* 3: "compagnies continuelles." Cf. *OC,* I, 666.
13. *OC,* I, 429–53; see also 699.
14. *OC,* I, 435, 712–13; Albert de Remacle, *Les Pascal en basse-Auvergne* (Clermont-Ferrand, 1923), 13–15.
15. *OC,* II, 43, 58, 101.
16. *OC,* II, 31, 50; I, 711, 716–17; Élie Jaloustre, "Histoire d'un village de la Limagne (Gerzat)," *Mémoires de l'Académie des Sciences, Belles-Lettres, et Arts de Clermont-Ferrand* 28 (1886): 142. Étienne had close official and political associations with this Jean Begon as well as the marital affiliation and godparental relationship; the two had served together in the tax court of the Election from 1618 to 1624, and Begon followed Pascal as the *échevin* of the municipality in 1625. Ambroise Tardieu, *Histoire de la ville de Clermont-Ferrand* (Clermont-Ferrand, 1872), I, 534, 588–89; II, 188.
17. Tardieu, *Histoire de Clermont-Ferrand,* I, 580, 583. The comte de Champflour, "L'Édit royal de 1630," *Bulletin historique et scientifique de l'Auvergne,* 2d ser. (1910): 125, n. 2. Despite the unprecedented numbers of new creations, the value of ennobling offices in the sovereign courts inflated significantly in the 1620s and 1630s. See R. Laroux, "La Cour des aides," *Revue d'Auvergne,* vol. 31 (1914): 47, 262–63; vol. 34 (1917): 199–201; Roland Mousnier, *La Vénalité des offices sous Henri IV et Louis XIII,* 2d ed. (Paris, 1971), 356–70.
18. Mousnier, *Vénalité des offices,* 291–94. Officers in the sovereign courts opposed this forced loan so vigorously that it was later halved for them.
19. In 1629, the King had created new Elections for Brioude, Issoire, and Thiers, all at a cost to Étienne's former colleagues in Clermont. The multiplication of courts meant a multiplication of offices and a one-time increase in royal revenues from the sales. *OC,* II, 41. Tardieu, *Histoire de la ville de Clermont-Ferrand,* I, 588–89.
20. For the text of the Edict, see Savaron and Pierre Durand, *Les origines de la ville de Clermont* (Paris, 1662), 532–37.
21. Bertrand Gille, "Études sur Clermont à l'époque classique," *Revue d'Auvergne* 86 (1972): 98. Some of the most vocal opponents of the relocation were the officers from Montferrand. There were serious attempts by the lesser city to reclaim its court as late as 1644. All of this must have made professional life within what was still a small corporation unpleasant at best, insecure at worst. Gille, "Études sur Clermont," 102–4.
22. *OC,* I, 727. The anonymous author, perhaps Jacques Audigier, specified a date, 1633, and the name and *qualité* of the successful rival, Annet Durant, *lieutenant-général* in the Présidial. This Durant was in fact elected this year, but Étienne's move cannot have been motivated by

political frustration alone. For the municipal elections, see Tardieu, *Histoire de Clermont-Ferrand,* I, 534–35, 573. The timing of Étienne's sale of his house (1633) and office (1634) does fit the chronology suggested by the anecdote. See *OC,* II, 58, 101.

23. The term is that of the intendant Trudaine, who had inherited what was still an administrative mess a century later. See Gille, "Études sur Clermont," 95–105.
24. *OC,* II, 53–55.
25. Roger Sève, "La vie à Clermont au temps de Pascal," in Francine Leclercq et al., *Clermont, ville de Pascal* (Clermont-Ferrand, 1962), 129. Pierre Charbonnier, "La peste de 1631 à Clermont," *Revue d'Auvergne* 79 (1965): 118–21.
26. Charbonnier, "La peste de 1631," 125.
27. The Chevalier de Jaucourt, "La peste," in the great Diderot *Encyclopédie* (1765).
28. Sève, "La vie à Clermont," 131.
29. Sève, "La vie à Clermont," 104.
30. *Érudits* have published one detailed travel journal of an unhappily eventful round-trip in 1661 that took seven days from Clermont to Paris and six days back from Paris to Clermont. The traveler, a bourgeois who set out with only a single retainer, spent as much in these two weeks on the road as Blaise Pascal was then paying for a full six months' house rental in Paris. Armand Delphy, "De Clermont à Paris en 1661," *Le vieux papier* 1 (1900): 194–97; cf. *OC,* II, 1335.
31. *VMP,* 2.
32. Savaron and Durand, *Les origines de Clermont,* 534.
33. The most detailed account is still Élie Jaloustre's old monograph, "Les anciennes écoles de l'Auvergne," *Mémoires de l'Académie des sciences, belles-lettres, et arts de l'Auvergne* 23 (1881): 208–36. For the establishment of the local *collège* by the municipality Clermont in the 1570s and for the (re-)establishment of the Jesuit *collège* in 1662, see 132 ff. and 237 ff. More recent references: de Champflour, "L'Édit royal de 1630," *Bulletin de l'Auvergne* (1910), 127–28; Sève, "La vie à Clermont," 134–38; Gille, "Clermont à l'époque classique," 101–5.
34. Jaloustre, "Les anciennes écoles," 212, 229.
35. Gustave Dupont-Ferrier, *Du Collège de Clermont au Lycée Louis le Grand* (Paris, 1921), vol. I. François de Dainville, S.J., *La naissance de l'humanisme moderne: les Jésuites et l'éducation de la société française* (Paris, 1940).
36. Ariès, *Centuries of Childhood,* 197, 269.
37. Roland Mousnier, *The Institutions of France under the Absolute Monarchy 1598–1789,* vol. II, *The Organs of State and Society,* trans. A. Goldhammer (Chicago, 1984), 4–12.
38. Baillet, *Des enfans devenus célèbres par leurs études ou par leurs écrits* (Paris, 1688), 303–4, cf. 286–87.
39. Gabriel Pérau, *Vie de Jérome Bignon, avocat général et conseiller d'État* (Paris, 1757), 8–23.

40. Jérome Bignon was born on 24 August 1589: Pérau, *Vie de Jérome Bignon,* 9. Étienne Pascal was born on 2 May 1588: *OC,* I, 459–60. For Bignon's legal education, see Pérau, 31–35. For Pascal's, see *OC,* I, 721, contrary to *OC,* I, 1077.
41. In 1647–48, while Étienne was still in Rouen, Blaise and Jacqueline spent about a year in his house in Paris. He was determined to rule from afar, depending on the domestic surveillance of a faithful servant in Paris. *OC,* I, 664–65.
42. John Bowlby, *Separation* (New York, 1973), 261–83, with references to previous scholarship cited on 264 and 282.
43. *VMP,* 2. Much later, when the same "reasons" no longer applied, Étienne Pascal was to keep his first grandson, Étienne Périer, with him at Rouen after the infant's mother, Gilberte, had returned with her husband to distant Clermont. See *OC,* I, 1083–84; II, 243, 281–83. From 1646 to 1648, he seems to have clung to the young mother herself, who had come north for a visit. See *OC,* I, 1086–87; II, 248, 248–441. Finally, from 1648 to his death in 1651, he clung to Jacqueline. See *OC,* I, 665–70. This begins to look like a pattern.
44. Ernest Jovy, "Deux documents relatifs à Domat," *Bulletin historique et scientifique de l'Auvergne* 2d ser. (1924): 165.

NOTES TO CHAPTER THREE

1. *OC,* I, 720–21.
2. *VMP,* 8–14, 18–19, 21.
3. *VMP,* Second Version, 71.
4. Florin Périer borrowed it from his wife's manuscript for his "Préface" to Blaise's posthumous *Traités* (1663); see *OC,* I, 683–84. Adrien Baillet took it from Périer for his inspiring collection of stories about bright little fellows, *Enfans devenus célèbres* (Paris, 1688), 303–13. Pierre Bayle expressed doubts but retold the story in his *Dictionnaire historique et critique,* 3d ed. (Rotterdam, 1720), s.v. "Pascal."
5. "In any triangle, if one of the sides be produced, the exterior angle is equal to the two interior and opposite angles, and the three interior angles of the triangle are equal to two right angles."
6. *VMP,* 13–15. There is no independent confirmation of Blaise's interaction with older savants in the Mersenne circle before the *Essai pour les coniques.* See *OC,* II, 119–22, 236–39.
7. There were skeptics. Gédéon Tallemant des Réaux was first into print with a version of the anecdote in which Blaise learned his geometry from the forbidden book. *OC,* I, 463–64. The most economical explanation for the discrepancies between his version and Gilberte's is that she reflects her father's understanding of what had happened, while Tallemant reflects Le Pailleur's more skeptical reconstruction. For Étienne's relationship with Le Pailleur, see *OC,* II, 587. For Tallemant des Réaux and Le Pailleur, see the *Historiettes,* ed. A. Adam, 2 vols.

(Paris, 1960–61), I, ix, xvii, 156, 839 n, 222, and 888 n; II, 99–101, and numerous other indexed references.

8. The catalog of the Bibliothèque Nationale lists editions of the Dounot version (1609, 1610, and 1613), the Henrion version (1615, 1621, 1631, and 1632), and the Le Mardelé version (1632). There would have been still other choices for the first six or nine books of Euclid's *Elements:* translators included Pierre Forcadel (1566), Jean de Tournes (1611), and J. Errard (1629).
9. *OC,* II, 712.
10. *OC,* II, 82–99.
11. *OC,* II, 329–41, 711–15; *VMP,* 18–19.
12. It is impossible to overemphasize the real and perceived burdens of direct taxation in this period. Richelieu compared all taxpaying subjects to mules who should be worked hard and to men who should be bled medicinally. And the Normans were rebels who deserved severe punishment. See *The Political Testament of Cardinal Richelieu,* ed. H. B. Hill (Madison, Wis., 1961), 31–33, 84–93. The King, Cardinal, and Chancellor also injured the pride and interests even of the privileged Robe. See *Diaire ou Journal de voyage du chancelier Séguier en Normandie,* ed. A. Floquet (Rouen, 1842), 384–85, and passim. Royal policy subjected even the Swords to the humiliation of having to prove their nobility—and so their exemptions—to the satisfaction of Étienne Pascal, an alien commoner! See Alexandre Bigot de Monville, *Mémoires sur la sédition des Nu-Pieds* (Rouen, 1876), 4.
13. *OC,* II, 280–83, and 116, 240, 271, 277, 300, 342. For the Pascals at Rouen: Charles de Beaurepaire, "Blaise Pascal et sa famille à Rouen (1640–47)," *L'Académie des sciences, belles-lettres et arts de Rouen* (1902): 211–312, especially 234–69; A. Debuc, "Étienne Pascal, conseiller du Roi à Rouen," *Actes du 88e Congrès national des Sociétés savantes* (Clermont-Ferrand, 1963), 32–47. Unsurprisingly, the familial tradition tended to gloss over unpleasant aspects of the situation. For the context, see Boris Porchnev, *Les soulèvements populaires en France de 1623 à 1648* (Paris, 1963), 303 ff.; Madeleine Foisil, *La révolte des Nu-pieds et les révoltes populaires normandes de 1639* (Paris, 1970).
14. Edmond Esmonin, *La taille en Normandie au temps de Colbert: 1661–1683* (Paris, 1913).
15. Pierre Goubert shows that even technically competent central administrators made gross errors, *L'Ancien Régime: la société* (Paris, 1969), 32, 42. The arithmetic of tax collection on the local level was even worse: see Esmonin, *La taille,* 422–23.
16. *OC,* II, 331–32.
17. Pascal realized the versatility of the new technology. Four of the surviving machines were intended for calculations of money, one for calculations of length, and three for other calculations in a purely decile system. See Jacques Payen, "Les exemplaires conservés de la machine de Pascal," in Costabel, *L'oeuvre scientifique de Pascal,* 230–41.

18. René Taton, "Sur l'invention de la machine arithmétique," in Costabel, *L'oeuvre scientifique de Pascal,* 209–13.
19. *OC,* II, 121.
20. *OC,* II, 282–83.
21. *OC,* I, 731. The *Clermontois* author of this otherwise admiring little memoir on "La maison de Pascal" was probably informed by one of the Périers. He would have had no reason to deny his illustrious compatriot any of his glory.
22. *Histoire de la Roulette, Oeuvres,* III, 337.
23. *OC,* II, 336–38, 340, 712–13.
24. *VMP,* 19; *OC,* II, 330.
25. Blaise referred to the heavy expenses of development in all three of his writings on the machine, but the money must have been Étienne's, not his own. During his father's lifetime, he never had an independent income. See *OC,* II, 333, 335, 713.
26. Mesnard, *Pascal,* 7–8, 27–28; *OC,* II, 318–19. For derogation, which became an important concern for the Pascals only after their ennoblement in 1645, see Roland Mousnier, *The Institutions of France under the Absolute Monarchy,* vol. I, *Society and the State,* trans. B. Pearce (Chicago, 1979), 131–34: "[W]hat derogated from nobility was any activity aimed at making money, especially any trade, and any manual labor. . . ." A nobleman could not dirty his hands or sell manufactured products. The *privilège* of 1649 that granted a monopoly to Pascal was apparently intended to prevent others from marketing inferior copies. His concern was honor, not profit. See *OC,* 338–39, 714.
27. De Remacle, *Les Pascal,* 12.
28. De Remacle, *Les Pascal,* 13. The principle of three generations in office for transmissible nobility was stated in Article 25 of the great Edict on the Tailles of March 1600; see François André Isambert, *Recueil général des anciennes lois françaises* (Paris, 1829), XV, 234. The applicability of this principle to the *trésoriers* was generally acknowledged; see Jean-Paul Charmeil, *Les trésoriers de France à l'époque de la Fronde* (Paris, 1964), 72–74.
29. This was a fundamental point of most French law. Wives and children followed the status of their husbands and fathers. On the Pascals de Mons, see de Remacle, *Les Pascal,* 5–11 and 13.
30. For *patre et avo consilibus,* see Mousnier, *The Institutions of France,* I, 129, 131; II, 368. For ennoblement by office, see François Bluche: *L'anoblissement par charges avant 1789,* in *Les Cahiers nobles* 23 and 24 (1962).
31. Mousnier, *La plume, la faucille, et le marteau* (Paris, 1970), 166. The number of new councillors was a matter of disparaging comment at the time and afterward: Olivier Lefevre d'Ormesson, *Journal,* ed. P. Chéruel (Paris, 1860), I, 424; Guy Patin to Charles Spon, 1 April 1650, in *Lettres du temps de la Fronde,* ed. A. Thérive (Paris, 1921), 187.
32. *OC,* II, 334.

33. Mesnard argues for November 1645 at the latest as the date for the presentation to Séguier: *OC,* II, 322, 330, 331. Étienne's letters of appointment were dated 27 December 1645: *OC,* I, 1079. For the formal significance of the letters, see Bluche, *L'anoblissement,* in *Cahiers nobles* 23 (1962), 41; Pierre Guyot, *Répertoire universel et raisonné de jurisprudence civile, criminelle, canonique et bénéficiale* (Paris, 1784), IV, 514–15.
34. *OC,* II, 245–46, 296–97, 329–41, 443–44. The most celebrated such presentation, to the Queen of Sweden (June 1652), did follow the Pascals' ennoblement and Étienne's death, but the episode is in many ways a postscript. See *OC,* II, 918–26 and cf. *OC,* II, 902–3.
35. This nobiliary coat of arms is missing only from the handsome machine presented to Séguier (1645) and from the much humbler six-digit machine (1652) now in the Musée du Conservatoire des Arts et Métiers. Other surviving machines bear the arms. See the "Description" with photographs in Costabel, *L'oeuvre scientifique de Pascal,* 230–41.
36. *OC,* II, 688.
37. *OC,* II, 350; cf. II, 590.
38. *OC,* II, 354.
39. *OC,* II, 352. Galileo, *Dialogue Concerning the Two Chief World Systems,* trans. S. Drake (Berkeley, 1953), 7 n on 467–68.
40. *OC,* II, 501, 502.
41. *OC,* II, 501.
42. *OC,* II, 498.
43. *OC,* II, 589–90.
44. *VMP,* 18.
45. Between the time of his father's death and that of his own Second Conversion, Pascal was quite willing to vulgarize this past work and to capitalize on whatever appeal it might have to the greats of the world: *OC,* II, 890 and 902–3, 890–91 and 918–26. The silence of the documents on new mathematical or scientific activity for about two and a half years after the loss of his father, but before the Conversion, is quietly impressive: *OC,* II, 651–52, 889–95.

NOTES TO PART TWO

1. John Bowlby, *Attachment and Loss,* 3 vols. (New York, 1969–80).
2. *VMP,* Second Version, 69.
3. *OC,* II, 269.
4. *VMP,* 1, 20.

NOTES TO CHAPTER FOUR

1. *OC,* II, 58, 101–2, 111–12.
2. For the *rentes* and related matters of public finance, see François Véron-Duverger de Forbonnais, *Recherches et considérations sur les finances de*

France depuis l'année 1595 jusqu'à l'année 1721, 2 vols. (Basle, 1758); Julian Dent, *Crisis in Finance: Crown, Financiers, and Society in Seventeenth-Century France* (New York, 1973), esp. 46–54.

3. *OC,* II, 101–2, 111–12.
4. Forbonnais, *Recherches,* I, 222–23, 225–26, 228–35.
5. *OC,* I, 660. On the episode, see also *OC,* I, 462–63, 729–30, 1087–89, 1093–94.
6. *OC,* II, 193, 194.
7. *OC,* II, 200.
8. *OC,* II, 200–1.
9. *OC,* II, 199, n. 1.
10. For the remarkable story, see François-Paule de Clermont, marquis de Montglat, *Mémoires* in Michaud-Poujoulat, *Mémoires pour servir à l'histoire de France* (Paris, 1838), V, 66–67. Victor Tapié is among the modern skeptics, but his few remarks on the marriage do help at the very least to explain contemporaries' credulity: *France in the Age of Louis XIII and Richelieu,* trans. D. Lockie (New York, 1975), 16, 92, 154, 161, 166, 375–76.
11. *OC,* II, 199.
12. *Vie de Jacqueline Pascal, OC,* I, 660.
13. *Vie de Jacqueline Pascal, OC,* I, 660–61.
14. She was to be confirmed, on her own initiative, at the age of twenty-one. *Vie de Jacqueline Pascal, OC,* I, 663.
15. See Jean Orcibal, *La Spiritualité de Saint-Cyran avec ses écrits de piété inédits* (Paris 1962), 154–55. At the age of seven, Jacqueline had at first resisted her elder sister's instruction, but there was little doubt about her precociousness; see the *Vie de Jacqueline Pascal, OC,* I, 658.
16. Jacqueline to Gilberte, 24 March 1656, *Oeuvres,* IV, 327.
17. *VMP,* 23. For general discussion of the sacrament in post-Tridentine Catholicism and for further references, see E. Mangenot, "Confirmation d'après le concile de Trente," in *Dictionnaire de théologie catholique,* ed. A. Vacant (Paris, 1923–50), vol. III, pt. 1, cols. 1088–93. For the issues of age and obligation, see T. Ortolan, "Confirmation, questions morales et pratiques," *Dictionnaire de théologie catholique,* vol. III, pt. 1, cols. 1100–02.
18. *OC,* II, 204–5; cf. 197–201.
19. *OC,* I, 664; cf. II, 205–6.
20. *OC,* II, 205–6.
21. *OC,* I, 660–61.
22. *OC,* II, 219, 255–60.
23. It would be naive to suppose that Corneille and his compatriots could have been perfectly disinterested when they solicited a poem for their Palinodes from the daughter of *Commissioner Pascal.* He had come to Rouen to reimpose what passed for fiscal order in a province that had just rebelled and been repressed militarily. Corneille seems not to have read Jacqueline's work before asking her, an alien Auvergnat and the

only girl in the competition, to submit a piece. Of course, she won the prize. Corneille himself struck off verses of his own in honor of "a twelve-year-old girl." For what little the correction is worth, she was fifteen but small for her age. The Normans bore the prize and the poem to the Pascals' house "with drums, trumpets, and great ceremony." Étienne must have enjoyed the show.

24. *OC,* II, 272–74.
25. The story improved with the telling: *OC,* I, 463, 661–62, 729–30, 1087–89, 1094–97. For Jacqueline's contemporaneous account in a letter to her father, see *OC,* II, 209–13.
26. *OC,* I, 214–15.
27. De Scudéry, *L'amour tirannique, tragi-comédie* (Paris, 1639), act 4, scene 5, page 66. On de Scudéry's play as an attempt to teach the world how to do it right after Corneille had done it wrong in *Le Cid,* see Virginia Farinholt, *A Critical Edition of Georges de Scudéry's L'Amour Tyrannique* (Chicago, 1938).
28. *OC,* II, 213.
29. The girls themselves welcomed all the fondling and kissing as evidence of the Cardinal's willingness to pardon their father, but from this immense distance it looks abusive, however "welcome." *OC,* I, 661–62; II, 211–12.

NOTES TO CHAPTER FIVE

1. *OC,* I, 663.
2. *OC,* I, 1079.
3. *OC,* II, 265.
4. *OC,* I, 663.
5. *OC,* I, 1078–79.
6. *OC,* I, 1079.
7. *OC,* I, 1098.
8. *OC,* I, 1098.
9. *OC,* II, 862.
10. *OC,* I, 663; Henri Gouhier, *Pascal et les humanistes chrétiennes: l'affaire Saint-Ange* (Paris, 1974), 15–16 nn on 122–23.
11. Jansenius's text is most accessible in Gustave Michaut, *Les époques de la pensée de Pascal* (Paris, 1902), 194–222.
12. Michaut, *Les époques de la pensée,* 221.
13. Jean du Vergier de Hauranne, abbé de Saint-Cyran, *Coeur nouveau,* in *Oeuvres chrétiennes et spirituelles* (Lyon, 1674), IV, 78, 79, 80–81.
14. *OC,* I, 712; Albert de Remacle, *Les Pascal en basse-Auvergne* (Clermont-Ferrand, 1923), 30.
15. *OC,* II, 43.
16. *OC,* II, 58, 101, 981.
17. See the Ojardias marginal notation in his copy of De Remacle, *Les Pascal in Basse-Auvergne,* 14. This precious copy is in the rich Pascal

collections of the Bibliothèque Municipale et Universitaire de Clermont-Ferrand.

18. Jansenist authorities were quite consistent in their warnings against curiosity. For Jansenius himself, see the *Discours,* 206–8. Saint-Cyran echoed these opinions, for instance in a relevant letter to Antoine Singlin on the direction of new converts: "[The convert must] avoid all sorts of curiosity. This is the second root of sin according to Saint Augustine, although few realize it. Adam and Eve lost themselves in this way. The Devil has hardly any more dangerous trap." See the *Lettres chrétiennes et spirituelles* (Lyon, 1674), I, 320. Singlin learned the lesson well and taught it to congregations including the Pascals: "All our reasoning does no more than to intoxicate us [with sinful pride]. . . . So we must stifle our intelligence in order to make room for God's." See *Instructions chrétiennes* (Paris, 1736), II, 136. Pascal himself left this thought in Pensée 744: "Man's chief malady is his restless curiosity about things he cannot know. . . ." Modern reconsideration of his examples of the unknowable, meteorology and medicine, might or might not humble proud reason.
19. *OC,* I, 1100.
20. *VMP,* 31.
21. *VMP,* 32.
22. Cf. *VMP,* First Version, 32, and *VMP,* Second Version, 21.
23. The absence of better documentation cuts both ways. Obviously, the limitations of the evidence must limit confidence in any historical diagnosis. Less obviously, silent or deficient sources are no better evidence of good health than of ill health. There are only two or three relevant paragraphs from Gilberte, another from Marguerite, and scattered remarks in Jacqueline's letter of 25 September 1647.
24. On the one hand, what we do know is suggestive of the polysymptomatic psychiatric disorder that has been called hysteria, Briquet's syndrome, or somatization disorder. On the other hand, we do not know enough to make any such diagnosis with any confidence, and there is no way to rule out a physical disorder or a more complicated case history of various physical disorders, perhaps further complicated by psychiatric difficulties. For the history of medical thinking, see Ilza Veith, *Hysteria: The History of a Disease* (Chicago, 1965); Paul Briquet, *Traité clinique et thérapeutique de l'hystérie* (Paris, 1859); G. Abricossoff, *L'hystérie aux XVIIe et XVIIIe siècles* (Paris, 1897). For discussion of the diagnosis in clinical situations, see Samuel B. Guze, "The diagnosis of hysteria," *American Journal of Psychiatry* 124 (1967): 491–98; Samuel B. Guze, Robert A. Woodruff, and Paula J. Clayton, "A study of conversion symptoms in psychiatric outpatients," *American Journal of Psychiatry* 128 (1971): 643–46; Paul Chodoff, "The diagnosis of hysteria: An overview," *American Journal of Psychiatry* 131 (1974): 1073–78; Ray Kimble, James G. Williams, Stewart Agras, "A comparison of two methods of diagnosing hysteria," *American Journal of Psychiatry* 132 (1975): 1197–99;

Donald W. Goodwin and Samuel B. Guze, *Psychiatric Diagnosis,* 2d ed. (New York, 1979), 70–87; American Psychiatric Association, *Diagnostic and Statistical Manual of Mental Disorders,* 3d ed. (DSM-III), ed. Robert L. Spitzer et al. (Washington, D.C., 1980), 241–52.

25. *VMP,* First Version, 31–32; Second Version, 21. Cf. also *VMP,* First Version, 47–50, 81; *Prière pour le bon usage des maladies, Oeuvres,* IX, 323–40.
26. *VMP,* Second Version, 21.
27. *OC,* II, 581.
28. *OC,* II, 583.
29. *OC,* II, 583.
30. *OC,* I, 665. Canon law did not require parental consent even for marriage, let alone religious profession. Civil law reinforced parental rights in the case of marriage before the age of 25 but did not strictly require consent for the profession of someone who had reached the age of "20 or 22 years." See François Richer, *Traité de la mort civile* (Paris, 1755), 635–41.
31. Jacqueline's letters of 19 June 1648, 5 November 1648, and 24 March 1649 provide contemporaneous documentation on the crisis of confidence. See *OC,* II, 614–19, 694–95, and 701–3.
32. Jacqueline's letter of 19 June 1648 does make her submissiveness to her father's will a matter of obedience as well as gratitude: *OC,* II, 614–19. On her withdrawal from secular society and relations with Port-Royal, see *OC,* I, 665–66, 670–71. Étienne decided soon afterward to leave Paris, taking his son and daughter with him to Clermont, where the three Pascals remained a full seventeen months. This was to enlist time and place as allies in his campaign to hold Jacqueline back from Port-Royal.

NOTES TO CHAPTER SIX

1. *VMP,* 30.
2. Blaise to Gilberte, 17 October 1651, *OC,* II, 857–58. See also Blaise and Jacqueline to Gilberte, 1 April 1648, *OC,* II, 582–83.
3. *OC,* II, 857–58.
4. *OC,* II, 862.
5. *OC,* II, 852–53.
6. *OC,* II, 856.
7. *OC,* II, 857.
8. *OC,* II, 857–58.
9. *OC,* II, 854, 858.
10. *OC,* II, 860.
11. *VMP,* Second Version, 71.
12. *OC,* II, 861–62.
13. *OC,* I, 664–71.
14. *OC,* II, 651.

15. *OC,* II, 861–62.
16. *OC,* II, 862.
17. *OC,* II, 822–40, including these references to Singlin: 826 twice, 828, 832, 836, 837, 838, 839. See also *OC,* I, 664–65, 669–70, where Gilberte provides authoritative testimony that Singlin served as the director of her conscience even before her entry into the convent. He continued in this role thereafter: *OC,* II, 972–75. In her *Relation* of 10 June 1653, Jacqueline honored him "as the common father both of this house [Port-Royal] and of my closest relatives." See *OC,* II, 993.
18. The theme is constant in Singlin's published sermons. See chap. 7.
19. Mesnard has found the inspiration for this line of thought in Singlin's sermons. See *OC,* II, 861, n. 1.
20. Flandrin, *Families in Former Times,* 118–45. Mousnier, The Institutions of France, I, 85–91. For excerpts from secular theorists, see Albert Chérel, *La famille française: le Moyen-Age et le XVIe siècle* (Paris, 1924), 173–200. For an extreme statement of the paternalist position, see Pierre Ayrault, *De la puissance paternelle,* in *Opuscules et divers traictez* (Paris, 1598), 231–356. For a more moderate statement by an author who is broadly representative of humanistic thinking on the subject, see Pierre de Charron, *De la sagesse* (1601 and later editions, here cited from that of Paris, 1836), III, 68 ff., esp. 120. A father is like God, and the child's duty of obedience seems neither to require discussion nor to admit exception.
21. *OC,* I, 666.
22. *OC,* II, 830.
23. Matt. 18:20.
24. *OC,* I, 670.
25. *OC,* I, 671.
26. Richer, *Traité de la mort civile,* 546 ff.
27. *OC,* II, 749, 750, 761.
28. *OC,* II, 911.
29. *OC,* II, 912.
30. *OC,* II, 913.
31. *OC,* II, 913–14.
32. *OC,* II, 916.
33. *OC,* II, 915.
34. *OC,* II, 917.
35. *Les constitutions du monastère de Port-Royal du S. Sacrement* (Paris, 1721), 69. This Rule had been written in 1647, although it was not to be published until 1665. See Ellen Weaver, *The Evolution of the Reform of Port-Royal* (Paris, 1978).
36. See Jean Mesnard's prefatory remarks to the "Relation de Jacqueline Pascal," *OC,* II, 954–98. Mesnard's two-part paper on the brother-sister dispute is indispensable: "Blaise Pascal et la vocation de sa soeur Jacqueline," *XVIIe siècle* 11 (1951): 69–92 and 15 (1952): 373–96.

37. Mesnard, "Pascal et la vocation," *XVIIe siècle* 11 (1951): 73, 85–90 and 15 (1952): 394.
38. Mesnard, "Pascal et la vocation," passim. For a contemporary statement of the ideals of the community, see "Antoine Godefroy," the pseudonym for Antoine Arnauld and Godefroy Hermant, *La conduite canonique de l'Église pour la réception des filles dans les monastères* (Paris, 1668). The work goes back to the 1650s.
39. Mesnard, "Pascal et la vocation," *XVIIe siècle* 15 (1952): 385–87. *OC,* II, 970–71.
40. For the 1648 delay, see *OC,* I, 666; for the 1651 delay, see *OC,* I, 670; for the 1652 delay, see *OC,* II, 917; for the 1653 delay, see *OC,* II, 971.
41. *OC,* II, 976.
42. *OC,* II, 977.
43. *OC,* II, 978–79.
44. *OC,* I, 828; see Mesnard, *Pascal et les Roannez,* I, 251–66.

NOTES TO PART THREE

1. *OC,* II, 980–81; *Oeuvres,* IV, 17–18.
2. *Écrit sur la conversion du pécheur,* in Mesnard, *Pascal* (1969), 113. *Oeuvres,* X, 422–26.
3. *Oeuvres,* IV, 15. The set of letters has now been reedited by Jean Mesnard in *OC,* III, 61–75.
4. I recommend pages 128 ff. and 311 ff. from the James Strachey translation (New York, 1965). For the standing of Freud's associative methods in an era of sleep laboratories and systematic research on dreams, see Richard M. Jones, *The New Psychology of Dreaming* (New York, 1970) and David Foulkes, *A Grammar of Dreams* (New York, 1978).

NOTES TO CHAPTER SEVEN

1. *Oeuvres,* IV, 15–16; *OC,* III, 67–68. Factors limiting this brief communication included Jacqueline's deference to the convert himself as the proper informant, time constraints and other communal restrictions on her letter writing as a newly professed nun, the uncertain outcome of the providential conversion that was still in process, and silence as a way of life related to the fundamental ideal of humility.
2. From untitled manuscripts edited by Jean Orcibal in *La spiritualité de Saint-Cyran* (Paris, 1962), 190. Saint-Cyran's lessons on the point were as invariable as they were influential; see also 325, 339–42, and so on.
3. Mesnard places Jacqueline's letters on the table as the first and best account of Blaise's conversion. So doing, he confronts a major difficulty, in that her testimony on her brother's rejection of worldly persons seems to undercut the very grouping of three converts, Blaise-Artus-Charlotte, that he seeks to establish. His solutions to this diffi-

culty are not fully convincing or even perfectly consistent: on the one hand, Jacqueline need not have meant to include the Roannez among the worldly; on the other, she who proudly reclaims her brother must have been motivated by a sort of jealousy, however conscious, of the Roannez. Mesnard, *Pascal et les Roannez,* I, 385, 389, 398–99. See also *Oeuvres,* IV, 66. Jacqueline reports that Blaise's "good friend," surely Artus, shed tears at the news of his impending retreat. The tears are not Blaise's, and she explains the retreat in large part as an attempt to put distance between the newly converted Pascal and the importunate de Roannez, who had recently returned from Poitou.

4. For his generally depressed spirits that fall, see her letter of 25 January, quoted at length in the next paragraph of the text. For his subsequent high spirits, see especially the good-natured banter in her letter of 19 January: *Oeuvres,* IV, 17–18; *OC,* III, 68–69.
5. The chronology is at once crucial and confused. This text from 25 January 1655 implies that there was one previous letter, not more; the surviving note from 8 December suggests no prior communication. So far, so good. But how could "8 December" have been "a few days" after "sometime toward the end of September"? Apparently, by late January, a month and a half after her hasty note, Jacqueline had forgotten just when she had sent her sister this long-delayed and quite sketchy first word.
6. Jacqueline to Gilberte, 25 January 1655, *Oeuvres,* IV, 61–62; *OC,* III, 71–72.
7. *Oeuvres,* IV, 63; *OC,* III, 72.
8. See Richard M. Golden, *The Goldly Rebellion: Parisian Curés and the Religious Fronde, 1652–1662* (Chapel Hill, N.C., 1981), 69–71, 97–111.
9. *Oeuvres,* IV, 63; *OC,* III, 72. Jacqueline's analogy of selecting a medical doctor had recently been used by the Jesuit preacher Claude de Lingendes in a sermon that created a notable brouhaha in April 1654. See Golden, *Godly Rebellion,* 109–10.
10. *VMP,* 35; *OC,* II, 1333–36. This move brought Pascal much nearer to Jacqueline at Port-Royal. For the melancholy brother, that must have been the primary "pull," but parochial politics added a powerful "push." Saint-Merri was the Pascals' Parisian parish from 1635 to at least 1648 and Blaise's probable place of worship from December 1651 to October 1654. The curacy was split between a Jansenist and an anti-Jansenist, who preached antiphonally on alternate Sundays. On 16 August, the turn of the Jansenist Henri Duhamel happened to come just after the news of the escape of the Cardinal de Retz from the fortress of Nantes. Duhamel took the occasion to support de Retz, oppose Mazarin, and threaten a new Fronde. On 17 August, the day after this dangerous and disruptive sermon, Blaise signed the lease for his new quarters. His new priest, Nicolas de Bry, was another very strong Jansenist in a parish that was less hotly contested. See Godefroi Her-

mant, *Mémoires sur l'histoire ecclésiastique du XVIIe siècle* (Paris, 1905–10) II, 573–84; René Rapin, *Mémoires* (Paris, 1865), II, 232, 283–84; the abbé Baloche, *Église Saint-Merry de Paris* (Paris, 1912), I, 276–324; II, 537–39; Golden, *Godly Rebellion,* 18–42; Jean Mesnard, "Les demeures de Pascal à Paris," *Mémoires de la Fédération des sociétés historiques et archéologiques de Paris et de l'Ile de France* 4 (1952): 21–61.

11. The best evidence on Singlin's health and movements comes from the correspendence of Mère Angélique and Mère Agnès. Angélique Arnauld, *Lettres* (Utrecht, 1742), II, 538–40, 542–43, 546, 549–50; Agnès Arnauld, *Lettres* (Paris, 1858), I, 345–48.
12. There is remarkable contemporaneous evidence on such sentiments in a letter from Singlin at Port-Royal des Champs dated 16 November 1654; see Eustoquie Flexelles de Brégy, *La vie de la mère Marie des Anges* (Paris, 1754), 572–75.
13. *Oeuvres,* IV, 65; *OC,* III, 73.
14. *Oeuvres,* IV, 15; *OC,* III, 68.
15. *Oeuvres,* IV, 64–66; *OC,* III, 72–74.
16. *OC,* I, 664.
17. *OC,* II, 993.
18. *Instructions chrétiennes* (1736), VII, 378–92. Among many other sermons on the Two Loves and the necessity of detachment, see I, 44–46, 334–35; II, 70; III, 277–81; IV, 7–8, 310–12; V, 218–24, 271–74, 325; VI, 308, 411–17, 435; VIII, 8–12, 449–54; IX, 200–202; XI, 255–56; XII, 60–61, 230–31.
19. *Instructions chrétiennes,* V, 364.
20. *Instructions chrétiennes,* VII, 68–70.
21. *Instructions chrétiennes,* XII, 104.
22. *Instructions chrétiennes,* XII, 228.
23. *Instructions chrétiennes,* XII, 336–37.
24. *Instructions chrétiennes,* III, 184–87.
25. *Vie de Singlin,* in *Instructions chrétiennes,* I, xxi–xxii.
26. Arnauld, *Fréquente Communion,* in *Oeuvres,* 43 vols. (Paris and Lausanne, 1775–83), XXVII, 592–93.
27. *Fréquente communion,* 216, 384–85. For the place of the Two Loves in Arnauld's work, see Jean Laporte, *La doctrine de Port-Royal: la morale d'après Arnauld* (Paris, 1951), I, 106–24.
28. *Fréquente communion,* 386.
29. *Tradition de l'Église, Oeuvres,* XXVIII, 156; Arnauld cites the *Traité de l'amour de Dieu,* book 10, chap. 6.
30. *Tradition de l'Église,* 161.
31. *Seconde Apologie, Oeuvres,* XVII, 305.
32. *Seconde Apologie,* 306–10.
33. *Seconde Apologie,* 308–9.
34. *Seconde Apologie,* 309–15.
35. *OC,* I, 664–71; *OC,* II, 822–40, 884–86; *Oeuvres,* IV, 17, 75–76.

36. *OC,* I, 1005.
37. Agnès de Saint-Paul Arnauld, *L'image d'une religieuse parfaite et d'une imparfaite* (Paris, 1665), 7–10.
38. *Manuel des ames religieuses,* in *Image d'un religieuse parfaite,* nouvelle édition (Paris, 1711), 453.
39. *Manuel des ames religieuses,* 466.
40. Mère Angélique Arnauld, *Entretiens ou conférences* (Brussels, 1757), 21–23.
41. Charles-Augustin de Sainte-Beuve, *Port-Royal,* ed. Maxime Leroy (Paris, 1953–55), I, 128 ff. and passim.
42. There is a well-organized "Généalogie des Arnaulds" at the head of the *Mémoires pour servir à l'histoire de Port-Royal et à la vie de la Révérende Mère Marie-Angélique de Sainte-Magdeleine Arnauld* (Utrecht, 1742), I, vi–xx. Louis Cognet is the modern authority on the reform of Port-Royal and the genealogy of the family. See his edition of Angélique's *Relation sur Port-Royal* (Paris, 1949), esp. 19–21, and his own *Réforme de Port-Royal, 1591–1618* (Paris, 1950), 251 ff. Following Cognet, Maxime Leroy drew up a useful genealogical chart, published with the second volume of his edition of Saint-Beuve's *Port-Royal.*

NOTES TO CHAPTER EIGHT

1. *OC,* III, 55.
2. Bibliothèque Nationale, fonds français, ms. 13913, 214–15. For a facsimile, see Lafuma, *Le manuscrit des Pensées de Pascal* (Paris, 1962), 344; cf. the earlier but less detailed certifications on 304, 305. *OC,* III, 55–56.
3. Pascal's Paper survives at the head of the *Recueil original* of the *Pensées,* B.N., f.f., ms. 9202, folio D. Louis Périer's Exact Copy of the Parchment, the original of which is lost, follows on folio E. Material aspects of the Paper and Parchment are described by Zachaire Tourneur in his *Pensées de Blaise Pascal: Édition paléographique* (Paris, 1942), 7–11. The best discussions are those of Henri Gouhier in *Blaise Pascal commentaires* (Paris, 1984), 11–65, 367–87, and Jean Mesnard in *OC,* III, 19–53.
4. The commonest horizontal strokes in surviving manuscripts are those used to separate noncontinuous notes or drafts made on the same large sheet. These strokes extend from beyond the *left* margin under a portion of the last line of a text that he wanted to discriminate from whatever was to follow. Such strokes separate Pensées 2 and 3, 3 and 4, and so on. Horizontal strokes extending from a line of autographic text to the *right* margin are quite another matter. The strokes on the Paper *Mémorial* (lines 14, 15, 20, 21, 22, 23, and the underscoring following line 17) are wholly exceptional. Pensée 14, where we also find the theme of separation, does provide one very suggestive comparison.
5. For tables of biblical citations in Pascal's work, see Jean Lhermet, *Pascal et la Bible* (Paris, 1931) and Philippe Sellier, *Pascal et la liturgie* (Paris,

1966). Jean Mesnard provides the most authoritative notes on the *Mémorial;* see *OC,* III, 52–53.

6. For *Mémorial* Line 2, Exod. 3:6 is primary; the quoted words recur in Exod. 3:15, 3:16, and 4:5, Matt. 22:32, Mark 12:26, Luke 20:3, and Acts 7:32. Line 16 is discussed below: Matt. 27:46 is the accepted reference, but Mark 15:34 also gives this Word from the Cross; Jesus recalled Ps. 21:2, and there is similar language in Ps. 26:9, 37:22, 70:18, and 118:8.
7. *VMP,* First Version, 36; Second Version, 35.
8. Fortunat Strowski provides an early and influential example of such imagination; see *Pascal et son temps* (Paris, 1921), II, 355.
9. *Blaise Pascal commentaires* (Paris, 1984), 35.
10. I count thirteen instances: Matt. 3:9; Luke 1:73, 3:8, 16:24, 16:30; John 8:39, 8:53, 8:56; Acts 7:2; Rom. 4:1, 4:12, 4:16; James 2:21.
11. *La Sainte Bible: Contenant le Vieil & Nouveau Testament; traduite de Latin en François, & approuvée par les Théologiens de Louvain* (Paris, 1586). Fortunat Strowski first made the case for this version as that of the Pascals; see *Pascal et son temps* (Paris, 1921), II, 355. Lhermet adopted it in his standard if dated work, *Pascal et la Bible,* 240–46.
12. Pensées 25, 741.
13. David Wetsel, *L'Écriture et le Reste: The Pensées of Pascal in the Exegetical Tradition of Port-Royal* (Columbus, Ohio, 1981).
14. Sellier, *Pascal et la liturgie* (Paris, 1966), 1.
15. Sellier, *Pascal et la liturgie,* 40–41. *Breviarium Romanum* (Venice, 1735), 908–11; *The Roman Breviary,* trans. John of Bute (Edinburgh, 1908), IV, 762–65. A hagiographical rationale related Saint Clement to the saving *fons.*
16. *Abrégé, Oeuvres,* XI, 71–72.
17. Professor Drake Bradley of the Department of Psychology, Bates College, has assisted me greatly with sampling techniques and the calculation of statistical significance. Faults are mine. Controls were selected in the following manner. My reference Bible is an undated Oxford edition of the King James Version, with the Old Testament on 1,158 pages and the New Testament separately paginated on another 348 pages. I renumbered the pages continuously and used a random-number-generating computer program to select 100 of the 1,506 total pages. On each page selected, I counted the first complete verse as one of the controls. I defined "contexts" and "associations" exactly as above, paying due attention not only to adjacent verses but also to marginalia from Pascal's Louvain Bible. Then I looked for instances of the two associations, scoring them liberally in cases of doubt. The chi-square calculations are a standard measure of statistical significance.

NOTES TO CHAPTER NINE

1. *The Interpretation of Dreams,* trans. James Strachey (New York, 1965), 128–54. This one-volume edition gives the text and apparatus from the

Standard Edition, vols. IV and V, which is the scholarly reference in the English language. Three more recent works help to bring this classic up to date: David Foulkes, *A Grammar of Dreams* (New York, 1978); Richard M. Jones, *The New Psychology of Dreaming* (New York, 1978); Alexander Grinstein, *Freud's Rules of Dream Interpretation* (New York, 1983). With Foulkes and many others, I would question the universality of wish fulfillment even while accepting the methodological breakthrough.

2. At the request of the biographer Maxime Leroy, Freud considered Descartes's Olympian dreams, then explained why he could not offer a methodical interpretation. For his response, see Leroy, *Descartes* (Paris, 1929), I, 89–90. For a close paraphrase of the lost dream record, see Adrien Baillet, *La vie de Monsieur Des Cartes* (Paris, 1691), I, 81–86. For a historical interpretation, see John Cole, *The Olympian Dreams and Youthful Rebellion of René Descartes* (Urbana, Ill., 1992).
3. *The Varieties of Religious Experience: A Study in Human Nature* (New York, 1923).
4. On Louis-Henri Loménie de Brienne, see Mesnard, *Pascal et les Roannez,* II, 882–87.
5. *Oeuvres,* XII, clii.
6. *OC,* III, 994 and note; *Oeuvres,* VI, 112 and n. 2.
7. On him, see Élie Jaloustre, "Un neveu de Pascal: Louis Périer," *Bulletin historique et scientifique de l'Auvergne* 2d ser. (1906): 125–220.
8. *OC,* III, 55.
9. In the course of efforts to normalize this behavior, Maurice Souriau cited other historical examples of supposedly similar practices, and Jean Mesnard and Henri Gouhier have both written as if the point were established. Souriau, *Les Pensées catholiques de Pascal* (Paris, 1935), 46. Souriau named names (Richelieu, La Vallière, and Vincent de Paul) and cited sources but did not discuss the cases critically. Gouhier repeated Souriau's list with a rhetorical indication of reserve but without citing, let alone examining, the sources; see *Blaise Pascal commentaires* (Paris, 1984), 17 and n. 13. Mesnard simply accepted as factual the "pious practice" in his *Pascal* (1967), 66.
10. Richelieu: the fervent Jansenist Godefroi Hermant is our sole informant, and his account is both late and hostile to Richelieu, the persecutor of Saint-Cyran and the opponent of contrition. He says that the Cardinal felt justified pangs of conscience and demanded from his confessor a written guarantee of salvation. So much for his own confidence in the sufficiency of attrition. Richelieu is supposed to have "carried" this all-too-human pledge "always up to his death." Even if this tendentious report were to be accepted uncritically, it would document only the carrying of a very different sort of text than the *Mémorial,* one that was not Richelieu's own, not copied, and not sewn. See Hermant, *Mémoires,* ed. A. Gazier (Paris, 1905), I, 80–81.

    La Vallière: the *Réflexions sur la miséricorde de Dieu* are traditionally attributed to the former mistress of Louis XIV, who says that she has written in her own hand "a register of your mercies and my most intimate resolutions." But there is no ecstatic experience, no copying, no sewing, not even any carrying. Furthermore, the detailed, reliable, and devout testimony on La Vallière's death fails to report the discovery of any such document. See *Madame de La Vallière repentante: Confessions intimes,* ed. Romain-Cornut (Paris, 1874), 309, 312, 315; Mère Madeleine de Saint-Esprit, circulatory letter dated 6 June 1710, in Gonzague Truc, *Louis XIV et Mlle. de La Vallière* (Paris, 1933), 201–12.

Vincent de Paul: over forty years after the Saint's death, Bossuet says that Vincent had said that, when tempted by heresy, "he would hold his profession of faith written on a paper, which he would place over his heart." Again, no ecstatic experience, no copying, no sewing, no explicit carrying. See Bossuet, *Témoignage sur la vie et les vertues éminentes de Monsieur Vincent de Paul,* ed. A. Gaste (Paris, 1892), 5–17.

11. The best handbook available to seventeenth-century Frenchmen was that of Scipion du Pleix or Dupleix, *Les causes de la veille et du sommeil, des songes, et de la vie et de la mort* (Paris, 1609). For a much broader selection of traditional materials on dreams, see Nicolas Lenglet Dufresnoy, *Recueil de dissertations anciennes et nouvelles sur les apparitions, les visions, et les songes,* 2 vols. (Avignon and Paris, 1751).
12. Mère Angélique can represent her community both in her caution and in her credulity. Within one conference, she both expressed her reservations about the "extraordinary ways" of dreams and visions and then, at second hand, reported three dream-visions that satisfied even her: Antoine Le Maistre, "Relations de plusieurs entretiens," in *Mémoires pour servir à l'histoire de Port-Royal* (Utrecht, 1742), II, 337–45. The Bible sanctioned belief in particular revelations of this sort: Job 33:14–16, Joel 2:28, Acts 2:17.
13. *Interpretation of Dreams* (1965), 311–85.
14. *A Grammar of Dreams,* 27–87.
15. *Interpretation of Dreams,* 312–39.
16. *Interpretation of Dreams,* 340–44.
17. *Interpretation of Dreams,* 374–75; Foulkes, *A Grammar of Dreams,* 65. Freud is clearer on the subject in the later *Introductory Lectures on Psychoanalysis,* trans. James Strachey (New York, 1977), 170–83, especially 175–77.
18. *OC,* II, 855.
19. Gouhier, *Blaise Pascal commentaires,* 65; *OC,* III, 36–37, 39–40.
20. *Imitation,* trans. Corneille (1654), 142: "D'une heure de travail doit naistre un long repos, d'un moment de souffrance une eternelle joye." *Mémorial,* Second Postscript: "Eternellement en joye pour un jour d'exercise sur la terre." For purposes of reference in other editions, the passage in question from the *Imitation* appears in book 1, chap. 25, "Of the Fervent Amending of All Our Life."
21. *Imitation,* trans. de Sacy (1663), 208.

22. *Imitation,* trans. R. Whitford, ed. Gardiner (New York, 1955), 110–11. The passage is from book 3, chap. 5.
23. Lélut, *L'amulette de Pascal pour servir à l'histoire des hallucinations* (Paris, 1846).
24. The scriptural associations for the less certain citation at line 5, apparently a very fragmentary reminiscence of Eph. 1:17, are properly spiritual. They do include "the Father of Glory" and the hope of immortality, but, in themselves, they do not connote a father-son relationship.
25. In late November, 10:30 P.M. is some six hours after nightfall at this latitude. Nicolas Fontaine gives 8:00 P.M. as a normal bedtime for the Solitaries at Port-Royal des Champs: *Mémoires pour servir à l'histoire de Port-Royal* (Utrecht, 1736), I, cii.
26. David Foulkes, *The Psychology of Sleep* (New York, 1966), 24. D. J. Kupfer and F. G. Foster, "Interval between onset of sleep and rapid eye movement sleep as an indicator of depression," *Lancet* 11 (1972): 684–86; Kupfer, "REM Latency: A psychobiologic marker for primary depressive disease," *Biological Psychiatry* 11 (1976): 159–74.
27. *Interpretation of Dreams,* xxvi.
28. Louis J. West, "A General Theory of Hallucinations and Dreams," in *Hallucinations,* ed. Louis J. West (New York, 1962), 275–91. Other pertinent papers from this same collection: Jay T. Shurley, "Hallucinations in Sensory Deprivation and Sleep Deprivation," 87–91; Eugene L. Bliss and Lincoln D. Clark, "Visual Hallucinations," 92–107; Harold Williams et al., "Illusions, Hallucinations, and Sleep Loss," 158–65; Edwin Weinstein, "Social Aspects of Hallucinations," 233–37. See also Ernest Hartmann, "Dreams and Other Hallucinations," in *Hallucinations: Behavior, Experience, and Theory,* ed. Ronald K. Siegel and Louis J. West (New York, 1975), 71–79. Among the many points that seem beyond any doubt is that sleep deprivation and social isolation promote waking hallucinations.
29. C. Murray Parkes, "Recent bereavement as a cause of mental llness," *British Journal of Psychiatry* 110 (1964): 198–204; "Bereavement and mental illness," *British Journal of Medical Psychology* 38, no. 1 (1965): 1–12, and 38, no. 13 (1965): 13–26; " 'Seeking' and 'finding' a lost object," *Social Science and Medicine* 4 (1970): 187–201; *Bereavement: Studies of Grief in Adult Life* (New York, 1972), esp. chap. 5; "Determinants of outcome following bereavement," *Omega* 6, no. 4 (1975): 303–23. Paula Clayton and coauthors have devoted many papers to the study of normal or "uncomplicated" grief; see esp. Clayton, Lynn Desmarais, and George Winokur, "A study of normal bereavement," *American Journal of Psychiatry* 125 (1968): 168–78.
30. "On the Care to Be Had for the Dead," 12–15, in *The Nicene and Post-Nicene Fathers,* 1st ser., ed. P. Schaff (Buffalo, 1887), III, 544–46.
31. Herodotus 7.16. *The Persian Wars,* trans. G. Rawlinson (New York, 1942), bk. 7, chap. 16.
32. Henri Gouhier, *Pascal et les humanistes chrétiens* (Paris, 1974), 15–16.

33. *De la fréquente Communion,* in *Oeuvres* (Paris, 1776–83), XXVII, 476.
34. Philippe Sellier, *Pascal et la liturgie* (Paris, 1966), 1–2, 40–41.
35. *OC,* III, 74; *VMP,* 72.
36. *The Roman Breviary,* trans. John, Marquess of Bute (Edinburgh, 1908), I, 764.
37. *OC,* III, 71–74.
38. *OC,* III, 73 and n. 2. For the crucial point of Singlin's location in late November, there is decisive evidence in two letters from Singlin at Port-Royal des Champs to Mère Marie des Anges Suireau in Paris, one dated November 16 and the other undated but written after an election held on November 26. See the texts in Anne-Marie Flécelles de Bregy, *Modèle de foi et de patience: Vie de la mère Marie des Anges (Suireau)* (n.p., 1754), 572–78. Singlin was back in Paris—and in Mère Angélique's more familiar correpondence—by the beginning of December; see *Lettres de la révérende mère Marie Angélique Arnauld* (Utrecht, 1742–44), II, 538–40.
39. For early signs of concern, see Angélique's letters from the end of October, before Singlin's retreat to Port-Royal des Champs: *Lettres,* II, 530–32.
40. "Remarques sur les premiers temps et les Abbesses de Port-Royal," in *Vies intéressantes et édifiantes des religieuses de Port-Royal* (Utrecht, 1751), III, 482–84.
41. *Lettres,* II, 528, 530, 534–35.
42. *Lettres,* 536–44.
43. De Bregy, *Vie de la mère Marie des Anges,* 572–78.
44. *Lettres,* II, 536–44.
45. Mesnard, "Pascal à l'Académie Le Pailleur," in Costabel, *L'oeuvre scientifique,* 11, 16.
46. *OC,* II, 1021–35, esp. 1031.
47. *Pascal et les Roannez,* I, 389–93.
48. For the attribution to Blaise and the date of Composition, see Mesnard's comments in *OC,* I, 102–3; IV, 35–39; cf. *Oeuvres,* X, 421. Jan Miel provides a balanced discussion in *Pascal and Theology* (Baltimore, 1966), 118–22 and n. 29.
49. *Pascal et les Roannez,* I, 394, 399–401, 404–5.
50. Philippe Sellier, *Pascal et Saint Augustin,* 37, 154, 163, 315, 334, 359–60, 426–27.
51. *OC,* IV, 40–41; *Oeuvres,* X, 422–24.
52. *OC,* IV, 41–44; *Oeuvres,* X, 424–26.

NOTES TO PART FOUR

1. Vulgate Ps. 118:16. Compare the closely associated verse, 118:8, "I will keep thy statutes; O foresake me not utterly." The long psalm ends with David's confession that he has strayed, his plea that God seek him, and a renewed promise to keep God's commandments.

2. *OC,* II, 1035, 1158.
3. *OC,* II, 712–15; 923–26.
4. *OC,* I, 43–44, 681, 685–89; II, 1036–1101.
5. *OC,* I, I, 3-37; II, 1166–1332.
6. *Oeuvres,* IV, 17.
7. American Psychiatric Association, *Diagnostic and Statistical Manual of Mental Disorders,* 3d ed. (DSM-III) (Washington, D.C., 1980), 220. Although my research was conducted using DSM-III, I have also consulted DSM-III-R and DSM-IV. Frederick Goodwin and Kay Jamison, *Manic-Depressive Illness* (New York, 1990), 332–67. See appendixes 2 and 3.

NOTES TO CHAPTER TEN

1. Pierre Courcelle's critical edition has sustained the scholarship of the past generation: *L'Entretien de Pascal et Sacy: ses sources et ses énigmes* (Paris, 1960). Its text of the *Entretien* is that excerpted from the manuscript *Mémoires* and first published posthumously by Pierre-Nicolas Desmolets in the *Continuation des Mémoires de littérature et d'histoire* (Paris, 1728), vol. V, pt. 2, 239–70. The *Entretien* in Fontaine's context can be studied in Michel Tronchai's first edition of the *Mémoires* (Utrecht, 1736), II, 55–73. Jean Mesnard's *Oeuvres complètes* now provides a new text with extensive commentary that is sure to be accepted as the basis for all further work: *OC,* III, 76–157.

   Sacy's conduct in other cases is the most reliable guide for historical judgment on his conduct in this case. See his *Lettres Chrestiennes et spirtuelles,* 2 vols. (Paris, 1690); *Choix des lettres inédites de Louis-Isaac Le Maistre de Sacy,* ed. G. Delassault (Paris, 1959). The most important secondary literature on Sacy and the *Entretien* in chronological order includes Geneviève Delassault, *Le Maistre de Sacy et son temps* (Paris 1957), esp. 67–79; Courcelle, *L'Entretien de Pascal et de Sacy;* Henri Gouhier, "*L'Entretien de Pascal avec M. de Sacy* et les origines de son apologétique," *Revue de théologie et de philosophie* 3e. sér. 13 (1963): 41–58; Jean Mesnard, "Introduction générale," *OC,* I, 236–50; André Gounelle, *L'Entretien de Pascal avec M. de Sacy: étude et commentaire* (Paris, 1966); Raymond La Charité, "Pascal's ambivalence toward Montaigne," *Studies in Philology* 70 (1973): 187–98; Jacques Malet, "Remarques à partir de *L'Entretien . . . :* La perspective spirituelle et littéraire de Pascal à son arrivée à Port-Royal," *Revue du Pacifique* 1 (1975): 74–82; the *Chroniques de Port-Royal* devoted an issue to Sacy on the tercentenary of his death in 1984; Odette Barenne, *Une grande bibliothèque de Port-Royal: l'inventaire inédit de la bibliothèque de Isaac-Louis Le Maistre de Sacy* (Paris, 1985).
2. Recent commentators have tended to give the great Pascal his head, so to speak, without adequately appreciating that Sacy had reined him in. Perhaps the most startling example of this undervaluation of the historical director comes in Geneviève Delassault's most learned monograph

on Sacy, where the priest's contributions to the *Entretien* are given just two summary sentences: *Le Maistre de Sacy,* 68. Courcelle's commentary does attempt to redress this imbalance: *L'Entretien de Pascal et Sacy,* 107–26, 149–63, 166–70. Gounelle's commentary respects Sacy's role as director but concedes far too much to Pascal's genius and makes much too much of Fontaine's assertions of fundamental agreement: *L'Entretien de Pascal avec M. de Sacy,* 34–39, 48–52, 73–79, 111–13, 119–29.

3. Fontaine's foreword and afterword are both suspect (Mesnard par. 7–10 and 39–40; Courcelle lines 1–69 and 600–607). In the three speeches of Pascal, I also suspect the following lines, Courcelle's 138–39 (Mesnard par. 15), 366–74 (par. 26), 462–69 (par. 32), 487–90 (par. 33), 522–31 (par. 35). The first intervention of Sacy begins with Fontaine's incredible report on what the priest said *to himself* over forty years earlier (par. 23; lines 299–306), and the second begins with utterly implausible expressions of the director's wonder at his penitent's wisdom and elevation (par. 36; lines 541–45). The latter has aroused particularly well-justified suspicions. See Courcelle, *L'Entretien de Pascal et Sacy,* 109–12; Gounelle, *L'Entretien de Pascal avec M. de Sacy,* 74–75, 111–13; Mesnard, *OC,* III, 110. Unfortunately, along with the discarded trappings and the discounted conversation goes Fontaine's explicit testimony on the date (par. 7). Nevertheless, no date seems possible either before or long after the conventionally accepted January 1655. For the most recent opinion and best-informed discussion, see Mesnard in *OC,* III, 13, 68 n. 3, 111–16.
4. Sacy had been an intimate disciple of the first abbé de Saint-Cyran, the modern master of Port-Royalist spirituality. The Pascals, too, had made particular use of Saint-Cyran's letters and devotional works. Letter 124 offers an extended and impersonal treatise addressed "to a gentleman who wanted to give himself to God" that was published as "an excellent instruction for worldly persons whom God has moved to convert and seriously to consider their salvation." See *Lettres chrétiennes et spirituelles* (Lyon, 1674), III, 13–94. On Saint-Cyran's teachings more generally, see Jean Orcibal, *La spiritualité de Saint-Cyran avec ses écrits de piété inédits* (Paris, 1962).
5. Pascal's high social standing and higher intellectual achievement made him doubly subject to pride. See Saint-Cyran, *Lettres inédites,* ed. Annie Barnes (Paris 1962), 23. The circumstances of Pascal's Second Conversion increased the risk of spiritual pride. The prescription was humility and silence. See Saint-Cyran, *Lettres,* I, 4, 7, 14–15, 96, 136–37, 139, 142, 244–53, 315, 324, 358, 448, 451; II, 48–50, 418–24, 480–87, and so on.
6. Saint-Cyran, *Textes inédits,* in Orcibal, *Spiritualité,* 523: "There are so many good books to study that, if we behave properly, we won't have time left for profane books that . . . incline us toward pride, presumption, and independence. . . . God seems to have cursed this

sort of study. . . . The true way to treat spirits who have been wounded by philosophy isn't to philosophize with them, but to rise above them with a reason nourished and fortified in the light of faith, Scripture, and piety."

7. Cf. Epictetus, *Manual,* 31, trans. Jean de Saint-François Goulu (Paris, 1609), and Fontaine, *Entretien,* par. 11.
8. While remaining perfectly faithful to the spirit and close to the letter of Goulu's Epictetus, this passage recalls Job 1:21 and perhaps also I Peter 2:11. I owe these references to Gounelle, *L'Entretien de Pascal avec M. de Sacy,* 56.
9. Jacqueline to Gilberte, 8 December 1654, *Oeuvres,* IV, 16; to Blaise, 19 January 1655, *Oeuvres,* IV, 19.
10. Cf. Epictetus, *Manual,* 22, Goulu translation and title, with Fontaine, *Entretien,* par. 13. The "parallel" is justifiable textually, but the lines of thought and belief are divergent.
11. For the Thinking Machines, see *OC,* II, 296–97, 329–41, 920–26; for the Vacuum Experiments, see *Lettre dédicatoire à Monseigneur le Chancelier, OC,* II, 331 ff.; *Expériences nouvelles, OC,* II, 501, 502–3; *Grande expérience, OC,* II, 677 ff.
12. Jacqueline to Gilberte, 8 December 1654 and 25 January 1655, *Oeuvres,* IV, 16, 62, 65–68. Christian Huygens to Mylon, 1 February 1655, *Oeuvres complètes* (La Haye, 1888–1950), II, 370.
13. Odette Barenne, *Une grande bibliothèque,* 36–37, 156.
14. Augustine, *Enchiridion,* ed. Jean Rivière (Paris, 1947).
15. See parallel texts in Courcelle, *L'Entretien de Pascal avec et Sacy,* 16–17. There is no warrant in the Greek text (*Manual,* 2.17 and 3.24) for Pascal's adaptation of the Goulu version.
16. Du Vair, *De la Sainte Philosophie* [and] *Philosophie morale des Stoïques,* ed. G. Michaut (Paris, 1945); Léontine Zanta, *La Renaissance du Stoïcisme au seizième siècle* (Paris, 1914), 240–331; Pierre Mesnard, "Du Vair et le néostoïcisme," *Revue de l'histoire de philosophie,* 2 (1928): 142–66; Paul Roques, "La *Philosophie morale des Stoïques* de Guillaume Du Vair," *Archives de philosophie,* 20 (1957): 226–39 and 379–91.
17. *OC,* I, 826–29.
18. Bernard Croquette, *Pascal et Montaigne* (Paris, 1974), 1; Léon Petit, "Le chevalier de Méré, introducteur de Pascal aux *Essais* de Montaigne," *Bulletin de la Société des Amis de Montaigne,* sér. 3, no. 16 (1960): 42–58.
19. Courcelle, *L'Entretien de Pascal et Sacy,* 95–99. It is appropriate to the subject in question that the most scholarly counts of partial "parallels" cannot be certain. Pascal's very familiarity with the *Essais* and his legendary memory would have allowed him to work without an open book, which would have guaranteed imprecision on his part and frustration for any scholar determined to count. See Mesnard in *OC,* III, 99–108.
20. Raymond La Charité argues vigorously that Montaigne was not just

more complex but also rather different from the skeptical immoralist portrayed by Pascal in the *Entretien;* see his "Pascal's Ambivalence toward Montaigne," *Studies in Philology* 70 (1973): 187–98, esp. 188–92.

21. In honor of Copernicus, whose revolutionary work Montaigne did know by reputation, let us consider astronomy. See *The Complete Essays of Montaigne,* trans. Donald Frame (Stanford, 1958), 328–31, 381, 400–401, 429.
22. Montaigne, "Apologie," in *Oeuvres complètes,* ed. Thibaudet and Rat (Paris, 1962), 555; Fontaine, *Entretien,* par. 22.
23. The passage here excerpted combines references to at least five Essays. The final contrast includes language on the subject of philosophy from "De l'institution des enfans" (I, 26) and language on the subject of nature from "De l'expérience" (III, 13). See Courcelle, *L'Entretien de Pascal et Sacy,* 48–53. This sort of composition suggests to me not "a collection of excerpta" made from an open book but rather a very free adaptation of materials from a very full memory.
24. La Charité, "Pascal's ambivalence toward Montaigne," 189–92.
25. De Sales, *Traité de l'Amour de Dieu,* book 1, chap. 17, in *Oeuvres,* ed. A. Ravier (Paris, 1969), 402. On the supposed Christianity of Epictetus, see also 463.
26. Montaigne, *Travel Journal,* trans. Donald Frame (San Francisco, 1983), 74–75, 91–92 and n. 23, 98, 101.
27. See Mathurin Dréano, *La Pensée religieuse de Montaigne* (Paris, 1936), 419–70; Alan Boase, *The Fortunes of Montaigne* (New York, 1970).
28. Jean Dagens and Andre Gounelle have suggested that Augustine's Sermon 156 provided an authoritative model for the Pascal of the *Entretien.* See Dagens, *Bérulle et les origines de la restauration Catholique (1575–1611)* (Paris, 1952), 338–39; Gounelle, *L'Entretien de Pascal avec M. de Sacy,* 90. However, Augustine's opposition of the Stoic intellectual and the Epicurean sensualist is very different from Pascal's opposition of Epictetus and Montaigne. Augustine's attitude toward the philosophers was uncomplicated; as he said more pithily in Sermon 240.6: "The Lord Christ, the Wisdom of God, has come; let frogs cease their croaking." Pascal emphasizes strengths as well as weaknesses in the philosophers and argues for spiritual utility of these readings. This was original, especially at Augustinian Port-Royal.
29. For the references to these other authors hidden away in Pascal's exposition "on Montaigne," see Courcelle, *L'Entretien de Pascal et Sacy,* 28–31, 36–37; for the omissions in Sacy's library, see Barenne, *Une grande bibliothèque.*
30. *OC,* III, 58 and n. 3.
31. The penitent here tells his director about his choice of readings rather than asking for advice. When other penitents did ask, the advice that Sacy gave time after time was this: read the Bible, the *Confessions,* and the *Imitation of Christ.* See *Lettres Chrestiennes et spirituelles* (Paris, 1690), I, 30–32, 326–28; II, 27, 74, 208, 572, 683. In the *Imitation,* which

Sacy was to translate for others' use, see esp. book I, chap. 2, 3, 5; II, 5; III, 3, 17, 43.

For Saint-Cyran, see above, n. 6.

32. For a maximal statement of lifelong Augustinianism, see Philippe Sellier, *Pascal et Saint Augustin* (Paris, 1970), 13–18 and passim. Sellier cites the testimony of Paul Beurrier, Pascal's confessor in 1662, that the Étienne Pascal household was a veritable school of Patristics even before the conversions of 1646 (*OC,* I, 869–70). This testimony is very late, at best indirect, and historically unconvincing. On the other hand, Sellier does argue effectively that Blaise's letters of 1648 and 1651 already show considerable familiarity with Augustine, whatever Fontaine's supposition of a later ignorance.
33. Fontaine's assertion that this was a conversational gambit by the antiphilosophical Sacy is quite incredible, not least because the text is not that of a conversation.
34. *Oeuvres,* IV, 17; *OC,* III, 68–69.

NOTES TO CHAPTER ELEVEN

1. P. Kuentz, "Un discours nommé Montalte," *Revue d'histoire littéraire de la France* 71 (1971): 195–206. Dominique Descotes, "Fonction argumentative de la satire dans les *Provinciales,*" in *Onze études sur l'esprit de la satire,* ed. H. Baader (Paris, 1978). Gérard Ferreyrolles, *Blaise Pascal: Les Provinciales* (Paris, 1984), 43–52.
2. See *OC,* I, 1023, for testimony that Pascal used "Montalte" as an alias, not a pseudonym, as early as February 1656.
3. The temptation to identify the literary "Provincial" with a historical person was too strong to resist, and some contemporaries speculated that the real person was Pascal's brother-in-law, Florin Périer: *OC,* I, 737, 894. It may be relevant that Périer was actually in Paris, not the provinces, lodging with Pascal during the heat of the campaign from April to October 1656: *OC,* I, 1022, 1126; *OC,* III, 450, 459, 904–7, 910–11, 971, 1051. For the false imprint, see Cognet, lxx–lxxi.
4. I am greatly indebted to three learned editors: Félix Gazier, Louis Cognet, and Jean Mesnard. Gazier is responsible for the texts and exceptionally full supporting documentation in the Grands Écrivains edition of the *Oeuvres,* vols. IV–VII. This edition also serves historical interests in two other ways, first, by providing the texts of the original pamphlets, not the collected *Provinciales* initially edited without Pascal's direct involvement in 1657; second, by interspersing these precisely dated Letters with other contemporaneous materials that were never part of this polemic. Cognet's edition of the *Provinciales* (Paris 1965) also includes related Pascalian compositions, especially the *Écrits des Curés de Paris.* It has been the scholarly reference for the past generation, but the decision to give the text of the last collected edition in Pascal's lifetime, the second impression from 1659, has been contested. Mesnard projects

a fifth volume of the *Oeuvres complètes* that will include the *Provinciales* and related compositions and documentation. His third volume includes historically crucial materials, especially the *Écrits sur la grâce,* documents concerning the Miracle of the Thorn, and the *Lettres à Mlle. de Roannez* with authoritative commentary and full bibliographies. The immense literature on the *Provinciales* proper includes two well-informed but admirably concise introductions: Walter E. Rex, *Pascal's Provincial Letters* (London, 1977), and Gérard Ferreyrolles, *Blaise Pascal: Les Provinciales* (Paris, 1984). Two sets of collected papers can be cited economically: *Méthodes chez Pascal,* Actes du Colloque tenu à Clermont-Ferrand 10–13 juin 1976 (Paris, 1979), 203–65; *Pascal et Corneille: Désert, Retrait, Engagement, Papers on Seventeenth Century French Literature* (Paris, 1984), 11–88. Recent monographs with further bibliographical references include Roger Duchêne, *L'imposture littéraire dans les Provinciales de Pascal,* 2d ed., with appended papers by Dominique Descotes, Michel Le Guern, and Philippe Sellier and with "Table ronde" (Aix-en-Provence, 1985); Louis A. MacKenzie, *Pascal's Lettres Provinciales: The Motif and Practice of Fragmentation* (Birmingham, Ala., 1988); Richard Parish, *Pascal's Lettres Provinciales: A Study in Polemic* (Oxford, Eng., 1989).

5. I cite the *Provinciales* from Cognet's edition (1965) and Lafuma's *Oeuvres complètes* (1963), the former as Cognet and the latter as the Intégrale. Cognet, 52 n. 1 and variant a; Intégrale, 382.
6. *OC,* I, 29–30.
7. *OC,* I, 826–27; Mesnard, *Pascal et les Roannez,* I, 251–53.
8. *OC,* I, 738, 1016, 1024.
9. Cognet, 52 n. 1; Lafuma in the Intégrale, 382 n. 9; Mesnard in the *OC,* I, 1016 n. 1 and 1024 n. 1.
10. *Oeuvres,* IV, 194–95; *OC,* I, 1016, 1024 variant a.
11. *OC,* I, 470, 475; cf. 896–97.
12. For documentation, see the notes in Cognet, 39–52.
13. Arnauld and Godefroy Hermant were later to publish a collaborative work under the joint name of "Antoine Godefroy." See *La conduite canonique de l'Église pour la réception des filles dans les monastères* (Paris, 1668). Must reading for anyone curious about such authorial disguises more generally is A[drien] B[aillet], *Auteurs déguisez sous des noms Étrangers, Empruntez, Supposez, Feints à plaisir, Chiffrez, Renversez, Retournez, ou Changez d'une langue en une autre* (Paris, 1690). Although A. B. did "sign" this work with his own initials, in another he listed twenty-seven fictitious books by twenty-seven Baillets in twenty-seven anagrammatic disguises. See Gregor Sebba, "Baillet's Life of Descartes," in Thomas Lennon, *Problems of Cartesianism* (Kingston, Ont., 1982), 17 n. 20 and 43–44.
14. *VMP,* First Version, 23; compare Second Version, 17.
15. See chap. 2 and *OC,* II, 42, 53–55. Étienne's cousin Martin was still fighting the good fight for the municipal *collège* in 1639, the year of Étienne's outlawry. On Martin and the school controversy, see Élie

Jaloustre, "Les anciennes écoles de l'Auvergne," *Mémoires de l'Académie des sciences, belles-lettres, et arts de Clermont-Ferrand* 23 (1881): 220.

16. Jaloustre, "Anciennes écoles," 212–13, 229–30. On Annat's career before his greatest prominence as the King's confessor and the Jansenists' archenemy, see Lucien Ceyssens, "François Annat, S.J., avant son confessoriat (1590–1654)," *Antonianum* 50 (1975): 483–529. On his role in the condemnation of the Five Propositions, see A. Janssen, "Un polémiste anti-janséniste: le père François Annat, S.J.," in *Mélanges d'histoire offerts à Charles Moeller* (Louvain, 1914), II, 349–58.
17. For other motivations, see chap. 2. Controversies swirling around the Jesuit *collège* of Clermont-Ferrand had not been finally resolved even in 1656. At the height of the pamphlet war in Paris, there was political maneuvering in Auvergne to block the Jesuits from moving their new establishment from Montferrand to Clermont. See *OC,* III, 816–27.
18. *OC,* II, 509–40, 556–76, 584–602. See also A. Koyré, "Pascal savant," in *Blaise Pascal: l'homme et l'oeuvre* (Paris, 1956), 278–80.
19. *OC,* I, 737; II, 799–818.
20. For the most detailed exposition, see Albert de Meyer, *Les premières controverses Jansénistes en France (1640–1649)* (Louvain, 1919). Other more general and more recent histories, less theological but very helpful: Antoine Adam, *Du mysticisme à la révolte: Les jansénistes du XVIIe siècle* (Paris, 1968); Alexander Sedgwick, *Jansenism in Seventeenth-Century France* (Charlottesville, Va., 1977).
21. Lucien Ceyssens, "Les cinq propositions de Jansénius à Rome," *Revue d'histoire ecclésiastique* 66 (1971): 449–501 and 821–86. Pascal, *Oeuvres,* IV, 85–88.
22. Ceyssens, "Les cinq propositions," 868–86.
23. These passages are conveniently gathered in Pascal, *Oeuvres,* IV, 93–98. I have also used the great eighteenth-century edition for the full *Seconde lettre:* Arnauld, *Oeuvres* (Paris and Lausanne, 1775–83), XIX, 337 ff. In this edition, the offending passages are on 379, 448, 464–66, and 534.
24. Arnauld, *Oeuvres,* XIX, 512–34.
25. Paule Jansen makes a very strong case for the Machiavellian interpretation. Mazarin was committed to two courses of action that strongly displeased the Pope. First, he had imprisoned the Cardinal de Retz, and, even after de Retz's escape and flight into exile in 1654, he refused to allow him to exercise his ecclesiastical functions as Archbishop of Paris. Second, he had formally allied France with Protestant England in the Treaty of Westminster and was continuing the foreign war against Spain, resisting Papal offers to mediate the conflict. The Sorbonne inquest gave the French minister an opportunity to please the Pope by supporting orthodoxy. See Jansen, *Le cardinal Mazarin et le mouvement janséniste français 1653–1659* (Paris, 1967).
26. René Rapin, *Mémoires,* ed. L. Aubineau (Paris, 1865), I, 40–41, 161–62: II, 25–27, 307, 339–51.

27. This brings us to the *Provinciales* and Pascal. See Mesnard's chronologies: *OC,* III, 11–17 and esp. 447–66.
28. *Oeuvres,* VII, 66–67.
29. Jan Miel began the argument for an early date for the *Écrits* in his *Pascal and Theology* (Baltimore, 1966), 195–201. Mesnard has added a magisterial exposition; see *OC,* III, 543–92.
30. *OC,* III, 548–55, 563–64, 566–71.
31. *OC,* III, 647–50, 653–57, 665–73, 680–83, 693–96, and so on.
32. *OC,* III, 71.
33. The well-informed author of the "Manuscrit Lamy" lists four factors that favored Pascal's inclination toward Port-Royal. In his order: esteem for Jansenist partisans, affection for his sister, gratitude for the miraculous cure of his niece, and lingering resentment at the insinuations of the Jesuit Médaille: *OC,* I, 733–34. Henri Gouhier also makes the most important point about Blaise's feeling for Jacqueline: "La tragédie des *Provinciales,*" *La Table Ronde* 171 (1962): 50.
34. *OC,* III, 393, 413–21.
35. *OC,* III, 680, 696–712.
36. Cognet, 51; Intégrale, 382.
37. See Aristide Douarche, *L'Université de Paris et les Jésuites: XVIe et XVIIe siècles* (Paris, 1888), 110–20.
38. On Simon Marion, father of Catherine, see Douarche, *L'Université de Paris,* 136–38. On Catherine de Sainte-Félicité Arnauld's exhortation to the younger Antoine, see *OC,* I, 1131.
39. Formally defined in appendix 2.
40. On Arnauld and the *Journal* of the sieur de Saint-Gilles, see *OC,* I, 468–69; on the sieur de Saint-Gilles's expectations of "distressing events" and the like, see Baudry d'Asson, sieur de Saint-Gilles, *Journal,* ed. E. Jovy (Paris, 1936), 113, 115, 116, 117, 121, and so on.
41. Saint-Gilles, *Journal,* 122–23, 130–33, 135–36, 141–42, 148–49.
42. Saint-Gilles, *Journal,* 118–20, 127, 128, 131. See wonderful detail in Louis Battifol, "L'impression clandestine des *Provinciales* de Pascal," *Revue Hébdomadaire* 8 (17 August 1912): 346–63; Henri-Jean Martin, "Guillaume Desprez: Libraire de Pascal et de Port Royal," *Mémoires de la Fédération des Sociétés historiques et archéologiques de Paris et de l'Ile de France* 2 (1950): 205–28.
43. Saint-Gilles, *Journal,* 118.
44. Saint-Gilles, *Journal,* 134, 138–41.
45. Saint-Gilles, *Journal,* 139.
46. Saint-Gilles, *Journal,* 135. On the Assembly, see Pierre Blet, S.J., *Le Clergé de la France et la Monarchie* (Rome, 1959), II, 204–20.
47. Saint-Gilles, *Journal,* 144–45.
48. Saint-Gilles, *Journal,* 150–53, 161–62. The reported chronology may well be correct, but the explanation for the delay, the desire to publish the Fifth and Sixth Letters simultaneously, is questionable.
49. *Lettres* (Utrecht, 1744), III, 193.

50. *Lettres,* III, 199, 200, 202, 206, 210–11, 215, 219.
51. *Lettres,* III, 196.
52. *Lettres,* III, 187.
53. *Lettres,* III, 191.
54. *Oeuvres,* IV, 324. This narrative, drawn from a *Relation* first published in 1737, is based on contemporaneous memoirs written in accordance with Mère Angélique's wishes.
55. *OC,* III, 994 and marginal note from manuscript.
56. *OC,* III, 904–22.
57. *OC,* III, 922–38.
58. The cruel dilemma of risking a natural death or a surgical killing is clearest in the father's deposition: *OC,* III, 905–6.
59. See Jacques Guillemeau, *Oeuvres de chirurgie* (Rouen, 1649), 516–17, 791–92.
60. Jacqueline's formal deposition is quite restrained; she does not mention the coincident summons or dwell upon the horrors of the prescribed remedy. For the summons, *OC,* III, 906, 910. For *le feu,* see her long poem on the Miracle, *OC,* III, 986–95.
61. On the pamphlet, see *OC,* I, 474–75; on the support of Arnauld and Nicole, see *Oeuvres,* VII, 68.
62. For documentation on the Miracle, see *OC,* III, 800–815, 868–42, 962–95, 1086–129. Much of this material is unavailable in the Grands Écrivains *Oeuvres,* but see the derivative traditions gathered in the appendix to vol. IV, 336–53.
63. His reported opinion that "faith had been extinguished" must mean that before the Miracle he had bemoaned the apparent triumph of the partisans of Molinist grace and laxist morals.
64. *Mémoire sur la vie de M. Pascal,* in *Recueil de plusieurs pièces* (Utrecht, 1740), 300–301; also *OC,* I, 970–71. Gouhier and Sellier are both skeptical: *Blaise Pascal commentaires,* 149, n. 5; *Pascal et Saint Augustin,* 602, n. 2. Shiokawa cautiously recalls Pensée 853 as circumstantial evidence for the the report; Tetsua Shiokawa, *Pascal et les Miracles* (Paris, 1977), 122–23, n. 16. I would add that Pensée 965, not yet published in 1740 and not copied onto working manuscripts, confirms that Pascal was eager to respond to unbelievers who did challenge him with the apparent failure of divine providence.
65. *Mémoire sur Pascal,* in *Recueil d'Utrecht,* 300–301.
66. *OC,* I, 416, 957.
67. Such "letters" would include the *Lettre sur la possibilité des commandements* (*OC,* III, 642–712), the *Lettres à Mlle. de Roannez* (*OC,* III, 1029–47), and, in the mind's eye, at least, an Apology in epistolary form (see Pensées 4, 5, 7, 9, 11).
68. *OC,* I, 1023.
69. The most scholarly effort, Ernest Jovy's, is an exercise in bibliographical arcana having nothing to do with Pascal's central concerns: "Essai de solution d'un petit problème d'histoire littéraire relatif à Pascal: Pascal

et Montalte," *Bulletin du Comité des travaux historiques et scientifiques: Histoire, archéologie, et philologie* (1894): 324–40. See Cognet, lxxi.

70. I use King James's English. Vulgate: "Iesus . . . ducit illos *in montem excelsum* seorsum et transfiguratus est." Louvain: "*une haute montagne.*" Sacy: "*une haute montagne.*"
71. Méré: *OC,* I, 825.
72. Sacy, reported by Fontaine: *OC,* I, 957–61. Angélique, *Lettres,* III, 219–20, 223–40; much of this is also included with relevant passages from later letters in *OC,* III, 868–90. Cf. Jacqueline Pascal's outspoken opinion that she could rejoice in the fact of the cure without fearing prideful inflation from any degree of personal responsibility for it; see Jacqueline to Gilberte, 28–31 March 1656, *Oeuvres,* IV, 390.
73. *OC,* I, 893.

NOTES TO CHAPTER TWELVE

1. Scholars as knowledgeable and sympathetic as Henri Gouhier have regretted Pascal's willful oversimplifications, his apparent eagerness to hunt down his game, and his violent denunciations of Jesuits in the name of God. See Gouhier, "La tragédie des *Provinciales,*" esp. 48, 50. Cf. Jean Mesnard, "Pascal et la contestation," *Revue d'Auvergne* 85 (1971): 185–97.
2. See Parish, *Pascal's Lettres Provinciales,* passim. The principal collection of materials from the counterpolemic is attributed to Jacques Nouet, S.J.: *Réponses aux Lettres Provinciales publiées par le Secrétaire du Port-Royal contre les PP. de la Compagnie de Jésus, sur la Morale des dits Pères* (Liège, 1657).
3. *Lettres,* III, 203.
4. Nicole's shifting explanations suggest rationalizations, Pascal's and perhaps his own, too. *Oeuvres,* VII, 67–69. Méré's claim of credit for having suggested to Pascal this change of direction is characteristically vain, but Pascal may have sought out his critical opinion and respected his literary judgment: *OC,* I, 850, 977–78.
5. Intégrale, 375, 383; Cognet, 20, 57.
6. Cognet, xlvii; the citation by this most meticulous editor is erroneous, but I have not succeeded in correcting it.
7. American Psychiatric Association, *Diagnostic and Statistical Manual,* 3d ed. (DSM-III) (Washington, D.C., 1980), 220. I have also consulted the revised version of DSM-III and the relevant portions of DSM-IV. See appendix 2.
8. DSM-III, 220. This language has been retained in DSM-IV.
9. *Oeuvres,* V, 176–82.
10. Intégrale, 409; Cognet, 159 and n. 2.
11. *OC,* I, 1022, 1137.
12. *Oeuvres,* VII, 67–69.

13. Intégrale, 471–91; Cognet, 404–59.
14. Intégrale, 385; Cognet, 65 and n. 1.
15. *OC,* I, 1074.
16. *OC,* I, 885.
17. On Pascal and Forton, see *OC,* II, 362–420; Henri Gouhier, *Pascal et les humanistes chrétiens: l'affaire Sainte-Ange* (Paris, 1974). On the "civil wars," *OC,* I, 1006, 1010–11, 1035 ff.; Mesnard, *Pascal* (1967), 125–29.
18. Cf. *VMP,* Second Version, 80.
19. Goodwin and Jamison, *Manic-Depressive Illness,* 50–51.
20. Gustave Lanson first made the case for Pascal's extensive mining of Arnauld's *Théologie morale des Jésuites extraite fidelement de leurs livres* (1643) and *Lettres de Polémarque à Eusèbe at d'un Théologien à Polémarque* (1643). See Lanson, "Les *Provinciales* et le livre de la *Théologie morale des Jésuites,*" *Revue d'histoire littéraire de la France* 7 (1900): 169–95. Arnauld's work is accessible in his *Oeuvres,* XXIX, 74 ff.
21. *VMP,* First Version, 40; Second Version, 39, 41.
22. See part 5.
23. *VMP,* 44.
24. *OC,* I, 1017.
25. *OC,* I, 1075.
26. René Rapin, S.J., *Mémoires,* in *OC,* I, 849; cf. Paul Beurrier, *Mémoires,* in *OC,* I, 873.
27. *OC,* I, 893.
28. *OC,* I, 1031 and n. 1.
29. See M. Gorce, O.P., *Introduction aux Provinciales de Pascal: Nicolaï et les Jansénistes ou la grâce actuelle suffisante* (N.p.: Éditions de la *Revue Thomiste,* 1932). Intégrale, 373–75, 376–78; Cognet, 13–19 and n. 1 on 14, 22–31.
30. Kenneth Krabbenhoft, "Pascal contre Caramuel," *XVIIe Siècle* 33 (1981): 435–42.
31. Intégrale, 455; Cognet, 333.
32. *OC,* I, 488–89.
33. *Journal,* ed. Jovy, 180–81; also in *OC,* I, 479 with n. 4; cf. Beaubrun, *Mémoires,* in *OC,* I, 1024.
34. Long after the fact, Père Rapin still supposed that Arnauld himself must have written Letters 1–3; *Mémoires,* in *OC,* I, 847.
35. *Arrest du Parlement de Provence contre l'autheur des Lettres au Provincial,* in *Oeuvres,* VI, 377–78; Hermant, *Mémoires,* III, 292 ff.
36. *La condemnation des dix-huit Lettres et autres escrits des Jansénistes,* in *Oeuvres,* VII, 229–32.
37. *Oeuvres,* X, 13–21.
38. Pensée 916.
39. *Réponse à la lettre d'une personne de condition, touchant les règles de la conduite des Saints Pères dans la composition de leurs ouvrages, pour la défense des Vérités combattues, ou de l'innocence calomniée* (1654), in *Oeuvres,* XXVII,

1–49. This tract was written to defend Le Maistre de Sacy's *Enluminures*. See also Arnauld's *Dissertation selon la méthode des géometres pour la justification de ceux qui emploient, en écrivant, en certaines rencontres, des termes que le monde estime durs,* in *Oeuvres,* XXVII, 50–70.

40. Intégrale, 422; Cognet, 203–6. Mesnard, "Pascal et la contestation," 194–95.
41. For Pascal's formal statement of what he had and had not read, see *OC,* I, 1075. Karl Weiss failed to make the case against Pascal, and Augustin Gazier succeeded in making the case for his veracity as a reader of Escobar. Weiss, *P. Antonio de Escobar y Mendoza als Moraltheologe in Pascals Beleuchtung und im Lichte de Wahrheit* (Freiburg-im-Breisgau, 1911); Gazier, *Blaise Pascal et Antoine Escobar* (Paris, 1912).
42. Cognet's judgment is justly respected: see his edition of the *Provinciales,* xl–xlii. See the notes and documentation assembled in the *Oeuvres,* vols. IV–VII.
43. Cognet, 204–5 and n. 1 on 205; Augustine's Letter 48 is cited in Arnauld's *Réponse à une personne de condition, Oeuvres,* XXVII, 44.
44. Intégrale, 387, 409, 434, 455; Cognet, 74, 157 and n. 2, 253, 332–33. See Ignatius of Loyola, *The Constitutions of the Society of Jesus,* G. E. Ganss, trans. (St. Louis, 1970), 161, 284.
45. "The *Lettres provinciales* as a Jansenist calumny: Pascal and moral theology in seventeenth-century France," *Seventeenth-Century French Studies* 8 (1986): 5–21.
46. *Ad sacram* reaffirmed the condemnation of the Five Propositions, specifying that they were in Jansenius's *Augustinus* and that the sense condemned was Jansenius's. See the text in *Oeuvres,* VI, 59–62. The Bull was dated in Rome 16 October 1656, but it was not presented in Paris until the second week of March 1657 (*OC,* III, 464); thus, it effectively followed the publication of Letter 17 but preceded the composition of Letter 18. See the Intégrale, 464–68; Cognet, 367–78.
47. Intégrale, 419, 424; Cognet, 194, 213. For these specific cases, see the Intégrale, 396, 404, 405, 407; Cognet, 110–12 and nn, 139–41 and nn, 142–43 and nn, 149–51 and nn.
48. For a summary, see Cognet, lxix–lxx.
49. Intégrale, 446–47; Cognet, 301–3.
50. Intégrale, 451–52; Cognet, 319, 322.
51. *Pascal et les Roannez,* I, 488.
52. Nicole in *Oeuvres,* VII, 67, 70; Brienne in *Oeuvres,* XII, cxlviii.
53. Charlotte's story as otherwise documented is dramatic enough. In August 1656, she was a twenty-three-year-old noblewoman about to be married off to the marquis d'Alluye, a young courtier and something of a libertine. On 4 August, she and her mother went to venerate the Holy Thorn at Port Royal; she returned cured of a minor eye ailment, converted to a newly fervent devotion, and determined to enter the Paris convent. Her brother and mother opposed this precipitous voca-

tion and, to forestall it, spirited her off to Poitou for seven months. After their return, she escaped into Port-Royal, from which they extracted with a *lettre de cachet*. She remained celibate for another decade before marrying unhappily. See Hermant, *Mémoires,* III, 504–18, 548, 560–61.

54. Readers of the surviving texts have concluded variously that Blaise loved Charlotte passionately but hopelessly (Prosper Faugère, in Pascal, *Pensées* [Paris, 1844], lxv–lxix); that he had little or no relationship with her before her conversion and no role in her vocation (Augustin Gazier, "Pascal et Mlle. de Roannez," in *Mélanges de littérature et d'histoire* [Paris, 1904]); that he dominated her, terrifying her into submission, turning her against a natural life in the world and thrusting her into the convent (Charles Adam, "Pascal et Mademoiselle de Roannez," *Revue bourguignonne de l'enseignement supérieur* 7 [1891]: 517–78); that he was a longtime family friend, trusted as older and wiser, who offered spiritual direction and a properly restrained, almost paternal affection (Jean Mesnard, *Pascal et les Roannez,* I, 209–45 and 437–546; *OC,* III, 996–1047).
55. In what follows, I adopt Mesnard's numeration and chronology. For tabular summaries, see *Pascal et les Roannez,* I, 490; *OC,* III, 1016.
56. Mesnard provides a circumstantially detailed and fully documented account of the marriage project. Then, unnecessarily and unpersuasively, he endorses the pious tradition of an instantaneous conversion and simultaneous vocation having nothing to do with the historical situation. Hermant, the regulative informant, attributes this prayer to the girl in her carriage *on the way* to Port-Royal on 4 August: "My God, if you want to touch my heart so as to make me a nun serving only you, I'd be delighted. . . ." See the *Mémoires,* III, 505. Mesnard does accept that the familial opposition to the vocation was related to the marriage project: *Pascal et les Roannez,* I, 441–59.
57. *OC,* III, 1029–31.
58. *OC,* III, 1031–32.
59. The "condemnation" in question must have been the Formulary based on *Cum occasione* that was voted by the assembly of the Clergy in Paris, 1 September 1656: *Formule pour la réception et souscription de la Constitution de nostre saint Père le Pape Innocent X portant condemnation de la doctrine des cinq propositions de Cornelius Jansenius.* See *Oeuvres,* V, 337–38.
60. *OC,* III, 1033–34.
61. *OC,* III, 1035–37.
62. *OC,* III, 1037–40.
63. *OC,* III, 1041–42.
64. *OC,* III, 1043.
65. He was to repeat it in a remarkable fragment, Pensée 924. Sellier has suggested a bookish source for the image of God "as a mother protecting and guiding her child." See his preface to André Bord, *Pascal et Jean de la Croix* (Paris, 1987), 12. However, the maternity attributed to

God is perhaps the less striking aspect of Pascal's repeated image; the more startling and more suggestive aspect is the painful, even horrific, prospect of violent separation or loss in infancy.

66. *OC,* III, 1043–45.
67. *OC,* III, 1045–46.
68. Intégrale, 468–69; Cognet, 381–84.

NOTES TO PART FIVE

1. *VMP,* First Version, 42, 44; Second Version, 53, 56. Carcavy to Huygens, 14 August 1659, in Huygens, *Oeuvres complètes,* II, 456–57.
2. *OC,* II, 665; IV, 24–27, 323–30, 579–96.
3. There is an extensive modern literature on the medical case history. In addition to the article cited in n. 6 below, see P. Just-Navarre's still useful "La maladie de Pascal: étude médicale et psychologique," *Mémoires de l'Académie des Sciences, Belles-Lettres, et Arts de Lyon. Sciences et lettres.* 3d ser., 11 (1911): 295–404. More recent papers have been helpful: Robert de Sinéty, "La maladie de Pascal," *Archives de philosophie* 1.3 (1923): 1–32; Jean Torlais, "Au chevet de Pascal," *Le progrès médical* No. 1 (10 January 1954): 16–22; P. Wertheimer and A. Bouchet, "Les maladies et la mort de Pascal," *Comptes rendus du 88e congrès national des sociétés savantes. Section des sciences.* (Clermont-Ferrand, 1963), III, 3–25; M. Dordain and R. Dailly, "La maladie et la mort de Pascal: hypothèses nouvelles," *Bulletin historique et scientifique de l'Auvergne* 59 (1978): 151–58; P. Rentchnick, "Pathographies (71): Blaise Pascal," *Médecine et hygiène* 41 (1983): 4530–36. Jean Mesnard provides an overview with a fuller bibliography in *OC,* IV, 1469–1503. I caution readers against an ambitious but historically and medically amateurish dissertation: Murkje Scholtens, *Études médico-psychologiques sur Pascal* (Utrecht, 1958).
4. *OC,* I, 1026–27, 1084, 1121; IV, 574. Mesnard, *Pascal et les Roannez,* II, 747–48.
5. *Préface,* Intégrale, 497.
6. Just-Navarre, "Les médecins de Pascal," *Mémoires de l'Académie de Lyon. Sciences et lettres.* 3d ser., 14 (1914) 283–84; Pascal, *Oeuvres,* X, 306.
7. For Voltaire's relative scrupulousness in citations of Pascal, see Jerolyn Scull, "Voltaire's reading of Pascal: His quotations compared to early texts," *Studies on Voltaire and the Eighteenth Century* 161 (1976): 19–35. For his casual misrepresentation of Leibniz, see Voltaire to s'Gravesande, 1 August 1741, Besterman 2359; compare the much vaguer remark actually attributed to Leibniz in the posthumous *Otium Hanoveranum sive Miscellanea* (Leipzig, 1718), 165–66. In a very later letter, Leibniz says that his informant on Pascal's mental condition was Huygens, who had met the Frenchman but was neither intimate personally nor sympathetic confessionally; Leibniz to Remond, 14 March 1714, in *Philosophical Papers and Letters,* ed. L. E. Loehmer (Dordrecht, 1969), 656.

NOTES TO CHAPTER THIRTEEN

1. For "P.R." as Pascal's abbreviation for Port-Royal, see Pensées 63 and 955. I punctuate the three letters as on the table of contents and in all recent literature; Pascal did not punctuate them in the heading of his original manuscript.
2. Ernst's work is in press as I write. I am grateful to him and the Université de Paris-IV for the opportunity to examine the text, tables, and photographs of his ambitious and impressive thèse.
3. Mesnard has written that Pensée 6 was "doubtlessly" prior and Pensée 12 is "perfectly" concordant with "the order followed in the twenty-eight chapters." He also supposes that Pascal must have filed Pensée 12 first in the dossier "Ordre," which would seem to entail a subsequent filing of a superseded plan, and he concedes that, "strictly speaking," Pensée 12 corresponds only to the dossiers conventionally numbered 11–25. See *Les Pensées de Pascal* (Paris, 1976), 46–47, 179–80. It is important that the twenty-eight titles from the two columns of Pascal's table are not consecutively numbered on any of the manuscript copies of that document; see below for a facsimile.
4. *VMP,* Second Version, 41–54; "Preface," in Intégrale, 494–501.
5. For the most ambitious efforts to provide detailed commentary on the "classified" fragments in light of Pascal's plan, see Pol Ernst, *Approches pascaliennes* (Gembloux, 1970), and Anthony Pugh, *The Composition of Pascal's Apologia* (Toronto, 1984). Henri Gouhier is the most prominent skeptic; see his *Blaise Pascal commentaires,* 173–85. Ernst remains faithful to the traditional conception of a single, orderly plan, about which he writes in the language of instantaneous creation even in a book in which the central concerns are chronological and the dominant image is geological: *Géologie et stratigraphie des Pensées* (thèse Paris-IV, 1990, vol. 1, 174–75).
6. Périer, "Préface de l'édition de Port-Royal," in Intégrale, 495; Filleau de La Chaise, "Discours sur les *Pensées* de M. Pascal," in *Oeuvres,* XII, cxcix–cciii. See Annie Barnes, "La conférence à Port-Royal et les liasses de Pascal," *French Studies* 10 (1956): 231–40; Barnes, "Le discours sur les *Pensées* de Filleau," and Lafuma, "Réponse à Mrs. Annie Barnes," in *Écrits sur Pascal* (Paris, 1959), 81–115.
7. Mesnard, *Pascal et les Roannez,* II, 645–49.
8. For chronology, see *OC,* IV, 16–27. This dates the onset of incapacitating illness to the winter of 1659. For Gilberte's early dating of the onset (before Pascal's thirty-fifth birthday, 19 June 1658), see *VMP,* First Version, 44; Second Version, 53.
9. The question remains where it was left forty years ago in the learned perplexity shared by Mesnard and the abbé Cognet: none of the voluminous correspondence of Port-Royalists mentions any such conference, but there is no other plausible explanation for Pascal's "A.P.R." See the

Royaumont Conference, in *Blaise Pascal: l'homme et l'oeuvre* (Paris, 1956), 100–101; Gouhier, *Commentaires,* 179. See note 1 above.

10. See also Pensée 122.
11. Intégrale, 356–57, 372–77.
12. Mesnard finds a precise definition of "misère" in Pensée 75: "vouloir et ne pouvoir." See *Les Pensées de Pascal,* 186–87. It seems imprudent to place too much weight on the single fragment, but, if we are to do so, it is incumbent upon us to give further meaning to the "incapacity" in question; Pascal singles out two frustrated "wants"—happiness and truth. Pensée 6 more simply opposes "misère" to "félicité." Pensée 148, which concludes part 1 and prefaces part 2 as we have it, also provides more reliable evidence on the structure of the whole; here, the one great unsatisfied "want" is happiness.
13. Pierre Charron begins a "general portrait of man" in his *De la Sagesse* (1601, rev. ed. 1604), book 1, chap. 37: "All sages seem to agree in their representations and descriptions . . . , emphasizing these four traits: *vanité, faiblesse, inconstance, misère.*" Charron then summarizes this summary in a word, namely, *misère.* Each of the four traits then gets a chapter. The chapter on "Misère" is especially gloomy: "This is his dominant trait. . . . He is *misère* incarnate. . . . Man's lot is to be *misérable;* only man, every man, is always *misérable.*" Somewhat similarly, Pascal entitles his first substantive *liasses* in the First Part "Vanité" and "Misère," and his summary, too, singles out "Misère" (Pensée 6). In addition, he used Charron's chapter titles as headings for fragments: "Vanité" (Pensées 16, 32, 46), "Faiblesse" (Pensée 28), "Inconstance" (Pensées 17, 54, 55), and "Misère" (Pensée 69). It seems obvious that Pascal had read Charron and been influenced by him, equally obvious that he makes these commonplaces his own, expressing his own more powerful personality and greater genius.
14. Mesnard, *Pascal* (Paris, 1967), 169–70.
15. Croquette, *Pascal et Montaigne,* 3–13.
16. *Essais,* III, 4, in *Oeuvres complètes,* ed. Thibaudet and Rat, 814–15.
17. See Croquette, *Pascal et Montaigne,* 5, for the reminiscence of the *Essais,* III, 4, 814, in Pensée 43.
18. Croquette, *Pascal et Montaigne,* 5–10.
19. See Croquette, *Pascal et Montaigne,* 6, for the reminiscences of the *Essais,* III, 8, 911, in Pensée 44.
20. Montaigne's fondness for Plutarch is well known. Plutarch, in turn, was fond of his warrior-heroes, but not equally fond. He thought that the Greek Alexander had won by "virtue," while the Roman Caesar won by "fortune." See *De Alexandri magni fortuna aut virtute,* 326D–345B, and *De fortuna Romanorum,* 316B–326C.
21. *Essais,* III, 8, 917. See the textual parallels in Croquette, *Pascal et Montaigne,* 6.
22. *Essais,* I, 50, 291.

23. See Croquette, *Pascal et Montaigne,* 11–12, for the reminiscences of the *Essais,* I, 3, 18, in Pensée 47.
24. See Croquette, *Pascal et Montaigne,* 14, for the reminiscence of the *Essais,* I, 2, 328, in Pensée 56.
25. See Croquette, *Pascal et Montaigne,* 30–31, for the reminiscence of the *Essais,* I, 20, 82, in Pensée 133.
26. It may be relevant that Montaigne's mother lived on and on—which led to rather different problems. See Donald Frame, *Montaigne: A Biography* (San Francisco, 1984), 23–28.
27. For the successive states of this very important pensée, see Michel Le Guern, "Pascal au travail: La composition du fragment sur le Divertissement," *Revue de l'Université d'Ottawa* 36 (1966): 209–31.
28. See Croquette, *Pascal et Montaigne,* 31, for the first relevant reminiscence of the *Essais,* I, 42, 252–53 in Pensée 136.
29. See Croquette, *Pascal et Montaigne,* 32, for the second relevant reminiscence of the *Essais,* I, 42, 254, in Pensée 136.
30. See Croquette, *Pascal et Montaigne,* 32, for the third relevant reminiscence of the *Essais,* II, 12, 548–49, in Pensée 136.
31. See Croquette, *Pascal et Montaigne,* 33, for the fourth relevant reminiscence of the *Essais,* I, 4, 25, in Pensée 136.
32. See Croquette, *Pascal et Montaigne,* 34, for the reminiscence of the *Essais,* I, 39, 235–36 in Pensée 139.
33. Ironically, even this claim is itself an echo of sorts, *Montaigne* having said much the same thing about *his* reading of Plato. See "De l'institution des enfans," *Essais,* I, 26, 150. There is deeper irony in Pascal's apparent unawareness that in his case, as Montaigne's reader, it was not simply a matter of agreement with a prior thinker but rather of subtle but fundamental changes imposed unconsciously on materials gathered from his great predecessor.
34. Intégrale, 355.
35. Annie Barnes, "La Table des titres de la Copie des *Pensées:* Est-elle de Pascal?" *French Studies* 7 (1953): 140–46.
36. See Hugh M. Davidson and Pierre H. Dubé, *A Concordance to Pascal's Pensées* (Ithaca, N.Y., 1975).
37. Henri Gouhier long ago raised many of these objections to the now dominant emphasis on the orderliness and planfulness of the "classified" fragments. He considers it imprudent to seek evidence even of provisional planning; see *Blaise Pascal commentaires,* 181–83. This skepticism seems excessive.
38. See Richard Parish, "Mais qui parle? Voice and persona in the *Pensées,*" *Seventeenth-Century French Studies* 8 (1986): 23–40; Henri Gouhier, *Blaise Pascal: conversion et apologétique* (Paris, 1986), 56. Earlier students of these problems include Jacques Demorest, *Dans Pascal* (Paris, 1953) and Patricia Topliss, *The Rhetoric of Pascal* (Leicester, 1966).

NOTES TO CHAPTER FOURTEEN

1. A prominent and persistent dysphoric mood that is associated with other symptoms of the depressive syndrome is "the essential feature" of that common affective disorder as now conceived. DSM-III, 205–6, 210–15; DSM-IV, 320–27. See appendix 2.
2. For Gilberte's reports of *langueur: VMP,* First Version, 44; Second Version, 53, 56. For her son Étienne: *Préface, Oeuvres,* XII, clxxxviii–clxxxix. For her husband Florin: *OC,* I, 688.
3. See the *Trésor de la langue française,* ed. Paul Imbs (Paris, 1978–).
4. See Zachaire Tourneur's "paleographical edition": *Les Pensées de Pascal* (Paris, 1942), 304.
5. *Les Pensées de Pascal,* 92.
6. Editors have rightly respected a "literary" sequence for this fragment, beginning with Pascal's "Ennui" as a heading and placing his marginal afterthought at the midpoint.
7. *VMP,* 68, 70.
8. This is as straightforward a translation of Pensée 931 as the manuscript text allows. Despite the paragraphing in Tourneur's indispensable paleographical edition of the *Pensées* (page 127) and in the less daunting editions of Lafuma (no. 931), Sellier (no. 759), and Le Guern (no. 655), there is no good textual warrant for internal breaks other than those before and after what I present as a middle paragraph. Pascal began this as an interlinear revision and then greatly extended it as a marginal afterthought, clearly written after my last paragraph. I have generally been quite free in my paragraphing, but here there is particular justification for some such disposition of the text. The more important textual point, reflected in the editions of Tourneur and Le Guern but not those of Lafuma and Sellier, is that the "self-portrait" on folio 104 is the continuation of a passage begun on the *recto,* folio 103. See my discussion in the following paragraphs.
9. *Recueil original,* 104.
10. *Provinciales,* Seventeenth Letter, Intégrale, 454–55; Cognet, ed., *Provinciales,* 330–31.
11. *Recueil original,* 103.
12. Jansenius, *Discours de la réformation de l'homme intérieur,* in Gustave Michaut, *Les époques de la pensée de Pascal* (Paris, 1902), 194–222. For Pascal's "three orders," Pensée 308, 933.
13. Phillipe Sellier, *Pascal et Saint Augustin* (Paris, 1970), 463–64.
14. Augustine, *Enarratio in Psalmum CXXXVI,* 2. This long commentary is built on the opposition of the two cities, Babylon and Jerusalem. Augustine presents the paradox of the Christian in Babylon, who should "weep in joy and rejoice in sorrow." Pascal's source may very well have been Antoine Arnauld's *Réflexions sur le Pséaume CXXXVI,* in *Oeuvres* (Paris, 1776), V, 1–18. Arnauld incorporated great chunks from Augustine and remarks of his own on the Two Loves that emphasize the

perishable nature of all objects of earthly attachment. Neither Augustine nor Arnauld could have been the source for the nostalgic regression, if that is the proper term, that I sense in Pascal's anguished words.

15. Pascal to Fermat, 27 October 1654, *OC,* II, 1158. Compare the letter of 10 August 1660, also to Fermat, *Oeuvres,* X, 4–6.
16. Jean Mesnard, "Pascal à l'académie Le Pailleur," *Revue d'histoire des sciences* 16 (1963): 1–10, reprinted in P. Costabel et al., *L'oeuvre scientifique de Pascal* (Paris, 1964), 7–16.
17. *OC,* II, 1031.
18. Pensées 780, 887.
19. Jacqueline to Gilberte, 8 December 1654, *Oeuvres,* IV, 15.
20. Paulette Carrive has devoted a paper to this pensée, which she regards as "cynical," even "bitter": "Lecture d'une pensée de Pascal: 'Qu'est-ce que le moi?' " *Les études philosophiques* 3 (1983): 353–56. Many other pensées bear directly on the possibility and the propriety of human love, among them the famous Cleopatra fragments (Pensées 46, 197, 413). The doctrine of the Two Loves is perhaps less memorable but certainly more pervasive and more consequential: Pensées 142, 151, 198, 373, 381, 396, 503, 618, 764, and so on.
21. Pensée 792; cf. Pensée 978. Pascal's pensées on friendship ought to be cautionary even with respect to his now celebrated friendship with the Roannez, especially Artus.
22. Lafuma's Pensée 552 is the sixth of six paragraphs on a single sheet (*Recueil original* 127), each paragraph break marked by the characteristic traits that Pascal drew from the left margin of his papers upon the conclusion of a thought. The great editor's Pensée 550 groups the first four, and his Pensée 551 designates the fifth paragraph.

    Pensée 550 begins with Christ's agony in the garden and the sleepy Disciples; references to Luke 22–23 reflect meditation on the part of the Gospel that inspired the *Mystère de Jésus.* Here, Pascal's focus is on Peter's failings. There can be no question but that this is an intensely personal page on which *this particular* penitent meditates *his own* sense of temptation as a sinner and *his own* sense of obligation as a convert.

    Pensée 551 concerns the contrary powers of our "imagination" to fill itself with "little things" made fantastically great and to reduce even the very greatest, God, to its own petty measure. Pascal's reflection is in the spirit of Montaigne's "Apologie," but, to my knowledge, no parallel texts have been suggested.

    If there ever was a coherent line of thought on this page, it may have followed something like this course. Pascal felt called, like Peter, but also tempted, like Peter. As to the nature of his temptation, Pensées 551 and 552 together suggest an unhealthy preoccupation with self that could have limited the convert's capacity to affirm his own faith and to strengthen that of others.
23. A good humanist would also recall the almost identical language of

Virgil's *Aeneid* 4.6: ". . . *lustrabat lampade terras.*" The context here is Dido's dawning love for Aeneas.

24. See Lane Heller, "Note on a pensée (Brunschvicg 107 [=Lafuma 552]): Pascal and Montaigne," *Orbis Litterarum* 29 (1974): 216–20. Montaigne's theme of instability evidently appealed to Pascal; see the headings of Pensées 54 and 55 and the reminiscences in Pensées 55, 136, 629, catalogued in Croquette, *Pascal et Montaigne,* 14, 33–34, 59.
25. *Essais,* II, 1, 316–17.
26. Croquette, *Pascal et Montaigne,* 4, 8–9, 10, 32, 54.
27. *Essais,* II, 12, 547.
28. *Essais,* II, 12, 948–49.
29. *Essais,* III, 13, 1091.
30. *Essais,* III, 9, 951.
31. *Essais,* II, 1, 318.
32. For de Roannez, see *Oeuvres,* IV, 66. There is no simply correct way to edit the *Mystère.* Sellier numbers it Pensée 749 and ends it with the first two paragraphs translated below; he edits what follows as Pensée 751. The emotional tone of the former does contrast with that of the latter, in which there are the clearest indications of a date late in 1654 or early in 1655. Le Guern groups these materials under a single number, his Pensée 717. Both recent editors provide very helpful notes.
33. *Oeuvres,* IV, 67.
34. For the physical evidence of folding and carrying, see Tourneur, *Les Pensées de Pascal,* 27, n. 3. For alternative dispositions of Pascal's text(s) on the printed page, cf. Louis Lafuma's Pensées 927–29 in my edition of reference, the *Oeuvres complètes* (Paris, 1963), to Philippe Sellier's Pensée 756 in his well-regarded edition (Paris, 1976) and Michel Le Guern's Pensée 722 from his also respected *Pensées* (Paris, 1977). These more recent alternatives are superior in respecting the common provenance of the disparate paragraphs assigned three numbers by Lafuma. See the facsimile in Lafuma's magnificent *Le manuscrit des Pensées de Pascal* (Paris, 1962).
35. *Entretien,* par. 24, citing Augustine, *Confessions* 4.16.
36. *Oeuvres,* IV, 67.
37. *Oeuvres,* IV, 15, 63–65, 67. Angélique Arnauld, *Lettres,* 3 vols. (Paris, 1742–44), II, 538–40, 542–43, 546, 549–50; Agnès Arnauld, *Lettres,* 2 vols. (Paris, 1858), I, 345–48.
38. *Recueil original,* 93–94.
39. *OC,* III, 1043.
40. *VMP,* First Version, 38–40; Second Version, 38–41.
41. Louis Lafuma, *Histoire des Pensées de Pascal* (Paris, 1954), 91–92; Gouhier, *Blaise Pascal commentaires,* 149–62.
42. *Recueil original,* 415.
43. *VMP,* 39–40; *OC,* I, 689; *Oeuvres,* XI, 405; *Oeuvres,* XII, clxxxi and clxxxix–cxcv.

44. For a systematic concordance that enables the modern reader to see how the old edition was put together, see Thérèse Goyet, "Le visage de 1670," in *Les Pensées de Pascal ont trois cents ans* (Clermont-Ferrand, 1971), 43.
45. Dernières remarques 50, in *Oeuvres complètes,* XXXI, 16.

NOTES TO CHAPTER FIFTEEN

1. I have abbreviated these criteria from the American Psychiatric Association, *Diagnostic and Statistical Manual of Mental Disorders,* 4th ed. (DSM-IV) (Washington, D.C., 1994), 327. See appendix 2 for formal presentation of criteria from this DSM-IV; this diagnostic system, with few significant differences, was introduced in DSM-III, 213–14.
2. Pol Ernst's *Géologie et stratigraphie des Pensées* tends to date Pascal's work on the Apology to the one year from mid-1657 to mid-1658, one Pentecost to the next. Of course, the *Pensées* also include other texts from other periods, most spectacularly the earlier *Mémorial.* Even observable "strata" of materials that are at least arguably apologetic are complicated by fault lines that disappear beneath the surface. Take, for instance, Pensées 403 and 622, texts reproduced in facsimile in the first section of my chap. 14. The paper of Pensée 403 is from the earliest of Ernst's four "major strata," but this "original" is clearly a secretary's fair copy, so it presupposes a still earlier author's draft. Furthermore, what makes it so compelling is that—on another paper—Pascal virtually identified himself as a "Solomon" and that he came back to this paper—at an unknown time or times—to scrawl and to retrace in his own hand the telling "Misère." Somewhat similarly, Pensée 622, from the second of Ernst's "major strata," is most compelling for marginal afterthoughts that may have been added at any later date.
3. DSM-III, 210, 214; Aaron Beck, *Depression* (Philadelphia, 1970), 18–20, 29–30, 35.
4. For Pascal's intentions concerning the Arithmetic Machine, see *OC,* II, 318–26, 711–15; for the Vacuum Experiments, see *OC,* I, 43–44, 679–81; for *the Traité du triangle arithmétique,* see *OC,* I, 33–37, 690; II, 1166.
5. *VMP,* 45–46. See *Oeuvres,* VII, 337; IX, 181. Francois Russo, "Pascal et l'analyse infinitésimale," in *L'oeuvre scientifique de Pascal* (Paris, 1964), 137.
6. See Pascal to Fermat, 10 August 1660, *Oeuvres,* X, 3–6.
7. *OC,* I, 680, 688.
8. *OC,* I, 670, 1087; II, 652.
9. *Pascal et les Roannez,* I, 311–38; II, 618–45.
10. Mesnard, *Pascal et les Roannez,* II, 631.
11. Mesnard, *Pascal et les Roannez,* I, 249–310; II, 594–97. Pascal did inform Fermat that he planned a trip to Poitou for fall 1660, but this visit never took place. See *Oeuvres,* X, 5–6.

12. *Journal de voyage à Paris et à Londres,* ed. H.-L. Brugmans (Paris, 1935), 137.
13. *Journal de voyage,* 135, 139–40.
14. For speculation, see Huygens, *Oeuvres complètes,* XVII, 258; Mesnard, *Pascal et les Roannez,* II, 712–13.
15. For the description of the flying machine with Pascal's address, see Mesnard, *Pascal et les Roannez,* II, 713, n. 1.
16. *Journal de voyage,* 135, 137.
17. *VMP,* First Version, 53 (= Second Version, 62) documents that Pascal had a financial stake in the scheme and wanted to anticipate profits for charitable donations even before they had been earned on the streets. Two manuscript copies of *VMP* 53, made by others during Gilberte's lifetime, add a gloss on the "affair of the carriages," asserting that "it was his invention"; see *OC,* I, 589, variant *a,* with editorial remarks on 546 and 550–58. The added assertion is not familial, although it is historically defensible with this important qualification: it ignores de Roannez, who certainly shared in the original conception, certainly invested much more capital in the enterprise, and almost certainly played the most active role in its organization and operation. For the late "on dit," see Henri Sauval, *Histoire et recherches des antiquités de la ville de Paris* (Paris, 1724), I, 192–93; excerpted in *OC,* I 619–21.
18. See the chronology in *OC,* IV, 15–27.
19. For a wonderfully erudite discussion that gives Pascal a very active role in 1662, see Mesnard, *Pascal et les Roannez,* II, 765–813. Mesnard may overstate the case. If he does not, that still leaves a period of no known or suspected activity by Pascal from the original conception in 1658 or 1659 to the signature of a contract on 6 November 1661. The duc de Roannez and the marquis de Crenan, not Pascal, had taken the lead in securing the crucial support of the *grand prévôt,* the marquis de Sourches, on 29 October. These two principals did bring their agreement to Pascal, an investor, for his signature.
20. Pierre de Courcelle, *Entretien de Pascal et Sacy* (Paris, 1960); Bernard Croquette, *Pascal et Montaigne* (Geneva, 1974).
21. On the dating of the *Écrits sur la Grace,* see *OC,* III, 543 ff.
22. Mesnard, *Les Pensées de Pascal,* 38–50, 53, 358–61.
23. Mesnard, *Les Pensées de Pascal,* 44–45. Pol Ernst, "Les autographes de Gilberte dans l'original des *Pensées,*" *Chroniques de Port-Royal* 31 (1982): 69–92.
24. Preface of the Port-Royal *Pensées, Oeuvres,* XII, clxxxix.
25. *VMP,* 42.
26. *VMP,* I, 35, 43, 47.
27. *VMP,* Second Version, 28.
28. *VMP,* 35; *OC,* I, 1084, 1086.
29. *VMP,* 47.
30. *VMP,* 48.
31. One striking anecdote concerns Gilberte's surveillance of her daugh-

ters—when they were in their forties: *OC,* I, 1153. The mother's writings remain the best evidence of her piety.

32. *VMP,* 48–49.
33. Jansenius, *De la réformation de l'homme intérieur,* in Michaut, *Les époques de la pensée,* 203–5.
34. Pensée 919.
35. *VMP,* Second Version, 55.
36. See Beck, *Depression,* 40–42.
37. DSM-III, 210; Beck, *Depression,* 41.
38. Jacqueline to Gilberte, 25 September 1647, *OC,* II, 480–81; deposition of Antoine Arnauld, 21 December 1684, *Oeuvres,* X, 373; "Propos de M. Arnoul," *OC,* I, 885; *VMP,* 41–42, 44, 47.
39. "Pourquoi les *Pensées* de Pascal se présentent-elles sous forme de fragments?" *Papers on French Seventeenth-Century Literature* 10 (1983): 635–49. See also Mesnard, *Les Pensées de Pascal,* 37.
40. "Pourquoi . . . fragments," 642.
41. Beck, *Depression,* 41.
42. DSM-III, 210–11.
43. Beck, *Depression,* 35–36; cf. 27–30. Writing to Gilberte on 25 September 1647, Jacqueline remarked in passing that Blaise was usually worse in the morning. See *OC,* II, 480.
44. *Oeuvres,* IX, 163; X, 5.
45. On the date of *Prière pour le bon usage des maladies,* see *VMP,* Second Version, 58; see also *OC,* IV, 976–82; on Pascal's "vigor," see *Oeuvres,* IX, 324.
46. Carcavy to Huygens, 14 August 1659, in Huygens, *Oeuvres complètes,* II, 456.
47. *VMP,* Second Version, 53, 56.
48. *Préface des Traités de 1663, OC,* I, 688.
49. Preface of the Port-Royal *Pensées, Oeuvres,* XII, clxxxviii–clxxxix.
50. DSM-III, 211.
51. Philippe Sellier suggests an Augustinian source: *Pascal et Saint Augustin* (Paris, 1970), 591, n. 12. That Augustine could be quite self-reproachful is clear enough from the *Confessions,* for instance, 7.16 and 8.7–12. Pascalian self-hatred remains extreme. Having acknowledged the Fall, an Augustinian may reconsider the *Confessions,* 7.14: "It is the mark of an unsound mind to be displeased with any single thing in your creation."
52. See Madeleine Defrenne, "A propos d'une pensée de Pascal, 'Le moi est haïssable,' " *Revue des langues vivantes* 34 (1968): 5–8. Therèse Guyot, "Le visage de 1670," in *Les Pensées de Pascal ont trois cents ans* (Clermont-Ferrand, 1971), 71.
53. The coextensiveness of "self-love" and "the self" can also be argued persuasively by starting from the greatest of the texts devoted to the former theme. Pensée 978 requires an extensive conception: "The nature

of self-love and of this human self is to love only the self and to consider only the self."

54. *Oeuvres,* IX, 331, 333.
55. Mère Angélique had died in 1661. Mère Agnès consoled Gilberte in 1662 with the thought that Blaise had been "rich with the riches of God." More impressively, Agnès also wrote to another nun, neither a relative nor a close friend, that Blaise had been "one of our best friends" and "a true servant of God." This was more than charity alone would have required of her. See *Oeuvres,* X, 322–23, 324. The Arnauld men were, if anything, more respectful of the departed Pascal. See *Oeuvres,* X, 326–28.
56. Rapin, *Mémoires,* in *OC,* I, 839, 843–44, 846, 848–49, 859–61.
57. Huygens, *Oeuvres complètes,* II, 310.
58. Huygens, *Oeuvres complètes,* II, 345.
59. Huygens, *Oeuvres complètes,* II, 456–57.
60. *VMP,* 42, 44, 47, 72.
61. *OC,* I, 680–81, 688–89.
62. Preface of the Port-Royal *Pensées, Oeuvres,* XII, clxxxi–clxxxii, clxxxviii–cxc. Cf. Pensées 542, 656.
63. *Oeuvres,* XII, cxc.
64. Beck, *Depression,* 25–26.
65. DSM-III, 211, 214.
66. Pascal's last word is either *nostre* or *vostre,* leaving us all a last, unhappy choice. The fragment is written on a paper that Ernst has identified by its watermark as "FNIC"; this is the last of his "major strata," which he dates to the spring of 1658. I believe that a somewhat later date is quite possible, but that summer 1662, the only period that would make medical sense of this Proposition Five for the author if not his readers, can be ruled out on the strength of Gilberte's testimony.
67. *VMP,* Second Version, 59.
68. *VMP,* 81.
69. *VMP,* First Version, 84.
70. On him, see A. Durengues, *Monsieur Boileau de l'Archêveché* (Agen, 1907).
71. *Lettres de M. B[oileau] sur differens sujets de morale et de piété* (Paris, 1737), 206–7.
72. Louis Moréri, *Le grand dictionnaire historique* (Paris, 1759), vol. II, pt. 2, 22; Jacqueline to Gilberte, 25 January 1655, *Oeuvres,* IV, 66. Four letters from Boileau after de Sacy's death in 1684 document their close relationship: *Vies édifiantes des religieuses de Port-Royal* (Paris, 1752), IV, 91–92, 92–94, 105–7, 422–29.
73. The one old monographic study of Pascal's Abyss regards the perceived void on his left side as the hallucinatory effect of migraine headaches: René Onfray, *L'abîme de Pascal* (Alençon, 1923). Even a layperson can reevaluate this old thesis in light of current work on migraines. See

Oliver Sacks, *Migraine: The Evolution of a Common Disorder,* abr. ed. (Berkeley, 1973), esp. 67–108. Onfray's evidence consisted primarily of manuscript pages on which Pascal had left broad margins and of two suggestive zigzag lines on page 254 of the *Recueil original* (Pensée 771). However, Occam's razor cuts cleanly through both arguments. It is more economical to suppose that the careful author often left broad margins for later additions and revisions. Onfray's own reproductions show subsequent use of the space for such purposes. And the zigzag lines are most economically "read" as illustrations (or mere doodles) inspired by nothing more than the accompanying text on the natural phenomena of flux and reflux, particularly the tides. Robert Arnauld d'Andilly had already used the tides as an image of spiritual progress-and-regress. See Michel Le Guern's note on what he numbers Pensée 646 (Lafuma Pensée 771). Furthermore, Pascal's zigzags were rectilinear, not circular or curved, as they are in common representations of migraine scotoma. See Sacks, *Migraine,* figures 2A, 2B, 2C, 2D, 2E, 3A, 3B.

74. Voltaire to 's-Gravesande, 1 August 1741, in *Correspondance,* ed. T. Besterman (Paris, 1965), II, 514.
75. For Pascal's carriage accident on the Pont de Neuilly, see *OC,* I, 885. Condorcet put together the anecdotes of the accident and the Abyss as an explanation of the Second Conversion: *Éloge de Pascal,* in *Oeuvres* (Paris, 1847), III, 592–93. His history was surely mistaken, but his supposition that Pascal's Abyss must mean a literal fear of heights still seems to be influential: Gouhier, *Blaise Pascal commentaires,* 382–87; Mesnard, *Pascal* (1967), 66–67, and *OC,* I, 968–69.
76. Donald W. Goodwin and Samuel B. Guze, *Psychiatric Diagnosis,* 2d ed. (New York, 1979), 90, 99. I am particularly grateful for a private communication from Dr. Goodwin on this subject. Deficiencies in my discussion are my own. See also DSM-III, 234–35. N. L. Gittleson, "The phenomenonogy of obsessions in depressive psychosis," *British Journal of Psychiatry* 112 (1966): 261–64.
77. Saint-Cyran on the Devil's invasion of the soul, which becomes a living Hell: "The Demon . . . , not yet being confined to the Abyss, which won't happen until Judgment Day, . . . makes an abyss of our hearts, into which . . . he often precipitates himself with entire legions." See *Lettres chrétiennes et spirituelles* (Lyon, 1674), I, 454. Cf. "the abyss of muck" into which man has fallen and "the abyss and precipice" of his love of creatures, in *De la grâce de Jésus-Christ,* ed. Jean Orcibal in *La spiritualité de Saint-Cyran avec ses écrits de piété inédits* (Paris, 1962), 233, 235.

    Sacy was particularly fond of the image. See his instruction on our Christian duty to acknowledge "the abyss of weakness and sin" within us all: *Lettres chrétiennes et spirituelles* (Paris, 1690), II, 2; cf. 254, 329. On "the frightful abyss of nothingness, misery, and meanness in all that seems great and magnificent according to the world": *Lettres,* II, 72; cf.

82, 145. On "the profound abyss of nothingness, sin, weakness, pride, ingratitude, and darkness in each of us": *Lettres,* II, 363–64.

Singlin on our sins and consequent miseries, which thrust us into the "precipice" and the "abyss": *Instructions chrétiennes* (Paris, 1736), III, 58. On the "abyss of unhappiness" for those who have withdrawn from God: *Instructions,* III, 186. And so on.

78. See *Lettres,* 206, 342, 350.
79. Boileau, *Lettres,* 209–10.

NOTES TO CONCLUSION

1. See above, note 3 to the Introduction.
2. *VMP* 1, 3–18, 33–34. Mesnard, *Pascal,* 8–9, 11–20, 64–65.
3. *VMP,* First Version, 2, 30, 59–60; Second Version, 2, 19–20, 69–71. Cf. Mesnard, *Pascal,* 8, 47–48, 126, 129.
4. In his more scholarly monograph, Mesnard does include very preceptive remarks on the impact of the loss of Étienne followed by the withdrawal of Jacqueline in 1651–52: *Pascal et les Roannez,* 169–70; cf. his treatment of the deaths of Antoinette and Jacqueline, 33 and 749–50.
5. *Pascal et les Roannez,* 11, 15.
6. *VMP,* First Version, 60–64; Second Version, 71, 75–78.
7. *Pascal,* 120–21; Mesnard's emphasis.
8. *OC,* III, 1016, 1031. Pascal makes no such personal reference, but his reference to the liturgy for this 24 September makes the dating certain: *Pascal et les Roannez,* I, 474–75.
9. *OC,* IV, 999–1004.
10. In this sarcastic paraphrase and in his more formal citation of the offending passage, the philosophe quietly drops the all-important qualification that what makes a love spiritually suspect is "attachment." Gilberte had written about the man in his last year, after Jacqueline's death on 4 October 1661: "He was not at all attached to those persons whom he loved [family members, particularly Jacqueline]. . . . But he didn't let it go at that: not only did he permit himself no attachment to others, but also he didn't at all want others to have any to him."
11. In his *Éloge,* Condorcet seems ready to question the historicity of Gilberte's account on just this point as so much Jansenist hagiography, but then he steps back, as if conceding that perhaps Pascal really was so detached, after all. He infers a personality trait (emotional insensitivity) as an alternative to the orthodox inference of spiritual gifts (saintly detachment), but he does not look backward in time or attempt anything like an analysis of Pascal's apparent indifference to the living and apparent failure to grieve for the dead. See *Oeuvres complètes,* III, 625.
12. *OC,* I, 663–64. Saint-Cyran, *Le coeur nouveau,* in *Oeuvres chrétiennes et spirituelles,* IV, 71–88.
13. *VMP,* 22; *OC,* I, 663. Mesnard, *Pascal,* 29–34.
14. *VMP,* First Version, 33–34; Second Version, 25–27.

15. *OC,* III, 19–53, 61–75; IV, 35–44. *Pascal,* 64–67. *Pascal et les Roannez,* 393–401.
16. Lélut, *L'amulette de Pascal: pour servir à l'histoire des hallucinations* (Paris, 1846); Gouhier, *Blaise Pascal commentaires,* 382–84.
17. See particularly Binet-Sanglé, "La maladie de Blaise Pascal," *Annales médico-psychologiques,* 8th ser., 9 (1899): 177–99.
18. *VMP,* 44 ff., esp. 76 ff. Condorcet, like Bayle a century earlier, reacted particularly against the sentiments in *VMP* 81; see *Oeuvres complètes,* III, 568–69, n. 1.
19. *OC,* IV, 1494, 1498.
20. Lélut, *L'amulette de Pascal,* 190; Binet-Sanglé, "Maladie de Pascal," 178, 191–99.
21. *OC,* IV, 976–82, 996.
22. *OC,* IV, 1000–1003.
23. *OC,* IV, 1004–10.
24. *OC,* IV, 1006–10.
25. *Pascal* (1967), 169, 179.
26. *Pascal et les Roannez,* I, 11.
27. *VMP,* 88.

NOTES TO APPENDIX I

1. Erna Furman, *A Child's Parent Dies: Studies in Childhood Bereavement* (New Haven, 1974). Bowlby's respectful criticism concerns what might be called a "sampling bias." Eight of the twenty-three cases were patients or children of patients who were already in therapy at the time of a parent's death. The other fifteen were referred for various emotional difficulties afterward, so that the "sample" as a whole is skewed toward pathological outcomes. Bowlby, *Loss,* 265–68. Nevertheless, the lay historian can learn an immense amount from these studies.
2. The fifth point is most open to question. See Bowlby, *Loss,* 295–380.
3. Furman, *A Child's Parent Dies,* 1–4, 168, 267–69.
4. Furman, *A Child's Parent Dies,* 12.
5. Bowlby, *Loss,* 81–262.
6. Furman, *A Child's Parent Dies,* 16, 102, 178.
7. Bowlby, *Attachment* (New York, 1969); *Separation: Anxiety and Anger* (New York, 1973); *Loss: Sadness and Depression* (New York, 1980). For summaries, see "Attachment Theory, Separation Anxiety, and Mourning," in *The American Handbook of Psychiatry,* 2d ed. (New York, 1975), VI, 292–309, and "The making and breaking of affectional bonds," *The British Journal of Psychiatry* 130 (1977): 201–10 and 421–31.
8. Bowlby, *Loss,* 39.
9. Bowlby, *Loss,* 39–41; *Attachment,* passim.
10. Bowlby, *Attachment,* 198–209, 235 ff.
11. Bowlby, "Attachment Theory," 294; "Making and breaking of affectional bonds," 203.

12. Bowlby, *Attachment,* 299–330.
13. Bowlby, "Attachment Theory," 294; "Making and breaking of affectional bonds," 203.
14. Bowlby, "Attachment Theory," 294; "Making and breaking of affectional bonds," 203; *Loss,* 40.
15. The literature on parental loss and hypothesized pathogenic effects is fundamental to this inquiry. It is also immense. Here, I merely list the names of the authors who have most directly influenced me. In addition to John Bowlby and Erna and Robert Furman, I would mention especially John Birtchnell, author of many particularly impressive epidemiological studies. The layperson interested in looking further into the psychiatric literature might begin with review articles, some by skeptics, that provide more extensive references than are practical here: C. M. Heinicke, "Parental Deprivation in Early Childhood: A Predisposition to Later Depression?" in *Separation and Depression,* ed. J. P. Scott and E. C. Denay (Washington, D.C., 1973); C. Lloyd, "Life events and depressive disorder reviewed: Events as predisposing factors," *Archives of General Psychiatry* 37 (1980): 529–35; T. Crook and J. Eliot, "Parental death during childhood and adult depression," *Psychological Bulletin* 87 (1980): 252–59; C. Tennant, P. Bebbington, and J. Hurry, "Parental death in childhood and risk of adult depressive disorders: A review," *Psychological Medicine* 10 (1980): 289–99; H. Finkelstein, "The long-term effects of early parent death: A review," *Journal of Clinical Psychology* 44 (1988): 3–9; C. Tennant, "Parental loss in childhood: Its effect in adult life," *Archives of General Psychiatry* 45 (1988) 1045–50.

NOTES TO APPENDIX 2

1. Formal citation: American Psychiatric Association, *Diagnostic and Statistical Manual of Mental Disorders,* 3d ed. (DSM-III) (Washington, D.C., 1980). American Psychiatric Association, *Diagnostic and Statistical Manual of Mental Disorders,* 4th ed. (DSM-IV) (Washington, D.C., 1994). My research was accomplished using DSM-III; I have presented it following the related criteria of DSM-IV.
2. The five sources of unreliability are drawn from Robert L. Spitzer, Jean Endicott, and Eli Robins, "Clinical criteria for psychiatric diagnosis and *DSM-III,*" *American Journal of Psychiatry* 132 (1975): 1187–88. For agreement on the relative importance of the fifth, see Julian Leff, "International variations in the diagnosis of affective illness," *British Journal of Psychiatry* 131 (1977): 329–38.
3. John P. Feighner et al., "Diagnostic criteria for use in psychiatric research," *Archives of General Psychiatry* 26 (1972): 57–63; Robert L. Spitzer, Jean Endicott, and Eli Robins, "Clinical criteria for psychiatric diagnosis and DSM-III," *American Journal of Psychiatry* 132 (1975): 1187–92, and "Research diagnostic criteria: Rationale and reliability," *Archives*

of General Psychiatry 35 (1978): 773–82; and the American Psychiatric Association, *Diagnostic and Statistical Manual,* 3d and 4th eds. (Washington, D.C., 1980 and 1994). See Gerald L. Klerman, "The Significance of DSM-III in American Psychiatry," and Robert Kendell, "DSM-III: A Major Advance in Psychiatric Nosology," in *International Perspectives on DSM-III* (Washington, D.C., 1983), 3–25 and 55–67. For most purposes, the changes in the understanding of mood disorders incorporated in DSM-III-R and DSM-IV are inconsequential.

4. I cite two reviews of the literature that emphasize cultural differences, both by Anthony J. Marsella: "Depressive Experience and Disorder across Cultures," in *Handbook of Cross-Cultural Psychology,* ed. Harry C. Triandis and Juris G. Draguns (Boston, 1980), VI, 237–89; "Cross-Cultural Studies of Depressive Disorders" (1985), in *Culture and Depression: Studies in the Anthropology and Psychiatry of Affect and Disorder,* ed. Arthur Kleinman and Byron Good (Berkeley, 1985), 299–324.
5. See P. Pichot, R. Bailly, and J. E. Overall, "Les stéréotypes diagnostiques des psychoses chez les psychiatres français: comparaison avec les stéréotypes américains," in *Neuro-Psycho-Pharmacology: Proceedings of the Fifth International Congress of the Collegium Internationale Neuropsychopharmacologicum (Washington, D.C., 1966),* International Congress Series, no. 129, 16–26. See also F. Engelsmann et al., "International comparison of diagnostic patterns," in *Transcultural Psychiatric Research* 7 (1970): 130–37.
6. N. Sartorius et al., "WHO collaborative study: Assessment of depressive disorders," *Psychological Medicine* 10 (1980): 743–49; A. Jablensky et al., "Characteristics of depressive patients contacting psychiatric services in four cultures: A report from the WHO collaborative study on the assessment of depressive disorders," *Acta Psychiatrica Scandinavica* 63 (1981): 367–83; World Health Organization, *Depressive Disorders in Different Cultures* (Geneva, 1983).
7. A. Jablensky et al., "Characteristics of Depressive Patients," 378. This study agrees with those summarily reported above in its finding that guilt is more prevalent in Western depressives (68 percent in Basle and 58 percent in Montreal, compared with 48 percent in Tokyo, 41 percent in Nagasaki, and 32 percent in Teheran) and somatization less prevalent in the West (27 percent in Montreal and 32 percent in Basle but 57 percent in Teheran).
8. Jablensky, "Characteristics of Depressive Patients," 368.
9. *Melancholia and Depression from Hippocratic Times to Modern Times* (New Haven, 1986), ix. There are also two particularly relevant French histories: Maxime Laignel-Lavastine and Jean Vinchon, *Les maladies de l'esprit et leurs médecins du XVIe au XVIIe siècles* (Paris, 1930); Jean Starobinski, *Histoire du traitement de la mélancholie des origines à 1900* (Basle, 1960). A few pertinent papers: A. Brink, "Depression and loss: A theme in Robert Burton's *Anatomy of Melancholy* (1621)," *Canadian Journal of Psychiatry* 24 (1979): 767–71; Edward Hare, "The two manias: A study

of the evolution of the modern concept of mania," *British Journal of Psychiatry* 138 (1981): 89–99; T. H. Jobe, "Medical theories of melancholia in the seventeenth and eighteenth centuries," *Clio Medica* 11 (1976): 217–31; J. S. Madden, "Melancholy in medicine and literature: Some historical considerations," *British Journal of Medical Psychology* 39 (1966): 125–30; M. J. Sedler, "Falret's discovery," *American Journal of Psychiatry* 140 (1983): 1127–33.

10. Page 56.
11. DSM-III, 207–8; DSM-IV, 363–66.
12. DSM-III, 213, 333; DSM-IV, 326–27.
13. DSM-IV, 327.
14. DSM-IV, 365–66.
15. DSM-IV, 338.

NOTES TO APPENDIX 3

1. Aristotle, *Problemata*, 953a.
2. Raymond Klibansky, Erwin Panofsky, and Fritz Saxl, *Saturn and Melancholy: Studies in the History of Natural Philosophy, Religion, and Art* (New York, 1964).
3. Montaigne, "De l'affection des pères aux enfans," in *Oeuvres complètes*, ed. Thibaudet and Rat (Paris, 1962), 364. See M. A. Screech, *Montaigne and Melancholy* (Selinsgrove, Pa., 1984), esp. 22–36.
4. On André Du Lauren's *Des maladies mélancholiques*, see *Toutes les oeuvres* (Paris, 1613), 25r; on Jean-François Senault's *L'homme criminel*, see the epigraph for this volume. Senault's work, published at Paris in several editions—1644, 1647, and 1663—provides a very useful background for Pascal's similarly Augustinian teachings on human *misère*.
5. Goodwin and Jamison, *Manic-Depressive Illness* (New York, 1990), 15–124, esp. 74–84.
6. "Behavioral paradigm for identifying persons at risk for bipolar depressive disorder: A conceptual framework and five validation studies," *Journal of Abnormal Psychology Monograph* 90 (1981): 381–437, esp. "Study 1," 392–403.
7. "The Zurich study: A prospective epidemiological study of depressive, neurotic, and psychosomatic syndromes," *European Archives of Psychiatry and Neurological Sciences* 234 (1984): 13–37.
8. The review essays: "The Bipolar Spectrum: New Concepts in Classification and Diagnosis," in *Psychiatry Update: The American Psychiatric Association Annual Review*, ed. L. Grinspoon (Washington, D.C., 1983), 271–92; "Cyclothemic and Related Disorders," in *Depression and Mania*, ed. Anastasios Georgotas and Robert Cancro (New York, 1988), 86–95. Other relevant work: "Cyclothemic disorder," *American Journal of Psychiatry* 134 (1977): 1227–33; "The Nosological status of neurotic depression," *Archives of General Psychiatry* 35 (1978): 756–66; "Cyclothemic temperamental disorders," *Psychiatric Clinics of North America* 2

(1979): 527–53; "External validating criteria for psychiatric diagnosis: Their application in affective disorders," *Journal of Clinical Psychiatry* 41:12, sec. 2 (1980): 6–15; "Subaffective disorders: Dysthymic, cyclothemic, and bipolar II disorders in the 'borderline' realm," *Psychiatric Clinics of North America* 4 (1981): 25–46.

9. H. S. Akiskal and K. Akiskal, "Reassessing the prevalence of bipolar disorders: Clinical significance and artistic creativity," *Psychiatrie et Psychobiologie* 3 (1988): 34s.
10. Nancy Andreasen and Arthur Canter, "The creative writer: Psychiatric symptoms and family history," *Comprehensive Psychiatry* 15 (1974): 123–31.
11. "Creativity and mental illness: Prevalence rates in writers and their first-degree relatives," *American Journal of Psychiatry* 144 (1987): 1288–92.
12. "Mood disorders and patterns of creativity in British writers and artists," *Psychiatry* 52 (1989): 125–34.
13. *Touched with Fire* (New York, 1993), 89–99.
14. Dr. Nancy Andreason with Pauline Powers, "Creativity and psychosis," *Archives of General Psychiatry* 32 (1975): 70–73; "Mood disorders and creativity," separately paginated offprint from *Creative Psychiatry* 13 (New York, 1977); "Creativity and psychiatric illness," unpaginated reprint from *Psychiatric Annals* (New York, 1978); "Mania and Creativity," in *Mania: An Evolving Concept,* ed. Robert Belmaker and H. M. van Praag (Jamaica, N.Y., 1980), 377–85.

    Professor Kay Redfield Jamison, with three coauthors, "Clouds and silver linings: Positive experiences associated with primary affective disorders," *American Journal of Psychiatry* 137 (1980): 198–202.

    Ruth Richards, "Relationships between creativity and psychopathology: An evaluation and interpretation of the evidence," *Genetic Psychology Monographs* 103 (1981): 261–324; with others including Dennis Kinney (Boston) and Inge Lunde (Copenhagen), "Creativity in manic-depressives, cyclothemes, their normal relatives, and control subjects," *Journal of Abnormal Psychology* 97 (1988): 281–88; "Assessing everyday creativity," *Journal of Personality and Social Psychology* 54 (1988), separately paginated offprint; with Dennis Kinney, as principal author, et al., "Perceived influences of moods on creativity in bipolar, unipolar, and cyclothymic patients," prepublication typescript (1988).

Bibliography of Primary Sources

I. Pascal's Life and Works

I have made regular use of three editions of the collected works. The Brunschvicg-Boutroux-Gazier Grands Écrivains edition of the *Oeuvres* (1904–14) remains the most nearly complete scholarly reference, although its presentation of the *Pensées,* particularly, has been superseded. Mesnard's *Oeuvres complètes* (1964–) will replace all previous editions; four of the projected seven volumes have appeared as of this writing. Both of these great editions include much supporting documentation. Pending completion of the latter, the Lafuma Intégrale edition of the *Oeuvres complètes* (1963) is the standard reference; its one-volume format offers great advantages of convenience. I also list frequently used editions of some separate works, here ordered by date of composition.

Given my subject, Pascal's loves, it is worth mentioning that I do not consider the *Discours sur les passions d'amour* to be his work. This is to side with Lafuma and Mesnard and against Brunschvicg-Boutroux-Gazier. In his otherwise exhaustive "Introduction générale," Mesnard deferred critical discussion to a subsequent volume; see *OC,* I, 227. That discussion comes in *OC,* IV, 1628–54, where the *Discours* is relegated to a section of "Textes écartés." See also his *Pascal et les Roannez,* I, 213–26, and Georges Brunet, *Un prétendu traité de Pascal.*

A. COLLECTED WORKS

Pascal, Blaise. *Oeuvres.* Edited by Léon Brunschvicg, Pierre Boutroux, and Félix Gazier. 14 vols. Paris, 1904–14. Cited as the *Oeuvres.*

Pascal, Blaise. *Oeuvres complètes.* Edited by Louis Lafuma. Paris, 1963. Cited as the Intégrale.

———. *Oeuvres complètes.* Edited by Jean Mesnard. 4 vols. to date. Paris, 1964–92. Cited as the *OC*. The First Version of Gilberte Périer's *Vie de Monsieur Pascal* from vol. 1 is cited as *VMP* with Mesnard's paragraph numbers so as to facilitate comparison of the two versions.

B. SINGLE WORKS

Pascal, Blaise. *Entretien de M. Pascal avec M. de Sacy sur la lecture d'Epictète et de Montaigne.* In *Continuation des mémoires de littérature et d'histoire,* Pierre-Nicolas Desmolets. Vol. V, pt. 2, 239–70. Paris, 1728.

———. [*Entretien de M. Pascal avec M de Sacy.*] In *Mémoires pour servir à l'histoire de Port-Royal,* Nicolas Fontaine. Vol. II, 51–74. Utrecht, 1736.

———. *L'Entretien de Pascal et de Sacy.* Edited by Pierre Courcelle. Paris, 1960.

———. *Les Provinciales ou les Lettres escrites par Louis de Montalte à un Provincial de ses amis et aux RR. PP. Jésuites sur le sujet de la morale et de la politique de ces Pères.* Cologne, 1657. First collected edition.

———. *Les Provinciales.* Edited by Louis Cognet. Paris, 1965. Based on collected edition of 1659. Cited as Cognet.

———. *Le manuscrit des Pensées de Pascal.* Edited by Louis Lafuma. Paris, 1962. Facsimiles from the *Recueil original* (B.N., mss., f.f., no. 9202) reordered according to the First Copy (B.N., mss., f.f., no. 9203).

———. *Pensées.* Paris, 1670. First edition, called "Port-Royal Edition," ordered arbitrarily by the editors.

———. *Les Pensées de Pascal disposées suivant l'ordre du cahier autographe.* Edited by G. Michaut. Fribourg, 1896. A first objective edition, following the *Recueil original.*

———. *Pensées de Blaise Pascal: Édition paléographique.* Edited by Zachaire Tourneur. Paris, 1942. The author's strikeouts and additions are represented typographically.

———. *Pensées sur la religion et sur quelques autres sujets.* Edited by Louis Lafuma. 3 vols. Paris: Luxembourg, 1951. Lafuma's scholarly edition, following the order of the First Copy.

———. *Pensées.* Edited by Philippe Sellier. Paris: Mercure, 1976. Follows the order of the Second Copy (B.N., mss., f.f., no. 12449).

———. *Pensées.* Edited by Michel Le Guern. 2 vols. Paris, 1977. Follows the order of the First Copy but not the editorial numeration of Lafuma.

———. *Pensées.* Edited by Philippe Sellier. Paris: Garnier, 1991. Follows the order of the Second Copy.

C. MISCELLANEOUS

Pascal, Blaise. *Textes inédits.* Edited by Jean Mesnard. Paris, 1962.

———. *Trois pensées inédites de Pascal.* Edited by Louis Lafuma. Paris, 1945.

II. Other Sources

[Annat, François]. *Défense de la vérité catholique touchant les miracles contre les déguisements et artifices de la response faite par messieurs de Port-Royal.* Paris, 1657.

———. *Rabat-joie des Jansénistes ou Observations nécessaires sur ce qu'on dit être arrivé au Port-Royal au suject de la Sainte-Épine.* Paris, 1656.

Arnauld, Agnès. *Image d'une religieuse parfaite et d'une imparfaite.* Paris, 1665.

———. *Lettres.* 2 vols. Paris, 1858.

———. *Manuel des âmes religieuses.* In *Image d'une religieuse parfaite,* new edition. Paris, 1711.

Arnauld, Angélique. *Entretiens ou conférences de la révérende Mère Marie-Angélique Arnauld.* Brussels, 1757.

———. *Lettres.* 3 vols. Paris, 1742–44.

———. *Relation sur Port-Royal.* Edited by Louis Cognet. Paris, 1949.

Arnauld, Antoine. *Oeuvres.* 43 vols. Paris and Lausanne, 1775–83.

Arnauld, Antoine, and Godefroy Hermant. *La conduite pour la réception des filles dans les monastères.* Paris, 1668.

Arnauld, Robert. *Arnauld d'Andilly, Défenseur de Port-Royal (1654–1659): Sa correspondance inédite avec la Cour.* Edited by Paule Jansen. Paris, 1973.

Augustine, Bishop of Hippo. *Against the Academicians.* Translated by M. P. Garvey. Milwaukee, 1957.

———. *City of God.* Translated by M. Dods. New York, 1950.

———. *Confessions.* Translated by Rex Warner. New York, 1963.

———. *Earlier Writings.* Translated by J. H. S. Burleigh. Philadelphia, 1963.

———. *Enchiridion.* Translated by J. F. Shaw. Chicago, 1961.

———. *On the Care to Be Had for the Dead.* In *The Nicene and Post-Nicene Fathers.* Edited by P. Schaff. Vol. 3. Buffalo, 1887.

———. *Sermons on the Liturgical Seasons.* Translated by M. S. Muldowney. New York, 1959.

Ayrault, Pierre. *De la puissance paternelle.* In *Opuscules et divers traictez,* 231–356. Paris, 1598.

Baillet, Adrien. *Auteurs déguisez sous des noms Étrangers, Empruntez, Supposez, Feints à plaisir, Chiffrez, Renversez, Retournez, ou Changez d'une langue en une autre.* Paris, 1690.

———. *Des enfans devenus célèbres par leurs études ou par leurs écrits.* Paris, 1688.

———. *La vie de Monsieur Descartes.* 2 vols. Paris, 1691.

Bayle, Pierre. Notice of Gilberte Périer's *Vie de Monsieur Pascal* from *Nouvelles de la république des lettres,* December, 1684. In *Oeuvres diverses.* Edited by E. Labrousse. Vol. I, 194–95. Paris, 1964.

———. *Dictionnaire historique et critique,* 3d edition. 3 vols. Rotterdam, 1720.

Besoigne, Jérôme. *Histoire de l'abbaye de Port-Royal.* 6 vols. Cologne, 1652.

Bigot de Monville, Alexandre. *Mémoires sur la sédition des Nupieds.* Edited by d'Estaintot. Rouen, 1876.

B[oileau, Jean-Jacques]. *Lettres de Monsieur B. sur différens sujets de morale et de piété*. Paris, 1737.

Bossuet, Jacques Bénigne. *Témoignage sur la vie et les vertus éminentes de Monsieur Vincent de Paul*. Edited by A. Gaste. Paris, 1892.

Bregy, Anne-Marie Flécelles de. *Modèle de foi et de patience: Vie de la mère Marie des Anges (Suireau)*. N. p., 1754.

Burton, Robert. *The Anatomy of Melancholy*. Edited by Holbrook Jackson. New York, 1977.

Charron, Pierre de. *De la sagesse*. Edited by A. Duval. 3 vols. Paris, 1836.

Descartes, René. *Oeuvres de Descartes*. Edited by Charles Adam and Paul Tannery. 11 vols. Paris, 1897–1913.

Diderot, Denis, et al. *Encyclopédie ou dictionnaire raisonné*. 17 vols. Paris, 1751–65.

Dufresnoy, Nicolas Lenglet. *Recueil de dissertations anciennes et nouvelles sur les apparitions, les visions, et les songes*. 2 vols. Avignon and Paris.

Du Laurens, André. *Des maladies mélancholiques*. In *Toutes les oeuvres*. Paris, 1613.

Dupleix, Scipion. *Les causes de la veille et du sommeil, des songes, et de la vie et de la mort*. Paris, 1609; Paris, 1969–73.

Du Vair, Guillaume. *De la Sainte Philosophie* [and] *Philosophie morale des Stoïques*. Edited by G. Michaut. Paris, 1945.

Epictetus. *Discourses* and *Manual*. Translated by P. E. Matheson. In *The Stoic and Epicurean Philosophers*. Edited by Whitney Oates. New York, 1940.

Fontaine, Nicolas. *Mémoires pour servir à l'histoire de Port-Royal*. 2 vols. Utrecht, 1736.

Forbonnais, François Véron-Duverger de. *Recherches et considérations sur les finances de France depuis l'année 1595 jusqu'à l'année 1721*. 2 vols. Paris, 1758.

François de Sales. *Oeuvres*. Edited by A. Ravier. Paris, 1969.

Furetière, Antoine. *Le dictionnaire universel*. 3 vols. The Hague, 1690.

Galileo Galilei. *Dialogue concerning the Two Chief World Systems*. Translated by S. Drake. Berkeley, 1953.

Guillemeau, Jacques. *Oeuvres de chirurgie*. Rouen, 1649.

Guyot, Pierre. *Répertoire universel et raisonné de jurisprudence civile, criminelle, canonique et bénéficiale*. Paris, 1784.

Henri IV. *Recueil de lettres missives de Henri IV*. Edited by Berger de Xivrey. 9 vols. Paris, 1843–76.

Hermant, Godefroy. *Mémoires sur l'histoire ecclésiastique du XVIIe siècle*. Edited by A. Gazier. 6 vols. Paris, 1905–10.

———. *Tradition de l'Église sur le Silence chrétien et monastique et les paroles inutiles en général et en particulier contre la trop grande fréquentation des Parloirs des Religieuses*. Paris, 1697.

Héroard, Jean. *Journal de Jean Héroard sur l'enfance et la jeunesse de Louis XIII (1601–1628)*. Edited by E. Soulié and E. Barthélemy. 2 vols. Paris, 1868.

Huygens, Christian. *Oeuvres complètes*. 22 vols. The Hague, 1888–1950.

———. *Journal de Voyage à Paris et à Londres.* Edited by H.-L. Brugmans. Paris, 1935.

Ignatius of Loyola. *The Constitutions of the Society of Jesus.* Translated by G. E. Ganss. St. Louis, 1970.

Isambert, François André. *Recueil général des anciennes lois françaises.* 29 vols. Paris, 1821–33.

———. *Le cardinal Mazarin et le mouvement janséniste français 1653–1659.* Paris, 1967.

Jansenius, Cornelius. *Discours de la réformation de l'homme intérieur.* In G. Michaut, *Les époques de la pensée de Pascal,* 194–222. Paris, 1902.

Jovy, Ernest. "Deux documents relatifs à Domat." *Bulletin historique et scientifique de l'Auvergne* 2d ser. (1924): 163–65.

Jurgens, Madeleine, and M.-A. Fleury. *Documents du Minutier central concernant l'histoire littéraire (1650–1700).* Paris, 1960.

La Vallière, Louise de. *Madame de La Vallière repentante: Confessions intimes.* Edited by Romain-Cornut. Paris, 1874.

Le Maistre, Antoine. *Relations de plusieurs entretiens.* In *Mémoires pour servir à l'histoire de Port-Royal.* Utrecht, 1742.

[Le Maistre, Antoine, presumed primary author]. *Response à un escrit publié sur le suite des Miracles qu'il a pleu Dieu de faire à Port-Royal.* Paris, 1656.

Leibniz, Gottfried Wilhelm. *Otium Hanoveranum sive Miscellanea.* Leipzig, 1718.

———. *Philosophical Papers and Letters.* Translated by L. E. Loemher. Dordrecht, 1969.

Mazure, Nicolas. *L'obligation des fidèles de se confesser à leur curé.* Paris, 1653.

Mémoire sur la vie de M. Pascal. In *Recueil de plusieurs pièces pour servir à l'histoire de Port-Royal.* Utrecht, 1740.

Méré, Antoine Gombaud, chevalier de. *Oeuvres complètes.* 3 vols. Paris, 1930.

Mitton, Damien. *Bons mots de feu M. M.* In *Portefeuille de Monsieur L. D. F.* Carpentras, 1694.

Montaigne, Michel de. *Oeuvres complètes.* Edited by Thibaudet and Rat. Paris, 1962.

———. *The Complete Essays.* Translated by Donald Frame. Stanford, 1958.

———. *Travel Journal.* Translated by Donald Frame. San Francisco, 1983.

Montglat, François-Paule de Clermont, marquis de. *Mémoires.* In *Mémoires pour servir à l'histoire de France.* Edited by Michaud and Poujoulat. Vol. V. Paris, 1838.

Pérau, Gabriel. *Vie de Jérome Bignon, avocat général et conseiller d'État.* Paris, 1757.

[Port-Royal]. *Les constitutions du monastère de Port-Royal du S. Sacrament.* Paris, 1665 and 1721.

———. *Mémoires pour servir à l'histoire de Port-Royal et à la vie de la Révérende Mère Marie-Angélique de Sainte-Mageleine Arnauld.* Utrecht, 1742.

———. *Recueil de diverses pièces concernant les Miracles de la Sainte Épine de Port-Royal.* Bibliothèque Mazarine, manuscripts, A 17119.

[Port-Royal]. *Vies intéressantes et édifiantes des religieuses de Port-Royal.* 4 vols. N. p., 1750–52.
Racine, Jean. *Abrégé de l'histoire de Port-Royal.* Edited by G. Truc. Paris, 1933.
Rapin, René. *Mémoires.* Edited by L. Aubineau. 3 vols. Paris, 1865.
Richelet, Pierre. *Dictionnaire françois contenant les mots et les choses.* Geneva, 1679.
Richelieu, Armand du Pléssis, Cardinal. *The Political Testament of Cardinal Richelieu.* Translated by H. B. Hill. Madison, Wis., 1961.
Richer, François. *Traité de la mort civile.* Paris, 1755.
Sacy, Louis-Isaac Le Maistre de. *Lettres chrestiennes et spirituelles.* 2 vols. Paris, 1690.
———. *Choix de lettres inédites.* Edited by G. Delassault. Paris, 1957.
Saint-Cyran, Jean Duvergier de Hauranne, abbé de. *Écrits de piété inédits.* Edited by Jean Orcibal. In his *Origines du jansénisme.* Vol. V. Paris, 1962.
———. *Lettres chrétiennes et spirituelles.* 3 vols. A fourth volume is entitled *Oeuvres chrétiennes et spirituelles.* Lyon, 1674.
———. *Lettres inédites.* Edited by Annie Barnes. In Orcibal, *Origines du jansénisme.* Vol. IV. Paris, 1962.
Saint-Gilles, Baudry d'Asson, sieur de. *Journal.* Edited by E. Jovy. Paris, 1936.
Savaron and Pierre Durand. *Les origines de la ville de Clermont.* Paris, 1662.
Scudéry, Georges de. *L'amour tirannique.* Paris, 1639.
Séguier, Pierre. *Diaire ou Journal de voyage du chancelier Séguier en Normandie.* Edited by A. Floquet. Rouen, 1842.
Senault, Jean-François. *L'homme criminel.* Paris, 1663.
Singlin, Antoine. *Instructions chrétiennes.* 12 vols. Paris, 1736.
Tallemant des Réaux, Gédéon. *Les Historiettes.* Edited by A. Adam. 2 vols. Paris, 1960–61.
Thomas à Kempis. *L'imitation de Jésus Christ mise en vers françois par Pierre Corneille.* Paris, 1654.
———. *L'imitation de Jésus Christ, traduction nouvelle par le Sieur de Breüil, Prieur de Saint Val.* Paris, 1663.
———. *The Imitation of Christ.* Edited by H. C. Gardiner. New York, 1955.
Vallambert, Simon de. *De la manière de nourrir et gouverner les enfants des leur naissance.* Poitiers, 1565.
Voltaire, François-Marie Arouet de. *Correspondance.* Edited by T. Besterman. 107 vols. Geneva, 1953–65.
———. *Oeuvres complètes.* Edited by Louis Moland. 52 vols. Paris, 1877–82.

General Index

Pascal's written works are listed only summarily under the author's name in the General Index; for detailed references to specific passages, see the Index of Passages Cited.

Index of Passages Cited